D0073042

THE PHILOSOPHY OF THE AUSTRIAN SCHOOL

THE PHILOSOPHY OF THE AUSTRIAN SCHOOL

Raimondo Cubeddu

Translated by
Rachel M. Costa, née Barritt

London and New York

First published 1993
by Routledge
11 New Fetter Lane, London EC4P 4EE

Simultaneously published in the USA and Canada
by Routledge
29 West 35th Street, New York, NY 10001

Typeset in Garamond by
Ponting–Green Publishing Services, Chesham, Bucks

Printed and bound in Great Britain by
Mackays of Chatham PLC, Chatham, Kent

British Library Cataloguing in Publication Data
A catalogue record for this book is available from
the British Library

Library of Congress Cataloging in Publication Data
Cubeddu, Raimondo, 1951–
The philosophy of the Austrian School / Raimondo Cubeddu.
p. cm.
Simultaneously published in the USA and Canada.
Includes bibliographical references and index.
ISBN 0–415–08647–7
1. Social sciences–Austria 2. Social sciences–Philosophy.
3. Austrian school of economists. I. Title.
H62.5.A9C83 1993
330.15'7–dc20 92–46097
CIP

ISBN 0–415–08647–7

to Giuliano Marini

CONTENTS

PREFACE

This book is an exploration of the consequences that the various issues raised by the Austrian School's[1] 'theory of subjective values' may have on *political philosophy* understood as a *critical and practical science*. Its aim is to analyse the contribution made to the theoretical social sciences by exponents of this School and the model of *political order* that follows from their emphasis on individualism.

The specific subject of this work is the methodology and political philosophy of Menger, Mises and Hayek. Reference to questions of a more strictly economic nature will be made only when it is deemed necessary in order to understand the way these thinkers approached methodological and political matters. Consequently, I will make only passing mention of Böhm-Bawerk and Wieser. Although the latter writers dealt with political issues of great importance – think, for example, of the political implications of Böhm-Bawerk's critique of the Marxian theory of value[2] and of Wieser's[3] historical, political and sociological works – they do not truly form part of the field of political philosophy; rather, they should be considered as contributing to the field of political thought. For, unlike Menger, Mises or Hayek, they gave only superficial attention in their scientific activity to the philosophical foundations of politics.

Whatever the differences observable between Menger, Mises and Hayek, economics was for them part of a philosophical system. It would thus be misleading and reductive to regard them merely as economists who took an interest in philosophy and the social sciences. Despite the prominent place they have come to occupy in contemporary political philosophy, however, they should perhaps not be classed with the great systematic thinkers of the history of philosophy. Even so, as well as systematic conceptual frameworks, the period when they were at work also saw a great ferment of innovative ideas that rocked established views. Seen in this perspective, the Austrian School's most important contribution to the philosophy of the social sciences arguably consists in having emphasized the need to reconsider the systematic structure of these sciences in the light of the findings of the *theory of marginal utility*.

If the impact of the sphere of economics in political life was one of the most important aspects of 'modernity', then the approach taken by the exponents of the Austrian School to the relation between *economics* and *politics* may provide a significant contribution to an understanding and explanation of the contemporary world. For no other school of thought has carried out such an influential investigation, or one yielding such significant results, into the political repercussions of individual and collective economic choices. The School's *philosophy of the social sciences* can be seen as an attempt to understand and explain history and social institutions in the light of the natural limits of human knowledge. History and social institutions accordingly appear as the often involuntary products of individual actions directed to the achievement of subjective ends. Thus, Menger, Mises and Hayek were not so much economists who also delved into politics, or dreamers conjuring up visions of a utopian better world, but rather thinkers who elaborated a theory of the 'best political regime' on the basis of a conception of human action and the nature of society.

In other words, if it is true that the beginning of the modern era was marked by the emancipation of political economics from ethics and politics – i.e. by its assumption of the status of a 'science' – it is equally true that today the question of the best regime appears inextricably bound up with economic issues. For the spread of information and the success of certain models of social behaviour have meant that no ideology or political regime can now hope to endure unless it is able to satisfy subjectively understood individual needs. Such an observation appears trivial today, but gave rise to more than a few reservations when Mises and Hayek embarked on their critique of socialism. Their contention was that socialism would be bound to turn into chaos or tyranny precisely on account of its inability to reconcile planning with individual freedom. At that time the prevailing belief was that no such danger existed, and that their critique was inspired chiefly by ideological motivations and a mistaken view of the mechanisms of economic development.

If the pre-eminence of individual rights appears to be the distinctive feature of the modern era, the latter in its turn, for better or for worse, appears closely bound up with the birth and enhancement of the capitalistic mentality and of modern science. Therefore it may not be far-fetched to claim that repudiation of the market economy will also lead to rejection of liberal-democratic political organization. For the liberal-democratic state and its system of civilization, the rule of law, cannot be considered independent from the outcome of what has effectively been the *capitalist revolution*.[4] The idea that democratic structures can be maintained without the market economy implies a failure to realize that this link can be severed only at the price of the breakdown of civilized social relations. If this nexus is neglected, the end result is an inability to understand what lies at the foundation of modern democracy. For democracy consists not so much in an unreal government by the people, nor in the possibility of choosing one's government élite, but rather in political recognition of the subjectivity of choices.

This set of problems allows an assessment to be made of the Austrian School's contribution to contemporary political philosophy. Certainly, their critique of historicism and scientism enables the exponents of the Austrian School to be classified among the critics of modernity. But in their case modernity – unlike the most common reading of this movement – was understood not as a secularization process (whereby the gradual shift away from the message of Christian revelation would eventually pave the way to relativism and nihilism), but rather as an overestimation of the powers of human knowledge and reason, which was doomed to tend towards totalitarianism. The theological and eschatological implications of secularization having thus been swept aside, modernity then appeared as the trend towards underestimation of the fact that the abuse of reason is among the causes of that endemic scourge of politics that is tyranny. Therefore the viewpoint of the Austrian School may be seen as an internal critique of modernity and its products: a critique focusing on the schools of thought, such as contractualism, historicism, marxism and idealism, which exercised hegemony over philosophical and political affairs in the last few centuries.

Just as it cannot be maintained that the exponents of the Austrian School were acritical supporters of modernity, neither can it be claimed that they were pure democratic thinkers. They were liberal thinkers who had grasped the value of democracy as a feature intimately bound up with the subjectivist dynamics of the market economy, and had incorporated it into their liberal tradition. But this by no means prevented them from seeing and speaking out against both the degeneration of modernity as represented by *constructivist scientism*, and also the degeneration of democracy in the welfare state. In the case of Hayek – who dealt most exhaustively with the problem – this critique started out from an analysis of the contrast between *naturality* and *artificiality*, going on to recast the history of the ideas of Western civilization and their evolution. Hence the problem of the foundation of the best regime took on a rather different form from either that of the discovery and imitation of a *natural order*, or that of the creation of a *rational order* which is the fruit of a contract. The concept of the 'best regime', understood as rationalistic construction of political order – undeniably one of the distinctive features of modernity – thus appeared as the chief target of Hayek's criticism. Despite identifying this concept as the theoretical premise of what was later to turn into totalitarianism, Hayek showed in his analysis that he was nevertheless fully aware that this ideal line of development was not the ineluctable outcome of the entire evolutionary process of Western political philosophy; rather, it was no more than an overestimation of the role that reason can play in human affairs.

The theoretical problem of the Austrian School can be summarized as the attempt to understand why the pursuit of subjective ends should result in situations that are objectively valid. In a perspective of this kind, the market (understood as a system for information transmission) and political society are none other than the consequences – at times unforeseen – of the meeting of different aims and bodies of knowledge that enrich society with their constant differentiation and evolution. But such a process requires there to be inbuilt safeguards of continual exchange. The principle that every action is to be seen as a shift from a situation believed to be *subjectively* worse to one believed to be *subjectively* better thus appears as an explanatory principle of human action valid in all fields of the social sciences.

The philosophical premise of this liberalism was, then, that the best solution to the problem of how to live together in society must spring from comparing and contrasting different subjective solutions. But this also meant denying the existence of a concept of political society and of value systems stemming from any origin other than the more or less involuntary products of human action. By the same token, it implied that history, like society, economics and morals, was none other than the succession of solutions individuals have proposed in order to solve their own problems.

Unless it is kept in mind that the factors which engendered society were typified by the concepts of *need*, of *exchange* in its broadest meaning and of *scarcity* leading to the alternative use of resources, a true understanding of the nature of politics will continue to elude us. Scarcity, above all, may be defined as one of the fundamental laws of politics, valid both in relations between individuals and also in relations between states. And untenable though it may be to imagine a *pure economic theory of politics*, political philosophy can derive nothing but benefit from an economic assessment of its theoretical and practical problems. Economic science thus proves to be invaluable for political philosophy, as can readily be supported by pointing to the interest that the solution of theoretical problems of political economy indisputably arouses in the field of political philosophy. This conviction is equally well supported by the fact that, if political philosophy lacked a solid economic component, it would be tantamount to a mere intellectualistic reflection on the best political regime. That is, it would end up being simply a speculative, ethical, metaphysical interpretation, under another guise, of the origin of *civil society* and its nature, or else it would turn into the violent construction of a regime producing subjects rather than citizens.

In other words, political philosophy can overcome the vanity of the theoretical constructions that have so often been its hallmark only by positively reappraising the political-economic aspect of its objects. Such a view appears to hold true with particular force at the present time. For after political philosophy succeeded in freeing itself from the clutches of revelation and theology, it was subjected to the fierce grip of historicism, modern natural science and nihilistic relativism. The ensuing impasse leads first and foremost to the crucial necessity of a critical assessment of modernity with all its myths, and it is thus that the philosophical and political reflections of the Austrian School thinkers may be read and interpreted.

An additional consideration regarding the influence of Aristotle on the

Austrian School may be mentioned here. This influence, so strong and decisive in Menger, waned progressively until it all but disappeared. For Mises and Hayek did maintain Menger's method (*methodological individualism* in its subsequent conceptual refinements) but not the Aristotelian content that explained the shift from simpler forms of social aggregation (the family) to more complex groupings with reference to the concept of 'essence' [*Wesen*]. The root of the differences betwen Menger, Mises and Hayek can be traced in the position they took vis-à-vis this problem.

The reflections of Menger, Mises and Hayek unfolded in a setting and an era characterized by the success of the phenomenon of socialism. Their attacks on this phenomenon and the opposition they showed to it may now appear to have been overtaken by the course of events. Nothing could be further from the truth, however, than the assumption that their teachings are no longer of any relevance: firstly, because socialism is simply the most high-profile aspect of a mentality that is far from being defeated; secondly, because the degenerative phenomena in Western democracies pinpointed by Hayek have only just begun to be critically reconsidered. Beyond the undeniable merits of their analysis of socialism and interventionism, and apart from the historical confirmation of their predictions, it appears that their theses have most definitely not been falsified. It would be a grave mistake to disregard their political philosophy by recognizing that they were right on the issue of socialism and forgetting that what they elaborated was indeed precisely that, a political philosophy, i.e. reflections on the *best political order.* For, as such, it has a theoretical status that, paradoxically, cannot be discarded along with socialism; it is closely bound up with a reflection on the history of political philosophy that raises a number of interesting and topical questions.

This book can thus be taken as an attempt to show how the consequences that the *theory of subjective values* has for the theoretical social sciences, and in particular for the concept of 'good', affect the concept of *common good*, which constitutes the focal point of the explorations of political philosophy as the *search for the best regime.* It is an investigation of the way the exponents of the Austrian School, and in particular Hayek, approached the problem of political philosophy, taking into account the transformations of the concepts of *good* and *value*, and the need to avert a relativistic outcome. The Austrian School's political philosophy therefore assumes an antithetical position with regard to socialist ideologies. But it also represents a critical stimulus directed towards democratic and liberal theories which have not yet realized that the philosophical and economic presuppositions of their theory of human action no longer stand up against the evidence of reality. A simple example will suffice: one need only think of the unwanted consequences of democracy.

NOTES

1 In general on the Austrian School, see Howey, 1960; Kauder, 1965; Hayek, 1968a, pp. 458–62; Mises, 1969; Streissler, 1972, pp. 426–41; 1988, pp. 191–204 and 1990b, pp. 151–89; White, 1977; Taylor, 1980; Hutchison, 1981, pp. 176–232; Shand, 1984 and 1990; Barry, 1986b, pp. 58–80; Craver, 1986, pp. 1–32; Leser, 1986a; Pheby, 1988, pp. 95–113; Negishi, 1989, pp. 279–317; Boehm, 1990, pp. 201–41; De Vecchi, 1990, pp. 311–47; Hébert, 1990, pp. 190–200; Kirzner, 1990a, pp. 242–9; Parsons, 1990, pp. 295–319; Rosner, 1990.

2 See Böhm-Bawerk, 1896, 1921.

3 See in particular Wieser, 1914, 1926.

4 See Berger, 1986, where the references to Mises and Hayek are on pp. 188–9, and pp. 4, 6–7, 21, 80, 82, 88, 205, respectively; Pellicani, 1988; Seldon, 1990, opens with the claim that «Capitalism requires not defence but celebration» (p. ix).

1

METHODOLOGICAL PROBLEMS

Wieso vermögen dem Gemeinwohl dienende und für dessen Entwickelung höchst bedeutsame Institutionen ohne einen auf ihre Begründung gerichteten *Gemeinwillen* zu entstehen?
(Menger, *Untersuchungen*)

1. *Methodological foundations*; 2. *The* Methodenstreit *and its legacy*; 3. *The critique of historicism*; 4. *The critique of scientism and of constructivist rationalism*

§ 1. METHODOLOGICAL FOUNDATIONS

Menger's *Untersuchungen über die Methode der Socialwissenschaften, und der politischen Oekonomie insbesondere*[1] occupies a pre-eminent position in the history of the social sciences. For it is in this work that the first steps were taken towards an investigation of epistemological problems that are still wide open today, while at the same time the methodological and political implications of *Historismus*[2] were brought to the fore. Indeed, not only did the *Untersuchungen* play a fundamental role in clarifying the basic issues at the heart of the theoretical social sciences; they also enabled a new framework to be established for relations between the social sciences and the two phenomena that have been the overriding feature of the study of these sciences for the last several centuries, namely the tendency to study them from an empirical-naturalistic point of view, and the trend towards studying them from a historical viewpoint.

But much of the importance of this work also resides in its position as the focal point of the Austrian School's philosophy of the social sciences and epistemology. Apart from the misunderstandings of Mises's and Hayek's occasionally diverging views, it has exerted constant influence both over methodological, philosophical and political questions and also over the objectives around which the polemics revolved. The arguments put forward by Hayek and Mises against the theories of knowledge of historicism and socialism are inevitably drawn into this complex of issues.

The *Untersuchungen*, however, not only represent a treatise on the theoretical social sciences and a polemical tract, but can also be seen as the first attempt to forge a link between the study of the social sciences and the marked shift in the science of economics that goes under the name of the 'marginalist revolution'. Menger thus has the merit of having made clear that the *theory of subjective values* would lead to a profound change in the theoretical approach to the social sciences, for his conception of economics was that of a discipline capable of opening up new perspectives in the interpretation of motivations and prediction of the outcome of human action. This stood in contrast to the predominant approach in the Germanic region, which regarded economics as occupying a lower-ranking position within the framework of the *allgemeine Staatslehre*.[3] Menger, on the other hand, reshaped the web of relations between politics, ethics and economics, reclaiming the latter from the purely instrumental and subordinate status previously assigned to it, and drew up a new theory of the origin and development of social institutions.

Once attention has been focused on these innovative aspects, the question arises whether the criticisms levelled against the Historical School of German Economists can be restricted simply to the epistemological problems involved in the reduction of the science of economics to the history of economics.[4] For this line of interpretation does not give a satisfactory explanation of why Menger should have devoted so much time and energy to criticizing a research programme when he was aware of the triviality of the epistemological foundations on which it rested. In fact, his criticisms were directed not only against the methodological approach, but against the ideological programme of the Historical School of German Economists as well. He identified this programme as consisting not just in the reduction of the science of economics to economic history, but more particularly in a refusal to acknowledge the relevance of the 'marginalist revolution', and furthermore in an attempt to consider economics as a tool of politics and ethics.

The conceptual scheme of the *Untersuchungen* unfolds through a series of criticisms directed towards (1) the positivist doctrine of science (F. Bacon, Comte, J.S. Mill), (2) the role of rationalist knowledge in human affairs (Smith) and (3) the claim that theoretical knowledge of human concerns can be derived from history (Roscher, Knies, Hildebrand, Schmoller). In other words, Menger refused to accept the positivist conception of science together with the fragmenting of knowledge; he rejected the pragmatism of 'abstract rationalism', and he contested the validity of the founding theories of knowledge and the conclusions of the Historical School of German Economists.

A salient feature of the *Untersuchungen* is thus their criticism of the theoretical and cultural presuppositions of the Historical School of German Economists, in particular the latter's attempt to ground all knowledge in history. Yet Menger did not cast doubt on the value of historical knowledge in the field of political action; rather, he drew on examples taken from Plato, Aristotle, Machiavelli, Bodin or the Physiocratics, Voltaire, Montesquieu, Smith and Savigny to deny any originality in what were purported by the exponents of the Historical School to be important discoveries.[5]

Another important feature of this critism concerned the classification of the economic sciences and their method. Menger distinguished three groups:

> first, the *historical* sciences (history) and statistics of economy, which have the task of investigating and describing the individual nature and the individual connection of economic phenomena; second, *theoretical* economics, with the task of investigating and describing their general nature and general connection (their laws); finally, third, the *practical* sciences of national economy, with the task of investigating and describing the basic principles for suitable action (adapted to the variety of conditions) in the field of national economy (economic policy and the science of finance).[6]

This subdivision was to be found again, structured in greater detail, in the concluding part of the work.[7] Menger reproached the Historical School of German Economists for what he saw as a confusion between the three types of science and for deducing norms of practical action from a mistaken conception of economic science. Any social policy founded on a false conception of human life will be doomed to failure.[8] This classification, which appears as the systematic nucleus of the *Untersuchungen*, may be helpful for a better understanding of Menger's critical assessment of the Historical School. It may also provide insight into the relation between empirical-realistic orientation, and exact orientation and between *empirical laws* and *exact laws*. Finally, it can shed light on the function of economic science.

The fundamental mistake made by the Historical School of German Economists was that of conceiving society as an *empirical and organic-naturalistic whole*. This led members of the school to study society by means of a method of investigation – the inductive-comparative method – which proved to be unsuited to its nature as a whole. Consequently, the goal pursued by this school of discovering the laws governing society and history could not lead to theoretically acceptable results.

Unlike the Historical School of German Economists, which tended to regard social bodies as data and underestimated the role of individuals in their formation, Menger considered such bodies to be the product, at times involuntary, of individual choices. Thus a theoretical knowledge of society cannot, in his view, be founded on empirical generalizations, but rather will have to start out by splitting up more complex facts into their simpler component parts. Just like other 'exact laws', then, theoretical economics will be called upon to investigate «the concrete phenomena of the real word as exemplifications of a certain regularity in the succession of phenomena, i.e. genetically». Therefore his discovery model was to consist in an attempt to explain «the complicated phenomena of the research field peculiar to it as the result of the coworking of the factors responsible for its origin. *This genetic element is inseparable from the idea of theoretical sciences.*»[9]

Thus the problem facing Menger was that of understanding and providing an answer to the following question: «*how can it be that institutions which serve the common welfare and are extremely significant for its development come into being without a* common will *directed towards establishing them*?» But he had no intention of theorizing the pre-eminence of economics within the framework of the social sciences. For among the institutions which «are to no small extent the unintended result of social development» he numbered law, religion, language, state, money, market, prices of goods, interest rates, ground rents, wages and many other phenomena of social life and in particular of economy.[10]

This marked a shift from the organicist naturalism of the Historical School of German Economists, from positivism and the individualistic tradition of rationalist liberalism, for Menger's interpretation saw the history of mankind as an *evolution* that was in some sense underpinned by a 'naturality' or 'essence' [*Wesen*] inherent in man. This conception of history may also be viewed as an extension of the concept of society Menger derived from Aristotle,[11] now seen as embracing the entire historical process.

This approach led Menger to deny that the phenomena of the human world can be considered on a par with phenomena belonging to the natural world. But he was also critical of the interpretation of the origin of human institutions – which he defined as 'pragmatistic' – put forward by those who consider these institutions to be the products arising from individual or collective human will. He objected on the grounds that not all institutions can be explained in this manner. This «pragmatic» interpretation – an approach Menger also ascribed to Smith – was to his mind typical of a «one-sided rationalistic liberalism [*einseitiger rationalistischer Liberalismus*]», of a «partially superficial pragmatism [*zum Theil oberflächlicher Pragmatismus*]». By the very attempt to wipe the slate clean of any irrational aspects and create new, more rational institutions, this approach, in Menger's view, was doomed and «contrary to the intention of its representatives inexorably leads to socialism».[12]

Menger did not extend to the philosophy of the social sciences the method and aims of the science of economics. But he did extend to the theoretical social sciences (including economics) a theory of human action and of the rise and development of social institutions. The revolutionary nucleus of his thought thus consists of the new avenues his *theory of subjective values* opened up in the study of social phenomena.

Confirmation of the view that Menger did not aim to formulate an economic interpretation of the birth and development of society comes from his conviction that the earliest reaction to pragmatism arose in the field of law. For it was Burke, «trained for it by the spirit of English jurisprudence», who was able to understand «with full awareness the significance of the organic structures of social life and the partly unintended origins of these». This interpretation, previously put forward by Montesquieu, achieved full actualization in Germany, where Burke's ideas acted as the spur «for an attack on pragmatism in jurisprudence». And indeed first Gustav Hugo, followed by Savigny and then by Barthold G. Niebuhr, conceived of the law as «the unintended result of a higher wisdom, of the historical development of the nations», and rejected the contentions of those who, while claiming to be using the tools of «pure abstract understanding», were actually pressing for a «comprehensive construction of the law».[13]

Far from regarding existing social institutions as unalterable, the founders of the Historical School of Law were in effect aiming to achieve a more thorough understanding of such institutions. In opposition to the reformism of 'one-sided rationalism' they urged not so much a return to the past as a greater emphasis on the wisdom and flexibility of institutions shaped by the course of history, an approach which abstract rationalism would not countenance, driven as it was by its ambition to make reality conform to reason.[14]

Thus when faced with the positivism of Comte and Mill,[15] with *Historismus* which made no distinction between history, politics and economics and, furthermore, with *abstract rationalism* as an offshoot of English tenment, Menger did not disguise his affinity with the method of the Historical School of Law. Nor did he conceal his close relation to Savigny, who had had considerable insight into the importance of historical and environmental affairs in the shaping of language and the law without however eschewing a theoretical account of these issues.[16]

But as well as dissenting from the Historical School of Law, his criticism of the Historical School of German Economists also encompassed remarks of a philosophical nature linked to the relation between the practical, historical and theoretical sciences,[17] and likewise to the distinction between

> two main orientations of research in general and in the realm of economic phenomena in particular: the *individual* (the historical) and the *general* (the theoretical). The former strives for the cognition of the individual nature and the individual connection of phenomena, the latter for that of their general nature and general connection.[18]

Thus the aim of the theoretical sciences is to establish

> the types (the empirical forms [*die Erscheinungsformen*]) and the typical relationships (the laws [*die Gesetze*]) of phenomena. By this they are to provide us with theoretical understanding, a cognition going beyond immediate experience, and, whenever we have the conditions of a phenomenon within our control, control over it.[19]

For Menger's aim was to bring together «in strict types the phenomena of the real world as they are presented in their empirical reality and by obtaining their strictly typical relationships – 'laws of nature' [*'Naturgesetze'*]». He was fully aware that «the desire to determine strict categories of empirical forms comprising 'all empirical realities' (according to their full content) is therefore an unattainable goal of theoretical research». An objective of this kind would thus appear to be even harder to obtain through realistic investigation that endeavours to discover general laws by starting out from observation of regularities in the overall behaviour of phenomena.[20] «Aristotle recognized this correctly when he denied the strictly scientific character of induction» («the inductive method perfected essentially by Bacon»), asserting that this method did not open up the means to achieve strict laws of phenomena (*strenge exacte Gesetze der Erscheinungen*).[21]

Setting out from a critique of the investigative limits of the inductive method, therefore, Menger's goal was to reach «*exact laws of nature* [*exacte Naturgesetze*]».[22] These were not to be the «result of an empirical realistic research» but rather an 'exact' investigation valid in the fields of natural and social phenomena and «essentially different from Bacon's empirical-realistic induction». The confusion surrounding the *exact laws of nature* and how to succeed in obtaining them thus lay at the root of the mistake made by those social philosophers who attempted to obtain «exact social laws» by means of empirical research.[23] All this

> has had the consequence of causing some of them to try to attain *exact* laws of social phenomena in an 'empirical' way, that is, not in an *exact* way. But it induces others of them to apply the standards of *exact* research to the results of empirical research in the realm of the social sciences and conversely the standards of empirical research to the results of exact social research. These are two errors which have had an equally pernicious effect on the development of the social sciences. We must attribute to them the greater part of the misunderstandings which dominate theoretical social research in its present-day form and in its present endeavors.[24]

But if the critique of inductivism retains much of its topical interest and goes far beyond the theoretical horizon of positivism represented by the Historical School of German Economists, the whole issue of the 'nature' of the «exact laws of nature» is nevertheless far more complex. This concerns, in other words, those

> strict laws of phenomena, of regularities in the succession of phenomena which do not present themselves to us as absolute, but which in respect to the approaches to cognition by which we attain to them simply bear within themselves the guarantee of absoluteness. It is the determination of laws of phenomena which commonly are called 'laws of nature'

> [*Naturgesetze*] but more correctly should be designated by the expression '*exact laws*' [*exacte* Gesetze].[25]

If the aim is to strive to formulate 'exact laws', then theoretical investigation must start out from the search for the «*simplest elements* of everything real» and conceive of them «as strictly typical». Thus they can only partly be determined on an empirical-realistic basis, for the whole point of the research is to determine «empirical forms which *qualitatively* are strictly typical». This means attaining *typical concepts* which

> must not be tested by full empirical reality (for the empirical forms under discussion [. . .] exist in part only in our ideas). However, these results correspond to the specific task of the exact orientation of theoretical research and are the necessary basis and the presupposition of obtaining *exact laws*.[26]

Inasmuch as science strives to formulate «typical relationships (exact laws) of phenomena», exact science does not concern itself with the way facts really happen: it examines, rather, how more complicated phenomena develop from the simplest, in part even unempirical elements of the real world in their (likewise unempirical) isolation from all other influences, with constant consideration of exact (likewise ideal!) measure'.[27]

Exact science is thus 'striving' to discover «strict laws». Its starting point is that there do exist «strictly typical elements» which can be thrown into sharp relief if they are imagined «in complete isolation from all other causative factors». In this manner Menger gave voice to his belief that it is possible to achieve the formulation of «laws of phenomena which are not only absolute, but according to our laws of thinking simply cannot be thought of in any other way but as absolute». He then set about discovering these «exact laws», i.e. the «'laws of nature' of phenomena».[28] If applied to social phenomena, this approach consists

> in the fact that we trace back [*zurückführen*] human phenomena to their most original and simplest constitutive factors. We join to the latter the measure corresponding to their nature, and finally try to investigate the laws by which more complicated human phenomena are formed from those simplest elements, thought of in their isolation.[29]

Despite reference to our «laws of thinking», these 'exact laws of nature' cannot be interpreted along Kantian lines. Never, however, did Menger establish a direct correlation between the concept of an 'exact law of nature' and Aristotle.[30] Certainly, though, the combination of a conception of 'law' as a 'natural relation of phenomena' to be discovered by 'exact science' , with a recognition of the intangible quality of the subjectivity inherent in human relations, did indeed raise problems of a philosophical order which could appear to be insoluble unless they are conceived within the Aristotelian framework. Thus it is helpful here to mention Aristotle in order to grasp Menger's theory of value, goods and needs.[31] Both in Aristotle and in the leading figures of the Austrian School (though references to Aristotle in Mises and Hayek are very infrequent and somewhat controversial) one finds a theory of rational action that rests on the premise that human knowledge is finite, and sets itself the goal of achieving a «good» that cannot be taught. This good admits of no physical, metaphysical or cosmological derivation, for it belongs instead to the sphere of human knowledge.

Menger's interests thus focused on the complex of laws of nature that forms the basis of the satisfaction of human needs and their evolution over time as the range of human activities and needs expands. It follows that the starting point is not represented by a rationalist perspective, or a hedonistic approach as in Jevons, but rather by the *naturality of the needs*.[32] One may therefore speak of 'exact laws of nature' since it is clear that whenever the results of the subjective choices made by those who are endeavouring to appease their (natural) needs come into contact with the results of an infinite number of other individual choices, the outcome does not degenerate into *chaos*, but rather 'arranges itself' according to a certain *order* that is natural to man.[33] The laws of nature thus tend to be identified with the *genetic essence* [*Wesen*] of phenomena.[34] Essentially, then, Menger was not setting himself the aim of imposing a rational order on human reality. Rather, he wished both to discover how human action directed towards ends that are known to be influenced by the finiteness of human knowledge succeeds in producing an order, and also to obtain insight into the latter's *Wesen*.

In effect, the philosophical issues which concerned Menger had more affinities with Aristotelian philosophical themes (although not necessarily filtered through neo-Aristotelian authors or Thomists, who are given no mention in the *Untersuchungen*) than with natural-right, Kantian or positivist philosophical issues.[35]

Together with the *Untersuchungen*, the most significant works for an understanding of the philosophical and methodological foundations of the Austrian School, and of the differences between its exponents,[36] are the collection of essays by Mises, *Grundprobleme der Nationalökonomie*, of 1933,[37] and the essay by Hayek 'Scientism and the Study of Society', published between 1942 and 1944.[38]

In these works Mises and Hayek reaffirm the continuity between their methodology and that of Menger (though they diverge in the emphasis placed on various aspects, and at times there are significant distinctions). By contrast, the whole question of whether the external world can be truly known reveals a Kantian influence that was alien to Menger.

The problem to which we will now turn, however, consists only in part in reconstructing the genesis and foundation of the philosophy of the theoretical social sciences espoused by the exponents of the Austrian School. Rather, it appears more interesting to explore the different ways of thinking that distinguished its three major figures. Certainly Menger, Mises and Hayek all believed *order* to derive from a complex of individual actions which are composed into more complex social phenomena. But while in Menger's view this 'composition' came about *genetically*, according to «a certain regularity in the succession of phenomena»[39] that is grounded in the naturalness of the satisfaction of needs, for Mises and Hayek the assuaging of needs was not so much 'natural' as 'subjective'.

This difference can be made clearer by comparing Menger's general theory of goods and needs with those of Mises and Hayek.

For Menger, the task of economic science was «to attempt to classify the various goods according to their inherent characteristics, to learn the place that each good occupies in the causal nexus of goods, and finally, to discover the economic laws to which they are subject». He therefore classified goods into *three orders*, believing that «human beings experience directly and immediately only needs for goods of the first order – that is, for goods that can be used directly for the satisfaction of their needs».[40]

Mises, on the other hand, in dealing with the question of the transformation brought about in economic science by subjectivist economists and the general theory of choice and preference, stated in *Human Action* that

> choosing determines all human decisions. In making his choice man chooses not only between various material things and services. All human values are offered for option. All ends and all means, both material and ideal issues, the sublime and the base, the noble and the ignoble, are ranged in a single row and subjected to a decision which picks out one thing and sets aside another.

Further on, he pointed to

> the impulse to live, to preserve one's own life [. . .] present in every living being. However, to yield to this impulse is not – for man – an inevitable necessity [. . .] man has the power to master even these impulse [. . .] To live is for man the outcome of a choice, of a judgment of value.[41]

Hayek's view, as put forward in 'Scientism and the Study of Society', recognized that «every important advance in economic theory during the last hundred years was a further step in the consistent application of subjectivism». Giving Mises credit for having pursued this line of development further than any other scholar, he proceeded to connect methodological individualism to «subjectivism of the social sciences».[42]

The contrast is thus seen to lie in the fact that for Menger the ability to understand and give an account of human action was made possible by the existence of a *natural* component in the succession of phenomena – 'exact laws of nature' common both to concrete phenomena of the real world,[43] and to the thought processes of our minds – whereas Mises and Hayek held the view that it was the structure of the human mind itself that made it possible to classify, describe and explain individual actions and social phenomena.

The differences between Menger and Mises have their origin in diverging assumptions concerning the relation between laws governing phenomena of the natural and social world, on the one hand, and thought processes on the other. Menger, like Aristotle, believed this relation to be of a natural order, whereas Mises thought that «reason and experience show us two separate realms: the external world of physical [. . .] phenomena and the internal world of thought, feeling, valuation, and purposeful action. No bridge connects [. . .] these two spheres.»[44]

If one browses through Mises after reading the *Untersuchungen* one soon becomes aware of an overall approach to theoretical problems and a kind of terminology both of which show no influence from Menger, but rather bear the stamp of neo-Kantian philosophy. The very fact that Mises proposed to endow the sciences of human action with the same logical character and universal validity as the nomothetic sciences provides a striking distinction from Menger's thought. It may thus be deemed pointless to look to Menger in the search for the foundations of Mises's praxeology, quite apart from the misunderstandings of Menger's methodology that appear in Mises.[45]

In *Human Action*, Mises explicitly asserted the a priori character of the science of human action:

> praxeology is a theoretical and systematic, not a historical, science [. . .] It aims at knowledge valid for all instances in which the conditions exactly correspond to those implied in its assumptions and inferences. Its statements and propositions are not derived from experience. They are, like those of logic and mathematics, a priori. They are not subject to verification or falsification on the ground of experience and facts. They are both logically and temporally antecedent to any comprehension of historical facts. They are a necessary requirement of any intellectual grasp of historical events. Without them we should not be able to see in the course of events anything else than kaleidoscopic change and chaotic muddle.[46]

The starting point for praxeology is thus a «reflection about the essence of action»[47] founded on the «essential and necessary character of the logical structure of the human mind». In other words, its basis is a «*methodological apriorism*», the presupposition for which consists of «a set of tools for grasping reality» which are «logically prior to any experience».[48] This a priori structure of the mind is what makes *praxeology* possible. In this perspective, «action is the manifestation of a man's will»,[49] yet, equally, it is the «essence of his nature and existence». Inasmuch as it is «satisfaction of some desire of the acting man», «human action is necessarily always rational». Hence the impossibility of distinguishing and discriminating between ends, while any distinction between 'natural' and 'rational needs', on the one hand, and 'artificial' and 'irrational needs', on the other, is obliterated. For Mises, «to live is for man the outcome of a choice, of a judgment of value»[50] concerning which science can make no pronouncements.

The categories of *means* and *ends*, *cause* and *effect* accordingly rose to the status of presupposition for an understanding of human action, which was seen as taking place in a world governed by causality:

> in a world without causality and regularity of phenomena there would be no field for human reasoning and human action. Such a world would be a chaos in which man would be at a loss to find any orientation and guidance.

By 'guidance', Mises did not mean conforming to the natural order of the cosmos or the «search after the ultimate cause of being and existence», but simply the quest for causal linkages in order to discover the point where one has to «interfere in order to attain this or that end». This was, then, an external world lacking in ontological dignity of its own, in which it was necessary to interfere with the causal regularities in order to achieve subjective ends.[51]

What had disappeared in Mises's framework was the relation between individual interest and the naturalness of phenomena (and of action) which characterized Menger's thought. It was replaced by *subjectivism* aiming at discovering the universal and a priori laws that regulate action itself and allow the achievement of individual ends. The presupposition of the knowability of the world thus ceased to be the natural structure, common both to the external world and the human mind. The 'exact laws of nature' were replaced by a priori laws, logical considerations endowed with universal validity.

But a further distinction between Mises's position and that of Menger concerning the nature of society lay in the differing *general theory of goods and needs.* While the opening chapters of the *Grundsätze* clearly show that for Menger goods and needs had a 'natural' foundation, in Mises's view not only were needs and goods treated as 'subjective' entities, but indeed the function of economic science took on a very different configuration.

Let us consider a brief illustration of the respective positions and the distance between them.

In the first edition of the *Grundsätze*, Menger asserted that «needs arise from our drives and the drives are imbedded in our nature [. . .] the satisfaction of our needs is synonymous with the attempt to provide for our lives and well-being».[52] Despite the fact that in the 1923 edition Menger placed somewhat more emphasis on elements of a cultural order,[53] distance from the position of Mises remained considerable. In this latter edition Menger wrote that

> the quality of a good frequently depends on knowledge, and therefore error and ignorance may influence our relations with things [. . .] The more civilized a people becomes, and, moreover, the deeper its knowledge of human nature and of relations with the outside world, so also there is an increase in the number of its real goods and, consequently, a decrease in the number of imaginary goods.[54]

Mises, on the other hand, does not constantly refer to 'human nature' in the manner so characteristic of Menger's line of argument. For Mises, indeed, «goods, commodities and wealth and all the other notions of conduct are not elements of nature; they are elements of human meaning and conduct».[55] Although he did maintain Menger's classification and distinction between 'first-order goods' and 'remote or higher-order goods', and likewise between «man's "real" needs and imaginary and spurious appetites», Mises felt that «such judgments are beside the point for a science dealing with the reality of human action. Not what a man should do, but what he does, counts for praxeology and economics».[56] In accentuating the subjective character of the evaluation of goods, Mises seemed to be going so far as to reject the function ascribed to economic science of pointing towards the best way of satisfying an agent's needs by teaching him or her how to distinguish between 'real' and 'imaginary' needs.

In the early 1940s, Hayek's position differed from that of both Menger and Mises,[57] although he did follow rather more clearly in Menger's footsteps than Mises did. But while crediting Mises with opening up new fertile avenues to economic and social research through his 'subjectivism', Hayek's application of subjectivism to methodology of the theoretical social sciences did not reach the extremes of Mises. As early as his essay 'Scientism and the Study of Society', Hayek revealed a clear awareness that the object of theoretical social science did not consist of «our given concepts or even sensations». Rather, it comprised «a new organization» of the relation between individual experience and the external world, which was to come about by reformulating subjective sensations and, with the aid of abstraction, classifying phenomena according to theoretical criteria.[58]

Foreshadowing problems that would later be developed in *The Sensory Order*,[59] Hayek put forward the view that perception of the external world takes place through «sensations and concepts which are organized in a mental structure common to all of them». The task of science was therefore to provide a continuous re-elaboration of the «picture of the external world that man possesses».[60] Theoretical science was no longer to concern itself with relations between things but rather with the way perception and knowledge of the external world have a determining effect both on individual and collective action and on the involuntary effects of such action. This means that it would concern itself not so much with things *in se* as with the way 'things' assume certain configurations in the minds of agents and thereby influence the latter's action.[61]

While not denying the existence of «laws of nature» more or less analogous to those of the natural sciences, Hayek tended to look beyond the issue of whether or not they may be objectively true, and focused his interest on an attempt to grasp how the agent understands them, and the consequences deriving therefrom.[62] The presupposition for an understanding of human action was thus no longer, as in Menger, the existence of a *natural-genetic order* of succession of phenomena, but rather the way in which this order is subjectively understood by agents. Consequently, identification of the component elements of human relations was grounded on the fact that these elements «are known to us from the working of our own minds».[63] Knowledge of the external world was thus assured not by a uniform succession of phenomena but by the sheer fact that phenomena become understandable through the conceptual workings of the human mind.

The different philosophical approaches brought to light through analysis of the theory of knowledge underpinning the works of Menger, Mises and Hayek naturally have important consequences as regards political philosophy. A mitigating force can, however, also be seen in their common identification of the object of theoretical social science, centring on the belief that social institutions are the result – frequently involuntary – of actions by means of which individuals endeavour to solve their problems.

§ 2. THE *METHODENSTREIT* AND ITS LEGACY

The dispute between the Historical School of German Economists and the Austrian School has gone down in the history of the social sciences as a methodological one. In fact, the points of contention lay not so much in different methodological approaches (which are nevertheless undeniable and run extremely deep) as, far more importantly, in philosophical, economic and political motivations. For the Austrians, discussion revolved around five main themes: (1) the nature and origin of social institutions; (2) the method by which they should be studied; (3) the nature and aims of economic science; (4) the political conclusions of these investigations and (5) the role of the Historical School of Economy in German affairs.

The methodological problem, viewed by Menger as an opposition between an *empirical* and a *theoretical* perspective, has waned in interest when seen from the present-day vantage point.[64] From an epistemological point of view, the discussion thus became one of whether positivistic methods, aimed at the inductive establishment of general laws of dubious theoretical value, could be applied to the social sciences. In this regard, not even Menger, after *Die Irrthümer des Historismus* and 'Grundzüge einer Klassifikation der Wirtschaftswissenschaften', felt the need to go back over the earlier issue any further. Thus the interest raised by this discussion appears to have been linked to the great esteem in which the inductive method was held at the time, and this contributed to an underestimation of its philosophical and political implications.

It was only with Mises's work *Die Grundprobleme der Nationalokönomie* that the full consequences for the theoretical social sciences became apparent. For by starting out from what he believed to be Menger's «intuitions», Mises highlighted the repercussions of the *theory of subjective values* on the whole investigative framework of the social sciences, and in particular on the theory of human action.

With the *Untersuchungen*, as had been the case earlier with the *Grundsätze*, Menger had established the premises for a new conceptual structure in the social sciences. But the implications of these developments either failed to be noted or were misunderstood, or else it was thought that this 'revolution' was restricted to economic science. Consequently, discussion centred on the 'historicity' or 'theoreticity' of the method of the social sciences, i.e. according to the schemas and issues of the day. Menger himself, imbued with pessimism, had kept silent on methodological matters since 1889 (or, alternatively, he was working on notes and outlines for a new 'philosophical anthropology' of which no more than a handful of unrelated jottings have come down to us).[65] Wieser and Böhm-Bawerk – their confidence bolstered by the success of the 'theory of marginal utility' in economic science and neglecting its philosophical and political implications – believed that the *Methodenstreit*, all things considered, had been a waste of time.[66] Wieser, furthermore, dealt with the problems of method from a psychologistic and empiricist perspective that was alien to Menger,[67] which certainly did not help to clarify the originality of the Austrians' contribution to the social sciences.

The triumph of the marginalist revolution in the field of economic science had thus not been matched by similar success in the field of the social sciences. For in accusing Menger of 'atomism', the exponents of the Historical School of German Economists not only failed to recognize where there was a break with the tradition of classical economics, but were also unable to grasp the implications of the theory of subjective values in the framework of the social sciences. This failure was compounded by their constant refusal to recognize its import within the framework of economic science inasmuch as they persisted in viewing it as a historical science.

The *Methodenstreit* thus has the virtue of underlining that the theory of subjective values brought about a change not only in the conceptual and methodological structure of the theoretical social sciences, but also in the very manner of interpreting history and politics. For this reason, the Austrians' arguments, directed against those who endeavoured to deduce practical norms for individual and political action from the presumed discovery of the laws and meaning of history, are still of considerable topical interest. This can be attributed to their concern with the problem of the validity and effectiveness of practical norms derived from false general laws: one of the central problems not only of economic science but also of political philosophy.

Indeed, if the theory of Austrian marginalism concerning the origin and satisfaction of needs has a bearing on the other social sciences, then the entire conceptual framework of political philosophy will have to be rebuilt. The latter will no longer enjoy a privileged relation to ethics or law, but rather one to economics, in which the latter is understood not so much as a technique for the satisfaction of needs, or as a tool for statalistic power, but instead as a valid instrument for an understanding of *human action*. Economics, in this sense, results from the realization that human action is grounded in the problem of *scarcity*.

In the light of the dispute with Schmoller,[68] in 1889 Menger returned to the theme of the systematic configuration of economic science in his essay 'Grundzüge einer Klassifikation der Wirtschaftswissenschaften'. Here he distinguished between: (1) the historical sciences of economics, economic statistics and economic history; (2) the morphology of economic phenomena; (3) economic theory; and (4) practical or applied economics.[69] After reaffirming his own position, Menger identified the mistake made by the exponents of the Historical School of German Economists as residing in the connection set up between 'economic theory' and 'applied economics'. The reason was that, far from offering 'recipes' on how to behave in «every single concrete case», the applied sciences can only show «how generally determined human goals of a special kind can be most effectively realized in the light of diverse circumstances».[70] More than «sciences in the strict sense of the word», they were thus «scientific studies», attempts to provide rational answers to rational problems.[71] But Menger also believed that 'practical economic science' must draw its inspiration from an 'economic theory' that was free from error. Any social policy founded on a mistaken representation of life, even if operating under the best of intentions, will be doomed to failure.[72]

The unifying characteristic of the Austrian critique of the Historical School thus lay in the conviction that the latter's exponents (such as Marx and his followers) had not reached an understanding of economic science. Therefore the ensuing attempt to found a 'new' economic science rested on an inadequate understanding of the nature of this science, and on the attempt to group together disciplines – history, ethics and economics – which should be kept rigorously distinct. Having failed to grasp either the importance of the development of economic science or its character as a universally valid theoretical science, their plan to transform the discipline could not succeed. It is no coincidence that their project was politically rather than scientifically motivated, arising from the the desire to create a new economic science that would provide an alternative to the liberal-individualistic model in the form of a collectivist and organicist model idealized as the peculiar character of German culture.

But if in the *Grundsätze* Menger frequently worked on the ideas of Hildebrand, Knies and Roscher,[73] albeit adopting a critical stance, the atmosphere underwent a marked change in the *Untersuchungen.* For here Menger's dissent began to take on the sharp tone of clear-cut disagreement concerning the nature and articulation of economic science. Contesting the legitimacy of the comparison between Roscher's method and that of Savigny-Eichhorn, made by Roscher himself, Menger seized the opportunity to specify his criticisms in a series of objections to Roscher that can be extended to the entire Historical School:

> the vagueness about the nature of political economy and of its subdivisions; the lack of any really strict distinction of the historical, the theoretical, and the practical point of view in research in the economic field; the confusion of individual orientations of theoretical research and of the philosophy of economic history in particular with theoretical economics and with political economy at large; the vagueness about the nature of the exact orientation of theoretical research and its relationship to the empirical-realistic orientation; the opinion that the historical-philosophical orientation is the only one justified in political economy and is analogous to historical jurisprudence; the failure to recognize the true nature of the historical point of view in our science, especially as regards its theoretical aspects; the exaggerated importance which is attributed to the so-called historical method; the vagueness about the nature of the organic approach in economy and about the problems resulting therefrom for social research.[74]

This was in effect a series of «methodological errors» that were to spell disaster for the development of theoretical economics in Germany,[75] and which originated from the rash placement of excessive trust in the inductive method. These mistakes, together with the fact of having wrongly conceived of social institutions as biological organisms, were, in Menger's view, common both to the founder of the Historical School of German Economists, Roscher, and also to its followers.

While granting Hildebrand due merit for having distinguished «theoretical economics from the practical sciences of economy», Menger was critical of his denial of the existence of «"laws of nature" in economy». He also censured Hildebrand's belief that the essence of the historical method consisted in studying social phenomena from a collectivistic point of view and in the discovery «of the laws of national economic development».[76] Consequently he disagreed with the way Hildebrand conceived the task of the science of the economy of nations[77] and, equally, he dissented from the belief that there exists an «ethical orientation» of theoretical economics. An acceptance of the idea that the tasks of economics can be associated with the tasks of ethics would in fact lead to a blurring of the borders between two types of investigation of the real world that are legitimate but distinct.

Therefore Menger did not restrict himself to rejecting the idea of an «ethical orientation of exact economics», but indeed upheld the view that it had no place even among the *practical* economic sciences. For once the trivial consideration according to which all economic activity obeys moral rules on a par with juridical regulations and customs had been swept aside, such a belief could be laid bare as an affirmation of the need to subject economic science to ethical considerations, like a «moral writing about economy». Consequently, «an *ethical orientation of economics* has no greater justification than, for instance, that of an economic orientation of ethics». Otherwise, this would be tantamount to denying «the nature and peculiar problems of the theoretical and practical sciences of national economy» and underestimating «the economic aspect of national life in relation to other more highly esteemed aspects».[78]

The criticisms directed towards Knies were principally concerned with the subdivision of economics into three groups of sciences;[79] with the independence of the «economic element» as against the «total complex of the life of the state and nation»;[80] with the attempt to deduce the impossibility of «economic laws» from the demonstration of the falsehood of the dogma of individual interest;[81] and with the conception of economic theories as the result of historical development and, therefore, of their status as relative to the various stages of historical evolution.[82] Menger did not deny that Knies had given a boost to economic science, but reproached him for not having given a clear account of the question of the «nature and problems of the historical orientation of economy and its subdivisions», for denying the autonomy of exact economics and for regarding historical investigation as the only legitimate approach in the field of economic science understood as the science of collective economic phenomena.[83]

In his assessment of Roscher, in addition to the issues mentioned above, Menger was also critical of Roscher's scant comprehension of the aims of theoretical research,[84] and reproached him for confusion between the tasks of theoretical economics and those of history and economic statistics.[85] A serious misunderstanding of the nature of historical science thus led him «to the illusion that, from the study of history in general and of economy in particular, insight may be gained into the general nature and the general connection of the phenomena of human economy *in general*».[86] These mistakes were compounded by the belief that objective truths concerning politics could be derived from historical knowledge obtained by the comparative method[87], and furthermore by the concept of «economics as the science of the laws of development of national economy, of the economic life of a nation».[88]

As far as Schmoller's ideas were concerned, apart from the battle against the 'dogma of human self-interest',[89] Menger restricted himself to pointing out the triviality of the belief that it is well not to separate the understanding of economic phenomena from the complex of social and political phenomena.

In Menger's view, such problems are «not made more profound by Schmoller's categories, but are made obscure».[90]

The criticisms levelled against the exponents of the Historical School of German Economists in the *Untersuchungen* thus lead to a recognition that their attempt to open up new perspectives in economic science rested on a series of grave misunderstandings. In contrast to the *Grundsätze*, in the *Untersuchungen* Menger's criticisms were not without sarcasm. But the polemical vein foreshadowed in this work came more fully to the fore in *Die Irrthümer des Historismus*, where Schmoller rose from the status of bit-part-player to that of chief protagonist.

Apart from its effective polemical form, however, *Die Irrthümer des Historismus* contains few conceptual innovations. Rather, the novel elements are of a different nature. The first lay in Menger's choice of Schmoller as the target of his polemics. Menger was aware that the success of his own ideas within German culture was linked to the outcome of his dispute with the figure who had become the most authoritative and influential exponent of the *Kathedersozialisten*. Unfortunately this strategy was destined to involve a series of largely undesired repercussions. Menger knew of the differences between Schmoller and the first exponents of the Historical School of German Economists. Indeed, the chief subject of the controversy – aside from the usual methodological themes – concerned the possibility of considering history as «the empirical basis of the practical sciences of economy»,[91] an issue only touched on in the *Untersuchungen*. A further innovation consisted in extending the term *Historismus*, which in the *Untersuchungen* was used to designate the thought of Georg G. Gervinus, to the entire Historical School.

Menger thus intended to demonstrate the impossibility of founding a 'new economic science' on the basis of the theories of the Historical School of German Economists. Moreover, as early as the *Untersuchungen*, he had claimed that the denial of the subdivision of economics into *historical, theoretical and practical sciences* would lead to a «strict socialistic organization of society, indeed to a type of organization in which the only forms to exist would be a collectivist economy and not private individual economies». Only a «social economy [*Volkswirthschaft*]» would exist, in which the «economic subject would be the people [*Volk*] (or the representatives of it)», and its aim «would be the fullest possible satisfaction of the needs of all members of society». Economic science would in this way be reduced to «one practical economic science», that is, to a science «of the basic principles by which the collectivist economy [*Gemeinwirthschaft*] [...] could be most suitably instituted and conducted. What in our day are designated with extreme inaccuracy as 'socialistic *theories*' are the beginnings of this *practical* science».[92]

Menger's criticism thus focused on the validity and effectiveness of practical norms of action derived from historical knowledge. In effect he had pinpointed problems which were nevertheless to remain on the fringe of the discussion that had arisen around the human sciences at that time, a debate characterized by the spread of positivism, historical materialism and a 'return to Kant'. Drawing inspiration from Kant, such thinkers as Dilthey, Windelband and Rickert set up a distinction between the sciences and the aims and methods of the sciences which showed only superficial affinities with Menger's classification.[93] Admittedly, they dealt with 'types', 'nomothetic knowledge', 'idiographic knowledge', 'the historical', 'theoretical', 'individual' or 'universal' orientation of scientific knowledge, the relation to inductive knowledge and the value of historical knowledge. But both premises and conclusions were vastly different.

Menger's project was more ambitious than that of the above thinkers. While they were endeavouring to find a justification for the two types of scientific investigation, ultimately accepting the positivistic model, Menger set himself the task of dealing with the relation between theoretical, historical and practical sciences within the framework of a *unitary conception of knowledge*. He did so, however, in a way that failed to raise any interest among philosophers of the day, who were generally indifferent to the issues and theoretical constructs of economic science.

It is the more striking, therefore, that Menger's theses were taken up as early as Weber's writings on 'Roscher und Knies und die logischen Probleme der historischen Nationalökonomie' (with which Weber intended to conclude the long debate centring on method), although only to be misunderstood. It is hard to recognize Menger's views under the surface of Weber's work.[94] Weber was undoubtedly influenced by Menger, but the impression remains that Weber interpreted «abstract economics» (and its 'exact laws') within the perspective of neo-Kantism – as was to be expected given his philosophical background. For in his writings Weber replaced the expression 'Theorie des subjectiven Wertes' by 'subjektive Wertlehre', thus shifting 'subjectivity' (as relativity) from *values* to *theory* (i.e. the typical ideal schemas through which the reality of phenomena can be known). This usage would seem to indicate the distance separating Weber from the Austrians, since for him (like the other exponents of the Historical School of German Economists) it summarized in one single expression everything that had been put forward in a series of writings concerning the historicity of the theory of marginal utility and economic organizations.[95] This was very opposite of what had been stressed by the Austrians as they investigated the 'exact laws' and unexpected results of human action.

The *Untersuchungen* may give the impression of indifference on Menger's part towards many of the problems of economic epistemology of his time, though this should not be mistaken for a poor understanding of the issues.[96] One can quote the case of Walras and likewise Jevons, whose epistemology, curiously, Menger neglected to compare and contrast with his own stance, despite being well aware of the significant differences between their economic epistemology and his.[97] The following years, however, were to show how different would be the lines of development of their social philosophies, which would thus have proved unreconcilable.[98]

Yet this does not mean that Menger avoided contemporary epistemological problems.[99] But rather than moving towards a true exploration of the influence of economists who had dealt with methodological problems, he seemed to be interested, firstly, in fighting against the tremendous contemporary popularity (and not only in Germany) of the misguided attempt to found a 'new economic science', the political outcome of which he could foresee, and secondly, above all, in revising the entire theoretical framework of the social sciences in the light of the consequences the theory of marginal utility was likely to have for the overall configuration of these sciences. If this is identified as his chief concern, then whether or not he cited various authors becomes of secondary importance.

As already stated, the echo of the economic *Methodenstreit* is absent from the work of other thinkers who enquired into the problem of method in the social sciences during those years.[100] Scanning the accumulated literature on the methodology of the human sciences and *Historismus* (allowing, naturally, for different impacts in the field of economic theory), one finds little trace of Menger. But even in the field of economic epistemology, until just a few years ago historical investigation was mainly focused on the moment of the birth of the 'marginalist revolution' at the expense of the implications of the theory of subjective values for the social sciences.[101]

If such is the legacy of the *Methodenstreit* in the history of the philosophy of the social sciences, from the perspective of Mises and Hayek the question appears vastly different. Here the *Methodenstreit* was at once understood as a clash between two differing conceptions of the role of the individual in the world, and their interest in the work of the Historical School of German Economists appears to arise from the fact that the latter effectively laid the theoretical foundations for totalitarianism. Certain distinctions should be made, however. Menger's position should be kept distinct from that of Mises and Hayek, if for no other reason than chronological faithfulness. But in his case too, it is helpful to call to mind the dangers foreseen in attributing ethical goals to economic science. To this should be added the realization that a failure to achieve political recognition of individual choices in the economic field would lead to political-economic organization of a socialist type, in which the subject of choices would not be the individual but rather a super-individual entity – the state – which would subordinate individual choices to its own ends.

Consequently, it was in the affirmation of the historicity of knowledge and economic organization,[102] together with the simultaneous negation of a theoretical science of human action and of an economic science whose laws could be universally valid and perennial, that Mises identified the roots of criticism directed against the market economy. Here also he exposed the claimed plausibility of socialistic economic, social and political organizations.[103]

It is thus no coincidence that the Historical School of German Economists was transformed into a movement advocating a sort of 'state socialism' characterized by sharp hostility towards economic liberalism. Nevertheless, despite its grave responsibility within German history, Mises and Hayek saw the Historical School as no more than the German version of a more general entanglement of social philosophy with statalism and collectivism. Mises's words afford a glimpse into their awareness of the importance of the *Methodenstreit*; for in this matter

> and in the discussion between the school of John Bates Clark and American Institutionalism much more was at stake than the question of what kind of procedure was the most fruitful one. The real issue was the epistemological foundations of the science of human action and its logical legitimacy.[104]

The sparring match with the Historical School of German Economists extended up to 1933. Subsequently, these themes tended to turn into a sort of cultural legacy hardly worth any further in-depth theoretical treatment. To explain these developments, one need probably only mention that Mises and Hayek felt they were no longer compelled to dwell on a question they now considered to be closed on account of the epistemological inconsistency of the Historical School.

Thereafter, Mises and Hayek appear to have taken a greater interest in identifying the effects of the methodological positions of *Historismus* on the approach to economic and political problems. They tried to show how collectivist and totalitarian doctrines had been influenced by the *Historismus* of the Historical School of German Economists. In this manner a link of continuity was established between *Historismus*/historicism and the rise of the totalitarian mentality.

§ 3. THE CRITIQUE OF HISTORICISM

In the Austrian tradition, *historicism* is predominantly taken as being the English translation of the term *Historismus* in the meaning attributed to it by Menger in the *Untersuchungen* and in *Die Irrthümer des Historismus*: that is, the belief that through the study of historical events it is possible to discover their meaning and derive the laws regulating their unfolding.[105]

Both Mises's and Hayek's critiques of historicism (and, one could add, their critiques of *positivism* and *scientism*) are still solidly anchored in the *Untersuchungen*. For there was no change in the theoretical and historical outline of the concept of historicism, since the latter, enriched though it might have been by new issues, still corresponded to Menger's *Historismus*. Nor, above all, was there any change in the resolutely critical attitude to the application of the empirical-inductive method to the theoretical social sciences.

Therefore the critique of *Historismus*/historicism, and of constructivist scientism, allows one, albeit indirectly, to highlight how discovery of the implications of the theory of subjective values was followed by profound changes in the conceptual and methodological structure of the theoretical social sciences.

As a first approximation, a common critical objective may be observed, represented by historicism understood as speculation on the unfolding of history. But deep within the same tradition there existed – as Hayek had duly and vainly pointed out – both absolutistic designs (interpretations of historical development as a whole dominated by a prime cause and moving towards a single goal which may be transcendent or immanent) and also individualistic designs which aimed to capture the different and at times intractable contributions of individuality to universal history.[106]

This situation may make it appear necessary to find a term capable of standing more exactly for both of the meanings of *Historismus.* So far, however, this has not come about and is unlikely to happen. This is in part attributable to the twofold origins of *Historismus*, which were intimately bound up with the Historical School of German Economists – who wished to study historical events in order to uncover their recondite meaning and the general laws of becoming[107] – but also with the Historical School of Law, the inspiration behind which was congenial both to Menger and to Hayek. In this light, the location of Savigny within the broadly evolutionistic tradition that was passed on to Hayek from Mandeville and Hume may have some foundation, since his stance contrasted with the Hegelian historical-philosophical and juridical-political tradition.[108]

A common feature of the Austrians' reflections is that history is conceived as an often quite random intertwining of the ways in which individuals endeavour to pursue their own subjective ends, with the results, desired or otherwise, of their actions. Such a view rules out the possibility of interpreting history as motion proceeding forwards towards something that will be realized through the more or less conscious contribution of the deeds of man, and which can be unveiled by means of revelation or by philosophical speculation. But it also rules out an interpretation of history as the flowering of a reason that lies beyond earthly matters and directs its endeavours, through laborious effort, overcoming ignorance and individual prejudice, towards a configuration of human relations according to its own dictates. The exponents of the Austrian School rejected these two complementary attempts to assert sovereignty over the meaning of life, and restored to the latter a quality that transcends the natural limits of human knowledge. For these limits are so manifold, they objected, that any attempt to interpret history on the basis of conscious human action or human reason would be tantamount to affirming that it is possible to know the meaning of the process of becoming. Indeed, it would imply that this meaning is something other than the set of infinite meanings individuals try to give to their existences.[109]

Alternatively, this would be equivalent to maintaining the existence and knowability of a prime cause. Yet the problem would not be solved here either. If the prime cause were fully known to the whole of mankind there would be no history, nor philosophy. If, on the other hand, it were not fully known to all of mankind, the problem of its knowability would ultimately be confused with that of the way different and contrasting interpretations cluster together and give shape to history. The fact remains, however, that this knowledge would not exclude the possibility of individual or collective behaviour contrary to what has been established theoretically: a possibility that can only be ruled out by thinking of an efficient totalitarian organization. This argument formed the basis of the critical views held by Hayek and Mises (as well as Popper), who believed totalitarianism to be an outcome of historicism.

The impossibility of founding economic science on the accumulation and classification of data concerning the historical facets of human action need not mean that history is a useless discipline for economic science and political philosophy. In this connection one may quote Menger's objection to Schmoller, in *Die Irrthümer des Historismus*, concerning the relations between economic, historical and ethical science:

> It is in fact immediately self-evident that even the deepest knowledge of various peoples of the world cannot be deemed a sufficient basis for taking adequate measures in the economy; in other words it does not guarantee that action will be truly commensurate with intended purposes. The economic aspect of the life of different peoples constantly sets new tasks for those who watch over them [. . .] tasks which cannot be carried out by turning exclusively to study of the past but rather can be performed only on the basis of knowledge that goes beyond mere historical and statistical facts and involves the requirements of the statalistic life of the moment.[110]

On these grounds, while reasserting the frutifulness of history and statistics for an understanding of human phenomena, Menger challenged the view that valid norms of practical action can be deduced from the study of history and the discovery of its supposed laws. If the object of history and statistics consists of the historical manifestations of human life, these cannot be confused either with theory, which «has to do with the forms and laws of those manifestations», or with the «practical social sciences», which, in their turn, have to do «with the principles of political-social action that is tailored to an end».[111] Thus the attack was levelled against the principal assumption of the philosophy of history of the Historical School of German Economists, namely the possibility of deducing practical rules of action from the comparative study of history and from discovery of its supposed laws.

The origins of this school, in Menger's eyes, were not to be thought of as stemming from Hegel, Fichte or Friedrich List, but rather from that particular group of historians and economists active in Tübingen and Göttingen towards the end of the eighteenth. century, who endeavoured to found politics on a 'philosophy' of history and, in the attempt to do so, frequently mingled the two disciplines and the two types of knowledge.[112] Unlike the founders of the Historical School of Law, conservative in their outlook, these forerunners of the Historical School of German Economists were in fact of liberal orientation («even if not [. . .] abstract liberal») who intended to use their «fine and solid knowledge in political history for the science of politics».[113]

The Historical School of German Economists, then, arose from a confusion between *history* and *politics* and between *historical* and *theoretical knowledge*[114], the result of which was a mistaken conception of nature and of the purposes of the social sciences. The object of Menger's critical enquiry was thus represented by the possibility of a comparison between phenomena (conceived as empirical facts), political systems and economic systems, in order to gain an overall vision of these phenomena.[115] His criticism was chiefly directed against the attempt to extend the method of anatomy and physiology to the field of human sciences, understood in the same manner as 'natural organisms'.[116]

From a political point of view, the conception of society and of political economy held by the Historical School of German Economists led to a type of political organization in which – as has been seen – individual choices were subordinated to collective choices. But, rather than focusing on the «rare spectacle of a *historical* school of economists with socialistic tendencies» – i.e. on the political valences – Menger turned his attention to the inherent error of considering «social economy [*Volkswirthschaft*] [. . .] as a special unit differing from the singular phenomena of human economy [*menschliche Wirthschaft*]». He also concentrated on the fact that the «aspiration to reduce [*Zurückführung*] the phenomena of social economy [*Volkswirthschaft*] to the singular phenomena of human economy [*menschliche Wirthschaft*], was characterized as 'atomism'». Laying the basis for what later became the common feature of the Austrian School's critique of collectivist economy, Menger claimed that

> the phenomena of social economy [*Volkswirthschaft*] are by no means direct expression of the life of a nation [*Volk*] as such or direct results of an "economic nation" [*wirthschaftendes Volk*]. They are, rather, the *results* of all innumerable individual economic efforts in the nation [*Volk*], and they therefore are not to be brought within the scope of our theoretical understanding from the point of view of the above fiction.[117]

The underlying fallacy of *Historismus* thus sprang from conceiving of historical reality and social institutions as organic entities of a naturalistic type obeying laws that can be discovered through methods typical of naturalistic-comparative knowledge, together with the belief that it was possible to deduce knowledge of a theoretical and practical order having a bearing on social phenomena from these laws themselves.[118] This conception of human affairs was linked to an organicist political perspective, which considers the individual to be an exponent of a genus. In political and economic terms, this results in a critique of the individualistic foundation of classical economy (which Menger, in contrast, defends). It also leads to 'communitarian' conception of economic activity, within whose framework the political and ethical aspects prevail over those of an individual nature.

Like Menger, Mises too tended to identify *Historismus* with the Historical School of German Economists and with the *Kathedersozialisten*. More generally, he also tended to consider it a construct of the social sciences founded on the belief that the only method suitable for the study of human affairs is the 'historical' one. Within this framework, however, Mises drew a distinction between those who would deny the possibility of a theoretical science of human action and those who chose not to exclude this possibility, postponing it until the fruits of wider historical investigation might become available.[119]

Seen in this light, the *Methodenstreit* appears essentially to be a contest between the champions of historical social science and the supporters of theoretical social science. The implications go far beyond the dispute between Menger and the Historical School of German Economists.

Mises felt an affinity with the attempts by Windelband, Rickert and Weber to provide a theoretical foundation for historical knowledge and to reaffirm its peculiar character. But he also considered that their position revealed an underlying inability «to conceive of the possibility of universally valid knowledge in the sphere of human action». However much they might have opposed the opinion that the only true sciences were those constituted on the model of Newtonian mechanics, Mises could not share their claim that «the domain of social science comprises only history and the historical method». The theoretical core of the problem was in Mises's view represented by the implications of subjectivist economics for the theory of human action. Through failing to take note of these implications, even Windelband and Rickert assessed the discoveries of subjectivist economics «in the same light as the Historical School. Thus, they remained bound to historicism (which is not incompatible with empiricism)». They did not realize that, by restricting the scope of the science of human action to history and its method, one would ultimately deny the possibility of constructing a theoretical system of the social sciences. Consequently, for these scholars too, the understanding of historical events as irreducible individual entities appeared to be «the only appropriate method of the social sciences».[120]

The theoretical premises of Mises's critique of historicism also become evident in his examination of Weber's methodology and distinction between sociology and history.[121] Like the exponents of historicism, Weber, Windelband and Rickert approached the study of history with conceptual instruments that were inadequate for the object of study. The former looked to collections of data devoid of any theory in their search for the foundation of historical knowledge, while the latter turned to 'ideal types' not endowed with universal validity. For both had failed to understand that the transformation of the conceptual framework of the theoretical social sciences brought about by «subjectivist economy» made it possible

> to construct, by the use of the axiomatic method, a universal praxeology so general that its system would embrace not only all the patterns of action in the world that we actually encounter, but also patterns of action in worlds whose conditions are purely imaginary and do not correspond to any experience.[122]

Essentially, then, Mises regarded historicism as a wide-ranging and variegated field, of which the Historical School was simply just one component, even if it was the most important. For alongside the historicism criticized by Menger, another form had also developed, characterized by the conviction that «the only appropriate method of the social sciences is the specific understanding of the historically unique».[123]

The criticisms levelled against this brand of historicism are worth mentioning if only because several recent developments concerning the theory of knowledge of the Austrian School appear to have obliterated them from memory. It was Mises's belief that to consider understanding (*das Verstehen*) as an instrument which enables one to grasp the meaning of human action signified conceiving the latter as standing outside «a theoretical science having in view the attainment of universally valid principles of human action». This had resulted in failure to realize that the theory of human action is «logically *prior* to history» and that «without recourse to propositions accepted as universally valid» it is impossible to understand either of them. Since the method of *Verstehen* does not admit the possibility of a theoretical science of human action, it is a method that appears to be «the specific comprehension of the unique and the irrational, as the intuitive grasp of the historically nonrepeatable, in contrast to conception, which is attainable by rational methods of thought».[124]

Mises's answer to the theory of human action proposed by historicism and to *Verstehen* was *praxeology*. This was founded on logic and the universal valid presuppositions of human action, and was seen «as an a priori category», on a par with «the principle of causality». In this manner, the *science of human action* became the theoretical foundation of social science.[125]

The theme of the opposition between historicism and praxeology, already stated in the *Grundprobleme der Nationalökonomie*, was later to be taken up again in *Human Action.* Here Mises stressed the sharp distinction between praxeology, on the one hand, and historicism and positivism (understood as «an illusory social science which should adopt the logical structure and pattern of Newtonian mechanics»), on the other. And here too he emphasized that the thesis of historicism, according to which «the logical structure of human thought and action is liable to change in the course of historical evolution», renders knowledge and human rationality impossible, and with it theoretical social science as well.[126]

The problems connected with history and knowledge of history formed the nucleus of *Theory and History.* Here Mises developed the theme of the evolutionism of social institutions already mentioned in *Human Action* and transformed praxeology into the basis for his criticism of historicism, scientism and Marxism. His aim was thus to reconsider Western cultural history in the light of the adverse effects the above schools of thought had exerted on the development of the theoretical social sciences. Also in this work, in a notable shift away from Menger and Hayek, Mises made a distinction between historicism and *philosophy of history.*

Mises also blamed the philosophy of history – taken both as the belief that «God or nature or some other superhuman entity providentially directs the course of events toward a definite goal different from the ends which acting men are aiming at» and as a source of historical judgment[127] – for having long hindered the birth of theoretical social science. It was no coincidence that this science arose in the seventeenth century, when Smith and Mandeville cast doubt on the belief in a providence directing the course of human events, and began to look at the latter «from the point of view of the ends aimed at by acting men, instead of from the point of view of the plan ascribed to God or nature». This was not a univocal process, however. For, as well as the theoretical social sciences, the secularization of the Christian philosophy of salvation led to the new philosophies of history of Hegel, Comte and Marx.[128]

From this ambivalent situation, historicism arose. Mises considered it to have originated from opposition to the «social philosophy of rationalism» and from «the concern to preserve existing institutions», or indeed to revive those already extinct, whereby in its eagerness to preserve, «against the postulates of reason it appealed to the authority of tradition». But the original conservative connotation was short-lived, for very soon the movement metamorphosed into opposition to capitalism and became «ancillary to socialism and to nationalism».[129] Unlike Menger, who had distinguished *Historismus*/historicism from the Historical School of Law, Mises identified its origin as triggered by a reaction to the rationalistic excesses of English tenment, and by a turning away from the American and French Revolutions, with which both Menger and Hayek felt an affinity.

But Mises's real concern was not so much with the motivations behind reaction against the Enlightenment as with the epistemological doctrine of historicism. This doctrine was identified (1) in the belief that, apart from mathematics, logic and the natural sciences, any other type of knowledge derives from history; (2) in the conviction that «there is no regularity in the concatenation and sequence of phenomena and events in the sphere of human action»; and (3) in the negation of a theoretical science of economy and its laws.[130] So here too, interest revolved around the theme of epistemological economics. Debate centred on the Historical School's intention of founding a historical economic science and on the claim that knowledge and economic organization are epoch-specific.[131]

To dwell so insistently on the critique of a theoretically inconsistent epistemology may appear eccentric. Yet this is not the case at all. For it was precisely in the negation of a theoretical science of human action and of an economic science endowed with laws having universal and perennial validity that Mises identified one of the foundations of the belief in the possibility of socialistic organizations. He thus regarded historicism as one of the sources of socialism and interventionism.[132] Accordingly, the possibility of a socialistic economy was seen as linked to the demonstration of the historicity of the market economy and of the theory of human action by which it is underpinned. Should it be shown that the theory of subjective values is merely a historical realization of economic science, it would lose its universal value, thereby paving the way for the possibility of other types of economic organization.

Mises returned to the correlation between historicism and the Historical School of German Economists in *The Historical Setting of the Austrian School of Economics*. In this work he voiced the idea that the correlation arose from an interpretation of classical economists, and of Mill, as subscribers to the doctrine that economic theory derives from experience. Once transformed into the negation of the universal validity of economic theorems,[133] this interpretation gave rise to the *Methodenstreit.* In Mises's interpretation of the *Methodenstreit*, in addition to the topics already touched upon, his claim that «Menger was too much under the sway of John Stuart Mill's empiricism to carry his own point of view to its full logical consequences»,[134] is one in which his distance from and lack of understanding of Mengerian epistemology come clearly to the fore.[135]

Another interesting point concerns awareness of the political implications attaching to the idea of the historical and cultural relativity of economic and social institutions. The social philosophy of the Historical School of German Economists was indeed destined to turn into a sort of 'state socialism' characterized by defiant hostility towards the market economy and its political implications. Its influence over the future of Germany led Mises to write that the essence of German economic science could be perceived in the process going from «Schmoller's glorification of the Hohenzollern Electors and Kings to Sombart's canonization of Adolf Hitler».[136]

Mises's critique thus concentrated on the epistemological character of historicism. In terms of the history of ideas, his views appear less persuasive, as regards the identification of both the origins and the political outcome of *Historismus*, which was not exclusively socialistic and nationalistic.[137] But his restriction of the perspective of investigation to economic methodology did have the merit of calling attention to the impact of the theory of subjective values on the methodological debate. And this debate saw the participation during Mises's lifetime not only of exponents of the Austrian School and the Historical School of German Economists, but also of Windelband, Rickert, Dilthey and Weber.

Basically, then, Mises's problem can be stated as the recognition of the consequences economic science has had for the other theoretical social sciences.[138] Admittedly, his picture of the debate was one-sided. Yet the true focus of his attention included the epistemological and gnoseological aspects of historicism in relation to their influence on historical development. From this point of view, it cannot be denied that his cautioning against the political dangers inherent in historicism's conception of the history evinced a lack of elements worthy of reflection.

But Mises's aim was above all to reconsider the social sciences in the light of praxeology, on which he hoped to found both catallactics (the exchange principle) and liberalism. This was a plan that led him, just as it led Hayek, to concentrate on those schools of thought that had achieved greatest influence over the course of contemporary affairs. What was at stake was the 'restoration' of the liberal political philosophy – the principal goal of both Mises's and Hayek's strivings, as they sought to free it from what they saw as the bonds of a mentality that in one way or another was connected with historicism and positivism.

The essay 'Scientism and the Study of Society' can be considered the first systematic foundation of Hayek's methodology of the social sciences, and a fresh look at Menger's criticism of *Historismus* and 'pragmatism'. By merging the epistemological part with the critical assessment of the direction taken by social studies, Hayek highlighted the latter's share of responsibility in encouraging the growth of totalitarian ideology.

The claim made by Hayek was that historicism, which also included historical materialism, was not the antithesis of the «treatment of social phenomena on the model of the natural sciences», but instead a form of scientism. Hayek was well aware that the term historicism had two distinct meanings. The first, the older of the two meanings, «justly contrasted the specific task of the historian with that of the scientist and [. . .] denied the possibility of a theoretical science of history». The second meaning, which is more recent, consists in the belief «that history is the only road which can lead to a theoretical science of social phenomena». Like Menger, Hayek distinguished the Historical School of German Economists from the Historical School of Law. He was critical of Meinecke's re-interpretation of the development of the latter in *Die Entstehung des Historismus*, reproaching him for having blurred the issue by designating it with the term *Historismus*, which

Menger had instead used to refer to the conception of history of Gervinus, Roscher and Schmoller.[139]

Hayek's historicism thus corresponds to what Menger termed *Historismus*. This differs from Meineckian *Historismus* in that the latter also includes the Historical School of Law. Both Menger and Hayek, by contrast, considered the Historical School of Law to be a movement of ideas, with which they felt they had considerable affinity, that could not be simply identified with the Historical School of German Economics.[140]

Hayek's attempts at more precise formulation did not, however, resolve the uncertainty. On the contrary, the confusion was compounded by reactions to Popper's *The Poverty of Historicism*, with the misunderstanding arising from the general failure to realize Popper's connection with the works of Menger and Hayek. Nevertheless, Hayek did not give up his attempt to bring order into the terminological dispute. In 'Comte and Hegel' he reiterated the need to distinguish the 'historical method' of Comte and Hegel from «the approach of the great historical school of a Niebuhr or a Ranke». Faced with «the confused state of terminology on these matters», he felt it was appropriate to establish

> a sharp distinction between the 'historical school' of the early nineteenth century and the majority of the later professional historians, and the historicism of a Marx, a Schmoller, or a Sombart. It was the latter who believed that with the discovery of laws of development they had the only key to true historical understanding, and who in an altogether unjustified arrogance claimed that the earlier writers, and particularly those of the eighteenth century, had been 'unhistorical'.[141]

For Hayek too, therefore, the historical method of the 'old Historical School' was of a different nature from that of historicism.[142] Hence the need to avoid confusing the Historical School of Law with *Historismus*/historicism, in particular since the latter's attempts to discover the law of historical development revealed a positivistic mentality alien to the Historical School of Law. As for Menger, so for Hayek the Historical School of Law was a reaction to the «generalizing and 'pragmatic' tendencies of some, particularly French, eighteenth century views». In opposition to the 'pragmatic' interpretation, «which regards social institutions as the product of conscious design», «a 'compositive' theory» was put forward, founded «on the singular or unique [*individuell*] character of all historical phenomena which could be understood only genetically as the joint result of many forces working through long stretches of time». The task of this 'compositive method' consisted in explaining «how such institutions can arise as the unintended result of the separate actions of many individuals». While agreeing with Menger in placing Burke among the precursors of this approach, Hayek believed that Smith also «occupies an honorable place».[143]

Unfortunately this interpretation of social institutions did not meet with immediate success. Furthermore, the lack of a philosophical formulation of its opposition to 'pragmatism' unjustly earned it the reputation of «an anti-theoretical bias», which in its turn gave rise to the belief that «the main difference between the methods appropriate to the study of natural and to that of social phenomena was the same as that between theory and history». In this way, «the belief that the search for general rules must be confined to the study of natural phenomena, while in the study of the social world the historical method must rule, became the foundation on which later historicism grew up». By accentuating its positivistic inspiration, Hayek recast historicism as an empirical study of history, one that could serve as the basis for «a new science of society» that would «produce what theoretical knowledge we could hope to gain about society».[144]

As well as reaffirming its distinction from the «great historical schools», in *The Constitution of Liberty* Hayek also defined historicism as «a school that claimed to recognize necessary laws of historical development and to be able to derive from such insight knowledge of what institutions were appropriate to the existing situation». His attempt to forge ahead of his own time by availing himself of this knowledge «to remake our institutions in a manner appropriate to our time», however, was to lead historicism, like legal positivism, «to a rejection of all rules that cannot be rationally justified or have not been deliberately designed to achieve a specific purpose».[145] But the construction of a social system based on fallacious premises was destined to bring about such a vast array of adverse consequences that it was bound to try to buttress itself with measures directed towards the limitation of individual freedom.

The starting point was thus the critique of the historicist distinction between theoretical history and a historical theory, and of the inconsistency of the claim that there was a necessary correlation between objects investigated and methods applied in order to attain knowledge of those objects. Rather, like Menger, Hayek believed that «for the understanding of any concrete phenomenon, be it in nature or in society, both kinds of knowledge are equally required».[146] The difference thus effectively came to consist in diverging investigative interests. Furthermore,

> the object of scientific study is never the totality of all the phenomena observable at a given time and place, but always only certain selected aspects: and according to the question we ask the same spatio-temporal situation may contain any number of different objects of study. The human mind indeed can never grasp a 'whole' in the sense of all the different aspects of a real situation.[147]

In his early methodological essays Hayek ascribed a fundamental role to theoretical reconstruction in the explanation of a phenomenon. He therefore believed that «the unique wholes which the historian studies» were not 'individuals', «natural units of which he can find out by observation which features belong to them», but theoretical constructions formulated on the basis of a system of relations designed to connect its parts. However, if the task of the theoretical social sciences is to elaborate the wholes to which history refers, then the historian's task in its turn also presupposes theory, and is thus «an application of generic concepts to the explanation of particular phenomena».[148] The historian is thereby furthermore committed to preventing construction of the wholes from becoming an operation purely instrumental to the investigative interests and ends of the scholar.

All this becomes possible because differences between individuals do not prevent utilization of the «familiar categories of our own thinking» to explain social phenomena. Naturally, this interpretation must remain in the sphere of mere conjecture, and not much more is known about it than that it generally works. Nevertheless, it provides the premises that pave the way for a proper understanding of the intentions and actions of others and opens up the possibility of historical knowledge. Thus Hayek, in the manner of Kant, believed in the existence of «universal categories of thought» that allow observations to be explained by analysing them in accordance with these categories.[149]

These epistemological considerations are essential for a critique of the historicist thesis that observation can reveal «'laws' of the development of these wholes». Historicism thus went astray when it endeavoured to «find laws where in the nature of the case they cannot be found, in the succession of the unique and singular historical phenomena». The affinity of historicism with positivism, then, rests on the shared belief in the possibility of constructing a theory, or a philosophy of history, on an empirical basis. Flawed by an empiricist prejudice concerning the nature of objects in the social worlds, historicism thus reached the fallacious conclusion that human history, «the result of the interaction of innumerable human minds, must yet be subject to simple laws accessible to human minds».[150]

To have reached such a conclusion was a poor show indeed in terms of theory alone. It also had extensive and serious consequences on the cultural and political level, to the analysis of which Hayek devoted *The Road to Serfdom* and the political sections of *The Counter-Revolution of Science*. Passing themselves off as «representative results of social sciences», the 'philosophies of history' of Hegel, Comte, Marx, Sombart and Spengler «exercised a profound influence on social evolution». Among the most widely acclaimed ideas were, firstly, the belief in the mercurial nature of the human mind, from which they derived the conviction that «all manifestations of the human mind are unintelligible to us apart from their historical setting»; secondly, their confidence in the ability «to recognize the laws according to which the human mind changes»; and thirdly, the belief that without knowledge of these laws it is impossible to understand any particular manifestation of the human mind.[151]

Consequently,

> historicism, because of its refusal to recognize a compositive theory of universal applicability, unable to see how different configurations of the same elements may produce altogether different complexes, and unable, for the same reason, to comprehend how the wholes can ever be anything but what the human mind consciously designed, was bound to seek the cause of the changes in the social structures in changes of the human mind itself.[152]

The first phase of Hayek's philosophical production thus appears to be characterized by greater emphasis on the issues pertaining to the constancy of the human mind. Subsequently, in his works following *The Sensory Order*, this element was reduced in an evolutionistic perspective. The way this affected the question of historicism can be seen in the treatment of the birth of the evolutionistic tradition in *Law, Legislation and Liberty*. Here, the references to the Historical School of Law, and to Savigny in particular, became more significant, and the «'historical schools' of linguistics and law» were assumed to be essential parts of the development of the evolutionistic tradition. Hayek again focused on the historiographical thesis of the Mengerian *Untersuchungen*, attributing to it the merit of having drawn the attention of social science scholars to «the problem of the spontaneous formation of institutions and its genetic character». He distinguished between this evolutionism and the claimed laws of global evolution that characterize «the altogether different conceptions of the historicism of Comte, Hegel and Marx, and their holistic approach».[153]

Hayek thus sketched a conception of history as the involuntary result of individual ends that come about as individuals strive to solve their problems with the tools of limited knowledge and limited reason. In some ways this conception resembles that of the authors of Meinecke's *Historismus*;[154] and on closer inspection they perhaps should be seen not as two different traditions but rather as one and the same ideal tradition. However, the term used by Meinecke to refer to this tradition had already taken on a different meaning shaped by a debate in which a relationship had been established between the epistemological problems of the social sciences and the very milestones in the development of economic science that were doomed to be ignored by the majority of authors who dealt with these matters. Mises himself pointed this out. Under the impact of these discoveries, the philosophy of the social sciences of the Austrian School was to develop in a direction away from the eventual outcome of the failure to heed economic science's findings concerning human action.

The exploration of historicism contained in the two principal essays in *The Counter-Revolution of Science* can thus be seen as Hayek's most analytical treatment of this question. In his later works, and above all in *The Fatal Conceit: The Errors of Socialism*, although the term itself does not appear, many references are made to the problem, together with a host of comments and clarifications, though these hardly modify the original picture. But what is important is the historical and conceptual mould in which the evolutionistic theory of history and social institutions (including language, tradition, law, reason and morals) was worked out, together with identification of the thinkers to whom Hayek's evolutionism owes most: Mandeville, Hume, Smith, Burke, Savigny and Menger.

In this work, as in the incidental comments concerning historicism contained in the *Studies* and the *New Studies*, Hayek's interpretation underwent no change. Nor indeed did his assessment change, for he continued to view historicism predominantly in terms of its affinity to positivism. Such a view had considerable historical and theoretical merit, but its end result involved more or less total neglect of the hermeneutic component and evolution of *Historismus*, whereas these features had been stressed several times, and effectively, by Hans Albert. In *Traktat über kritische Vernunft*, he defined the hermeneutic type of *Historismus* as a new form of *German ideology*, nothing less than «the attempt to extend the model of textual analysis to reality in general, and to hold up the speculative style of theology as a philosophical ideal». Because Albert brought criticisms against *Historismus* of a methodological and positivistic type that looked back to the Austrian and Popperian tradition, and because he extended his attention to the hermeneutic type of *Historismus* – understood as the use of conceptual instruments of Hegelian and Heideggerian derivation with the aim of transforming scientific knowledge into «the handmaiden of theology»[155] – his *critical rationalism* took on the appearance of a completion of what can be defined as the character of the Austrian School's critique of historicism. This was a highly significant development from a theoretical point of view, particularly at this time when the reception of hermeneutics among Mises's American students was coupled with a phase of psychologism in which the peculiarity of the contribution made by the exponents of the Austrian School to the theoretical social sciences seemed to fade into the background.[156]

§ 4. THE CRITIQUE OF SCIENTISM AND OF CONSTRUCTIVIST RATIONALISM

Opposition on the part of exponents of the Austrian School to the proposal to extend the methodology and investigative aims of the natural sciences to the social sciences was sparked off by Menger's criticism of the adoption of the inductive method in the social sciences. This unwarranted extension was felt to be the chief cause of the severe credibility problem experienced by the social sciences in the modern age. For the use of scientific methodology is intimately bound up with the principal expression of this problem, namely the widespread myths of collectivism and planning, understood as a prelude to totalitarianism. Unlike the majority of critics of modernity, however, Menger,

Hayek and Mises did not question the investigative value of modern science. Rather, their attention was more narrowly focused on its mythicization and its instrumental use as a technical tool.

In the *Untersuchungen*, Menger's criticism of the use of methods of naturalistic derivation in the theoretical social sciences arose from his distaste for the inductive method, in particular its comparativistic variant. It was a question less of the existence of two specific modes of knowledge than of two different manners of acquiring it, which were held to vary according to the specific purposes of the types of knowledge. As has been seen, Menger's position was characterized by denial that practical norms of action could be deduced, and *rigorous knowledge* of social phenomena obtained, simply by starting out from the gathering of inductively obtained observations and their comparativistic generalizations. The *Untersuchungen* can thus definitively be credited with having highlighted what links historicism to 'pragmatic rationalism'.

The same conceptual schema can also be found in Hayek, although not in Mises. As a result of his poor understanding of the *Untersuchungen*, Mises's criticism of historicism and of positivism stemmed from different origins and put forward different lines of argument. Yet his thinking did not substantially differ from Hayek's on the question of cautioning against the dangers of a political society built using methods derived from the natural sciences.

The prevailing trends of the era thus appeared to Hayek and Mises as the tendency to shape the theoretical, methodological and practical tools of the social sciences according to the mould of the natural sciences. Against this tendency, understood as leading towards the collectivist and totalitarian mentality, the criticisms levelled by Hayek and Mises were so ceaseless and uncompromising as to become one of the distinctive features of their thought.

Consequently, it would be misleading to embark on an analysis of the more specifically political aspects of their thought without also dealing with the theory of knowledge on which it is based. For the risk involved here is that of transforming a political philosophy into a political ideology. In other words, the political theory of the exponents of the Austrian School did not arise from a generic desire for political affairs to improve, or for so-called «social injustices» to be remedied, but from a precise awareness of the limits of human knowledge.

But their enquiry into the *best political order* was also implicitly related to a critical attitude towards the concept of *common good*. In this, the object of their inquiry encompassed not only man's limitations in discerning the 'good' and striving to achieve it, but also the concept of 'good' itself, analysed penetratingly and highly critically in terms of the findings of the *theory of subjective values*. In other words, one can find fault with the concept of 'common good' in politics, just as one can attack the classical concept of *value* in economics. Therefore the concept of *political order* founded on the so-called 'common good' appears to be untenable. The relevance of the theory of subjective values for political philosophy thus comes into play as soon as the latter's main problem is touched upon.

From the point of view of the Austrian School, then, the political history of the last two centuries can be seen as the crushing success of that multi-faceted mentality which perceives liberalism as its greatest enemy, and which holds the use of gnoseological tools derived from the natural sciences and mathematics to be the only means for solving those recalcitrant problems of the social sciences that over two thousand years of debate have not managed to disentangle.

In the case of Hayek, his aversion to the idea of extending the method of the natural sciences to the social sciences was already noticeable in 'The Nature and History of the Problem', the introductory essay of *Collectivist Economic Planning*. Here the objective was «to show how it came that in the era of the great triumphs of empiricism in the natural sciences the attempt to force the same empirical methods on the social sciences was bound to lead to disaster».[157] And yet, even if the role played by Neurath in studies of economic planning was already clearly evinced in this essay, there was still no more than a mention of the bond between scientism and collectivism that was soon to assume a central role. As early as 1937, in his essay 'Economics and Knowledge', having elaborated an organic theory of the knowledge of social facts, Hayek was to be in a position to launch an attack on what he at first termed scientism, and later renamed *constructivist rationalism*.[158]

Opposition to scientism was to remain constant regarding the two fundamental points around which controversy revolved, which also had important political implications. The first point, of a theoretical nature, concerned the critical assessment of inductivism, seen as a false method of science and as a confusion between the data of the social world and empirical data. The chief feature of the second, which concerned the history of ideas, involved the demonstration of the detrimental influence of the spread of scientism and constructivist rationalism on political philosophy and the development of the social sciences. In both cases, criticism was based on the contestation that false premises regarding the nature of social institutions cannot be taken as a source from which to deduce reliable indications about political action. Above all, however, the first point also highlights the fact that Hayek used conceptual tools derived from subjectivist economics.

The tremendous reception given to the theory of planning in the 1930s and the general confidence it inspired were thus grounded in the fallacious belief that the most appropriate manner of solving social problems was to apply the method of the natural sciences to the social sciences.[159]

After presenting his objections to the gnoseological foundations and political-economic implications of the confusion between the concept of 'datum' in the empirical sciences and that prevailing in the social sciences, in the essays 'Economics and Knowledge', 'Scientism and the Study of Society', and 'The Counter-Revolution of Science', Hayek went on to examine scientism itself, describing it as a «slavish imitation of the method and language of Science».[160]

From the very first pages – as was later to be repeated, even more clearly, in the introduction to the publication of these essays in book form, where reference was made to Popperian criticism of inductivism – Hayek pointed out that the distinction between the two types of science was linked to the names of figures such as Bacon («the prototype of the 'demagogue of science'»), Comte and the 'physicalists' (Neurath and the *Wiener Kreis*). The «claim for the exclusive virtues of the specific methods employed by the natural scientists» was thus «advanced by men whose right to speak on behalf of the scientists were not above suspicion». But despite these theorizations, and for all the fascination the success of physics exerted over social science scholars (spurring them to imitate its models and language more than its true spirit), no genuine contribution to the progress of the social sciences ensued.[161] The object of Hayek's criticism was thus the false method of science that goes by the name of *inductivism*, together with the damage wrought by its backers in the field of social sciences through the gradual spread of the 'engineering mentality'.

Hayek's basic intent, it may be concluded, was to show that the fundamental error of scientism resided in its taking an 'anthropomorphic' view of society.[162]

In opposition to this vision of inductivist and 'physicalist' science, the task of science was consequently defined as the re-elaboration of man's experience of the external world in the light of the fact that «people perceive the world and each other through sensations and concepts which are organized in a mental structure common to all of them». Hence, the task of the theoretical social sciences was now envisaged as the study of ideas (about the external world, one's fellow beings and oneself as well) that determine individual action. Therefore these sciences should not set themselves the goal of establishing the proper or *objective* relation between 'events' and human beings, but should instead enquire into the way individuals' construal of 'facts' or 'data' leads them to hold their particular views about the world and consequently to engage in action. If the object of the said sciences is composed of human actions, then their goal should be to explain the «unintended or undesignated results» of such actions.[163] Attention must therefore not be directed towards the quest for true and objective laws of nature but rather must focus on how the manner in which they are conceived influences human action.[164]

Hayek's statement on the subject of economic science could thus be extended to the theoretical social sciences; according to Hayek, «every important advance in economic theory during the last hundred years was a further step in the consistent application of subjectivism». If this were the case, their task would become that of obtaining insight into the meanings individuals intend their actions to embody.[165]

Those who backed scientism were thus bent on creating a 'new and objective science of society' that would banish from its scope all considerations regarding the subjective nature of knowledge. If this was the spirit of John B.

Watson's 'behaviourism' and Neurath's 'physicalism', their starting point was the mistaken belief that individuals all have the same feelings about the same objects and exactly the same reactions to the same stimuli.[166] Hence the political bankruptcy of scientism. Far from solving problems that social science or the market economy were unable to solve, building a society founded on mistaken theoretical premises of this kind would a recipe for disaster.

Scientism and constructivism, as well as the constructivism associated with these schools of thought, thus in effect mistook for «facts what are no more than provisional theories, models constructed by the popular mind to explain the connection between some of the individual phenomena which we observe». The misunderstanding therein lies in representing the 'social wholes' as «natural units» rather than as «constructions of our mind».[167] Seen in this perspective, historicism too stands out as «a product of the scientistic approach».[168]

In the field of politics, as befitted the theory of knowledge on which it was premised, scientism regarded social institutions 'pragmatically', i.e. as the result following from human actions intended to achieve precisely that very goal. Its 'constructivist contractualism' was not restricted to considering social institutions as the outcome ensuing from a human plan, but also embraced the idea that they must be 'built' in accordance with the methods and ends of its own conception of natural science. It was only natural, therefore, that the need should be felt to prevent this planning effort from being thwarted by individual subjectivity; but it was considered equally necessary for all tokens of behaviour to be 'rational' and directed towards the intended goal. This in its turn leads to an increasingly pressing drive to control and direct social processes. Hayek made shrewd observations apropos of what he called «one of the most characteristic features of our generation», unceremoniously debunking it as the «unfounded superstition» that runs something like this: «processes which are consciously directed are necessarily superior to any spontaneous process». The thrust of Hayek's comments was that attitudes of this kind are liable to usher in a spate of calls for one single mind to direct the whole of society, followed by «conscious control on the growth of the human mind itself».[169]

What we have here is a «super-rationalism» whose hallmark is the conviction that the human mind has now reached an adequate state of development for the building of the perfect society. In this society there will be no place for individual subjectivity, for everything will take on the form of *objective relations*. The actual components of society will undergo a conversion from *ends* into *means*, and will be evaluated in terms of their contribution to the achievement of social ends. The aspiration to a «conscious direction of all forces of society» is thus ultimately identified with *collectivism*, of which scientism appears to be the 'scientific' premise. *Methodological collectivism* is thus the intellectual source of *political collectivism*.[170]

Underlying the criticism of scientism and of the thesis of collectivist planning is thus a set of arguments of a gnoseological order. In his essay 'The Counter-Revolution of Science', Hayek developed these themes in a historical perspective, exploring the rise and growth of the scientistic mentality with the Ecole Polytechnique, Saint-Simon and Comte, thereby identifying Saint-Simon's ideas on *physicisme*, on the unification of knowledge in a new *Encyclopédie* and on the need «to plan life in general on scientific lines» as the source of positivism and modern socialism.[171]

Subsequently, Hayek's enquiry into scientism was to develop along four main lines: (1) the search for the philosophical sources of the scientistic mentality; (2) criticism of the view that rationalistic scientism is the distinctive trait of European philosophical and scientific thought; (3) recognition of the harmful effects of the constructivist-rationalistic tradition on the value system and moral doctrines of the West; and (4) demonstration of the erroneousness of the inductive method.

The first stage of this interpretation of the history of the social sciences consists of the distinction between the two souls of the individualistic tradition, as outlined in '"Individualism": True and False', the introductory essay to *Individualism and Economic Order*. For these souls are, in fact, diverging philosophical and political traditions. And while in 'Scientism and the Study of Society' attention was limited to scientism, seen as positivism, in the essay on individualism the perspective broadened, with the scientistic-rationalistic mentality viewed as originating with Descartes.[172] Two main traditions in Western political thought were thus distinguished. The first – that of *true* individualism – started out from Locke and, above all, Mandeville and Hume, but included Tucker, Ferguson, Smith, Burke, Tocqueville and Lord Acton. It may be defined as the English tradition, having a liberal political connotation. The second – that of *false* individualism – includes Descartes, the *Encyclopédistes*, Rousseau, the Physiocrats and Bentham, and may be defined as the French or continental tradition, which tended to develop into socialism or collectivism.[173]

Hayek characterised *true individualism* above all as a *theory* of society, «an attempt to understand the forces which determine the social life of man, and only in the second instance a set of political maxims derived from this view of society». He expressed the opinion that, contrary to the frequently held but mistaken view, true individualism is not animated by the «existence of isolated or self-contained individuals», but rather by «men whose whole nature and character [are] determined by their existence in society».[174]

The *false individualism*, or 'rationalistic individualism', of the Cartesian tradition, on the other hand, drew its inspiration from the conviction that social institutions are the result of deliberate human planning or contractualism. It thus lies at the root of the mistaken view of social phenomena that throttled development of the theoretical social sciences, namely the «belief in inevitable laws of historical development and the modern fatalism».[175] The contrast between 'true' and 'false' individualism thus revolves around the fundamental question of the *nature of social institutions*. For it is the contractualism of 'false' individualism[176] that underlies the assertion that the goal of the social sciences should be to determine what constitutes strictly rational human behaviour, and likewise underlies the belief that all moral rules must be subjected to the assessment of individual reason.

Having established these theoretical and historical premises, which can be analysed as stemming from a supervaluation of reason, in 'Kinds of Rationalism' Hayek went on to probe more deeply into the thesis of the two souls of Western political philosophy, coming to the defence of the 'anti-rationalistic' tradition, i.e. of 'true' individualism. He set up an opposition between a kind of rationalism that acknowledges no limit to the power of reason, and one that holds reason to be possessed of natural limits in just the same manner as all human products. The tradition of constructivist rationalism, believing as it did that «all institutions which benefit humanity have in the past [been] and ought in the future to be invented in clear awareness of the desirable effects that they produce», was thus singled out as the cradle of «modern socialism, planning and totalitarianism».[177]

To eliminate any residual ambiguity from the term 'rationalism', in his essay 'The Errors of Constructivism', Hayek used the term 'constructivism' for that widespread mode of thought which claims that «since man has himself created the institutions of society and civilization, he must also be able to alter them at will so as to satisfy his desires or wishes».[178]

The points at issue thus do not represent ongoing discussion between two souls within one and the same tradition. On the contrary: there is an opposition between traditions of thought with which are associated contrasting conceptions of the philosophy of the social sciences.

Hayek rejected the view of those who contend that scientific progress could jeopardize civilization. In his eyes it was not scientific progress that constituted a threat but rather the presumption of knowledge when knowledge has not been genuinely attained. He took as his starting point the conviction that the task of science should be to underscore the fact that whatever value choice is made will always involve sacrifice of some other value. His critical commentary is directed not towards the Humian claim according to which «from our understanding of causal connections between facts alone, we can derive no conclusions about the validity of values», but, instead, against the distortion of this claim when rendered as the belief «that science has nothing to do with values», along with the political implications of this misconstrual. This mode of thought was in Hayek's opinion connected with the conviction that common ends are required for the existence of a social order. In addition, it was related to the notion that the premise of a science free of values allows one to draw the conclusion that value problems cannot be resolved rationally.[179]

The havoc wrought by extension of the positivistic 'paradigm' to the social sciences thus had to be rectified by restoring the model of social science sketched out in the works of the seventeenth-century English individualists as well as in Menger's writings. Here Hayek's criticisms went well beyond censure of the constructivist mentality and its cultural, social and political effects. For the Mengerian account of the origin of social institutions argued that no single one of the main spheres of social life springs up before the others and establishes dominion over them. The attempt by constructivist rationalism to organize the spheres of social life according to the dictates of positivistic science thus turns out to be analogous to the attempt to organize them according to the dictates of religion, ethics or economic science. Far from looking to a hierarchical organization of the various spheres with a view to the achievement of some aim, which would result in attributing to one or other of them a pre-eminent position tantamount to a leading function, one should concentrate on the global complex of the social sciences in the sense of their reciprocal contribution to the formation of a spontaneous order. From this outlook there derives an innovative conception of order, of the philosophy of the social sciences and of the role of political philosophy.

Compared to this wide variety of themes and arguments, Mises's perspective, despite its thematic relevance, appears much more restricted. This remains true even if Mises is granted the merit of having been the first to realize that, in the face of the joint attack by positivism, historicism and collectivism, liberal principles could not be successfully defended or favourably reappraised with the theoretical tools of the philosophy of social sciences of classical liberalism.

Mises saw positivism as a movement that from the mid-nineteenth century onwards exercised considerable influence over cultural trends and political and social affairs. It was by no means a beneficial influence, however, since it too was one of the cultural seeds of collectivism and totalitarianism. But the analysis put forward by Mises differed from that of Hayek. Unlike the latter, Mises did not reach a reinterpretation of the history of the social sciences in the era of modernity; instead he explored the way several contemporary cultural movements were swayed by the myth of a science capable of solving human problems. Mises employed the term 'positivism' to define what Hayek calls 'scientism' and constructivist rationalism, ascribing the same adverse consequences to this movement as did Hayek; but his transition from the criticism to the indication of an alternative path appears less convincing. To some extent, as Hayek pointed out, this can be attributed to Mises's failure to sever his links with utilitarian rationalism. For at the end of the day the latter remained an aspect of that complex of contemporary ideologies which stand in contrast to evolutionism.

Consequently, the premises serving as the foundations of the evolutionism of *Theory and History* (the subtitle of which is *An Interpretation of Social and Economic Evolution*) seem weak and obsolete both from an epistemological point of view and from that of historiographic reconstruction. The strong point of Mises's critique of the mentality induced by positivism remains his demonstration of the extent to which the downfall of this mentality was brought about by the refusal to pay any heed to the findings of praxeology.

In *Theory and History*, positivism is defined as a movement asserting that «the experimental methods of the natural sciences are the only appropriate methods for any kind of investigation. They alone are scientific, while the traditional methods of the sciences of human action are metaphysical.» Positivism proclaims that the task facing science consists in the description and interpretation of sensory experiences. In so doing, it underestimates the impact of the findings of economic science; and, above all, with Comte it enhances the role of sociology, seen as social physics, raising it to a privileged position compared to the other social sciences.[180]

This precipitated a dramatic reversal of the path previously followed by theoretical social science ever since its beginnings with the English individualists. The discovery of the peculiarity of spontaneous social formations was set aside, and the further development of this theory through the work of Menger was greeted with indifference. Just as happened with Marxism, the social philosophy of positivism also evolved without taking into account the implications of marginalism for the theoretical social sciences. The very concept of 'theoretical social science' was rejected, and only a rigorously empiricist and organicistic conception of the social sciences was endorsed. In fact, the *Methodenstreit* was none other than the clash between these two different perspectives: between a philosophy of social sciences which avails itself of the discovery of the principle of marginal utility, and pursues its implications and ramifications, and one that disregards this principle or fights against it chiefly on account of its individualistic valences.

With Comte there developed a conception of science founded on a «biological and organic interpretation of social phenomena». When its absurdity became blatant, the neo-positivist movement, and Neurath in particular, elaborated a more sophisticated social theory founded on «pan-physicalism». The political hallmark of this movement was an «idiosyncratic abhorrence of the market economy and its political corollary: representative government, freedom of thought, speech, and the press». The neo-positivist movement thus claimed that «the procedures of physics are the only scientific method of all branches of science», and, anticipating a 'unified science', it denied the existence of an essential difference between the natural sciences and the sciences of human action.[181] Hand in hand with behaviourism, positivism went on to devise a philosophy of the social sciences founded on behavioural automatism and unconscious reactions.[182] But the aftermath of all this was the trivialization of positivism, which eventually forged a *de facto* link between scientism, realism and organicism seen as fated to usher in collectivism, a forecast Mises could not but share. The epistemological doctrine of positivism was transformed in this way into an ethical doctrine characterized by a strong anti-individualism.[183] Overall, Mises's central theme was always that of a philosophical and cultural movement that ended up exercising hegemonic dominion over the cultural and social life of the West, even with all its inconsistencies and shaky premises.

The manner in which this transition came about is dealt with in *Theory and History* and *The Ultimate Foundation of Economic Science*. In the latter the target of Mises's polemics now became the neo-positivism of the *Wiener Kreis*. Besides the conjectures some of his positions may give rise to – first and foremost that of forging an uncomfortably close link between Popper's epistemology and the neo-positivist movement[184] – Mises's familiarity with the ideas of the *Wiener Kreis* was far from superficial. Certainly he underlined the aspects that were most congenial to his own purposes, which need not mean that his criticisms were unfounded. Similarly, the grounds for his charges cannot have resided in an aversion to Neurath's ideas. Mises admittedly maintained an unceasingly critical attitude towards his ideas, but this did not prevent him from giving Neurath's works due consideration and recognizing their importance and influence. Besides, the *Wiener Kreis* owed a tremendous debt to Neurath in terms of the profound influence exercised by its epistemology over the methodological foundations of political science and contemporary sociology.

Mises regularly moved in Viennese scientific circles during the first three decades of the century and was therefore well acquainted with the issues explored by the *Wiener Kreis*.[185] It is surely no coincidence that his criticisms were prompted by epistemological considerations regarding the a priori structure of the human mind and the concept of probability, and concluded by exposing the role played by the neo-positivist movement in ushering in a mentality favourable to totalitarianism and in paving the way towards decadence in Western civilization. He was thus among the first to point out the harmful effects neo-positivistic culture would have on the social sciences: what has recently, and with reason, been defined as 'the tragedy of political science'.[186]

Mises's criticism was not motivated by analysis of the motives that determined the success of positivism, but from a statement of the reason behind the opposition between natural science and the science of human action. Focusing on the positivistic belief that ascribes the backwardness of the social sciences to a failure to adopt the methods of the natural sciences as codified by 'unified science', his aim was to show that, if such a belief is applied, even more undesirable effects will be caused than the original situation it was supposed to rectify. The science of human action cannot therefore be reduced to 'Pan-physicalism'. As a result of their basic inability to understand the new horizons opened up by economic science in order to explain human action, positivism and historicism thus rendered the theoretical problems of the human sciences far more complex.[187] Mises's goal was to set up praxeology in opposition to the social science born of positivism, identifying the core of praxeology as the negation of the «cognitive value of a priori knowledge», and as the claim that «all a priori propositions are merely analytic».[188] This was an opposition sparked off by epistemological considerations regarding the human mind and its structure, in which Mises critically explored the hypotheses of Russell, Carnap, Reichenbach and materialism.[189] As an outgrowth of these reflections he went on to reaffirm the main claims of *Human Action* concerning the foundations of knowledge, concluding with an examination of the chief errors of scope and method of the German Economists.

The elaboration of a social science founded on fallacious epistemological assumptions and on lack of knowledge of the results of the 'science of human action' could, in Mises's view, only lead to conceptual confusion. His defence of the science of human action was also carried out on two complementary planes, that of epistemology and that of culture. The latter consisted mainly in the formulation of a social science free from the defects of the social science of the past. After stressing that every action consists in the transition from a situation thought to be worse to one regarded as better, and stressing that the merit of liberal society lies in its having identified freedom with exchange, he went on to reaffirm the theory of subjective values as the foundation of a theoretical social science identified with *praxeology*, and with liberalism purged of its dependence on classical economic theory.[190]

The critique of the positivistic mentality must not, however, ignore those problems that the natural sciences are not yet capable of resolving and that cannot be shelved by relegating them to the 'nonsenses' of metaphysics, as neo-positivism did. A critical reappraisal is therefore needed of the very prestige that surrounds the natural sciences. This is particularly true for neo-positivism's fundamental claim, namely that «the experimental procedures of the natural sciences are the only method to be applied in the search for knowledge», together with its corollary that picks out 'social engineering' as the solution for social problems.[191]

Confirmation of the view that great ideologues of science have not truly left their mark on the history of science is provided by the tendency of Neurath's 'Unified Science' movement to transform science first and foremost into a myth, endowed with miraculous resources, and thence into the handmaiden of Communism and supporter of totalitarianism – in short, into nothing less than a threat to the survival of Western civilization.[192] Thus the mistake of positivism, and consequently of the social science that developed under its influence, was to set off along a path bristling with snares. Mises sought to show that the positivistic and historicist mentality, which in conjunction with collectivism had resulted in totalitarianism, had not yet been crushed. His exposure of the mistakes was associated with the indication of an alternative route founded on the extension to the social sciences of the disoveries of *subjectivist economics* and, above all, of *praxeology*.

From this standpoint, collectivist social philosophy and the social philosophy of classical liberalism alike seemed to him to be the residue of an outmoded philosophy of the social sciences. Both were founded on a specific premise that was now untenable, namely the principle of value-labour that could no longer be upheld after Böhm-Bawerk's refutation. Mises had recognized this as early as in *Socialism*, and the same problem also forms the object of discussion in *The Anti-Capitalistic Mentality*. His aim was to emphasize that the solution of social problems (if indeed any solution can ever be found) cannot be achieved simply by applying the method of the natural sciences to the various questions, but rather requires a different philosophy of the social sciences.

The critique of historicism and constructive rationalism is thus moulded, in the work of Mises and Hayek, into the first demonstration of the fallacy of the premises of science and of the social philosophy that led to totalitarianism. Their stance should be seen as the first steps in an attempt to fashion a link between the 'new' philosophy of the social sciences and a new interpretation of the history of Western political ideas. They aimed to prevent recognition of the effects of the predominant tendencies of our century from being taken as evidence of the inevitable demise of Western civilization. For, according to their approach, its decline was the result of errors of historicism and rationalism, i.e. of the prevailing, *but not the only existing*, cultural traditions of the West.

The political philosophy of the Austrian School can be seen, then, as part of a wider philosophy of the social sciences that grew out of a theory of human action which was in its turn inspired by the *theory of subjective values*. The latter was first taken as the basis for a critical review of conceptions of the social sciences of a historicist or positivistic kind; subsequently it became the foundation for the search for a model of spontaneous political order drawing its inspiration from the value of individual freedom.

The crisis and downfall of the prevailing philosophical tradition provide a further reason for turning our attention towards the evolutionistic and liberal component of Western philosophical and political culture, which gave the findings of modern natural science and of subjectivist economics a cooler reception. Critical assessment of the historicist and the rationalistic-constructivist mentality, together with a clear statement of the consequences of both mentalities, and of the end results for which they may be held responsible, can therefore be seen as the necessary premise for the elaboration of a different philosophy of the social sciences. This latter is better qualified to overcome an outcome which need no longer be regarded as a kind of inexorable destiny; instead, that outcome now appears simply to be the necessary conclusion of a tradition of thought grounded in a mistaken conception of human action and the latter's social consequences. The seriousness and wide-ranging repercussions of this crisis indicate the importance of Hayek's attempt. Marxist socialism, however, is only the most tragic expression of a mentality which (in spite of its failure) has not yet moved towards a critical re-examination of its own premises. Thus the most urgent task to result from the Austrians' critical considerations is a broader revision of the prevailing trends of the last two centuries. And this reconsideration will of necessity have to concentrate on the philosophical and political premises and the institutional outcome of contemporary democratic theory.

NOTES

1 On Mengerian methodology in general, see: Wicksell, 1921, pp. 186–92; Pfister, 1928, pp. 25–45; Hayek, 1933, pp. v–xxxviii; Bloch, 1940, pp. 431–3; Dobretsberger, 1949, pp. 78–89; Albert, 1963, pp. 352–80, in particular p. 364; Kauder, 1965; Spiegel, 1971, pp. 530–7; Hutchison, 1973, pp. 14–37, and 1981, pp. 176–202; Streissler and Weber, 1973, pp. 226–32; Kirzner, 1976a, pp. 41–2; Littlechild, 1978, pp. 12–26; Vaughn, 1978, pp. 60–4, and 1990; Zamagni, 1982, pp. 63–93; Ekelund and Hébert, 1983, pp. 282ff.; White, 1985, pp. vii–xxi and 1990; Antiseri, 1984, pp. 44–60; Boos, 1986; Galeotti, 1988, pp. 123–37; Alter, 1990a and 1990b; Birner, 1990; Lavoie, 1990b; Mäki, 1990b; Milford, 1990; Smith, B., 1990a. For Alter, see especially 1990a, which can be regarded as the reference work on Menger's philosophy of the social sciences, and on the cultural background within which his ideas evolved.

2 The general criterion followed in use of the terms *Historismus* and *historicism* is that of using the same term as did the author in the work in question.

3 To understand the cultural atmosphere that forms the background to Menger's work and the attitude towards economics in German and Austrian universities at the time, see Schiera, 1987, pp. 185–205, in particular p. 187, where Menger's position is outlined. It is hardly a coincidence that Menger rejected the notion of relegating economics to a subordinate position under the heading of 'science of administration'.

4 See Milford, 1988a and 1988b.

5 Among these discoveries were the importance of the lessons of history in the field of politics, and the certainty that «*the same constitution and legislation [are] not adequate for all nations and times. Rather, each nation and each age needs particular laws and state institutions corresponding to its own character.*» See Menger, 1883, pp. 187–99; the quotation is on p. 191 (Engl. trans. p. 166).

6 Ibid., pp. 8–9, (Engl. trans. pp. 38–9); Kauder, 1957, referring to pp. 35 and 79–80 of the *Untersuchungen*, wrote: «Plato and Aristotle, so repeats Menger time and again, are the authors who have helped to create his philosophy of science» (pp. 414–15 and n.)

7 See Menger, 1883, pp. 252–6 (Engl. trans. pp. 208–11). The «*historical* economic sciences» – subdivided into *Statistik* and history of human economy according to whether they focus on simultaneity or evolution – have the task of studying the individual nature of phenomena and of economic relations. Investigation of the general nature of phenomena and of economic relations is, on the other hand, the task of the «*theoretical* sciences of human economy», which, taken as a whole, constitute the «*theory of national economy* [*Theorie der Volkswirthschaft*], and when taken singly «correspond to the various orientations of theoretical research in the field of national economy». Finally, one finds the «practical economic sciences [*praktischen Wirthschaftswissenschaften*]», which have the task of teaching the most suitable means of achieving economic goals. Within these fields Menger distinguished between «*economic policy* [*Volkswirthschaftspolitik*]» and the «*practical doctrine of individual economy* [*praktische Singularwirthschaftslehre*]». The former was «the science of the basic principles for suitable advancement, appropriate to conditions of 'national economy' on the part of the

public authorities». The latter was «the science of the basic principles according to which the economic aims of individual economies, (according to conditions) can be realized most completely»; this can in its turn be subdivided into (1) «*science of finance* [*Finanzwissenschaft*]» and (2) «practical *science of private economy* [praktische *Privatwirthschaftslehre*]», i.e. «the science of the basic principles according to which private people, (living in our present-day social circumstances!) can best institute their economy, (according to conditions)».

Menger, 1884, e.g. p. 13, once again criticized the exponents of the Historical School of German Economists for having neglected the distinction between theoretical and practical sciences of economy. And the problem, as will be seen, was taken up again analytically in Menger, 1889b, pp. 185–218; see Alter, 1990a, pp. 84ff.

8 See Menger, 1883, pp. 208–18, 215–16 in particular. On this problem, see also Menger, 1884, pp. 44–5.

9 See Menger, 1883, pp. 87–9 (Engl. trans. pp. 93–4). Compare these pages with Aristotle's statements in *The Politics*, I, 1252a, 19–24. On Menger here, see Nishiyama, 1979, pp. 34ff., although there is no mention of Aristotle.

10 See Menger, 1883, pp. 163–5 (Engl. trans. pp. 146–8).

11 The first to demonstrate the influence of Aristotle on the theory of value of Menger, Böhm–Bawerk and Wieser was Kraus, 1905, pp. 573–92. On the same topic, see also Kraus, 1937, pp. 357ff. The claim put forward by Kraus fell more or less on dead ears. Sugimura, 1926; Stark, 1944, p. 3; and Dobretsberger, 1949, pp. 78–89, all maintained that Menger's methodology showed the influence of Kant. This latter view appears to be untenable, both on account of the lack of references to Kant in the *Untersuchungen*, and also as a result of Kauder's studies on unpublished Mengerian papers that have been preserved, together with a large portion of his library, at the Hitotsubashi University. These studies have highlighted the influence of Aristotle on Menger's theory of value, on his distinctions between the sciences and on his methodology of the social sciences. In particular: Kauder, 1953a, pp. 638–9, on the 'theory of value'; 1953b, p. 572 and n. (on the penetration of Kantian philosophy in Austria); 1957, pp. 414–15, (on the influence of Aristotle and Kant); 1959, pp. 59ff. (criticism of the claim of Kantian influence, and outline of the influence of Aristotle); 1961, pp. 71–2, (on neo-Kantian philosophy); 1962, pp. 3–6, (on the influence of Aristotle and on Menger's knowledge of the philosophy of Kant). On Kauder's interpretation of the Austrian School, see Johnston, 1972, pp. 86–7, (also useful for a general picture of Austrian culture in those years). On the influence of Aristotle on Menger, see Rothbard, 1976b, pp. 52–74, in particular pp. 69–71. Alter, 1982, pp. 154–5, wrote that Menger «Just like Aristotle [. . .] distinguishes sciences according to subject matter and not on the basis of the divorce between the *Geisteswissenschaften* and the *Naturwissenschaften*, as was customary in Germany at the time». For further observations by Alter on this subject, see also, 1990a, pp. 112–21. Important elements for a reconstruction of the influence of Aristotle on Austrian culture and on Menger are contained in the writings of Smith, 1986, p. 36, and 1990a, pp. 263–88.

12 Menger, 1883, pp. 207–8 (Engl. trans. p. 177). The concept was reasserted, and broadened to include Smith's theory of profit, in Menger, 1891, pp. 224–5. As regards Menger's relation to classical economists, see Yagi, 1981, pp. 205–35; and Rothschild, 1986, pp. 11–27.

On the political ideas of Menger and the old Austrian School, see Kauder, 1957, pp. 421ff.; Kirzner, 1990b, pp. 93–106; Yagi, 1992, pp. 93–108. For the problem of how much of Menger's conception of socialism may be owed to his brother Anton, see Kauder, 1965, p. 64; and Johnston, 1972, pp. 92–4.

On Menger's criticisms of Smith, see Bloch, 1940, pp. 430–1; Hutchison, 1973, pp. 29–31, and, 1981, pp. 191–2; Alter, 1982, pp. 153–4. On the penetration of Smith in Austria, see Kauder, 1957, p. 420. In addition to his criticism, however, Menger defended Smith's economic individualism, and more generally that of the classical economists, against the criticisms levelled by exponents of the Historical School of Economics.

13 See Menger, 1883, pp. 200–2 (Engl. trans. pp. 171–5).

14 Ibid., pp. 207–8 (Engl. trans. p. 177). Menger did not fall into the error of exchanging the positions of Burke and Savigny with those of de Maistre and von Haller, also mentioned. On the political ideas of the Historical School of Law, see Tessitore, 1981, pp. 35–94; and Cesa, 1986, pp. 83–103.

15 See Menger, 1883, pp. 48–59, 124n.

16 Savigny is the author whose name is most frequently quoted in the *Untersuchungen*. The mentions are always made in a rather positive tone, and raise points in which Menger makes reference to his theory of the origin of law and of language, 1983, pp. 15 and n., 205 and n., and of money, p. 173 and n. (on money, see also Menger, 1871, p. 256n.), and contests the proclaimed affinity of Roscher with the 'historical method' of Savigny, pp. 221 and n. On the treatment of Savigny by Menger, see Alter, 1982, pp. 151–54, and, 1990a, pp. 43ff; and Marini, 1982b, pp. 197–209.

17 As Menger wrote in the *Untersuchungen*: «The *theory* of economy must in no case be confused with the *historical* sciences of economy, or with the *practical* ones». And dealing with the «laws of nature [*Naturgesetze*]» of economic phenomena – distinct from «empirical laws [*empirische Gesetze*]» – on the basis of which inferences «can be drawn beyond direct experience about the occurrence of future phenomena, or about the coexistence of simultaneous phenomena not directly observed», he added that all this does not imply denying that those

> theoretical sciences, too, which only exhibit empirical laws have accordingly a great practical significance for human life, even if a now greater, now lesser probability takes the place of complete certainty of the knowledge mediated by them. *Historical* knowledge and the historical understanding of phenomena *per se*, on the contrary, do not offer us this prediction, etc. at all and they can therefore never replace theoretical knowledge. Historical knowledge, on the contrary, can never be anything but the material on the basis of which we can determine the laws of phenomena, (e.g., the laws of development of economy). Even the practical politician must first gain more general knowledge, rules from history before he can draw his conclusions in respect to shaping future events. The circumstances that in the realm of economic phenomena results of theoretical research of an absolute strictness are viewed by individual schools as unattainable can indeed impart a separate character to theoretical research in the field of economic phenomena and establish certain characteristics of that field. But it can never bring it about that in the economic realm of the world of phenomena the historical or the practical orientation of research can take the place of the theoretical and substitute for it. The same is true of the circumstances that theoretical research in the economic realm does, indeed, encounter difficulties which are foreign to natural-sciences research in its individual branches. It is true, finally, of the circumstance that for theoretical economics the problems that arise are not always of exactly the same kind as for the theoretical natural sciences. *Theoretical* economics can never be viewed as a *historical* science, nor, as many wish, as a *practical* one.

Menger, 1883, pp. 26–7, 29 (Engl.trans. pp. 52–3).

18 Ibid., p. 32 (Engl. trans. p. 55).

19 Ibid., p. 34 (Engl. trans. p. 56), but see also pp. 259–61.

20 Ibid., pp. 34–5, (Engl. trans. p. 56). It is no coincidence that in these, and the following pages, in which Menger specified his concept of 'natural law' (*Naturgesetz*), the only quotations are from Aristotle and Bacon. On pp. 38–9, n. 18, he warned against the risk of confusion between «empirische Gesetze» and «Naturgesetze, (im eigentlichen Verstande dieses Wortes)». As well as this, he pointed to a fundamental flaw in the whole reasoning, asserting that it was

> likewise incorrect and has already contributed much to confusion in the theoretical problems of our science. The contrast between the theoretical *natural sciences* and the theoretical social sciences is merely a contrast of the phenomena which they investigate from a theoretical point of view. It is by no means a contrast of methods, as both the realistic and the exact orientation of theoretical research are admissible in both realms (natural and social) of the world of phenomena. A contrast exists only between the *realistic* and the *exact* orientation of theoretical research, and between the sciences comprising the results of both orientations, the empirical and the exact theoretical sciences. There are natural sciences which are not exact ones, (e.g. physiology, meteorology, etc.), and conversely there are exact sciences which are not natural sciences, (e.g. pure economics [*reine Nationalökonomie*]). Accordingly it is not an accurate expression when this latter is called a '*natural* science' [*Naturwissenschaft*]. It is in truth an *exact ethical* science [*exacte ethische Wissenschaft]*. It is just as wrong, finally, to speak of the *natural science* method in the social sciences in general and in theoretical economics [*theoretischen Nationalökonomie*] in particular. The method of the latter can be either the empirical or the exact one, but in truth never that of 'natural science' [*naturwissenschaftliche*].
> (Engl trans. pp. 59–60n.).

21 Ibid., p. 35, (Engl. trans. p. 57). Despite quoting Aristotle in these pages, Menger does not refer to any particular passage from Aristotle's work. In the following pages he pursued the topic further, stating that an investigation carried out from an empirical-realistic point of view would succeed only in attaining a definition of «*real types*, basic forms of real phenomena» and «*empirical laws*, theoretical knowledge, which make us aware of the actual regularities, though they are by no means guaranteed to be without exception in the succession and coexistence of real phenomena». Menger concluded by affirming that if one considers the phenomena from the point of view of their «'full empirical reality', only their 'real types' and 'empirical laws' are attainable. Properly there can be no question of strict, (exact) theoretical knowledge in general or of strict laws, of so-called 'laws of nature' [*Naturgesetzen*] in particular for them.» Ibid., pp. 36–7, (Engl. trans. pp. 57–8).

22 As well as *Nicomachaean Ethics*, V, E, 7, 1134*b*, 19–20, and *Metaphysics*, IX, Q, 7, 1049*a*, 1049*b*, 5–10, in scanning for ideas connected with this interpretation one may point to *The Politics*, I, (A), 2, 1252*b*, (a book quoted by Menger, 1883, on pp. 267–9, in appendix VII, which features a discussion expressing agreement with Aristotle's view that the state is a natural phenomenon intrinsic to human nature); and to *Parts of animals* I, (A), 1, 639 *b* 25, and 642*a* 35. *Nicomachaean Ethics* and *The Politics* are the only two works of Aristotle cited by Menger in the *Untersuchungen*. Lachmann, 1978, pp. 58–9, noted a contradiction between the determinism of the exact laws and the subjectivism of individual choices.

23 See Menger, 1883, pp. 40–1, 260 (Engl. trans. pp. 60 and 215).

24 Ibid., pp. 260–1 (Engl. trans. p. 215).

25 Ibid., p. 38 (Engl. trans. p. 59). On the *exacte Naturgesetze*, see Mäki, 1990a.

26 See Menger, 1883, pp. 40–1 (Engl. trans. p. 61).

27 Ibid., p. 42 (Engl. trans. p. 61).

28 Ibid., pp. 41–2 (Engl. trans. p. 61).

29 Ibid., p. 43 (Engl. trans. p. 62). This is a problem that Menger was to take up again in the following pages, see pp. 44–5. As will be seen later, *zurückführen* should not be translated by 'to reduce', but by 'trace back'.

30 On the nature of the 'exact laws', further to the observation by Menger, see Kauder, 1957, p. 416. In the same article, see p. 414 and nn. 10, 11, Kauder wrote: «Before Menger wrote his methodology he studied Aristotle very intensively. In later years he became acquainted with Wundt and Kant. The Kantian influence cannot be traced, for Menger studied Kant during the long period of his literary silence.» On the relation between *Wesen* and *exacte Naturgesetze* see Kauder, 1965, pp. 97–8. Here he wrote that for Menger, unlike for Jevons and Walras, both of whom reduced economic phenomena to ideal types by means of abstraction and isolations,

> the subjects of science are not the constructions of our mind but are rather the social essences. Essence means the reality underlying a phenomenon [. . .] The belief in essences is a principle of philosophical realism; Aristotle is the greatest author of this school [. . .] Menger's theory deals with the Aristotelian essences, with exact types, and typical relations, and these theoretical types provide knowledge which transcends the immediate information. Menger's theoretical analysis produces laws and concepts valid for all times and places. He combined an up-to-date theory with a philosophy which in 1883 [. . .] was already more than two thousand years old. Like his Greek master, Menger searched for a reality hidden behind the observable surface of things.

On the influence of Aristotle, see also Hutchison, 1973, pp. 19–23, and, 1981, pp. 179–83; Lachmann, 1978, pp. 58–9; Alter, 1990a. This influence, although not actually denied, was seen in a drastically revised light by Silverman, 1990, pp. 69ff., who was more inclined to identify a predominant influence of the cameralistic 'Austrian' tradition and maintained that Menger's references to Aristotle in the *Untersuchungen* are rather generic and do not constitute reliable evidence. Although Menger's issues and conjectures need not necessarily be resolved in the Aristotelian framework, a discussion on this topic should start out from an analytical examination of the citations of Aristotle; above all, the influence of Aristotle can also be traced in passages where he is not overtly mentioned.

31 See Kraus, 1905; and Kauder, 1953a, pp. 638ff. In the *Untersuchungen* Aristotle is not cited in this connection, whereas he is quoted in Menger, 1871, p. 4n. (on the distinction «between true and imaginary goods according to whether the needs arise from rational deliberation or are irrational» (Engl. trans. p. 53 n.)), p. 108n., (on the relation between 'use value' and 'needs'), p. 173n. (critique of the Aristotelian theory of the origin of prices). As regards citations on the origin of money, in the *Untersuchungen* Menger refers the reader to the *Grundsätze*.

Referring to Kraus, 1905, pp. 584ff. (who felt one could identify the influence of Aristotle's treatment of the criteria of preferability of goods as outlined in the *Topica* III, (G), 2, 117*a*, on Menger and Böhm-Bawerk), Kauder, 1965, p. 16, wrote that «Even Menger's theory of imputation based on loss calculation, [*Verlustgedanke*] can be found in Aristotle»; and elsewhere (p. 95):

> Hedonism, Unitarian ethics, and French Laicism did not form a part of Menger's thinking, which, like that of many other Austrian intellectuals of the second half of the nineteenth century, was still influenced by Aristotle. Menger's welfare scale is an application of *Nicomachean Ethics* to economics [. . .] For Aristotle the good life is the end and the self-sufficient goal for all forms of human activity. The good life becomes Menger's economic welfare. As

Aristotle started his ethics with a hierarchy of human aims, so Menger also constructed a scale of welfare gains and goals. A conflict between the region of pleasure and the realm of morals is not mentioned in his published work.

For the Aristotelian critique of the Platonic concept of «the good» understood as meaning what is unique and absolute, see *Nicomachaean Ethics*, I, (A), 6, 1096*b*, 1097*a*. Despite the lack of citations, it does not seem far-fetched to claim that Aristotle's commentary in *Nicomachaean Ethics*, I, (A), 7, 1097*a* 16–26, concerning the good, and in *Eudemian Ethics*, I, (A), 8, 1218*b* 5ff., may have influenced Menger and, subsequently, the other members of the Austrian School. The extent to which this may be deemed a correct interpretation of Aristotle is another question.

32 On the differences between Menger and Jevons, see Stigler, 1937, p. 230; Kauder, 1953b, pp. 571–2; Jaffé, 1976, pp. 511–24; White, 1977, p. 4; Gram and Walsh, 1978, pp. 46–56; Vaughn, 1978, p. 61.

33 The problem of the unwanted consequences of human actions directed towards attainment of goals is one of the central themes of Hayek's reflections. In this regard, he makes constant reference to Menger. See Hayek, 1952a, in particular pp. 36–43, 80–93; 1967, above all the essay 'The Results of Human Action but Not of Human Design', in particular pp. 100ff. and notes; and 1973–9, 'Notes on the Evolution of Systems of Rules of Conduct', pp. 66–81; 'Reason and Evolution', p. 22; 'The Errors of Constructivism', p. 3n.; 'The Three Sources of Human Values', now 'Epilogue' to 1973–9 III, pp. 153–76; 1988, pp. 98, 144–6. On this aspect of the issues dealt with by Hayek, see Radnitzky, 1984, pp. 9–34.

34 See Menger, 1883, p. 6, n. 4; and Menger's letter to Walras, in Jaffé, 1965, II, letter 602, p. 3, in which Menger wrote:

> Wir untersuchen doch nicht nur die Grössenverhältnisse, sondern auch das WESEN der volkswirtschaftlichen Erscheinungen. Wie vermöchten wir nun aber zu der Erkenntniss dieses letztern, (Z.B. des Wesens des Wertes, der Grundrente, des Unternehmer-Gewinnes, der Arbeitsteilung, des Bimetallismus u.s.f.) auf mathematischem Wege zu gelangen? Die mathematische Methode würde sich – selbst, wenn sie im übrigen schlechthin berechtigt wäre – jedenfalls nicht für die Lösung des obigen Theiles der nationalökonomischen Probleme als adäquat erweisen.

On these aspects, see Hutchison, 1973, p. 17, and 1981, p. 178; and Kirzner, 1976a, p. 42.

35 On the matter of the philosophical and cultural background within which the reflections of the Austrian School evolved, and those of Menger in particular, as well as Alter, 1990a, see Grassl and Smith, 1986. In the essays contained in this collection – in particular Smith, 1986; Nyiri, 1986, pp. 102–38; Haller, 1986, pp. 196–209 – the problem is raised of the existence of a peculiarly Austrian philosophical tradition within which Menger's own ideas and reflections took shape. The results achieved are indeed of considerable interest, even if it is not always clear – see Smith, 1990b, pp. 212–38 – how this tradition made its influence felt. Even the famed *Katalog der Carl Menger-Bibliothek in der Handels-Universität Tokio* does not seem to testify to any special attention paid by Menger to 'Austrian philosophy'. (It is known, though, that not all the works of Menger's library went to the Hitotsubashi-Universität). The index of names, works cited and reasons for the citations in the *Untersuchungen*, – see Cubeddu, 1985 – provides confirmation of this view (the innumerable misprints contained in this essay do not concern the presence or absence of authors). See also Alter, 1990a, pp. 23–77; Streissler, 1990a, pp. 31–68, and 1990b; in the same collection also Silverman, 1990, pp. 69–92.

Streissler and Silverman made a more positive reappraisal of the influence of the German economic tradition on Menger. But a number of points need to be clearly stated. Firstly, a comparison between Menger's works of 1871 and 1883 leads one to think that in the latter Menger had decided to 'settle his accounts' with that tradition. In particular, in this regard, see the appendices. In II, p. 243, for example, after having analysed the concept of *teoretischen Nationalökonomie und das Wesen ihrer Gesetze*, in Rümelin, Rau, Roscher, H. von Mangoldt, Hildebrand, Knies, J. Kautz, J.C. Glaser, K. Umpfenbach, Schaeffle, A. Wagner, M. Wirth, G. Schönberg, F.J. Neumann, H. von Scheel and G. Cohn, Menger wrote that

> the above definitions of our science reflect quite clearly the low status of theoretical investigations in the realm of political economy in Germany. We learn – needlessly – for the most part the special views of the authors concerned on the nature of economy, of national economy, even of society. But no unprejudiced person will deny that these – quite aside from the question of their correctness – do not even satisfy the formal presuppositions of a suitable definition of science.

(Engl. trans. p.201)

The second point is that in Menger, 1883, one finds no references to the authors that Streissler and Silverman indicate as examples of this influence: i.e. J.H.G. von Justi, K.A. von Martini, P. Mischler, J.H. von Thünen, and above all J. Kudler and J. von Sonnenfels, while there are references to K.H. Rau, (pp. 198n., 213n., 216n., 241, 247), G. Hufeland (p. 247), F. B. W. Hermann (p. 250).

The third question is that from the point of view of the influence of the German economic tradition the differences between Menger's works of 1871 and 1883 show greater complexity and are more articulated. Furthermore, in the interpretative perspective of Streissler and Silverman, there is almost total neglect of the fact that in the *Untersuchungen* Menger's real 'German' reference point consisted of Savigny and the Historical School of Law. In conclusion, the fact that as Menger's reflections on economic science unfolded, they focused to some extent also on the German economic tradition should not lead us to forget that with the *Untersuchungen* he re-examined this tradition critically. (If among the authors cited by Menger one does not find those to whom Streissler and Silverman attributed formative influence, this need not mean that one cannot extend these objections to them as well). Menger also opened up a number of avenues of research, leading in various different and opposing directions: in theoretical economics, in social philosophy and in the philosophy of the social sciences.

Thus in the Preface to the *Untersuchungen* (pp. xv–xxii), Menger acknowledged that

> the theory of economics, as the so-called classical school of English economists shaped it in the main, has not been able to solve the problem of a science of the laws of national economy satisfactorily. But the authority of its doctrine is a burden on us all and prevents progress on those paths on which the scholarly mind for centuries, long before the appearance of A. Smith, sought the solution of the great problem of establishing theoretical social sciences.

On the other hand,

> the desire to do away with the unsatisfactory state of political economy by opening up new paths of research has led in Germany to a series of partly misleading, partly one-sided views of the nature of our science and its problems. It has led to views which separate the German economists from the movement

in the literature of the subject of all other nations. Indeed, it has led to views which have caused the German efforts, on account of their one-sidedness, to appear unintelligible in individual cases to the non-German economists.

«The largely polemic character of this writing» is thus also due to the hope

of making research in the field of political economy in Germany aware of its real tasks again. I thought of liberating it from the one-sided aspects harmful to the development of our science, of freeing it from its isolation in the general literary movement, and thus of preparing for the reform of political economy on German soil, a reform which this science so urgently needs in the light of its unsatisfactory state.

(Engl. trans. pp. 29–32.) Considerations that allow a greater degree of overall agreement in this regard are to be found in Milford.

36 In general here, but with greater attention to economic issues, see Egger, 1978, pp. 19–39; and Mongin, 1988, p. 6.

37 In the Preface to, 1933, pp. vi (Engl. trans. pp. xvii–xviii), Mises wrote:

The inadequacy of empiricist logic hampered the endeavors of Carl Menger still more seriously than those of the English thinkers. His brillant *Untersuchungen* [. . .] is even less satisfactory today than, for example, Cairnes' book on methodology. This is perhaps due to the fact that Menger wanted to proceed more radically and that, working some decades later, he was in a position to see difficulties that his predecessors had passed over.

38 See Hayek, 1952a, where, explaining the fundamental principles of the 'individualistic' and 'compositive' method of the social sciences, Hayek wrote (p. 212, n.3): «I have borrowed the term *compositive* from a manuscript note of Carl Menger who in his personal annotated copy of Schmoller's review of his *Methoden der Socialwissenschaften* [. . .] wrote it above the world *deductive* used by Schmoller.»

39 Menger, 1883 p. 87 (Engl. trans. p. 94).

40 Consequently:

«it is above all a fact of the most common experience that the satisfactions of greatest importance to men are usually those on which the maintenance of life depends, and that other satisfactions are graduated in magnitude of importance according to the degree, (duration and intensity) of pleasure dependent upon them. Thus if economizing men must choose between the satisfaction of a need on which the maintenance of their lives depends and another on which merely a greater or less degree of well-being is dependent, they will usually prefer the former.

See Menger, 1871, pp. 7–8, 35, 88–9 (Engl. trans. pp. 56, 80, 122–23).

41 Mises, 1948, pp. 3, 19–20. On what may be defined as the 'relativism' of Mises, see also, 1961, pp. 117–34.

42 Hayek, 1952a, pp. 31, (and n.24 on pp. 209–10), 38.

43 Menger, 1883, pp. 87–9.

44 Mises, 1949, p. 18.

45 See, for example, Mises, 1933, pp. vi, 67n., 68 (Engl. trans. pp. xvii–xviii, 72, 124, n.5). An attempt to reconcile Mengerian methodology with the apriorism of Mises was carried out by Smith, 1990c, pp. 1–5.

46 Mises, 1949, p. 32.

47 Ibid., p. 39.

48 Ibid., pp. 34–5.

49 Ibid., p. 13.

50 Ibid., pp. 18–20.

51 Ibid., pp. 22–3.

52 Menger, 1871, p. 32 (Engl. trans. p. 77). On the Mengerian conception of causality, see p. 1 (Engl. trans. pp. 51–52).

53 See Menger, 1923, pp. 3–4.

54 Ibid., pp. 16–17 (Ital. trans. pp. 91–2). On the Mengerian distinction between 'real needs' and 'imaginary needs', see Mises, 1933, pp. 161ff. (Engl. trans., pp. 72ff).

55 Mises, 1949, p. 92.

56 Ibid., pp. 96–7. On the relation between subjectivism, praxeology and economy in Mises, see Boehm, 1982; Buchanan, 1982a; Lachmann, 1982; Vaughn, 1982; Butler, 1988, pp. 137–49.

57 For Hayek, for instance – given the assumption that «the structure of men's mind, the common principle on which they classify external events, provide us with the knowledge of the recurrent elements of which different social structures are built up and in terms of which we can alone describe and explain them»: Hayek, 1952a, p. 34 – what constitutes the object of social science is not so much the question of whether visions of the world (on the basis of which the individual engages in action) accord with reality, as the way in which these visions produce new realities. For Menger, on the other hand, 'exact science' must strive towards rigorous knowledge of «types (the empirical forms) and the typical relationships (the laws) of phenomena»; see Menger, 1883, p. 34 (Engl. trans. p. 56). In this regard, see Nadeau, 1987; and Shearmur, 1990b, pp. 189–212.

58 Hayek, 1952a, pp. 23–4. In general on the methodology of the social sciences of Hayek, see Barry, 1979, pp. 16–41, on p. 41; Butler, 1983, pp. 132–50; Gray, 1984a, pp. 1–26; Paqué, 1990, 281–94.

59 See Hayek, 1952b. On this work, see Gray, 1984a, pp. 8ff.

60 Hayek, 1952a, pp. 23–4.

61 Ibid., pp. 25–7.

62 Ibid., pp. 29–31.

63 Ibid., pp. 33–5. The claim that Hayek was crucially influenced by Kantian philosophy, put forward by Gray, 1984a, pp. 4–8, illuminating though it may be, tends however to underestimate the influence of the Mengerian *Untersuchungen*, despite the fact that this influence is noticeable and present fairly constantly from the earliest writings onwards, including this one. Gray, however, does not appear to explain successfully how the two strands are combined in Hayek. Concerning the influence of Kant on the philosophy of law and on Hayek's political philosophy, see also Kukathas, 1989. While the question of influences is surely of secondary importance compared to aspects of Hayek's originality, what was new in his contribution to the social sciences has less affinity with Kantianism than with the theory of subjective values. The crux of the comparison thus resides not in pointing to any generic affinity but rather in the attempt to understand the relation of Hayekian 'subjectivism' to Kantian 'subjectivism', and thence in the search for insight into the reasons behind their differing conception of order.

64 Even Gide and Rist, as early as, 1909, p. 473, in reference to the *Methodenstreit*, wrote that «heureusement, l'opposition des méthodes inductives et déductives soulevée par l'école historique ne présente plus de nos jours un très grand intérèt». On the epistemological problems underlying the *Methodenstreit*, see Milford, 1988b.

65 According to Kauder, 1965, pp. 88–9, 120–1, it was only after 1900 that Menger began to work on the plan of an anthropological foundation of his system, and in this perspective he studied W. Wundt, F. Brentano, C. von Ehrenfels, O. Kraus. On the reconstruction of relations between Menger and prevailing

Austrian philosophical thought, see Smith, 1986 and 1990a. See also Leser, 1986b, pp. 29–57; and Diamond, 1988, pp. 157–72.

66 See Hayek, 1926, pp. 560–1. Böhm–Bawerk, 1890, wrote: «The abstract-deductive method as presented in the German literature by C. Menger, Sax, myself and others is in its very essence a genuine empirical method», (p. 263).

67 In the pages dedicated to methodological problems in Wieser, 1914, the distance separating Wieser from Menger is distinctly noticeable. On Wieser, see Menzel, 1927, pp. 4–12; Morgenstern, 1927, pp. 669–74; Johnston, 1972, pp. 81–2 (the paragraph bears the title «Friedrich von Wieser as advocate of a mixed economy»); Mises, 1978, pp. 35ff; Streissler, 1986, pp. 59–82; Ekelund and Thornton, 1987, pp. 1–12. On Wieser's methodology, Kauder, 1965, pp. 120–3, pinpointed the issue when he wrote: «Wieser's main concern was with introspection. Unfortunately Wieser identified psychology with introspection, and so an unnecessary confusion was created.» (On Wieser's political ideas, see Kauder, 1957, p. 421.) But see also Mitchell, 1969, pp. 345–74; Ekelund, 1970, pp. 179–96; Alter, 1990a, pp. 222ff. On the position of Wieser and Böhm–Bawerk in the *Methodenstreit*, see White, 1977, p. 7; on Wieser's 'psychological' method, see p. 12. On the influence Dilthey and Simmel exercised over Wieser, see Kauder, 1957, pp. 415–16.

On relations between Mises and Wieser, see Mises, 1933, pp. 20–1 (Engl. trans. pp. 21–2); according to Mises, Wieser «was unable to rid himself of the influence of Mill's psychologistic epistemology, which ascribed an empirical character even to the laws of thought»; and Mises, 1978, pp. 35–6: «He never really understood the gist of the idea of Subjectivism in the Austrian School of thought, which limitation caused him to make many unfortunate mistakes.»

68 The *Methodenstreit* was sparked off by the work of Schmoller, 1883. While reviewing the Mengerian *Untersuchungen* together with *Die Einleitung in die Geisteswissenschaften* of Dilthey, Schmoller – see pp. 239ff. – responded here to the criticisms brought against him by Menger. Schmoller stressed again that the future of economic science is linked to its capacity to utilize historical and statistical material, and not to its capacity for technical elaboration. Assimilating Mengerian methodology to Mill's naturalistic logic, he showed not only that he had misunderstood the Mengerian text, but also – more seriously– that he had failed to realize the difference between exact economics and classical economics. On this, work see Faucci, 1988, pp. 141–64.

69 See Menger, 1889, pp. 199–200.

70 Ibid., p. 202.

71 Ibid., pp. 205, 209. On the issue of the distinction between the sciences, and in particular on the relation between 'pure science' and 'practical arts', see Keynes, 1891, pp. 31ff, 142ff. The reference point for Keynes, however, was not Menger, (though the latter is cited in other parts of the work) but rather L. Cossa and G.C. Lewis.

72 See Menger, 1889b, pp. 208–18.

73 Whose writings on the origin of money he recalls with respect; see Menger, 1871, pp. 250, 260, 264, 270–2. This continued to take place in Menger too, 1892, pp. 16–17 in particular. On the evolutionist theory of money in Menger, see O'Driscoll, 1986, pp. 601–16.

74 See Menger, 1883, pp. 223–4 (Engl. trans. pp. 187–88).

75 Ibid., p. 225 (Engl. trans. p. 188).

76 Ibid., p. 228 (Engl. trans. p. 190).

77 Ibid., p. 241 (Engl. trans. p. 199).

78 Ibid., pp. 288–91 (Engl. trans. pp. 235–7).

79 Ibid., p. 8n.

80 Ibid., p. 61 (Engl. trans. p. 75).
81 Ibid., pp. 71–2.
82 Ibid., pp. 119–20.
83 Ibid., pp. 228–31.
84 Ibid., pp. 6–7n.
85 Ibid., p. 13 and n.
86 Ibid., p. 123 (Engl. trans. p. 117).
87 Ibid., p. 220–1.
88 Ibid., p. 241 (Engl. trans. p. 199).
89 Ibid., p. 74 (Engl. trans. p. 84). On the polemic with Schmoller, as well as the writings of Mises, 1929, pp. 54–90 (Engl. trans., pp. 71–106), 1933 and 1969, see Pfister, 1928, pp. 6–13; Ritzel, 1950; Hansen, 1968, pp. 137–73; Bostoph, 1978, pp. 3–16; Häuser, 1988, pp. 532–42; Milford, 1988a and 1990, pp. 215–39; Alter, 1990a. A reconstruction of the *Methodenstreit* seen from the perspective of the Historical School of German Economists, and of Schmoller in particular, has recently been made by Gioia, 1990.
90 See Menger, 1883, p. 61n., (Engl. trans. p. 75n.).
91 See Menger, 1884, p. 44.
92 See Menger, 1883, p. 257 (Engl. trans., partially modified, pp. 211–12).
93 In the case of Dilthey one need only think of the foundation of the distinction between *Geisteswissenschaften* and *Naturwissenschaften*, or reflect on the conception of psychology and its impact on the process of *Verstehen*. Rickert, 1899, p. 7, called attention to the Mengerian *Untersuchungen* in a brief historical overview devoted to recent interest in the methodological problems discussed in the *Kulturwissenschaften*; but he failed to appreciate the extent of the implications of the *Untersuchungen*, discounting the work as «belonging to the kinds of research that are isolated and restricted to some particular field». For this reason Hayek, 1968b, p. 125, was surely mistaken to suggest that the Mengerian distinction between the sciences exerted some kind of influence over Rickert and Weber.
94 See Weber, 1903–6, pp. 3–4n.; 1904, pp. 187–90; 1906, pp. 227n.; 1918, pp. 534–8; 1908, p. 395. This distance, which neither Mises nor Hayek would fail to note, was to be denied on the very basis of the foundations of the *Verstehen* by some of Mises's American students, who were influenced both by Gadamerian hermeneutics and also by Lachmann's reading, 1970, of Weber.

For a critique of Weberian methodology from an 'Austrian' point of view, see above all Mises, 1933, where briefly outlined comparisons are to be found on pp. 71ff. (Engl. trans. pp. 75ff); 1948, pp. 30n., 126; 1978, pp. 122–3. In the catalogue of Menger's library one finds no mention of works by Weber.

On the relation between Menger and Weber, (a question which is very little studied), see Kauder, 1959, p. 60; Tenbruck, 1959, pp. 573–630; Lachmann, 1970, pp. 24, 55ff.; Nishiyama, 1979, pp. 34–5; Bryant, 1985, pp. 57–108; Ashcraft, 1987, pp. 289–324; Hennis, 1987, pp. 38, 51; Osterhammel, 1987, pp. 110–12; Schön, 1987, pp. 60–2; but above all Hennis, 1991, pp. 27–59, and Burgalassi, 1992, pp. 71–102.
95 See Weber, 1918, pp. 534–7.
96 See Menger, 1926–55, and the various works by Kauder already cited. A glance at the index of names and of works cited in Menger, 1883 – see Cubeddu, 1985 – indicates that Menger never mentions Cantillon, Ricardo, Malthus, Hume, Kant, Hegel, Fichte, Gossen, Marx, Walras or Jevons (yet the catalogue lists various works of all these writers, except for Kant and Hegel). In itself, the fact that they are not mentioned is not particularly significant, but it does provide us with a general overview of who «his authors» must have been. This may also

contribute to clarifying the problem that Johnston, 1972, p. 80 defines as the «formative influences on Menger». In the *Untersuchungen*, three names fail to turn up on the list of references (though this does not necessarily mean that they exercised no influence over him at a later stage): F. Brentano, J.F. Herbart, R. Zimmermann (of these, Menger possessed only one work by Zimmermann).

97 On relations between Menger and the other two exponents of the 'marginalist revolution', see Jaffé, 1965, I, letter 566, pp. 768–9, and II, letter 602, pp. 2–6, (letters by Menger to Walras); I, letter 569, pp. 771–3, and II, letter 769, pp. 179–80, and letter 794, p. 206 (letters by Walras to Menger). On relations between Menger and Walras, see: Antonelli, 1953; and Kauder, 1957, pp. 412ff.; 1959, pp. 62–3; 1961, pp. 69–70; 1962, pp. 15–16. Not only do Walras and Jevons fail to get a mention in the *Untersuchungen*, but indeed according to Kauder, 1961, pp. 69–70, «the names of Jevons and Walras, who discovered the marginal utility theory simultaneously with Menger, are not found in the whole manuscript» of notes that Menger put together for the second edition of the *Grundsätze*; on the differences between the first and the second edition, cf. Weiss, 1924. It apparently escaped Kauder's notice that in the *Einleitung* to Menger written by the latter's son Karl, 1923, pp. vii–viii, an extract is reprinted from an introduction composed by the father, which was subsequently not presented for publication, in which Jevons and Walras are mentioned.

On the differences between the Austrian School and the 'Lausanne School', see Morgenstern, 1931, pp. 6–42. On the differences between Menger, Walras and Jevons, see Stigler, 1937, p. 230; Kauder, 1953b, pp. 571–2, and 1965, pp. 66–80; Lachmann, 1966, pp. 161–2; Streissler, 1972, pp. 438–40; Jaffé, 1976, pp. 511–24; White, 1977, p. 4; Gram and Walsh, 1978, pp. 46–56; Vaughn, 1978, p. 61; Shand, 1984, pp. 32–41, 43–49; Alter, 1990a, pp. 151ff.

98 In this regard see Vannucci, 1990, pp. 141–77.

99 See Milford, 1988a.

100 For in the literature on *Historismus*, the name of Menger seldom makes an appearance; it is absent, for instance, in the work by Rothacker, 1920, despite the fact that this is a work dealing with *Historismus* and the 'Historical Schools'. The first document on the *Methodenstreit* is by Philippovich, 1886, pp. 27ff., 50n., 52–3n., 54n; concerning this work, see the review by Menger, 1887, pp. 212–15.

101 Indeed, even the references to Menger in Keynes, 1891, pp. 5, 21n., 124n., 266, 324n., lead one to believe that there must have been a misunderstanding of his claims. Naturally Keynes was well aware of the import of Menger's thought, but it would seem inaccurate to suggest that the importance of Mengerian methodology was fully recognized in this work, which had such profound influence over the developent of studies in economic methodology. In the work of Blaug, 1980, in the more general context of scant attention to Austrian methodology (see pp. 91–3), the *Untersuchungen* received no mention, whereas considerable coverage was devoted to the work of J.N. Keynes. The same was true for Boland, 1982, where however some interesting pages can be found on the relation of the Austrian School, and in particular Hayek, to Popper (see pp. 169ff.). This also holds true for Collini *et al.*, 1983, where there is likewise a chapter on political economics and the historical method in which mention is made of Roscher and Schmoller. On the import of Mengerian methodology, the following are still useful, though for differing reasons: Ingram, 1888, pp. 233ff.; Schumpeter, 1914 and 1951; Eucken, 1938, pp. 63–86, and 1940, pp. 37–51; Hutchison, 1953.

102 See Mises, 1949, pp. 200–1.

103 See Mises, 1952, p. 2.

104 See Mises, 1949, p. 4.

105 But the term 'historicism' – as used by Hayek and Popper, who, however, also used the term 'historism' – also includes the conceptions of history of the Hegelian and Marxist tradition. For instance, the German translation of the work by Popper, 1957, bears the title *Das Elend des Historizismus*, 1965, and here the term *Historismus*, (see p. 14) translates the English term 'Historism', see p. 17. Albert, 1988, p. 576, states: «historism is a product of a theoretically ispired philosophy of history which must reject the naturalistic approach to social reality due to its origin in the idea of the revelation of God in history»; and he observes in a footote: «I take this term as a translation of the German term 'Historismus', because Popper has coined his concept of 'Historicism' in such a way that its meaning does not coincide with the meaning of 'Historismus'.» This latter is however a term that Albert used as early as 1973 when dealing, on pp. 132–5, with the first *Methodenstreit*; see also Albert, 1957, p. 133; 1963, p. 364; 1977, pp. 59ff. For Albert's critique of '*methodologischer Historismus*', see, 1987, pp. 120–43.

On the critique of Hegelian and Marxist historicism, see Hayek, 1951a; and Popper, 1945 and 1957. On the connection between the Popperian conception of 'Historicism' and that of the Austrian School, see Nadeau, 1986, pp. 127ff.; Cubeddu, 1987b; Clontz, 1988, p. 51.

106 On this latter opposition, see Tessitore, 1987.

107 What we have here are two different philosophical standpoints. Menger himself did not establish any relation linking the conception of positivistic-comparativistic history held by Roscher, Knies and Hildebrand to that of Hegel.

108 On these aspects of the issues raised by Savigny, see Marini, 1977, 1982a and 1982b. The positive references by Hayek to Savigny are in 1960, pp. 148, 452n.; 1967, pp. 103n., 104n.; 1973–9, I, pp. 22, 74, 152–3n., II, pp. 161n., 163n., 1978 p. 265n.; 1988, pp. 35, 70, 170.

109 The most insightful critique of this tradition is still probably that expressed by Strauss, 1953, pp. 295–323, dedicated to the conception of history found in Burke.

110 Menger, 1884, pp. 44–5. On the critique of *Historismus* in Menger, and its relation to the Historical School of Law, see Alter, 1990a, pp. 42ff.

111 Menger, 1884, pp. 17–18.

112 These thinkers: L.T. von Spittler, H. Luden, K.H.L. Pölitz, H.B. von Weber, K.G. von Wächter, F.C. Dahlmann, Gervinus, were receptive to the results of the efforts made by L.H. von Jacob, List, G.F. Krause, E. Baumstark, Rau and F. Schmitthenner to ground economic science on experience and on history; see Menger, 1883, pp. 213–14n.

113 Ibid., pp. 209–13 (Engl. trans. pp. 178–80).

114 Ibid., p. 19.

115 The target of the criticism was Roscher. As has already been seen, the objection raised by Menger, ibid., pp. 122–3 (Engl. trans. p. 117), against his theories about history was that

> only those who completely fail to recognize the nature of the historical sciences can thus yield to the illusion that, from the study of history in general and of economy in particular, insight may be gained into the general nature and the general connection of the phenomena of human economy *in general*.

116 Ibid., pp. 139–52.

117 Ibid., pp. 84–7 (Engl trans. pp. 92–3).

118 Ibid., pp. 120, 123, 144, 221, 224, 226. On pp. 212–17 Menger distinguished the 'Historical School of Law' of Burke and Savigny from the above-mentioned group of thinkers, (see n. 112) whom he placed at the origin of the 'Historical School of Economists', pointing out that the fundamental idea of Burke and Savigny, 'the doctrine of the organic, unintended origin of a number of human phenomena', had remained «quite alien to them».

They are opponents of abstract speculation (even that of historicizing philosophy), but not usually of the literature of the seventeenth and eighteenth century Enlightenment and of liberalism in politics. They are opponents of a priori construction in the political sciences and history, but not of one-sided pragmatism in the conception of social phenomena.

See p. 212 (Engl. trans. p. 180). But even they did not fall into «one-sided empiricism», or even into «one-sided historicism [*einseitiger Historismus*]»; «one-sided historicism still is not to be found in the presentations of above-mentioned writers». It was only in the first thirty years of the nineteenth century that a shift occurred towards «one-sided historicism». And this was brought about through Gervinus, who «exerted considerable influence on the young minds of the Göttingen historical school and by a rare concatenation of events was to become of decisive importance for the conception of methodological problems held by German economists». See pp. 216–17 (Engl. transl, modified, pp. 182–3). On the influence of Gervinus's historicism on Roscher, see p. 220.

119 Mises, 1933, p. 104 (Engl. trans. p. 107). In this work the term *Historismus* will always be translated into English by the term 'Historicism'.

120 Ibid., pp. 4–7 (Engl. trans. pp. 5–7).

121 Ibid., p. vii (Engl. trans. p. xix). What divided them was the question of the nature of 'ideal types', which for Mises were «the conceptual instruments of historical, and not of theoretical, investigation».

122 Ibid., p. 14 (Engl. trans. p. 14).

123 Ibid., p. 5 (Engl. trans. pp. 5–6).

124 Ibid., p. 124–5 (Engl. trans., pp. 132–3). On the theme of *Verstehen*, see also Mises, 1949, pp. 47–64.

125 See Mises, 1933, pp. 13–14 (Engl. trans. pp. 13–14).

126 Mises, 1949, pp. 4–5.

127 Mises, 1957, p. 162.

128 Ibid., pp. 166–71. It is curious to note that Mises never mentioned either Hayek, 1952a, or Popper, 1957.

129 Mises, 1957, p. 198. On the Historical School of Law see also Mises, 1981, p. 460.

130 Mises, 1957, pp. 199–200.

131 Ibid., pp. 200–1.

132 See Mises, 1952, p. 2: «All the essential ideas of present-day interventionist progressivism were neatly expounded by the supreme brain-trusters of Imperial Germany, Professor Schmoller and Wagner.»

133 See Mises, 1969, pp. 22–3.

134 Ibid., pp. 27–8. The concept had already been expressed in Mises, 1933, pp. 20–1n. (Engl. trans. p. 23): «Menger's pioneering investigations are still further weakened by their dependence on Mill's empiricism and psychologism.» This is a misunderstanding which, however, has the virtue of highlighting the radical difference between Menger's epistemological premises and those of Mises.

135 See the passages which in Menger, 1883, are concerned with an inquiry into Mill's claims, pp. 49, 53, 124n., 125n., 240n., 244, 256n.

136 See Mises, 1969, pp. 31–4. As regards Sombart, Mises returned to a critical assessment of Sombart in various works; see, for instance, 1929, pp. 111–22 (Engl. trans. pp. 127–38); 1944b, p. 180; 1948, pp. 197, 751n., 841; 1978, pp. 7, 9, 65, 102–3; 1981, pp. 317n., 343n., 529–30, 531n.

137 See Tessitore, 1981.

138 See Mises, 1933, p. v (Engl. trans. p. xvii).

139 See Hayek, 1952a, pp. 64–5 and n. 56 on p. 215, 198–200 and n. 36 on p. 248. Concerning the work of Meinecke, 1936, Hayek wrote:

> the term historicism applied to the older historical school discussed by Meinecke is inappropriate and misleading since it was introduced by Carl Menger [. . .] with reference to Gervinus and Roscher [. . .] to describe the distinguishing features of the younger historical school in economics represented by Schmoller and his associates. Nothing shows more clearly the difference between this younger historical school and the earlier movement from which it inherited the name than that it was Schmoller who accused Menger of being an adherent of the 'Burke–Savigny school' and not the other way round.

See p. 215, n. 56, and p. 248, n. 36. In 1936, I, p. 1, Meinecke mentioned the work *Die Irrthümer*, by Menger, stating that in this work the term *Historismus* is used «in a derogatory sense» to indicate the «supervaluation of history in political economics», a pitfall to which, in his opinion, Schmoller also fell victim.

140 In the literature on Hayek – as in that concerning Mises – the attention devoted to his critique of historicism, and the stature ascribed to this critique within the overall configuration of his philosophical reflections, where it formed the foundation of his political philosophy (which was a search for the best political order, in the absence of historical teleologism or of the infallibility of human reason), has not been equal to the importance of the issue. The Hayekian line of argument has in general been viewed using the conceptual tools of the Anglo-American philosophical tradition, which tended to overshadow various references to 'continental' philosophy. Thus Shenfield, 1977, pp. 71–2, for example, restricted himself to observing that «historicism», is «the third feature of the scientistic approach», briefly illustrating its principal tenets; Barry, 1979, devoted only pp. 34–5 to this theme; for Hoy, 1984, the problem does not exist; Butler, 1983, pp. 140–1, states:

> Historicism is a doctrine much popularized by Marx, which rests on mistaken principles. The first is that there are no general laws of social behaviour which apply in different societies or historical epochs. The second is that the only general law is a law of history, which shows how one historical epoch turns into the next [. . .] This view, which was once very prevalent, has today been almost entirely driven out of social studies, so only a brief summary is needed here.

See also Shand, 1990, pp. 48–50.

141 See Hayek, 1952a, p. 199. Concerning the origins of «later historicism» (p. 199), Hayek referred to Popper and to K. Löwith, p. 248, n. 35. On p. 199, Hayek wrote: «I have little to add to the masterly analysis of the historicism by my friend Karl Popper [. . .] except that the responsibility for it seems to me to rest at least as much with Comte and positivism as with Plato and Hegel.»

142 Ibid. p. 215, n. 57.

143 Ibid., pp. 64–5. The question of the Mengerian interpretation of Smith was taken up again in Hayek, 1948, pp. 4–5n.:

> Carl Menger, who was among the first in modern times consciously to revive the methodical individualism of Adam Smith and his school, was probably also the first to point out the connection between the design theory of social institutions and socialism.

(Hayek then quoted p. 208 of the *Untersuchungen*). In other words, Hayek refrained from making mention of Menger's criticism of Smith; and his pages would seem to support continuity between Smith's theory of the origin of social institutions and that of Menger. Such a view can be defended, but it does not correspond to Menger's beliefs. For in the *Untersuchungen* – apart from Burke and Smith – few references can be found to the individualist tradition from which Hayek drew his inspiration.

144 See Hayek, 1952a, pp. 65–6.

145 See Hayek, 1960, p. 236. In the accompanying note, on p. 493, Hayek refers back to the Mengerian *Untersuchungen* and to Popper, 1957.

146 See Hayek, 1952a, pp. 65–7. Consequently, the interest in particular events cannot be held to be the distinctive feature of historical science, and

> the distinction between the search for generic principles and the explanation of concrete phenomena has thus no necessary connection with the distinction between the study of nature and the study of society. In both fields we need generalizations in order to explain concrete and unique events [. . .] and the explanation of the particular phenomenon presupposes the existence of general rules.

147 Ibid., pp. 69–70.

148 Ibid., pp. 71–3. See also p. 216, n. 64.

149 Ibid., pp. 76–8.

150 Ibid., pp. 73–4.

151 Ibid., pp. 74–6.

152 Ibid., pp. 76–7.

153 See Hayek, 1973–9, I, pp. 22–4.

154 This refers to the remarks made by Meinecke, 1936, p. 5:

> We thus wish to present the rise of *Historismus* as a stage in the evolution of the Western spirit. For 'evolutionary' thought and 'individualizing' thought are inseparably bound up with one another. Individuality, whether it be that of a man taken as a single subject, or that of real and ideal collective entities, is revealed only through evolution [. . .] We must distinguish the concept of the evolution of *Historismus*, which latter was highly spontaneous, malleable and thus admitting of numerous transformations, both from the narrower concept of the mere burgeoning of shoots that were already in place, and also from what we may agree to call the criterion of the perfecting of illuminism, which was subsequently to become faith in progress [. . .] Through the concept of evolution it proved possible to overcome what had prior to that time been the predominant manner of interpreting historical transformations, namely pragmatism.

155 Albert, 1968, pp. 131ff.

156 For a critical approach to this tendency – which was sparked off by Lavoie's essay, 1986, pp. 192–210 – see the essay by Albert, 1988, pp. 573–98; see also Gordon, 1986; Caldwell, 1988b, p. 79; Selgin, 1988, pp. 19–58; Rothbard, 1989, pp. 45–59, and 1992, pp. 4–8; Johnson, 1990, pp. 173–211.

157 See Hayek, 1935, pp. 11–12.

158 On the role of this essay in the evolution of Hayek's thought, see Hayek, 1967, p. 91; and Hutchison, 1981, p. 215. In relation to the treatment of scientism in this

essay, which was of fundamental importance for the development of the Hayekian methodology of the social sciences, see Shenfield, 1977, pp. 61–72; Shand, 1984, p. 7; Nadeau, 1986, pp. 125–56. On this problem see also Caldwell, 1988a, pp. 513–41, and, 1988b, pp. 71–85; here, on p. 79, he rightly stated that «*Scientisme et sciences sociales* est le plus importante ouvrage méthodologique de Hayek»; see pp. 81ff.

159 Re-emphasized in Hahn *et al.*, 1929, this hope, as is well known, was to meet with great apparent success; in this regard, see Cubeddu, 1984, pp. 179–206.

160 See Hayek, 1952a, p. 15.

161 Ibid., p. 14. On Hayek's criticism of Comte, see Brown, 1984, pp. 197–201.

162 See Hayek, 1952a, p. 18.

163 Ibid., pp. 23–5.

164 Ibid., p. 30.

165 Ibid., p. 31. In the note relating to this passage (n. 24, pp. 209–10), Hayek, as has already been seen, recognized the role played by Mises and acknowledged that he had been ahead of his times. This was a very important recognition – like that on p. 209, n. 20, concerning «'praxeological' sciences» – which contributes to a clarification of the sources of his methodology, or at least the influences during that period. See Hutchison, 1981, pp. 210ff. Barry, 1979, p. 20, wrote that «In fact, much of Hayek's early writing on methodology [is] elaborations of Mises's positions.» But this statement seems excessive, as does the assertion made by Gray, 1984a, who, in the course of a reference to Hutchison and to Barry, pp. 17–19, wrote that «Hayek never accepted the Misesian conception of a praxeological science of human action which take as its point of departure a few axioms about the distinctive features of purposeful behaviour over time» (p. 18), and that «Hayek never endorsed the Misesian conception of an axiomatic or *a priori* science of human action grounded in apodictic certainties» (p. 9). All this is true, but it is equally true that Mises's subjectivism, in those years, left its mark on Hayekian methodology; and so did Kant, Menger and Popper. But the figure who is left out in these discussions concerning influences is Menger. For instance, in his seminal comparison of Hayek with Kant and Hume, on the subject of the influence of Menger, Kukathas, 1989, p. 131n., confines himself to referring back to Shearmur's essay, 1986, though this is not to deny the excellent qualities of that essay. Yet it appears that the most important aspect of Hayek's early methodological essays is related to *methodological individualism*, and more generally to the problem of the gnoseological foundation of the social sciences, a question where the Mengerian derivation clearly makes itself felt. One could even regard these essays as an attempt to revise and update Mengerian methodology. When Shand, 1990, p. 14, apropos of Hayek and «apriorism», and summarizing the discussion between Hutchison, Barry and Gray on the predominance of the influence of Popper or Mises on Hayek's methodology, ends up identifying *praxeology* with the essence of the Austrian School, this is surely erroneous. On the contrary, what characterizes the Austrian School is the methodological continuity between Menger and Hayek, while Mises's praxeology is a separate phenomenon, not exactly unrelated, but distinct. Besides – apart from the differences between Mises and himself that Hayek politely noted: see, 1973–9, III, pp. 204–5n.; 1981a, pp. xxiii–xxiv – even in 1988, the school of thought which formed the backdrop to Hayek's philosophy of the social sciences included not Mises but Menger. And it seems to be significant that an allusion was made to this latter fact in 1967 when Hayek wrote: «The more recent revival of this conception seems to date from my own article on 'Scientism and the Study of Society'» (cf. p. 100n.).

166 See Hayek, 1952a, pp. 44–5.

167 Ibid., pp. 54–5:

They are not 'given facts', objective data of a similar kind which we spontaneously recognize as similar by their common physical attributes. They cannot be perceived at all apart from a mental scheme that shows the connection between some of the many individual facts which we can observe.

And again, on p. 57:

The mistake of treating as definite objects 'wholes' that are no more than constructions, and that can have no properties except those which follow from the way in which we have constructed them from the elements, has probably appeared most frequently in the form of the various theories about a 'social' or 'collective' mind.

168 Ibid., p. 64.

169 Ibid., pp. 87–8; the polemical objectives, in these and the following pages, are the ideas of L.T. Hobhouse, J. Needham and K. Mannheim. Above and beyond their differences, in Hayek's view, what they share is the «idea that the human mind is, as it were, to pull itself up by its own boot-straps».

170 Ibid., pp. 90–2.

171 Ibid., pp. 121–3. The reference is to the ideas of H.G. Wells, L. Mumford and Neurath. Hayek (see p. 136) was, however, prepared to acknowledge that Saint-Simon had shown awareness of the fact that

the organization of society for a common purpose, which is fundamental to all socialist systems, is incompatible with individual freedom and requires the existence of a spiritual power which can 'choose the direction to which the national forces are to be applied'.

172 On the critique of Descartes, see Nemo, 1988, pp. 23ff.

173 See Hayek, 1948, pp. 3–4. On the position of Menger within the framework of this tradition, Hayek wrote that he «was among the first in modern time consciously to revive the methodological individualism of Adam Smith and his school» (see p. 9 n.)

174 Ibid., pp. 6–7.

175 Ibid., pp. 8–10.

176 For Hayek's critique of contractualism, see Yeager, 1984, pp. 61–80.

177 See Hayek, 1967, pp. 84–5. Hayek quoted the names of Bacon and Hobbes besides Descartes, as champions of the constructive tradition; while Mandeville, Hume and Menger were quoted among those who championed the spontaneist tradition. Here Hayek declared that the term 'constructivism' was a more precise definition of what he had previously defined as 'scientism'.

178 Hayek, 1973–79, III, pp. 3–7.

179 Ibid. pp. 20–2.

180 See Mises, 1957, p. 241.

181 Ibid., pp. 242–4.

182 Ibid., pp. 245–6.

183 Ibid., pp. 250–63.

184 Mises, 1962, pp. 69–70.

185 Mises had known Neurath since they had attended, together with exponents of the trend that was later to develop into Austro-Marxism, the seminar held by Böhm-Bawerk; see Mises, 1978, p. 40. And as well as being Richard's brother, Mises was also acquainted with Karl Menger, with whom he had the opportunity to discuss problems concerning economic methodology (see Menger, K., 1979, pp. 259 and 279). The list of those taking part in Mises's private seminar sheds some light on the way the various cultural circles were closely intermeshed in Vienna at that time. See also Morgenstern, 1976, pp. 806–7; Mises, M., 1974;

Craver, 1986, pp. 16ff.; Haberler, 1981, pp. 49–52.
186 See Ricci, 1984.
187 See Mises, 1962, pp. xi–xii.
188 Ibid., pp. 3–5.
189 Ibid., pp. 11–33.
190 Ibid., pp. 73–7.
191 Ibid., pp. 120–8, the citation is on p. 120.
192 Ibid., pp. 128–33.

2

THE THEORY OF HUMAN ACTION

> The fundamental condition from which any intelligent discussion of the order of all social activities should start is the constitutional and irremediable ignorance both of the acting persons and of the scientist studying this order, of the multiplicity of particular, concrete facts which enter this order of human activities because they are known to some of its members.
> (Hayek, *New Studies*)

1. *The problem of knowledge in the social sciences*; 2. *Methodological individualism*; 3. *Evolutionism, order and catallactics.*

§ 1. THE PROBLEM OF KNOWLEDGE IN THE SOCIAL SCIENCES

The *theory of subjective value* is first and foremost a theory of knowledge concerning the whole array of the theoretical social sciences. Its foundation is a theory of human action which, in its turn, invokes a theory of human knowledge. These themes were set out by Menger and given their final shape in *Grundprobleme der Nationalökonomie* and *Human Action* by Mises, and in the essays Hayek wrote between 1935 and 1945.[1]

One could interpret the Austrian School's theory of knowledge as a development of the views Menger put forward in the *Grundsätze* concerning the role of uncertainty in the field of economics:

> the greater or less degree of certainty in predicting the quality and quantity of a product [. . .] depends upon the greater or less degree of completeness of their [consumers'] knowledge of the elements of the causal process of production, and upon the greater or less degree of control they can exercise over these elements. The degree of uncertainty in predicting both the quantity and quality of a product is determined by

> opposite relationships. Human uncertainty about the quantity and quality of the product (corresponding goods of first order) of the whole causal process is greater the larger the number of elements involved in any way in the production of consumption goods which we either do not understand or over which, even understanding them, we have no control – that is, the larger the number of elements that do not have goods-character. This uncertainty is one of the most important factors in the economic uncertainty of men, and, as we shall see in what follows, is of the greatest practical significance in human economy.[2]

If the degree of predictability of the production of goods depends on knowledge and dominion of a multiplicity of elements, prediction of the results of social processes is likely to pose an even more formidable challenge. The conundrum will be compounded by the fact that even though «needs arise from our drives», and «the drives are embedded in our nature»,[3] the goods required to satisfy them take on differing values for us. Their value thus corresponds to the «importance that individual goods or quantities of goods attain for us because we are conscious of being dependent on command of them for the satisfaction of our needs».[4] Consequently,

> Value is thus nothing that attaches to the goods themselves, nor is it a property of the goods, but rather it is exclusively formed by the importance we attribute first and foremost to satisfaction of our needs, i.e. of our existence and welfare, which we then transfer onto economic goods, holding them to be the sole cause of that importance.[5]

This means that *value*, far from being either intrinsic to the goods themselves, an inherent property of the goods or even «an independent thing existing by itself», is an act of evaluation that «does not exist outside the consciousness of men».[6] If one then enquires how all this affects the concept of 'common good' and the latter's relation to the concept of and quest for the *best political order*, it is clear that it acted as an immediate bombshell in the field of political philosophy. For in the process of attribution of 'value' it is possible to make mistakes due to the fact that the sundry kinds of satisfaction of needs and the importance ascribed thereto are «matters of judgement on the part of economizing men, and for this reason, their knowledge of these degrees of importance is, in some instances, subject to error». In Menger's view, this originated from the circumstance that «men often esteem passing, intense enjoyments more highly than their permanent welfare, and sometimes even more than their lives». Therefore, if human beings are often mistaken about themselves, they are all the more likely to fall into error when it comes to subjects or goods produced by others.[7]

This part of the Mengerian system should be seen as linked with the way the themes of nature and knowledge of the social sciences are treated in the *Untersuchungen*. The problem revolves around the way individual efforts towards needs satisfaction affect the overall situation in which other members of society will likewise endeavour to satisfy their own needs. For as the individual strives to satisfy his needs, he brings into play whatever individual knowledge he possesses in order to assess which goods are required to achieve his purpose. By the nature of things, however, his very actions determine *de facto* situations which must be taken into account by other individuals in society as they in their turn proceed to satisfaction of their own needs.

As has been pointed out, Menger made a distinction between *exact orientation* and *empirical-rationalist orientation*. The limitations of the latter derived from its inability to satisfy the aims of theoretical research. He was thus aware that the establishing of categories of phenomena embracing the whole of empirical reality was an ideal that theoretical research would not attain if it were carried out following an 'empirical-realistic' orientation.[8] The same cannot be said regarding the exact orientation, however, which, on a par with other types of investigation of the world of phenomena, hoped to attain

> strict laws of phenomena, of regularities in the succession of phenomena which do not present themselves to us as absolute, but which in respect to the approaches to cognition by which we attain to them simply bear within themselves the guarantee of absoluteness. It is the determination of laws of phenomena which commonly are called 'laws of nature' [*Naturgesetze*] but more correctly should be designated by the expression '*exact laws*' [exacte *Gesetze*].[9]

The procedure of theoretical investigation also formed the foundation of the 'compositive method'. This consists essentially in the search for the simplest elements of reality, portrayed in their rigorously typical aspect. In order to comply with the rules of rigorous knowledge, these elements cannot be picked out on the basis of an empirical-realistic analysis, but rather by striving to grasp them in their pristine purity. Identification of typical relations, of the phenomenic laws whose aim is the discovery of exceptionless regularities in relations between phenomena, likewise follows a similar procedure. The task of *exact science* thus emerges not as an investigation devoted to identifying uniformities in the successions of phenomena, but rather as the study of the way those elements of reality grasped in their natural pristine purity develop into the more complex phenomena of social life.[10]

This approach was, of course, adopted just as confidently in the field of social phenomena as in that of phenomena belonging to the world of nature. But Menger concentrated above all on the application of this principle to economic science. In this field, he identified the task of 'exact orientiation' as consisting in an enquiry into the foundations of human economy («needs, the goods offered directly to humans by nature [. . .] and the desire for the most complete satisfaction of needs possible»), and furthermore in the measurement and elaboration of the «laws by which more complicated forms of the phenomena of human economy develop from these simplest elements».[11] The conclusion was that

> the function of the exact orientation of theoretical research is to apprise us of the laws by which not real life in its totality but the more complicated phenomena of human economy are developed on the basis of the thus given situation from these most elementary factors in human economy, in their isolation from other factors exerting influence on the real human phenomena. It is to teach us this not only in respect to the nature, but also to the measure of the above phenomena, and thus to open up for us an understanding of these which has a significance analogous to that which the exact natural sciences offer us in respect to natural phenomena.[12]

However, this was not taken as meaning that economic science would have to refrain from considering that human action is subject not just to egoism but also to «error, ignorance and external compulsion». Failure to take this into account would be tantamount to adopting the same stance as those who believe that such circumstances make exact knowledge impossible. Consequently, «both the exact and the realistic orientation of theoretical research are therefore justified. Both are means for understanding, predicting and controlling economic phenomena, and to these aims each of them contributes in its own way.»[13]

Menger's problem lay in succeeding in the discovery of rigorous laws that guide the 'genetic' evolution of human institutions, starting from a twofold order of problems. The first was that these institutions have taken shape as the result of mankind's being unacquainted with these laws or due to blunders made in their interpretation and implementation. The second resided in the fact that these 'exact laws of nature', to the extent to which they are knowable, are independent of human will-power and produce their effect whether they are known or otherwise.

If the aim of exact science was thus to discover the *essence* [*Wesen*] of the *genetic element*, of the *nature* of human society, Mengerian *subjectivism* was limited to a 'genetic' conception of individual needs and society.

This orientation underwent important modifications at the hand of Mises and Hayek, the origin of which can be traced to an accentuation of the subjective and cultural character of individual choices and their results.[14] In other words, Hayek and above all Mises were less 'essentialist' than Menger as regards the nature of laws regulating human action and its consequences. In this connection, particular importance attaches to the shift from an Aristotelian 'paradigm' to a Kantian approach, in which knowledge is seen as deriving from the way the human mind organizes the data of experience. This meant not so much eschewing the Mengerian framework as reappraising it in a different philosophical perspective. This was particularly apparent in the case of Mises, whose references to Menger testify to continuity while at the same time pointing to a development along rather different lines. With Hayek, this approach to the problem of knowledge began to break down in *The Sensory Order*. For in this and following writings, the earlier approach was transformed into an evolutionary perspective embracing both reality and indeed the human mind and reason as well. Yet in Hayek too, the evolutionary process – despite the increased emphasis on its genetic character manifested in *The Fatal Conceit*[15] – still remained a cultural process set in the framework of a concept of the *nature* of social institutions different from that of the traditional dichotomy 'natural' vs 'artificial'.

The theory of human action contained in Mises's work *Grundprobleme der Nationalökonomie* can be considered as the first attempt to apply the principles of subjectivist economics to the theoretical social sciences.

Mises did not take the *Untersuchungen* as his starting point, but rather set out from the need to elaborate a system of a priori concepts (through which to link cause and effects), that would pursue the aim of attaining «universally valid knowledge of social phenomena». Consequently, Mises saw the scientific approach to the problems of the social sciences as beginning with the opposition shown by Cantillon, Hume, Ricardo and Bentham towards those who wished to fashion these sciences on the model of the mechanistic sciences.[16] Set against this background, even the *Methodenstreit* itself appears to be simply one episode in the clash between the two rival traditions, one in which the rationalistic orientation stood in opposition to the positivistic or historicistic orientation. Unfortunately the real grounds underlying the contrasting positions were not grasped, either by Menger, by Windelband or Rickert[17] or by any of the thinkers such as Senior, Mill, Cairnes, Wieser and Schumpeter who believed that the method of the natural sciences could also be put to use by economic theory.[18] In this sense, the controversy sprang from a mistaken interpretation of the nature of the laws of human action. This is what led Mises to conclude that the early marginalists' attacks on classical economics, and likewise Menger's attacks on the Historical School of Economics, prevented them from perceiving at once the revolutionary impact their theories could have on the social sciences.

It is thus pointless to search through Menger's work in quest of the foundations of Mises's philosophy of the social sciences. Despite the distinctions, his outlook bears all the hallmarks of neo-Kantian thought; indeed, his very research programme, especially as drawn up in that period, presents itself as an attempt to extend the *Kritik der reinen Vernunft* to the social sciences. In fact, a closer look at the clash with Windelband, Rickert and Weber reveals that the dispute stemmed precisely from their having considered the human sciences as historical rather than theoretical sciences, an attitude which meant that they had dissociated themselves from radical apriorism.

In invoking praxeology, Mises planned to overcome misguided approaches to the problem by means of a science of human action founded not on empirical or historical considerations, but instead on a logical a priori science that would set itself the aim of «comprehension of the universal» and would identify the essence of man as residing in the fact that human action is targeted towards accomplishment of subjective ends.[19] The path to be followed would therefore start not from *behaviour* but from an understanding of human action by means of a priori theorems[20] which must not be modifiable – nor should it be possible to demonstrate their falsity – by historical or empirical experience.[21] This ultimately led to an all-embracing concept of praxeology – given that the distinction between economic and non-economic phenomena was no longer deemed justifiable in the light of the new insights contributed by the theory of subjective values – so that praxeology was eventually extended to cover all aspects of human life. For every human action arises as a result of subjective value judgments and is directed by a variety of information (both true and false) concerning ends and means.

The neutrality of science with respect to ends did not, however, imply indifference on the part of economic science towards value judgments and ends. In the avenue of research opened up by Mises, the theoretical foundation of the social sciences was not made to derive from their relation to philosophy, metaphysics or history. Rather, it was underpinned by the fact that *scarcity*, taken as a universal and ineluctable phenomenon of the human condition, enables the rationality of economic calculation to be extended to every aspect of human life.

In this sense praxeology stood in contrast to the Weberian distinction between *rational action* and *irrational actions.* Since, according to Mises, every action is underlain by what we hold to be rational on the basis of our knowledge, «action is, by definition, always rational». Thus the main problem of the theoretical social sciences became one of defining the role of knowledge in action.[22] Weber's mistake, in this respect, was that of believing in the existence of human actions not referring to categories of ends and means, of success or failure, of profit or loss. This error was compounded by the fact that his denial of the existence of universal and a priori behavioural laws led him, just as it had led the despised positivists and historicists before him, to search in vain for a way to derive the laws of human action from history or from sociology.[23]

Even the Weberian difference between history and the science of action became a difference of degree within the *Kulturwissenschaften*. It is certainly no coincidence that there was never any suggestion that *ideal types* should be connected with the a priori character of human action, or with the necessary nature of its laws, the favoured relation being on the contrary a relation to history; *these were historical, not theoretical, ideal types*. Consequently, social science was logically conceived by Weber «only as a special, qualified kind of historical investigation».[24]

From this framework there unfolded a whole series of mistaken views. First and foremost was the claim that it is impossible to make a rational choice between conflicting values, a claim which appealed to the fictional dimension of free availability of goods and seemed to espouse the belief that any end can be achieved. Weber was well aware that the costs and undesirable consequences of an end can point to certain conclusions regarding choice of such values, but he argued that this should not additionally constitute the presupposition for a critique of values that would maintain their 'subjective' character. Accordingly, in Mises's opinion, Weber did not realize that the economic principle is the fundamental law of action, and that the character of this law is theoretical, not historical. His mistake thus lay in not having realized that in the perspective of the theory of subjective values all values, even the most bizarre, can be expressed in economic terms. His classification of human actions, and the ensuing distinction between actions definable as rational or irrational with respect to the aim, was therefore untenable. Rather than working in the framework of the theory of marginal utility, Mises felt, Weber seemed to be operating within the perspective of classical economics.[25]

Naturally he was not the only one. Menger and Böhm-Bawerk also, in Mises's eyes, failed to comprehend fully the implications of the transition they themselves had brought about from an objective to a subjective theory of value.[26] Or, put slightly differently, the error into which Weber fell was that of considering 'the theory of marginal utility' as the theoretical schema of the current moment of capitalism, i.e. as a historical fact rather than a theoretical breakthrough.

The 'Copernican revolution' in the social sciences was thus the discovery of the subjectivist theory of value, which «traces the exchange ratio of the market back to the consumer's subjective valuations of economic goods».[27] For, «it is not mankind, the state or the corporative unit that acts [on the market], but individual men and groups of men, and *their* valuations and *their* action are decisive, not those of abstract collectivities». In this manner it began to be understood that what establishes a link between valuation and use value is not exchange between «classes of goods» but that between «concrete units of goods».[28]

On these premises Mises elaborated not only his own theory of human action together with his philosophy of the social sciences, but also his own political philosophy. In a different perspective, in *Grundprobleme der Nationalökonomie*, the differences between Mises and Menger come clearly to the fore. Indeed, even the philosophical background they invoke does not encompass the authors quoted by Menger and Hayek, but rather appeals to the tradition of utilitarian rationalism and Neo-Kantism. The background sources consist predominantly of authors belonging to the Scottish tradition, interpreted rationalistically and utilitaristically by Mises, and as precursors of the theory of *spontaneous order* by Hayek, but this difference is by no means trivial. That these are not mere occasional references is to be confirmed both by a systematic examination of Mises's thought, and also by the fact that they reappear in mature works such as *Human Action* and *Theory and History*.[29]

This said, one cannot deny Mises the merit of having drawn attention to the important bearing the 'marginalist revolution' would have on the social sciences. Indeed, he must be credited with more than simply having provided a solution – even if it proved to be a landmark solution – to the «paradox of value». In other words, Mises realized that human action, like economic action, «is always in accord only with the importance that acting man attaches to the limited quantities among which he must directly choose», and that it pays but scant attention to the definitions of the good and of utility in general. The «recognition of this fact is the essence of the modern theory», and this also means that theoretical social science, like economics, «is independent of all psychological and ethical considerations».[30]

The reflections concerning the nature of the theoretical social sciences developed in the essay 'Epistemological Relativism' may be considered as the philosophical rendering of problems intrinsic to the relation between politics and economics, and pertaining to the role of economics in society. Mises's chief concern here was to make clear that the position held by economic science, which professes neutrality with respect to final ends, was not to be identified with *historicistic rationalism*. Seen from a slightly different point of view, however, he was equally anxious to demonstrate that the field of social sciences allows for the possibility of discriminating between values without necessarily demanding reference to ethical criteria, and that furthermore observance of ethical norms is not a sufficient condition for the attainment of human aims. Or rather, exclusion of the ethical sphere from the study of social phenomena does not automatically translate into a form of relativism. This meant that the relation between ethics and economics must begin with recognition that 'good intentions' are not sufficient to create a 'good society'.[31]

It follows that the relation between knowledge and action belongs to *praxeology*, understood as «general theory of human action» or «general theory of choice and preference». However, praxeology established its predominance in virtue of a twofold failure: on the one hand, of metaphysical systems striving «to ascertain the ends which God and Nature [were] trying to realize in the course of human history» and to pinpoint the laws involved; on the other, the failure of social philosophy systems which «thought that man could organize society as he pleased». The belief that social problems derived from citizens' lack of virtue – a belief which effectively transformed economic, social and political problems into ethical queries – was countered by praxeology's discovery of the interdependence of market phenomena. Subjective economics thus allowed the development of a general theory of choice and preference, the core thesis of which is represented by the statement that «choosing determines all human decisions».[32]

Yet praxeology should be thought of not as an aid to political struggle, but rather as a *general theory of human action* that refrains from passing value judgments. It does not designate specific ends, but springs from the ascertained fact that «human action is purposeful behaviour», chosen from among different options on the basis of given knowledge.[33] Granting this premise, since such action has the purpose of satisfying a desire which it is «vain to pass judgment on», «human action is necessarily always rational». This likewise means that it would be wrong to assume that the desire to procure for oneself the goods required for maintaining life and health «is more rational, natural, or justified than the striving after other goods or amenities». For one of the most characteristic features of man is his ability to control «both his sexual desires and his will to live». It was therefore quite arbitrary, Mises felt, to judge satisfaction of physiological needs to be 'natural' or 'rational' while labelling other needs 'artificial' or 'irrational'. An appeal to rationality cannot be countenanced when the question is one of choice of ends, but only as far as choice of means is concerned. And this is precisely the sphere of action encompassed by praxeology, a science of manner and means directed towards achievement of ends. The 'subjectivist' revolution was therefore held to reside in considering final ends as 'data', eschewing any evaluation, and in ascertaining «whether or not the means chosen are fit for the attainment of the ends aimed». This is what constitutes the difference between the modern 'theory of subjective values' and the 'theory of objective values' of classical economics, on the one hand, and the guarantee of its objectivity, on the other.[34]

If human action is characterized by the ability «to discover causal relations which determine change and becoming in the universe», knowledge of such relations forms a precondition for the attainment of human ends.[35] The task of praxeology is thus that of reaching an understanding of «the meaning and relevance of human action». So knowledge of praxeology pertains to what is universal and necessary, and stands in contrast to historical knowledge, which deals with whatever is unique and individual.[36] Accordingly, this latter type of knowledge will never succeed in discovering the universal laws of human action, for which it can provide no more than statistical profiles. Furthermore, in the absence of a theory of human action, it is doomed to flounder amid events and their manifestations without any certainty as to the object of the quest, or to give a representation of the facts that is culture-dependent and historically conditioned.

Any account of human action must therefore start from the insight that the aim of such action «is always the relief from a felt uneasiness». Praxeology deals with man's behaviour towards the external world and explores the way in which man turns elements he imagines to be useful for attainment of his ends into the actual means to achieve these ends. Therefore, the question of human action can legitimately become the object of rational knowledge and judgment. Similarly to economics, praxeology does not concern itself with intentions or actions as they could or should have occurred had the agents been omniscient and guided by principles of absolute validity; rather, it focuses on what agents genuinely do and the mistakes they make when facing known opportunities. In this perspective, preference is moulded by a scale of values and desires, and on the basis of the values and needs that this choice is believed to satisfy. These scales of value, which are clearly subjective just as the final ends are, vary from person to person, change over time and do not form the object of judgment. Individual action, then, springs from a rational calculation deriving from the way all these circumstances are apprehended at the moment of choice. The task of theoretical social science, for Mises, can thus be taken as that of understanding the subjective relation established between ends and means.[37]

These themes recur in Hayek, albeit in a somewhat different philosophical and methodological perspective, where they constitute the substance of the 'swing to subjectivism in the social sciences' that he claimed to share.[38]

This perspective was already foreshadowed in 'Economics and Knowledge', where it clearly emerges that Hayek's methodology rested on assumptions concerning the role of knowledge in human action quite different from the views held by Mises. In this above essay a theory of knowledge of human action is sketched out whose core consists of the demonstration that a society is built up and sustained by the diffusion of an infinity of *practical knowledges* that cannot be centralized. Consequently, the critique of various types of collectivist planning is grounded not so much in political or economic arguments as in arguments relating to the nature of human knowledge.

Where theories of economic planning went wrong was in their assumption that the 'facts' on which individuals base their options are 'objective' and perceived in the same manner by all subjects. Working against this hypothesis is the fact that «so-called 'data', from which we set out in this sort of analysis, are [. . .] all facts given to the person in question, the things as they are known to [. . .] him to exist, and not, strictly speaking, objective facts». Consequently, a new piece of information inducing the agent to change his plans disrupts the equilibrium that had been established among prior actions and those subsequent to the change in knowledge.[39]

Hayek was particularly keen to understand the relation between the subjective data different individuals possess and objective facts.[40] Regarding this question,

> economics has come nearer than any other social science to an answer to the central question of all social sciences. How can the combination of fragments of knowledge existing in different minds bring about results which, if they were to be brought about deliberately, would require a knowledge on the part of the directing mind which no single person can possess?[41]

The problem facing the theoretical social sciences does not therefore reside in determining the best use of available means, should one by chance happen to possess «all the relevant information» and should it be possible to «start out from a given system of preferences». In any case, this ideal situation does not exist in the real world; the social scientist finds himself confronted by 'data' which are considered such only for individuals or groups of individuals. Knowledge, far from existing in «concentrated or integrated form», is distributed in fragmentary fashion among different individuals and is only partially possessed, indeed at times only half sensed.[42] Observing that if the 'spontaneous mechanism' of the market had been the result of human planning it «would have been acclaimed as one of the great triumphs of the human mind», Hayek emphasized that this mechanism is not merely a feature of economic phenomena, but rather a peculiarity of all social phenomena.[43]

The implication of these observations is that the problem the social sciences found themselves grappling with was not how to formulate plans, but instead that of finding «the best way of utilizing knowledge initially dispersed among all the people».[44] The problem thus came to be identified with the search for an institutional framework such as would offer the best coordination of the knowledge scattered among the members of a society. This meant endeavouring to grasp the process by means of which human knowledge is communicated and exchanged, thereby giving rise to new and unforeseeable situations. This was an eminently practical situation, in other words, which could not be resolved by hypothesizing a repository of all aspects of universal knowledge. Rather, what was required was a two-pronged investigation, involving an endeavour to unravel the complex web of interaction between individuals, each of whom possesses only partial knowledge, without however neglecting to map out the spontaneous coordination which takes place within the scope of a wider and more complex structure. This analysis would, it was hoped, shed light on how these two aspects jointly give rise to *order* which cannot be considered to be the conscious product of human knowledge and will.

The attention paid to problems of knowledge reveals the Hayekian philosophy of the social sciences to be an attempt to capitalize to the utmost on its one and only objective datum: the insuperable limitedness of human knowledge. The fatal conceit of the human race can then be seen as the illusion of being able to transcend not only 'its own time' but also the very human condition. It is no coincidence that totalitarianism, just like the old tyranny[45], originated at least in part from the aspiration to attain glory by doing exactly what the greater portion of mankind has not succeeded in doing, either because of failure to realize that it represents the right course of action, or else on account of inability to pursue the course of action despite believing it to be right. At the same time, tyranny was no doubt also fired by some idea of attempting to speed up the course of history.

Hayek's philosophy of the social sciences thus blended imperceptibly with his theory of *political order* and his political philosophy. He set himself the target of elaborating a political philosophy which, while acknowledging the invincibility of human ignorance, would not thereby feel compelled to consign the problem of the *best political order* into the hands of casual, if spontaneous, evolution, or of a struggle between diverging visions of the world. By conceiving evolution essentially as *cultural*, he endeavoured to escape from the relativism towards which he would be driven by a theory of subjective values shorn of a concept of *naturality*. What Hayek had in mind here was a theoretical and practical system in which the subjectivity of values – the foundation of social life – could be discussed in the light of universalizable rules of conduct that will guarantee the existence of society.

Important implications derive from the above considerations. Firstly, once it has been established that the foundation of civil coexistence is not a community of moral values (a public ethics understood as a watered-down view of the *common good*) but natural diversity and scarcity, then sociality no longer retains the obligatoriness previously attaching to it. Secondly, state and politics alike can be justified only as a complex of rules which will contribute to achievement of the greatest number of abstract social advantages from the contrast between limited resources and unlimited needs and purposes.[46]

The state and, indeed, politics itself are thus effects of *scarcity*. Moreover, their power and the tasks they are entrusted with must be limited to the setting up of regulations to govern circumstances where the diversity of knowledge, availability and values foils development of a spontaneous solution. The Mengerian theory of the origin of economics and the state as deriving from property rights[47] cannot but mean that it arose to defend an institution for which no spontaneous recognition presented itself. But it also means that though lacking in spontaneous recognition, such an institution appeared better equipped than others to resolve the problem of scarcity by means of more efficient utilization of resources. And it is difficult to understand why individuals possessing common values (which presuppose common physical and intellectual faculties) who are not subject to the laws of scarcity should create a society aiming towards ends different from that of simply 'socializing' ennui.

Seen in this perspective, Hayek's political philosophy was shouldering a task analogous to that which Menger attributed to economic science in identifying the latter's mission as teaching the distinction between real needs and imaginary needs. Hayek did not exclude merit evaluations from the realm of political philosophy, but it was his intention to avoid its transformation into a normative ideal that would ultimately wipe out the positive effects of contrast and comparison between individual consciences. Therefore it could not take the place of individuals in prescribing or indicating choices, but instead it would intervene whenever such choices took on social or political relevance.

To Hayek's mind, it was not simply a question of preventing the distribution of knowledge from becoming a dispersion that would hamper civil coexistence, for he was also concerned with forestalling any transformation of political philosophy from a *search* into *organization*. This danger is all too real in those societies where relief from scarcity is made to depend on more just distribution of resources by the state. The outcome is the transformation of political philosophy into an instrument whereby subjective demands are legitimized, and of political life into a struggle for power where what counts is the determination to acquire positions of privilege. In other words, Hayek rejected both the belief that the task of political philosophy was to give shape to social and statal order on the basis of knowledge superior to individuals' knowledge, and also the conception of the state as an instrument purpose-built to champion every individual and social demand without paying any heed to their compatibility and universalizability. For the result of all this would be that political life either would end up being metamorphosed into a decision-making process based on numerical strength or social influence, or it would eventually endow the state – set up in order to guarantee property and exchange as the best remedies against scarcity – with the power of redistributing goods on the basis of non-economic considerations which would hardly resolve the problem of scarcity.

But before turning to this topic, it is necessary to examine the way individual wills are composed into larger entities.

§2. METHODOLOGICAL INDIVIDUALISM

Like all seminal ideas, the concept of *methodological individualism* has by now taken on a more or less independent life, assuming meanings at times quite far from the original. This confirms the ideas put forward by Popper concerning the origin and autonomy of the objects of 'World 3'. But it does not mean that enquiry into theories should restrict itself simply to taking note of the various meanings which periodically enrich and transfigure the theories, or else should be content with studying the whys and wherefores of such changes; rather, it must also consist in casting light on misunderstandings that lead to pointless conceptual and linguistic confusion.

One such confusion is, first and foremost, the tendency to confuse *methodological individualism* with *political individualism*.[48] Menger's critique of the 'atomism' and 'pragmatism' displayed by 'one-sided rationalistic liberalism' and Hayek's critique of the 'constructivist rationalism' shown by 'false individualism' make clear that what these two thinkers understood by methodological individualism was not a variant on political individualism of rationalistic derivation, but rather a genuinely different approach to social phenomena and the world of politics. In the Austrian perspective, political-individualism can thus be defined as a conception of society and politics that is inspired by a view of individuals deliberately planning social institutions. By contrast, methodological individualism is inspired by a conception of individuals as fully social entities, and sees institutions as the involuntary result of human actions which endeavoured to solve problems with the limited instruments of knowledge.[49]

However, we will not dwell at length on the various meanings assumed by the concept of methodological individualism.[50] (or ascribed to it). Instead, we will focus more specifically on what methodological individualism represented for exponents of the Austrian School, and how it ranked within their philosophy of the social sciences.

As understood by the Austrians, methodological individualism is the procedure by means of which the attempt is made to provide an answer to

Menger's query: *«how can it be that institutions which serve the common welfare and are extremely significant for its development come into being without* a common will *directed toward establishing them?»*[51] It follows that precisely because such institutions correspond to the set of phenomena which form the object of knowledge of the theoretical social sciences, methodological individualism cannot be considered an instrument with which to establish the hegemony of economic science over the other social sciences.

The first formulation of the principle of the *compositive method*, or methodological individualism, is to be found in the Preface of the *Grundsätze*. Here Menger, mentioning the method adopted, wrote:

> In what follows I have endeavored to reduce [*zurückzuführen*] the complex phenomena of human economic activity to the simplest elements that can still be subjected to accurate observation, to apply to these elements the measure corresponding to their nature, and constantly adhering to this measure, to investigate the manner in which the more complex phenomena evolve from their elements according to definite principles.[52]

This statement appears important not merely on account of its collocation, or because it was to reappear almost word for word in the *Untersuchungen*, but above all because it was representative of Mengerian philosophical and methodological issues and their interpretations within the framework of the Austrian School itself.

In 1942 it was explicitly taken up again by Hayek in 'Scientism and the Study of Society'. In the Hayekian version, «the individualist and 'compositive method' of the social sciences» has its nucleus in the claim that social facts are not empirical data, but conceptual elaborations produced by individuals or collective entities. It follows that one should be consistent and refrain from treating these pseudo-entities as 'facts', and start out systematically «from the concepts which guide individuals in their actions»; this is «the characteristic feature of that methodological individualism which is closely connected with the subjectivism of the social sciences».[53]

There is a general consensus among scholars that the concept of methodological individualism should be traced back to Menger, even though the expression was devised by Schumpeter.[54] It is notable that from Schumpeter on, excluding Hayek, Menger's position has not always been accorded due consideration. Indeed, discussions centring around the concept have most often been prompted by the Hayekian or Popperian version of methodological individualism, or else the version furnished by Weber in *Wirtschaft und Gesellschaft*.

Thus a 'return' to Menger does appear necessary, and not only on account of the extreme variety of meanings attributed to the expression 'methodological individualism'.

In the *Grundsätze* and the *Untersuchungen*, Menger did not actually use this term, as has already been pointed out, although he did make use of the concept. It was only in manuscript notes on Schmoller's review of the *Untersuchungen* that – as Hayek wrote in 'Scientism and the Study of Society' – he corrected the term 'deductive' with the term 'compositive' in reference to his own method. While Hayek merely reported this circumstance in the first edition of the essay[55], when it was republished in *The Counter-Revolution of Science* he tried to explain the reason why Menger used the term 'compositive', correlating it with Cassirer's reflections in *Philosophie der Aufklärung* on the issue of the 'resolutive' and 'compositive' method used in natural science.[56] However, this suggestion of Hayek's seemed to imply a link between the Mengerian 'compositive' method itself and the method of modern natural science, an innuendo that was misleading and destined to cause numerous misunderstandings.[57]

In the *Untersuchungen*, on the other hand – and especially as regards this particular issue – Aristotelian influence clearly makes itself felt. So much so, in fact, that on the page dealing with the method of the «theoretical social sciences», and above all in the passage defining its procedure, Menger gives a definition of his own method that indicates the decisive influence of what Aristotle writes in *The Politics*:

> As in other departments of science, so in politics, the compound should always be resolved into the simple elements or least parts of the whole. We must therefore look at the elements of which the state is composed, in order that we may see in what the different kinds of rule differ from one another, and whether any scientific result can be attained about each one of them. He who thus considers things in their first growth and origin, whether a state or anything else, will obtain the clearest view of them.[58]

Menger wrote:

> 'Scire est per causas scire'. Whoever wants to understand theoretically the phenomena of 'national economy' [*Volkswirthschaft*], those complicated phenomena which we are accustomed to designate with this expression, must for this reason attempt to take back to their *true* elements, to the *singular economies in the nation*, and to investigate the laws by which the former are built up from the latter. [. . .] He moves on the foundation of a fiction but at the same time he fails to recognize the most important problem of the exact orientation of theoretical research, the problem of reducing [taking back (*zurückzuführen*)] complicated phenomena to their *elements*. [. . .] Every theory, of whatever kind it may be and whatever degree of strictness of knowledge it may strive for, has primarily the task of teaching us to understand the concrete phenomena of the real world as exemplification of a certain regularity in the succession of phenomena; i. e. genetically [. . .] *This genetic element is inseparable from the idea of theoretical sciences»*.[59]

In these passages, there are two terms which attract the reader's attention. The first, in Aristotle, is «compound», which can be placed in relation to the Mengerian 'compositive' method. The second, in Menger, is '*zurückzuführen*, which cannot be translated with 'to reduce', for this – as will be made clear further on – would lead one to think of *reductionism* rather than the 'genetic' procedure inherent in Menger's meaning.[60] The importance attributed to these terms is due to the fact that they appear highly indicative of the Aristotelian philosophical context that forms the backdrop to Mengerian thought. This thesis can be corroborated by a philosophical analysis of the *Untersuchungen*, which strongly suggests that the misunderstandings surrounding the concept of the 'compositive method' derive from imprecise understanding of its conception of the origin and developmental laws of social institutions.

Besides, that Menger looked to Aristotelian philosophy as the core of his framework can be seen from the very first few pages of the work. Here he began to deal with the problem of the classification of economic sciences, sorting them into three groups and thereby elaborating a model closer to that of the Aristotelian tradition than to other contemporary models.[61] This type of classification of the sciences – which came to be the systematic nucleus of the *Untersuchungen* – can be useful for an understanding both of his critique of the Historical School of Economics, and also of the relation between *empirical-realistic orientation* and *exact orientation*, between *empirical laws* and *exact laws.*

Furthermore, this classification is fundamental when one seeks to understand the theory of the unintended consequences of intentional human actions and their products – in other words, the relation between *human action*, *practical economic sciences* and *exact laws.* For the practical sciences cannot exist without *one* theoretical science;[62] and should the configuration of the latter which serves as the foundation for the practical sciences prove to be wrong, the practical sciences themselves will give rise to social policies doomed to failure. The *unintended consequences* may thus be regarded as the outcome of the limits of knowledge within the practical sciences: as the product, shall we say, of ignorance of the *exact laws* regulating human action.

Important though the influence of Aristotle may be, however, it should not be overemphasized. There is a significant difference between Aristotle and Menger that must not be overlooked. If Aristotle believed 'nature' to constitute an *order* to be known and upheld, Menger on the other hand, and likewise later exponents of the Austrian School, contended that knowledge of the world must start out from the presupposition that the world is a product – albeit largely an involuntary one – of human action triggered by purposes and ends that are both subjective and limited. In other words, the world is regarded as the outcome of the scarcity of goods and knowledge, of the struggle between unlimited needs and limited resources. Significantly enough, Hayek strove to overcome the misleading distinction between 'artificial' and 'natural' in the classification and study of human phenomena, in favour of the Fergusonian definition as 'the result of human action, but not of human design'.[63] If this is genuinely the object of the theoretical social sciences, then it goes far beyond all Aristotelianism. Whereas Aristotle held that the philosopher's task was to discover the natural order of the world and to endeavour to imitate it, by contrast in the case of the Austrians the aim was to discover how it could be that individual actions inspired by subjective ends and limited knowledge can give rise to an objective order.

But even in the case of Hayek certain misunderstandings concerning the nature of the 'Mengerian compositive method' still slipped through the net, despite Hayek's acknowledgment of Menger as his forerunner, of whose spirit he believed himself to be a faithful and reliable interpreter. A comparison between the passages in Menger and their interpretation by Hayek may provide evidence that the *compositive method* and *methodological individualism* are not exactly the same thing. One is almost inclined to reproach Hayek for having grafted this method onto the individualistic tradition of English political philosophy without having given due consideration to the philosophical premises. Undeniably, in his essay '"Individualism": True and False'[64], Hayek did complete this philosophical tradition with a theory of the origin of social institutions (deriving from Menger) which he rightly considered to be more exhaustive than that of Ferguson, Mandeville, Hume, Smith or Burke. But above and beyond the synthesis carried out by Hayek, or Menger's acknowledgments of Burke, or his misunderstandings of Smith, one may well wonder if the two types of 'evolutionism' match exactly in all respects.

These aspects are centred on the goal of overcoming the dichotomy 'natural' vs 'artificial' in the theoretical social sciences, and on assimilation of Menger's 'evolutionist-genetic' model to the 'indeterministic' model of the English tradition. This goal was achieved, albeit with significant alterations compared to Hayek's previous writings, in *Law, Legislation and Liberty* and in *The Fatal Conceit*.[65] Nevertheless, Hayek arguably does stand within the Mengerian tradition; for, whatever the differences between the two traditions it may be said that the common theoretical problem was to find out how the most important social institutions (money, prices, language, law, state, religion) could arise spontaneously as the 'unreflecting' result of human action pursuing subjective ends. Despite the apparently explanatory nature of this problem, it implies a theory of human action which must be not only methodological but also philosophical-systematic, so that it may provide an answer to the question as to the nature of society.[66] Consequently, criticism of the Hayekian connection between methodological individualism and liberal political philosophy in the light of an ethical principle which would evaluate the political sphere is certainly possible, and undoubtedly helpful, but this would also mean endowing ethics with a predominance over politics and economics that may not be shared by other thinkers.

Turning again to Menger, he put forth his 'exact' method not merely as an explanatory system, but also as the only investigative method adequate to the nature of the object. Thus economic science, which dealt with 'exact laws of nature' and 'essences', was held by Menger to be directed towards the goal of teaching the distinction between 'real needs' and 'imaginary needs'[67]; in this sense, economics could guide individual choices by means of the 'practical sciences'. A different situation obtained, however, concerning the 'subjectivism' that came down to Hayek from Mises. Mises was led by 'subjectivism' to make a distinction between 'good' and 'bad' evolution of society on the basis of different considerations from those of Menger.

As has been seen, the factors allowing the more complex elements of social life to be traced back to simpler ones are not so much a process of reasoning which abstracts away from reality and 'reduces' the issue to a priori forms of knowledge. On the contrary, they involve the fact that all social phenomena, from the simplest to the most complex, follow a 'genetic' development and are the 'unreflecting' product of a series of individual actions that can be explained through the '*exact laws of nature*'.

Menger did not draw an explicit comparison between the *three orders of satisfaction of needs*[68] and the development of social institutions from simpler to more complex forms. Nevertheless, it does not appear us as at all far-fetched to do so. Granted that agents do not possess complete knowledge, and are subject to the restriction of living together with other subjects likewise lacking in such knowledge, the question becomes one of identifying the 'exact laws of nature' regulating the transition from simpler to more complex forms of social activity. This involves reverting to naturality in evolution, which has to be 'discovered' by distinguishing 'essence' from 'accident' and exploring the 'legal' ways through which subjective individual actions are 'composed' into social entities which assume objective value for those belonging to the society. Restating the matter slightly, the explanatory model can be said to consist in drawing a comparison between a real situation and what would have constituted the dynamics of the events had the situation unfolded according to the 'exact laws of nature'. But this is essentially equivalent to conjuring up a vision of the situation free from external interference that would derive mainly from the natural limits of human knowledge. Thus the premise for this kind of model is the fact that both factors, i.e. real events and also human knowledge, develop 'genetically'. As is the case for economic science, the theoretical social sciences too, within their own fields, can provide enlightenment concerning the distinction between real needs and imaginary needs.

But the argument can be taken further. The problem of methodological individualism cannot be divorced from the Austrian version of the theory of marginal utility. Certainly, one may cast doubt on whether Menger (although he did use the expression 'value subjective')[69] would have been in agreement with the political consequences of the subjectivism characteristic of Mises and, in those years, also of Hayek.[70] However, methodological individualism arose in connection with this nexus of problems, and hardly appears plausible if related to a different context from that of the theory of subjective values. It cannot be a coincidence that it was Menger himself who, in the *Grundsätze*, set up an indissoluble bond between *human economy* and *private property*, holding both of them to be the effect of the *scarcity of goods*.[71] Nor can it be mere chance that led him, in the *Untersuchungen*, to emphasize that the human economy was in general guided by «individual interests» which agents «regularly recognize [. . .] correctly, even if not in all cases and absolutely».[72] But Menger also added that should individuals be unable to organize their private economies in the manner deemed most suitable, the practical sciences of economy together with economics itself «would [. . .] assume a considerably different form». For in the «systematic approach to the socialist sciences in the socialist state», «the 'practical science of private economy' also, would cease».[73]

Any attempt to deny the legitimacy of establishing methodological individualism, in the interpretation of it sketched above, as the foundation of the Austrian School's liberalism would seem to indicate a failure to grasp the connection between the theory of subjective values, the theory of marginal utility and methodological individualism. Accordingly, the political philosophy of the exponents of the Austrian School was an outcome of their general theory of human action, and it follows from what has been seen concerning the origin and development of social institutions that it was not subordinated to economics. One might well concur with Hayek in saying that economics, similarly to politics, derives from the conception of society.[74] And yet, the link between 'compositive method' and 'subjective values' cannot but imply a brand of liberalism founded on an economy in which the value of goods appears to be the result of scarcity and of the very mechanism of market dynamics.

Consequently, Austrian liberalism was not an ideological option; indeed, if it were, this would mean disregarding the political implications of the theory of human action that is the very foundation of the theory of subjective values. For through the latter, given that economic institutions have the same origin as institutions such as language, law, religion or the state, no less than a general theory of human action is engendered which cannot fail to apply to the sphere of politics as well.

This sheds light on the reasons that prompted Mises and Hayek to devote a number of works to the issue of demonstrating the theoretical, rather than primarily practical, impossibility of an economic system claiming simultaneously to be collectivist and to show respect for individualities. Their arguments started out, first and foremost, from observations concerning the nature and limits of human knowledge, in a bid to show that collectivism and the theory of economic planning form part of the rationalist-constructivist tradition.

It is undeniable that methodological individualism, taken as an explanatory system, can be constructive in giving an account of collectivist social entities.

However, it is not solely an explanatory system, but rather forms part of a theory of the rise, development and dynamics of social institutions. To dispute this claim would, in the light of all that has been seen so far, mean severing the connection between the theory of human action and Austrian epistemology. Naturally, one is free not to share the Austrian school's political philosophy, but methodological individualism is truly an integral part of this philosophy. If such a link is denied, then its nature as a system fails to be recognized; this would be tantamount to reducing it to mere political thought and dissociating it from the general theory of human action and economic theory.

This thematic approach is to be found both in Hayek and in Mises.

The Hayekian treatment of the individualist or 'compositive' method sets out from theoretical considerations on the relation beween the human mind and 'data' developed in 'Economics and Knowledge', 'The Facts of the Social Sciences', 'The Use of Knowledge in Society', and 'Scientism and the Study of Society'.

Hayek reached the conclusion that in the field of social science one should avoid treating «these pseudo-entities as 'facts'», taking care to commence systematically «from the concepts which guide individuals in their actions».[75] Hence the need to understand more complex social phenomena by starting out from individual actions. In social science «it is the attitudes of individuals which are the familiar elements and by the combinations of which we try to reproduce the complex phenomena, the results of individual actions, which are much less known». This method, in an explicit allusion to Menger, was defined as «compositive or synthetic». And Hayek specified that

> it is the so-called wholes, the groups of elements which are structurally connected, which we learn to single out from the totality of observed phenomena only as a result to our systematic fitting together of the elements with familiar properties, and which we build up or reconstruct from the known properties of the elements. It is important to observe that in all this the various types of individual beliefs or attitude are not themselves the object of our explanation, but merely the elements from which we build up the structure of possible relationships between individuals.[76]

Thus the object of the social sciences is represented not by conscious individual actions but by actions giving rise to unforeseen results and likewise by spontaneous regularities. Consequently,

> if social phenomena showed no order except insofar as they were consciously designed, there would indeed be no room for theoretical sciences of society and there would be, as is often argued, only problems of psychology. It is only insofar as some sort of order arises as a result of individual action but without being designed by any individual that a problem is raised which demands theoretical explanation.[77]

On the basis of these presuppositions, Hayek reproached methodological collectivism for mistaking «for facts what are not more than provisional theories, models constructed by the popular mind to explain the connection between some of the individual phenomena which we observe». Moreover, these «social wholes» are not «natural units», but rather

> different complexes of individual events, by themselves perhaps quite dissimilar, but believed by us to be related to each other in a similar manner; they are selections of certain elements of a complex picture on the basis of a theory about their coherence.

It is therefore the human mind that applies the laws of thought common to all human beings, in order to select the elements required for assignment of the causal relation on the basis of criteria informed by rational or logical coherence. This means that for Hayek, unlike Menger, it was not a question of reaching the 'essence' of phenomena and their 'exact laws of nature'; such 'wholes' «exist only if, and to the extent to which, the theory is correct which we have formed about the connection of the parts which they imply».[78]

The manner in which Mises approached methodological individualism does not in appearance differ substantially from Menger's taking back of the more complex elements of social life to their simplest elements. For Mises too believed that

> all actions are performed by individuals, for a social collective has no existence and reality outside of the individual member's actions. The life of a collective is lived in the actions of the individuals constituting its body. There is no social collective conceivable which is not operative in the actions of some individuals. The reality of a social integer consists in its directing and releasing definite actions on the part of individuals. Thus the way to a cognition of collective wholes is through an analysis of the individual's actions.[79]

What is significantly different, however, is the foundation of their interpretation of the way individual actions aiming at achievement of subjective ends actually produce an order. In Mises the 'genetic element' so characteristic of Menger's evolutionism is no longer to be found. Its place was taken by marked subjectivism which can be synthesized in the statement that «all human values are offered for option» and that «to live is for man the outcome of a choice, of a judgement of value».[80] The prerequisite whereby human action and its social consequences become accessible to cognitive analysis no longer resides in awareness that it is natural to act for the purpose of attaining some end, but on the contrary in the existence and discovery of *a priori* universal laws regulating the results of action itself. The 'exact laws of nature' are replaced by a priori laws, logical considerations endowed with universal validity, by means of which the individual strives to bestow a subjective order on the world.

Here we have philosophical premises quite different from those of Menger or Hayek, neither of whom, as a matter of fact, are mentioned by Mises. This difference holds true even if the more analytic definition of methodological-individualism given in *The Ultimate Foundation of Economic Science* fails to provide a clear-cut and decisive distinction. In the latter circumstance,

> individualism as a principle of the philosophical, praxeological, and historical analysis of human action means the establishment of the facts that all actions can be traced back to individuals and that no scientific method can succeed in determining how definite external events, liable to a description by the methods of the natural sciences, produce within the human mind definite ideas, value judgments, and volitions. In this sense the individual that cannot be dissolved into components is both the starting point and the ultimate given of all endeavors to deal with human action.[81]

The truly important element here would seem to be the close connection established between individualism and praxeology, together with renewed emphasis on the claim that the object of the theoretical social sciences (the manner in which a subjective conception of external events induces individuals to act) cannot be determined by a scientific method informed by naturalistic views.

It must therefore be acknowledged that despite reference to one and the same source and use of practically shared terminology, even in the case of the Austrian School there emerge differing theoretical foundations of methodological individualism.

In the case of Menger, phenomena and social institutions can be explained both because their development is *exact-natural*, or *genetic*, thereby following the 'exact phenomenal forms' which can be grasped by the human mind, and also because human phenomena – like all natural phenomena – are subject to the *law of causality*.[82] The '*types*' («phenomenal forms») and the '*typical relations*' («laws of the phenomena») we use to trace complex phenomena back to simpler ones thus tend to be identified with their *genetic essence*.

In Hayek, on the other hand, phenomena have no natural meaning but receive order and objectivity from our mind. The process of decomposition and recomposition takes place by means of 'types' which tend to assume shape in a Weberian manner, though they differ from the latter in that they are not historical, but rather products of the 'constancy of the human mind'.

Mises in his turn viewed the possibility of 'methodological individualism' as resting on the fact that in his analysis human actions are 'composed' into objective results according to the universal and necessary rules of praxeology. Through this transition praxeology becomes the instrument for an assignment of the causal relations which enable the complex phenomenon to be traced back to the set of individual actions on which it rests.

§3. EVOLUTIONISM, ORDER AND CATALLACTICS

The theory of the rise and development of social institutions is undoubtedly one of the most important contributions made by the Austrian School to social science philosophy and the theory of *political order*. It is a conception whose roots can be traced as far back as the Aristotelian interpretation of the origin of the state,[83] standing in contrast to modern contractualist approaches as far as the state as interpreter and achiever of the 'common good' is concerned.

Hayek's evolutionism,[84] the consummate expression of the above tradition, can be portrayed through several statements of his according to which «*culture is neither natural nor artificial, neither genetically transmitted nor rationally designed*»,[85] and «*man is not and never will be the master of his fate: his very reason always progresses by leading him into the unknown and unforeseen where he learns new things*».[86] Into evolutionism as thus outlined flowed a number of different cultural traditions: Mengerian, 'Scottish', Darwinism, the 'epistemologic' evolutionism of Campbell[87] and Popper,[88] and Alchian's[89] evolutionistic determination of economic order. It is of very little use to attempt to demonstrate that these traditions are or are not compatible, or to debate whether certain interpretations are well founded, since they can be interpreted as the development of an idea.

Austrian evolutionism is first and foremost a critique of finalism, springing directly from a critical attitude towards philosophies which sought to find a *purpose* in history, and from the realization that the claims put forward by such philosophies could not be upheld. However, it was a solution that left open the problem of the 'ontological status' of the 'exact laws of nature' (the mistaken interpretation of which gives rise to the undesired consequences that shape social institutions), and likewise the problem of the relation of these laws to evolutionism. The issue was therefore twofold. On the one hand, it raised the question of why not everything that individuals desire is accomplished; and on the other, it drew attention to the fact that the mere fact of acting with a view to achieving the 'good' and following ethical norms (known or revealed) does not suffice to produce good individual and social consequences. If there were no 'exact laws of nature' which have to be known in order for individual actions to be successful, and hence for ends to be selected, then order could simply be the unlikely product of chance. But these 'laws' do exist, and they are not subject to an evolutionary process. Furthermore, the attempt to control them leads to the birth of civilization.

Yet the problem of the nature and knowledge of the 'exact laws of nature' is not clarified by these observations. Theoretical science[90] can be interpreted: (1) following Kant, as knowledge and dominion of *phenomena* rather than of *noumena*; (2) as a reflection on the laws of order that are unknowable because they are subject to constant change and evolution. They are definitely not the involuntary product of human action – even in *The Fatal Conceit* Hayek, referring to Menger, once again underlined their 'genetic' character[91] – but their knowledge conditions the success of human action.

One might also propose to interpret them as a set of prudential norms, cast in a negative or prohibitory mode, referring to an indefinite class of actions that must not be carried out if one is to avert the risk of drastic changes in the system that would usher in uncontrollable chaos. For if it should prove impossible to obtain the information on the basis of which to predict the outcome of individual actions, chaos would inevitably ensue. In this perspective, all that could be known of the 'exact laws of nature' would be those relating to the set of types of behaviour to be avoided if one wishes to keep the system alive. Thus they would not be seen in a prescriptive vein, but instead would take on the character of a prohibition motivated by the fact that there exist categories of actions whose consequences are impossible to know at any given moment, or which cannot but lead to negative repercussions for the whole of society. In this framework, the 'exact laws of nature' come to be identified with actions that are not to be carried out. One could even say that they come to represent the constant warning not to forget that human knowledge is limited and fallible, and that society is the product of a selection of behaviours in the light of the predictability and universalizability of their consequences. In other words, society is not goal-oriented but rather is a collection of knowledge that enables one to exclude certain ends on the basis of prediction of their social consequences. From a political point of view, this would involve the exclusion of changes deemed too drastic or revolutionary.

By focusing squarely on the problem of the unwanted consequences of human action and bringing this to the attention of the theoretical social sciences, the exponents of the Austrian School were dealing with two of the central problems of philosophical-political enquiry. These were, firstly, whether it is possible for philosophy, seen as research and experience, to embrace all knowledge and explain the world; and, additionally, were this to prove impossible, how to resolve human problems and assess their solutions.

Moreoever, in dealing with the way subjectively understood natural needs produce an unintentional but objective order, they also furnished insight into the relations between individuals and history, and the laws regulating the latter. In this manner they addressed the problem of natural inequalities between individuals in a fresh perspective, showing how the greatest possible social advantage could be drawn from such circumstances. Theirs can truly be deemed an analysis of the fundamental problems of political philosophy. Their reflection encompassed not only the difficulties laid bare by the downfall of finalistic philosophies of history, and by the demise of naive trust in reason – the limits of which had been only too painfully exposed – but also the quandary that emerged upon realization of the damage done by application of the (presumed) methods of natural science to social science.

A more analytical consideration of the problem should start out, once again, from the Mengerian theory of the origin and development of social institutions. For this theory makes it clear that Menger did not feel satisfied with the traditional answer that the *organicist tradition* and the *pragmatistic tradition* gave concerning the nature and origin of human society and its institutions. Rather, he chose to broach the classic theme of political philosophy: that of the nature and origin of the *best political order.*

It was Menger's intention to construct the theory of the political regime on the framework of the naturality of human society. A link can be discerned here with his interpretation of human history as a *spontaneous* or *genetic evolution*, in some sense sustained by a 'naturality' or 'essence' of man. This conception of history can be considered an extension to the entire historical process of the conception of the nature of society which, as has been seen, Menger derived from Aristotle.

In Menger's critique of organic-naturalistic and pragmatistic theories about the nature and origin of social institutions, though, Aristotle remains a shadowy presence in the background. Sooner than appealing to his authority, Menger preferred to link up to the exponents of the reaction against «pragmatism in the view of the nature and origin of civil society [*bürgerliche Gesellschaft*] and its institutions» that was taking place at the end of the eighteenth century in the field of jurisprudence. From Montesquieu onwards a new theory of social institutions had begun to take shape. And it was in Germany that the reception given to Burke's reflections on the spirit of English jurisprudence, on the «significance of the organic structures of social life» and on the «partly unintended origin of these» acted as the trigger «for an attack on pragmatism in jurisprudence». These developments were noticeable first of all with Hugo, then with Savigny and Niebuhr, who forged a conception of law as «the unintended result of a higher wisdom, of the historical development of the nation», and denied «pure abstract understanding either the competence for or [. . .] the task of comprehensive construction of the law».[92]

This brought up again the problem of what should be understood by the phrase 'nature of society'. This problem was to receive a number of different answers within the Austrian School, depending on the differing philosophical backgrounds of its exponents. But leaving aside the differences, a common attempt to find a connection between the concept of society and social policies can be identified , as was well put by Hayek when dealing with the tradition of 'true' individualism in '"Individualism": True and False'.[93]

Thus it appears that what Menger, Mises and Hayek aimed to do was to underscore that any social policy not taking into account the nature of society is destined to be unable to achieve its established goals. Yet this does not mean that it may not be extremely popular for a certain length of time, and may thereby represent an objective political problem. A distorted interpretation of the relation between theoretical science, then, and practical sciences may not be capable of spontaneously producing an *order.* In other words, the interpretation of the *exact laws of nature* may be distorted to such an extent that the impossibility of achieving subjectively expected ends will produce not order, but *chaos*. Consequently, order is not the natural product or the result of the a priori laws regulating the consequences of human action (and these laws cannot be indefinitely disregarded), but instead the product of evolution and *cultural selection*.

Thus in Menger one can find the first formulation of some of the themes that reappear in Hayek: positive reference to the Historical School of Law, critique of historicist organicism (understood as a source of totalitarianism), critique of pragmatic rationalism (understood as the premise that paves the way to socialism and constructivism). But rather than dwelling on shared elements, let us more profitably focus on their differences. While Mengerian 'evolutionism' looked back to these cultural sources, the roots of Hayekian evolutionism stretch back to embrace the teachings of Mandeville, Hume, Ferguson and Smith, whom Menger ignored or perhaps – Smith is a case in point – regarded somewhat differently.

When one turns to Mises, on the other hand, one finds that he makes reference to rather a different framework of thought.

The work in which he delved most deeply into history and its theoretical and methodological problems is *Theory and History*. Here the issues of the evolutionism of social institutions (a topic already brought up in *Human Action*) and of the relation between theory and history were treated in the light of the repercussions of praxeology in the field of historical knowledge. Mises's intention appears to have been to establish the critique of determinism, materialism and historicism on a much more solid epistemological basis. In contrast to historicism's avowed aim of rendering the historical process linear and free from unforeseen effects, he believed that history, human institutions and all other social phenomena are subject to an evolutionary process which must be preserved[94] because it is the fruit of the *rational structure* that man has imposed on his experiences.

Mises's subtitle, *An Interpretation of Social and Economic Evolution*, would lead one to expect a treatise on the historical, social and economic evolution of the human mind. However, the work restricts itself to stressing that the claims of historical determinism are untenable, showing them to be the product of individual effort endeavouring to achieve subjective ends. Misesian evolutionism thus came to coincide with the increasing prominence of the *idea of economic rationality*. Indeed, the need to preserve such an advantageous structure formed the genesis of the most interesting pages of the work, in which he took a stand against those who, in one way or another, attempted to bridle historical evolution.

In this circumstance the utilitarian basis of Mises's social philosophy comes to the fore, and the limit of his conception of order is displayed. What Mises understood by order was a set of behavioural norms that had evolved rationally in order to reach a form of society in which it was possible to achieve the greatest possible number of subjective ends.

The task of attaining this target was entrusted not to historical evolution taken as signifying progress, but rather to human reason, taken as what transforms the data of sensory stimuli into experiences and a coherent system, and thereby acts as a guide to action. In this function, reason not only avails itself of world views (interpetations of the universe and advice on how to act) but also makes use of ideologies (the set of «doctrines concerning individual conduct and social relations»). Mises considered both aspects to be «doctrines about the ought, i.e. about the ultimate ends which man should aim at in his earthly concerns».[95] Clearly this process is an evolutionary development, a growth of knowledge which, however widespread its realization may become in society, still remains an individual achievement.[96]

The differences between Menger, Hayek and Mises came into play as regards the origin of society and social institutions. The ideal society, in Mises's eyes, was a society enabling all its members to achieve subjective values or ends. Hence, underlying the 'best political order' was the ability of the market economy to satisfy individual needs better than other economic arrangements, and democracy understood as a system that does not evaluate individual ends and delegates conflict-resolving power to the majority. It was precisely this that justified the claim that capitalism, i.e. subjectivist economics, is the only possible form of democracy. Now this conception of society, even though mitigated by considerations regarding the division of labour and the function of co-operation (where co-operation is seen as the most efficient manner to overcome natural inequalities in human abilities and unequal distribution of natural resources),[97] has an instrumental and utilitarian flavour to it. Mises did in fact believe that satisfaction of individual needs can come about through the system of market co-operation, the superiority of which consists in managing to assimilate and transform every individual desire into social utility.

Viewing man as a «social being» and considering society as «the great means for the attainment of all his ends», and his conservation as the «essential condition of any plans»[98], Mises left no doubt concerning his belief that there could be an infinite variety of subjective ends coexisting at any one time. In his opinion, it was only religious controversies that could not be settled by rational methods. When earthly questions are at stake, on the other hand, men's natural affinity and the biological needs to preserve life make capitalistic societies into mighty instruments well equipped to pursue any and every type of subjective end. Through this mode of reasoning, Mises implicitly rejected the Weberian claim that different views of the world produce conflicts that cannot be reconciled, contending that the essential part of political programmes consists not of great philosophical themes but, quite simply, of promises about how to become «more prosperous and more content». The whole problem of the struggle between political ideologies is thus reduced to a question of means and manner, which can be settled by rational methods.[99]

Although as early as *Socialism* he had pointed out that one of the components of socialist ideology was rejection of the market in favour of a society informed by completely different values, Mises did not take into consideration that there may exist subjects who wish to forgo the advantages offered by the market.[100] Consequently, his conception of society as «joint action and co-operation in which each participant sees the other partner's success as a means for the attainment of his own»[101] presents itself as a theoretical 'ideal type' of political order founded on the conviction that: (1) market economy is the best form of economic organization and the only one to be rational; (2) it allows realization of all individual aims and reduces, or indeed eliminates, violence from political life; and (3) those who forsake or spurn these tenets are doomed to downfall.

But the area where the distance from Menger and Hayek stands out most conspicuously is in Mises's conception of society and social affairs. According to Mises, society and social affairs are «a product of human action», and since human action is guided by ideologies, it is fair to claim that «society and any concrete order of social affairs are an outcome of ideologies». Therefore, Mises argued, society was «thought out and designed before it could be realized». Unlike those whom he dubbed «utopians», however, Mises believed that the «temporal and logical precedence of the ideological factor does not imply the proposition that people draft a complete plan of a social system», nor does man make «plans and execute actions intended to construct society». But he did maintain that «society is always the creation of ideologies temporally and logically anterior. Action is always directed by ideas; it realizes what previous thinking has designed.»[102] Consequently, the state is not essentially different from an «apparatus of compulsion and coercion [. . .] an institution to cope with human imperfection», whose «essential function is to inflict punishment upon minorities in order to protect majorities against the detrimental consequences of certain actions».[103]

Underlying Mises's theory of the *best political order* was thus the conviction that proper economic and social policy can so drastically reduce unsatisfied needs as to make it superfluous, anti-economic and irrational to toil for their satisfaction in any manner different from that granted by the social co-operation of the market. Through this mode of reasoning, however, Mises ultimately drew a connection between the problem of order and the problem of power: 'A country's public opinion may be ideologically divided in such a way that no group is strong enough to establish a durable government. Then anarchy emerges. Revolutions and civil strife become permanent.'[104]

In other words, Mises appears not to have noticed that the formation of ideological divisions could not be averted simply by envisioning society as an instrument by means of which any individual end whatsoever can be achieved, with the state viewed as an instrument of coercion. And if divisions emerge, they can become so deep as to jeopardize the very existence of society and the state. This cannot be avoided merely by subjecting to rational calculation the means and manner by and in which ends are to be attained; instead it requires that political philosophy be entrusted with the task of evaluating individual and social ends in the light of their universalizability. From this point of view, and this is crucial, his position was unequivocally distinct from that of Hayek; and Mises can be singled out as a democratic thinker who saw order as deriving from power.

There still remains the problem of ascertaining whether political philosophy performs a function within the framework of a spontaneously produced order that places the various spheres of human action on a plane of formal equality and which rejects the idea that order derives from one such sphere achieving hegemony over the others. The solution offered by Mises to this set of questions appears inadequate, especially when compared to the rather different solution, certainly more realistic, but also philosophically more stimulating and seminal, put forward by Hayek.

In opposition to the 'pragmatic' interpretation, Hayek – as has been outlined above – urged «a 'compositive' theory» founded on the individuality of social institutions and on the possibility of understanding them «only genetically», as the involuntary result of «many forces working through long stretches of time». The task of this 'compositive method' thus consisted in explaining how they «can arise as the unintended result of the separate actions of many individuals».[105]

In this perspective, it becomes important to make a clear-cut distinction between «the motivating or constitutive opinions [. . .] and the speculative or explanatory views», which individuals formulate regarding the objects of the social sciences. Despite this, Hayek seems not to have become aware that even the conception of such objects, which may be considered «popular abstractions» and should not be mistaken for 'facts', can have consequences for the origin and evolution of social institutions.[106] This appears particularly important when attempting to understand how the *corruption of order* comes about. For though it is true that the utmost efforts should be made not to fall into the foregoing error, yet there can be no doubt that it is perfectly possible to lapse into it. This slip-up would not be free from repercussions linked to the understanding and explanation of phenomena such as collectivism and totalitarianism. What we have here are unquestionably myths, or *fatal conceits*, whose success was as ephemeral as it was tragic. But since tyranny is the endemic scourge of politics, such myths cannot be forestalled without insight into the social mechanisms through which they arise and subsequently become more widespread, gradually gaining currency.

Therefore if one reflects that even mistaken ideas concerning society can influence their development, the 'good order' ultimately turns out simply to have greater likelihood of occurring than disorder.[107] In other words, Hayek's problem was to safeguard the possibility of a spontaneous order while knowing that it does not rest on a finalistic philosophy of history, and that this order is not *natural*, but *cultural*.[108]

Hayek felt that this model of order is not known by thought and imposed by politics. Instead it is the involuntary result of individual actions which, in their intent to achieve subjective ends, have given rise to a set of rules, norms, communication systems and traditions that represent an *objective whole* for those who intend to achieve subjective ends within its scope. Order, then, is neither imitation of nature, nor the meaning of history, nor the way towards eternity, nor the requirement of reason, nor the fruit of a contract.

While Hayek drew the obvious conclusions from the failure of the political philosophies that led to totalitarianism or that were unable to impede it, his concept of order cannot be reduced to these experiences. Rather, its origins are to be sought in a 'minority' tradition of Western political thought: a tradition that had perceived, as early as Menger, that the outcome of the 'majority' tradition was blighted not just by the consequences of its social philosophy but more specifically, indeed primarily, by its mistaken view of society.

In this spectrum of erroneous conceptions, the one that was singled out as being the most dangerous was certainly that of 'constructivist rationalism', which conceives «the human mind as an entity standing outside the cosmos of nature and society». Regarding the human mind as a product of the evolutionary process, Hayek made a distinction between the tradition of 'evolutionary rationalism' (or, in Popperian terms, the 'critical' tradition) and that of 'constructivist rationalism' (or, again in Popperian terms, the 'naive' tradition).[109]

The former tradition had as its starting point the recognition that «*not all order that results from the interplay of human actions is the result of design*». For the latter, on the other hand, order is a product of human will guided by reason. This distinction led Hayek to explore in greater depth the origins of this conception of order and the anthropomorphic connotations it has taken on. Thus his problem was to find a suitable term to identify a spontaneously formed order. Hence his distinction, with reference to the Greek tradition, between *taxis* (the arrangement of human production so that specific ends may be achieved) and *cosmos* («an order which existed or formed itself independent of any human will»). Although originally it was not widely used in this sense, tending instead to be taken in the sense of «order of nature», this term seemed equally appropriate also to designate «any spontaneous social order». The substantial difference between «a spontaneous order or *cosmos* and an organization (arrangement) or *taxis*» therefore consists in the fact that «not having been deliberately made by men, a *cosmos* has no purpose». On the contrary, «every *taxis* (arrangement, organization) presupposes a particular end, and men forming such an organization must serve the same purposes». Consequently, if in a *cosmos* the knowledge and ends guiding action are those of the individuals themselves, in a *taxis* «the knowledge and purposes of the organizer will determine the resulting order». *Taxis* thus appears as a plan for the attainment of particular hierarchically ordered ends. There derives from this the statement that the *cosmos* is the result of the «regularities of the behaviour of the elements which it comprises», while the *taxis* is «determined by an agency which stands outside the order».[110]

Glancing back over the most significant milestones of the history of the two traditions, Hayek pointed to Cartesian dualism as the mistake of 'constructivist rationalism'. He attacked the conception of «an independent existing mind substance which stands outside the cosmos of nature and which enabled man, endowed with such a mind from the beginning, to design the institutions of society and culture among which he lives». The mistake of Cartesian dualism thus lay in failing to realize that

> this mind is an adaptation to the natural and social surroundings in which man lives and that it has developed in constant interaction with the institutions which determine the structure of society. Mind is as much the product of the social environment in which it has grown up and which it has not made as something that has in turn acted upon and altered these institutions [. . .] It is the result of man having developed in society.[111]

The above is nevertheless but one among the aspects of the relation between social institutions and the human mind. Hard on its heels comes the problem of the origin of the distinction between 'natural' and 'artifical' phenomena. In Greek philosophy the original terms were «*physei*, which means 'by nature' and, in contrast to it, either *nomos*, best rendered as 'by convention', or *thesei*, which means roughly 'by deliberate decision'».What had sparked off the confusion was the use of two different terms to express what comes about not 'by nature' but on account of «objects which existed independently and objects which were the results of, human *actions*, or between objects which arose independently of, and objects which arose as the result of, human *design*». The failure to distinguish between these two different readings of the term 'artificial' had been the source of a confusion that was cleared up only when Mandeville and Hume became aware of the existence of «a category of phenomena which, depending on which of the two definitions one adhered to, would fall into either the one or the other of the two categories». This category of phenomena, defined by Ferguson as the set of phenomena which were «the result of human action but not of human design», corresponds to the specific object of the 'theoretical social sciences'.[112]

In his outline of the origin and development of the evolutionary tradition, Hayek added to the above-mentioned thinkers Louis Molina and sixteenth-century Spanish Jesuits, the Historical School of Law and Language, Savigny and Humboldt. But this tradition had not met with immediate acclaim. Quite the contrary: between the sixteenth and the seventeenth centuries it very nearly disappeared following the rise of modern rationalism, which changed the meaning of the terms 'reason' and 'natural law'. In this process 'reason' lost its meaning of the ability to distinguish between good and evil, becoming synonymous with the «capacity to construct [. . .] rules by deduction from explicit premises»; 'natural law' became synonymous with 'law of reason'. This marked the beginning of the decline of the influence of evolutionistic ideas, which was halted only by their reformulation, in the field of economics, in the *Untersuchungen*.[113]

The origin of the evolutionistic tradition thus lies in a conception of society expressed through the contraposition of *spontaneous individualism* and *rationalist individualism*. Spontaneous individualism takes on the appearance of a challenge to rationalism, and its chief claim is that more than one approach can be taken to social phenomena. Not only can a natural and biological conception be outlined (organicism), and also a rationalistic conception (contractualist), but in addition it is possible to discern «a third possibility – the emergence of order as the result of adaptive evolution».[114]

The evolutionism in question here is not of a biological but a cultural nature. It was Hayek's belief that Darwin himself had been influenced by the theories of social evolution put forward by the Scottish philosophers and the 'Historical School of Language and Law'.[115] This did not imply denial that in its original meaning the term 'evolution' referred to the unfolding of genetic potentiality, but it did encompass the proposition that the theory of biological and sociological evolution is inadequate to explain the emergence and differentiation of complex structures. For this reason, in the fields of ethics, anthropology and law, the theory of evolution was confined to stating that these structures, which represent the object of social science, «can be understood only as the result of a process of evolution», and that, in this field, «the genetic element is inseparable from the idea of theoretical sciences».[116]

These themes recur in 'The Three Sources of Human Values', where Hayek underlines that the evolutionism he espoused was not biological but cultural, initially inspired by Mandeville, Hume and the Historical School of Law and Language and then little by little becoming more sharply defined as the selection of norms within the framework of a competitive process. Hayek placed emphasis once again on the fact that «*culture is neither natural nor artificial, neither genetically transmitted nor rationally designed*», but is a set of behavioural norms that are learned without their having been 'invented', and at times even without their function being understood. In this way he reached the conclusion that «mind and culture developed concurrently and not successively».[117]

The subsequent developments of these views, which began to take shape as early as the end of the 1930s, form the epistemological stepping-stones to the construction of Hayek's political philosophy. Its central feature was the preeminent position awarded to society, where the latter is taken to be spontaneous cultural order, and the important role played by the state, seen as construction. Order is thus not a natural or biological fact, but a breakthrough obtained by a lengthy process of comparison and trade-offs between different solutions, which eventually sedimented into tradition. And similarly to all great achievements of the human mind, it is subject to criticism and improvement.

The problem facing Hayek, then, was to understand the nature of moral and behavioural norms underpinning the proper functioning of society, and to make sure that compliance with such norms does not turn into dull conformity but rather encourages the appearance of innovations. Clearly, a system of this kind will need to be characterized by considerable flexibility in the norms on which it is founded. This flexibility would be a prerequisite not only for gradual evolution of the norms themselves, but also for «modifications and improvements», that is, «the opportunity for the selection of the more effective ones».[118] From this point of view, 'human nature' itself ends up being «very largely» envisioned as «the result of those moral conceptions which every individual learns with language and thinking».[119]

Hayek thus hypothesized the existence of 'social knowledge', believing it to be endowed with higher value than that possessed by the individual.[120] Yet he was not thereby induced to think that this knowledge was infallible, or that individual reason played no role in social affairs. Rather, once again, his proposal was more along the lines of calling attention to the limits of human knowledge, whether it be individual or social. This vision by no means inflamed him with ideas of a near-mystical defence of the spontaneity of evolution, but on the contrary, as in Hume, impelled him to take a critical look at reason itself.[121]

This perspective suggests that the propensity to evolutionism does not derive from the conviction that there exists a biologically good human nature. For this could lead to the conception that once human nature were freed from the sedimentation of the mistakes of history and reason, everything would spontaneously turn out for the best. Hayek, on the other hand, felt that evolutionism could perhaps better be thought of as cultural, as something concerning above all the institutions which allow optimum coordination between individual ends and social order. Thus it was a complex of traditions and norms of behaviour which are in constant flux as they strive to tackle new problems that could not have been foreseen either by tradition or by reason.

Looked at from a more strictly political vantage point, the evolutionistic theory of social institutions also forms the starting point of Hayek's resistance to the traditional explanation of political order founded on the distinction between those in command and those who obey commands. This enabled him to explain order in terms of a «mutual adjustment of the spontaneous activities of individuals» provided that «there is a known delimitation of the sphere of control of each individual». Order thus appears as the result of individual acts guided «by successful foresight» and by effective use of individual knowledge where such knowledge is linked to prediction of the behaviour of other members of society. If this is understood, as in Michel Polanyi, as spontaneous formation, as 'polycentric order', then it is impossible for it to be the product of a will and of a central rule of knowledge.[122]

Consequently, order does not have the aim of realizing collective ends (such as the 'common good') but, rather, general aims without any specification or requirement as to who shall be able to draw the greatest advantage from it. This abstractness also allows order to obtain coordination of individual actions and utilization of knowledge and skills so as to ensure satisfaction of many individual expectations (not, however, all of them). In the wake of these reflections, and consequently dissatisfied with the traditional conceptions of order and their foundations, Hayek set about reviving the distinction between 'economy' and 'market order' or 'catallactics':

> while an economy proper is an organization in the technical sense [. . .] that is, a deliberate arrangement of the use of means which are known to some single agency, the cosmos of the market neither is nor could be governed by such a single scale of ends; it serves the multiplicity of separate and incommensurable ends of all its separate members.[123]

Faced with the imprecise meanings associated with the term 'economy' when used to designate a market order that forms spontaneously by means of «numerous interrelated economies», and quoting Mises, Hayek proposed replacing the expression 'economics' by the term *catallactics*. This replacement had by then made itself necessary, he felt, because

> the confusion which has been created by the ambiguity of the word economy is so serious that [. . .] it seems necessary to confine its use strictly to the original meaning in which it describes a complex of deliberately co-ordinated actions serving a single scale of ends, and to adopt another term to describe the system of numerous interrelated economies which constitute the market order.

Catallactics is thus «the order brought about by the mutual adjustment of many individual economies in a market»: «the special kind of spontaneous order produced by the market through people acting within the rules of the law of property, tort and contract».[124]

In this respect Hayek's most valuable contribution was precisely a feature normally reckoned to be a serious flaw in his approach: that of not having «an agreed ranking of ends», thereby making «individual freedom and all it values possible». But given that catallactics allows the conciliation of disparate bodies of knowledge and aims regardless of whether they are known or not, it shows itself to be «an overall order so superior to any deliberate organization» that within its framework «men, while following their own interests, whether wholly egotistical or highly altruistic, will further the aims of many others, most of whom they will never know». In adopting this position, Hayek effectively took a stand against the conception that a hierarchically organized common scale of values and ends is «necessary for the integration of the individual activities into an order», and also expressed the belief that it constitutes the common matrix of nationalism and socialism.[125]

The importance of catallactics in order to keep a great society united did not, however, imply that all forms of civilization are reducible to 'economic ends'. On the contrary, Hayek denied the existence of ends that would, «in the last resort», be economic, interpreting them instead as instruments for the «allocation of means for the competing ultimate purposes which are always non-economic». In this manner the role of economic activity was seen as consisting in the evaluation of such ends and decisions concerning the question of selecting the ones for which «the limited means are to be used». In this perspective, the merit of the catallactics model resides in its success in conciliating the pursuit of different ends by means of a process offering advantages to everyone. And precisely because it denies the existence of a hierarchy of needs, and hence of any priority in their satisfaction, this process takes on the characteristic of being «the only known method» capable of functioning without a prior agreement «on the relative importance of the different ultimate ends».[126]

The model outlined above therefore has the merit of avoiding the degenerations so typical of democratic regimes that derive from a 'political' decision as to priorities among the various needs to be satisfied. Moreover, these reflections on catallactics, understood as the foundation of order, and as the simplest and most functional solution to problems of social coexistence, constitute the premise for an attempt to come to grips with the real nature of politics.

Hayek thus rejected the idea that rational politics requires shared concrete ends, since this would transform politics into an 'organization' having the achievement of specific ends as its goal. Consequently, in the catallactic model the primacy formerly accorded to politics, on the assumption that politics represented the moment of decision regarding which needs to satisfy and in what order, no longer prevailed. Admittedly, this conclusion is not explicitly stated. It is nevertheless easy to imagine that compression of the political sphere as seemingly indicated would lead to redesigning the systematics of the theoretical social sciences.

A perspective of this kind would seem to be behind Hayek's reasoning when he writes that politics does not consist in «striving for the achievement of particular results», but is more effectively described as «securing an abstract overall order» which can ensure the best chance of pursuing different or as yet unknown ends. Politics is thus shorn of many of the tasks previously falling within its purview. In this case, if one decides to adopt the view, as did Hayek, that its aim is to achieve an egalitarian increase in every individual's opportunity to pursue his own ends, while restricting coercion to application of universal norms whose aim is «to improve everyone's opportunities», then the tasks assigned to politics will undeniably be substantially curtailed or modified. For politics will be divested of any function of guidance. It follows that identifying the 'common good' with «abstract order», which «must leave undetermined the degree to which the several particular needs will be met»,[127] will inevitably lead to acknowledgment that a substantive concept of 'common good' can exist only in an 'organization'.

Hayek's aim, therefore, was to find a way of conciliating values, individual ends and the requirement of an order which will allow these. For the achievements of catallactics meant it was no longer possible to set up a hierarchy of purposes and organize a society in view of such a ranking, as this would in fact lead straight to totalitarianism.

Extension of the findings of catallactics to the complex of the social sciences, then, radically changed the latter's aims. The change was rendered necessary by the discovery that market rewards do not derive from what has been done, but from what one «*ought* to do». Hayek's conclusion was thus that

> *Men can be allowed to act on their own knowledge and for their own purposes only if the reward they obtain is dependent in part on circumstances which they can neither control nor foresee. And if they are to be allowed to be guided in their actions by their own moral beliefs, it cannot also be morally required that the aggregate effects of their respective actions on the different people should correspond to some ideal of distributive justice. In this sense freedom is inseparable from rewards which often have no connection with merit and are therefore felt to be unjust.*[128]

Faced with the changes springing from the rise of innovation in forms of trade, Hayek reflected, the task of politics, cannot be spelled out as the distribution of resources according to ethical or political criteria, but must instead be sought in assessment of the advantages and costs inherent in change. This is a duty that will have to be performed for the sake of consumers, not for the sake of producers.[129] For the decision to accord preference to various groups in order for them to be able to preserve their position in society can only mean giving up the benefits that change could bring to the whole of society. Any interference in this process would, by creating privilege, be transformed into an act of coercion. One should thus not cherish a fond dream of development free from afflictions and costs, but instead pin hopes on a society governed by laws that strive «to improve as much as possible the chances of anyone selected at random». The «most desirable order of society» is then identified with a society such that the «initial position [. . .] be decided purely by chance», and in which any future position is entrusted to fate.[130]

The kind of approach adopted by Hayek towards the problem of order can essentially be seen as an innovative answer to the fundamental question raised by political philosophy: that of the nature and conditions of *order* and the *best regime.* But the innovative aspects were not restricted to a critique of the stance taken by modern and contemporary political philosophy vis-à-vis political order. The new outlook urged by Hayek also pointed to the need to rethink the entire theoretical framework of the social sciences, and thence to the further need to set up a relation between the various spheres (law, economics, morals, politics, etc.) that will take into account the recognition that, if there exists no hierarchy of ends, none of them can assume a hegemonic position.

NOTES

1 As well as the works by Menger, by Böhm-Bawerk and by Wieser, 1889 and 1891, pp. 108–21, on the concept of 'value' in the Austrian School and on the 'theory of subjective values', see Smart, 1891; Anderson, 1911; Laird, 1929, pp. 16–32, 367; Kraus, 1937, pp. 357, 362, 365 (on Menger), pp. 29, 263, 383 (on Böhm-Bawerk), pp. 263, 365–6, 372, 380 (on Wieser), pp. 263, 382–3 (on Mises). On this question, see also the essays by Morgenstern, 1931, pp. 1–42; and Mises, 1931a and 1931b. Among recent literature, see Shand, 1984, pp. 43–62.

On subjectivism as the 'essence' of the Austrian School, as well as Kauder, 1965, see Streissler, 1972, pp. 426–7 in particular, (where it is emphasized that the essence of the school lies not so much in the principle of marginal utility, as in the 'theory of subjective values'); also Buchanan, 1969, pp. 23–6, and 1982a, pp. 7–20; Streissler, 1969b, pp. 243–60; Lachmann, 1977, p.51 (however, the link set up by Lachmann between Weberian *Verstehen* and Austrian subjectivism is unconvincing), and 1986, pp. ix–x, 143–8, 163–4, («The Austrian School has always been the school of subjectivism and methodological individualism. Its descent from the subjectivist theory of value has marked its style of thought»); White, 1977, p. 4 («Subjectivism has been, in short, the distinctive method of the Austrian School economists», and what distinguished it from the marginalism of Jevons and Walras) and p. 19 (for Menger, Mises and Hayek the difference between natural science and social science consists in the former's objectivism as against the latter's subjectivism); Barry, 1979, pp. 16–26 («Hayek's subjectivism in economics can be best understood in the context of the development of the Austrian School of economics», p. 17; there are doubts, however, concerning the claim that «much of Hayek's early writings on methodology are elaborations of Mises's positions», p. 20); Taylor, 1980, pp. 40–52; Shand, 1984, pp. 3–4 («It is on this issue of subjectivism that one of the greatest differences between the Austrian and neoclassical methods exists»); Kirzner, 1986a, pp. 133–55; Alter, 1990a, pp. 151–220; Shearmur, 1990b, pp. 189–212; Tabarrok, 1990, pp. 5–9.

2 See Menger, 1871, p. 26 (Engl. trans. p. 71).

3 Ibid., p. 32 (Engl. trans. p. 77).

4 Ibid., p. 78 (Engl. trans. p. 115).

5 Ibid., p. 81n. This note (see p. 116, n.4) is not translated in the English edition:

> Der Wert ist demnach nichts den Gütern Anhaftendes, keine Eigenschaft derselben, sondern vielmehr lediglich jene Bedeutung, welche wir zunächst der Befriedigung unserer Bedürfnisse, beziehungsweise unserem Leben und unserer Wohlfahrt beilegen und in weiterer Folge auf die ökonomischen Güter, als die ausschliessenden Ursachen derselben, übertragen.

6 Ibid., p. 86 (Engl. trans. p. 121).

7 Ibid., pp. 122–3 (Engl. trans. pp. 147–48).

8 Menger, 1883, pp. 35–6. If this wording reminds one of Kant, the following pages, on the contrary, are more reminiscent of Aristotle.

9 Ibid., p. 38 (Engl. trans. p. 59).

10 Ibid., pp. 40–2.

11 Ibid., p. 45 (Engl. trans. p. 63).

12 Ibid., p. 45 (Engl. trans. pp. 63–4).

13 Ibid., p. 46–7 (Engl. trans. p. 64).

14 Gray, 1984a, p. 17, wrote that «Hayek's extension of Austrian subjectivism about value to the realm of social objects in no way represents a deviation from the positions of his mentors, Menger and von Mises»; but also, and rightly, that

In one fundamental area, however, Hayek always differs from the Austrian School, especially as that was embodied in the person of von Mises. It was indefatigably maintained by von Mises that the economic laws were deductions from a few axioms about human action [. . .] Hayek never accepted this apodictic-deductive or (as von Mises called it) praxeological conception of economic theory.

In his turn, Shand, 1990, p. 19, writes that «The best account of Austrian subjectivism is probably Chapter 3 of Hayek's *Counter-revolution* and subjectivism remains a strong influence in his subsequent writings.»

15 See Hayek, 1988, pp. 143–7. the reference to Menger is on p. 146, (but there is a mistake in citation of the page number on which the quotation appears: not p. 183, but p. 88).

16 See Mises, 1933, p. 3 (Engl. trans. pp. 2–3).

17 Ibid., pp. iiiff. (Engl. trans. pp. xviiff.). On Windelband, Rickert, Weber and Dilthey, see also Mises, 1961, pp. 120ff. Mises recognized that they, unlike positivistic historicism, denied the possibility of a posteriori knowledge of the laws of history, but they did not think that behavioural laws were a priori; and this, above and beyond the influence their theory of knowledge exerted on Mises, is what separated them. On Menger in particular, see Mises, 1933, pp. 20–1n. (Engl. trans. p. 23).

18 Ibid., pp. 18–22 (Engl. trans. pp. 18–22); critical remarks on Schumpeter's positivistic-behaviouristic epistemology are also on pp. 45–6 (Engl. trans. p. 47).

19 Ibid., pp. 12–14 (Engl. trans. pp. 12–14).

20 Ibid., p. 22 (Engl. trans. p. 23). On these aspects of praxeology, see Fuerle, 1986, pp. 31–5, 63–147.

21 Mises, 1933, pp. 26ff. (Engl. trans. pp. 27ff.).

22 Ibid., pp. 29–35, with the citation on p. 33 (Engl. trans. pp. 30–7, citation on p. 35).

23 See Mises, 1961, pp. 129–32. Despite his friendship with Weber during the years of teaching in Vienna, and despite his conviction that social science owes much to Weber, Mises reproached him for being neither an economist nor a sociologist, but a historian, and for lack of familiarity with economic theory; see Mises, 1926, pp. 85–8 (Engl. trans. pp. 102–4), and 1978, pp. 69–70, 104.

24 See Mises, 1933, pp. 70–5 (Engl. trans. pp. 74–8). On epistemological relativism, historicism and the lack of a concept of a general science of human action in Weber, see also Mises, 1961, pp. 119, 121, 124ff. From this point of view, the mistake enshrined in his typology of human action appears similar to the mistake made by classical economists; it consists in making a distinction between actions that are purely economic and those that are not. On Weber in relation to Mises's critical views, see Schütz, 1932, pp. 242, 259, 274, and especially 278–81. Schütz was among those who took part in Mises's private seminar; see, 1978, p. 100; and Lachmann, 1982, p. 35. On relations between Mises and Schütz, see Kauder, 1965, pp. 122–3, and Mises, M., 1984.

25 See Mises, 1933, pp. 71–95 (Engl. trans. pp. 75–97).

26 Ibid., pp. 91ff. (Engl. trans. pp. 94ff.). Mises wrote here that: «even Menger and Böhm-Bawerk did not completely grasp this logical fundamental of the theory they founded and [. . .] not until later was the significance of the transition from the objective to the subjective theory of value appreciated». These critical objections addressed to Menger and to Böhm-Bawerk, reiterated and developed on pp. 156–69 (Engl. trans. pp. 167–82), in the chapter 'Remarks on the Fundamental Problem of the Subjective Theory of Value', are attenuated in the concluding section, where Mises recognized that Menger and Böhm-Bawerk had explained «the determination of prices in terms of the subjective theory of value».

At the beginning there is a statement asserting that it «makes no claim to originality», but merely proposes «to put an end to the serious misunderstandings that modern economic theory repeatedly encounters». Nevertheless, primarily on account of certain turns of phrase adopted by Menger and by Böhm-Bawerk, it does constitute important reading material – as does the paragraph 'Bemerkungen zu Böhm-Bawerks Lehre von der Höherwertung gegenwärtiger Güter', of, 1940, pp. 439–43, a part not included in 1949 – both for an understanding of Mises's interpretation of the 'subjectivism' of Menger and of Böhm-Bawerk, and also, above all, for an awareness that Mises adopted an independent stance within the Austrian School. The object of his criticism was formed by the residual 'naturality in the satisfaction of needs' which is still retained in the conceptions of Menger and Böhm-Bawerk.

For further remarks on the theory of subjective values, see Mises, 1953, pp. 38–45. On Mises's relation to Menger and Böhm-Bawerk, brief notes appear in Lachmann, 1982, pp. 36, 39.

27 Mises, 1933, p. 156 (Engl. trans. p. 168).
28 Ibid., pp. 143ff. (Engl. trans. pp. 153ff.).
29 This would seem to limit the thesis of Mises's affinity with the Aristotelian tradition of Menger put forward by Smith, 1990a, pp. 272ff.
30 Mises, 1933, pp. 157–58 (Engl. trans. pp. 168–70).
31 Mises, 1961, pp. 119–23.
32 See Mises, 1948, pp. 1–3. The claims made here do not belong to Mises's later works, but rather are to be found in his early works as well, in particular in those of 1933 and 1981. It is thus only for reasons of completeness that reference is made here to 1949, given the lack of significant modification during their evolution.
33 Mises, 1949, pp. 11–13. On the Austrian critique of the concept of *Wertfreiheit*, and that of Mises in particular, see Kirzner, 1976b, pp. 75–84.
34 See Mises, 1949, pp. 19–22.
35 Ibid., pp. 22–3.
36 Ibid., pp. 51–2.
37 Ibid., pp. 92–8.
38 On the subjective character of social science in Hayek, see, 1952a, pp. 25–35 and the corresponding notes. On p. 29 Hayek wrote:

> at the last in economics the term 'subjective' has long been used precisely in the sense in which we use it here [. . .] that the knowledge and beliefs of different people, while possessing that common structure which makes communication possible, will yet be different and often conflicting in many respects. If we could assume that all the knowledge and beliefs of different people were identical, or if we were concerned with a single mind, it would not matter whether we described it as an 'objective' fact or as a subjective phenomenon.

39 See Hayek, 1937, pp. 35–7. On these aspects, see Nadeau, 1988, pp. 47–67.
40 Hayek, 1937, pp. 51–2.
41 Ibid., p. 54.
42 See Hayek, 1945, pp. 77–8. On this issue, see Butler, 1983, pp. 20–4, 47–8, 71–2; and Gray, 1984a, p. 36.
43 See Hayek, 1945, pp. 87–8.
44 Ibid., pp. 78–9.
45 See Strauss, 1948.
46 See Hayek, 1973–9, III, pp. 74–5.
47 See Menger, 1871, pp. 56–7 (Engl. trans. pp. 97–8).
48 In the paragraph dedicated to methodological individualism in his Introduction, Nishiyama, 1984, pp. liv–lx, rightly wrote that «methodological individualism is

not sociopolitical individualism», (p. liv), and that «methodological individualism is not an assertion of 'economic man'. From the beginning methodological individualism has not had to do with egoism, selfishness, or anything of this sort, even in Mandeville, Hume, Ferguson, or Adam Smith», (p. lx). On pp. lvi–lvii there are well-founded observations on the formulation of methodological individualism in Menger and its development in Hayek: «He is a very good student of Carl Menger. He not only inherited Menger's thought but also created a rather innovative and quite extensive order of ideas out of it.»

49 On this issue see Menger's critique, 1883, pp. 207–8 of the «pragmatistic conception» of the origin of social institutions and of «one-sided rationalist liberalism»; and Hayek, 1948, pp. 6ff., 1967, pp. 82–95, and 1978, pp. 3–22, 119–51.

50 In this connection, see Galeotti, 1988. Even if one may not always be in agreement with him, especially as regards his conclusions, the broadest treatment of the problem of methodological individualism, the exponents of this tradition and the issues encompassed within it is to be found in Heine, 1983. In the last few years – although neither Menger, nor Mises, nor Hayek use the expression – it has become almost a fashionable trend to challenge the common view which would link the origin of the concept of methodological individualism to Mengerian methodology, (as is the case both in Hayek, and in Popper; see Popper, 1957, p. 141n.); rather, it is traced back to the Smithian concept of the 'invisible hand'. For example, Rosenberg, 1988, pp. 141ff., wrote: «the 'methodological individualist' attempts to explain large-scale phenomena – what the holist describes as social facts – by a strategy that goes back to Adam Smith» and defines this method as the «invisible hand strategy».

51 Menger, 1883, pp. 163–5 (Engl. trans. pp. 146–8). This need not mean that Menger, Mises and Hayek had an identical concept of the presuppositions and procedures of methodological individualism.

On Menger's individualistic method, see Hutchison, 1981, pp. 187ff. In the vast literature, apart from Schneider, 1963, pp. 3ff., and the brief but well-founded reference by White, 1977, pp. 23–4; very seldom is the conception of methodological individualism put forward in Mises and Hayek seen as linked to the 'compositive method' of Menger. Mention is made of Menger in Barry, 1979, p. 36, although here methodological individualism is regarded as claiming that «all statements about collectives are logically deducible from statements about individuals». Lachmann, 1969, pp. 93ff, constitutes a special case on account of the attempt to assimilate methodological individualism to the method of *Verstehen*.

52 Menger, 1871, p. vii (Engl. trans. pp. 46–7). This translation, like that of the *Untersuchungen*, is often unreliable; in particular, I have some doubts about the translation of *zurückführen* as 'to reduce'; and I think it may be better translated as 'to take back'.

53 Hayek, 1942–4, pp. 36–8.

54 Schumpeter, 1908, pp. 88–98.

55 See Hayek, 1942–4, p. 287, n.33.

56 See Hayek, 1952a, p. 212n.

57 The literature that has sprung up around the question of methodological individualism as reductionism does not make reference, however, to this significant Hayekian fragment.

58 Aristotle, *The Politics*, I, 1, 19–23, and 2, 24–5. This book, with an explicit reference to Aristotle's arguments concerning the birth of the state from the family, is mentioned in Menger, 1883, pp. 267–9.

59 Menger, 1883, pp. 87–8 (Engl. trans. pp. 93–4).

60 Another example of a translation that is not always effective is that of *Wesen* by 'nature'. Starting out from this translation, in an essay that proved extremely

influential, Watkins, 1952, p. 29, wrote: «Thus, on one version of the principle of methodological individualism, the social scientist is to 'continue searching for explanations of a social phenomenon until he has reduced it to psychological terms'.» This definition can be considered the birthright of the reductionist interpretation of methodological individualism.

The same definition was cited and taken up again by Nagel, 1961, p. 541, and re-elaborated in a more exhaustive formulation of the principle, once again quoted from Watkins, 1957, p. 100. Nagel's conclusion (pp. 541–2) is that

> Methodological Individualism thus subscribes to what is often advanced as a factual thesis (although it is perhaps best regarded as a program of research) concerning the reducibility of all statements about social phenomena to a special class of ('psychological') statement about individual human conduct; and we shall therefore be able to assess this thesis in the light of the general requirement for reduction that were stated in Chapter 11.

In the two essays mentioned above, Watkins makes no mention of Menger, preferrring to quote Weber, Hayek and Popper, and when he does go on to cite him – 1976, p. 711, revising the concept of methodological individualism as formulated in his writings dating from the 1950s – he does not actually refer to the above-quoted excerpt from Menger, but to p. 152 of the English translation where money is spoken of as a 'social phenomenon'. The later observation (cf. p. 716) that the expression 'methodological individualism' «as I know [. . .] has been invented by Ludwig von Mises. See his *Epistemological Problems*, pp. 40–1», only succeeds in compounding the confusion.

In his turn Nozick, 1977, p. 353 – another essay that proved influential and was widely discussed – wrote that «methodological individualism claims that all true theories of social science are *reducible* to theories of individual human action, plus boundary conditions specifying the conditions under which persons act». In the accompanying note, n.2 on p. 385) he adds that «A standard account of reduction is provided in E. Nagel, *The Structure of Science* [. . .], NY, Ch. 11». Hence this is an example, perhaps the most significant one, of the misunderstandings – i.e. one of the reasons behind the arguments – that have arisen around the issue of methodological individualism. Naturally, in the chapter on Nagel, 1961, indicated by Nozick, no mention is made of Menger, not even of the paragraph dedicated to methodological individualism, (see pp. 535ff.). Here only Mises and Hayek are cited, and as far as methodological individualism is concerned, reference is made to the above-cited definition of Watkins.

As can be seen, the reasons for the subsequent and further misunderstandings almost all cluster round this central nucleus. They spring from the fact that no effort was made to discern what exactly was meant by 'to reduce'. Likewise Buchanan and Tullock, 1962, while stressing the need to avoid confusing methodological individualism with 'individualism', nevertheless see it as «an attempt to reduce all issues of political organization to the individual's confrontation with alternatives and his choice among them», (p. vii).

On the conception of individualism as 'reductionism' in these authors, see Galeotti, 1987b, pp. 216–20. In general one may conclude that the debate on the nature of methodological individualism, was sparked off by the failure to give due consideration to the formulation of this term by Menger. This is confirmed by observing that in the bibliography methodological individualism, his name only puts in a few rare appearances; exceptions are Antiseri, 1987, pp. 11–73, and Antiseri and Pellicani, 1992, pp. 27–66; and Alter, 1990a.

61 Menger, 1883, pp. 8–9 (Engl. trans. pp. 38–9).

62 Ibid., pp. 252–58 (Engl. trans. pp. 209–13).

63 Hayek, 1973–9, I, pp. 20–1.
64 In Hayek, 1948, pp. 1–32.
65 See Hayek, 1973–9, I, pp. 22–4, and 1988, pp. 35, 70, 143–7 in particular. On this assimilation, see Shearmur, 1986, pp. 210–24.
66 See Hayek, 1948, p. 6:

> What, then, are the essential characteristic of true individualism? The first thing that should be said is that it is primarily a theory of society, an attempt to understand the forces which determine the social life of man, and only in the second instance a set of political maxims derived from this view of society.

67 See Menger, 1871, p. 4 (Engl. trans. p. 53); the reference in the note is to Aristotle; see also Menger, 1923, pp. 3–4, 16–17.
68 See Menger, 1871, pp. 7–8, 35, 88–9; and 1923, pp. 23–56.
69 See Menger, 1871, p. 86 (Engl. trans. p. 121).
70 What little is known about Menger's political ideas – see Kauder, 1957, pp. 420ff., and Kirzner, 1990b – leads one to think that this is not so. In this regard, see also Shearmur, 1990b, pp. 189ff.
71 See Menger, 1871, p. 56.
72 Menger, 1883, p. 47 (Engl. trans. p. 64).
73 Ibid., pp. 257–8 (Engl. trans. p. 212).
74 See Hayek, 1948, p. 6.
75 See Hayek, 1952a, p. 38. On the Hayekian concept of methodological individualism, see Madison, 1990, pp. 41–60.
76 See Hayek, 1952a, pp. 38–9.
77 Ibid., pp. 39–41.
78 Ibid., pp. 54–6.
79 See Mises, 1948, p. 42.
80 Ibid., respectively pp. 3, 20.
81 Mises, 1962, p. 82.
82 See Menger, 1871, p. 1 (Engl. trans. p. 51).
83 As well as what appears in Menger, 1883, see Mises, 1981, p. 259.
84 On Hayekian evolutionism, as well as Hayek, 1988, and its bibliography, see Barry, 1979, pp. 6–9, 64–5, 199–200; Vanberg, 1981 and 1986, pp. 75–100; Buchanan, 1982a, p. 5; Butler, 1983, pp. 33–40; Gray, 1984a, pp. 110–14, 134–7; Hoy, 1984, pp. 5–7; Radnitzky, 1986, pp. 899–927; Nemo, 1988, pp. 73–105; Kukathas, 1989, pp. 207ff.; Miller, 1989b, pp. 61–7; Hodgson, 1991, pp. 67–82; Kley, 1992, pp. 12–34. It is difficult, on the other hand, to understand the criticisms of Ferry and Renaut, 1985, III, pp. 139–55. Here, the paragraph dedicated to Hayek has as title 'La dissolution historiciste des droits-libertés: l'évolutionnisme d'Hayek'. The evolutionism of Hayek is defined as «un historicisme», (p. 149); and it is believed that «l'*hyperlibéralisme d'Hayek est un hyperrationalisme*, présupposant, comme chez Hegel, que 'dans l'histoire tout se déroule rationnellement'», and that «la convergence théoretique entre l'évolutionnisme hayékien et l'historicisme hegéliano-marxiste du 'procès sans sujet' va donc jusqu'au lexique», (p. 150).
85 See Hayek, 1973–9, III, p. 155.
86 Ibid. p. 176.
87 Ibid., pp. 154, 158, 174.
88 On this latter tradition see Radnitzky and Bartley, 1987.
89 In this regard, in the Epilogue to 1973–9, III, p. 203n., Hayek wrote: «This is perhaps as good a place as any other to point out that our present understanding of the evolutionary determination of the economic order is in a great measure due to a seminal study of Armen Alchian»; see Alchian, 1977.
90 See Menger, 1883, pp. 34.

91 See Hayek, 1988 p. 146. Prior to this, on p. 144, Hayek wrote:

> Cultural evolution, although a distinct process, remains in important respects more similar to genetic or biological evolution than to developments guided by reason or foreknowledge of the effects of decisions. The similarity of the order of human interaction to that of biological organism has of course often been noticed. But so long as we were unable to explain how the orderly structures of nature were formed, as long as we lacked an account of evolutionary selection, the analogies perceived were of limited help. With evolutionary selection, however, we are not supplied with a key to a general understanding of the formation of order in life, mind and interpersonal relations.

The Mengerian passage had already been mentioned in Hayek, 1967, p. 101n. On Hayek, 1988, see Miller, 1989a, pp. 310–23, and Yeager, 1989 pp. 324–35.

92 See Menger, 1883, pp. 200–2. The paraphrase of the title of Savigny's 1814 work appears clearly here.

93 See Hayek, 1948, p. 6.

94 See Mises, 1957, pp. 159ff.

95 See Mises, 1948, p. 178.

96 Ibid., pp. 177–8.

97 Ibid., pp. 157–8.

98 Ibid., pp. 165–6, similar considerations on p. 175.

99 Ibid., pp. 178–84.

100 Ibid.

101 Ibid., p. 169.

102 Ibid., pp. 187–8.

103 Ibid., p.70.

104 Ibid., p.191.

105 See Hayek, 1952a, pp. 64–5. Here Hayek appeals to the Mengerian interpretation of the 'older historical school' and adds: «it is significant that among the fathers of this view Edmund Burke is one of the most important and Adam Smith occupies an honorable place». But he fails to report the Mengerian interpretation of Smith. In this regard, see also Hayek, 1948, pp. 4–5n.

106 See Hayek, 1952a, pp. 37–8.

107 On this matter, see Barry, 1986b, pp. 14–16. Within the framework of the contemporary liberal political tradition, Barry saw A. Rand and Rothbard, (who agreed on the need to found individualistic political philosophy on a theory of human nature) as being in opposition to the tradition going from Hume to Hayek, (which held reason to be incapable of discriminating clearly between the different possibilities of social and economic organization).

108 A useful anthology of the passages taken from various works in which the problem of order is addressed is to be found in Hayek, 1989.

109 Hayek, 1973–9, I, pp. 5–6.

110 See Hayek, 1978, pp. 71–6. On the theme of the uncertainty characterizing every human action and the social consequences of uncertainty, see Zöller, 1979, pp. 117–29.

111 Hayek, 1973–9, I, pp. 15–17.

112 Ibid., pp. 20–1.

113 Ibid., pp. 22–3, 84–5.

114 See Hayek, 1960, pp. 58–9 and n.21 on p. 433. On the concept of order in relation to the concept of evolution, see Barry, 1982, pp. 7–58; Brough and Naka, 1984, pp. 83ff.; Gray, 1984a, pp. 27–55, 54–5, (here Gray, interpreting, as Nozick did, methodological individualism in terms of reductionism, reached very questionable conclusions); Hoy, 1984, pp. 30–67; Radnitzky, 1984, pp. 9–33, and,

1987b, pp. 49–90; MacCormick, 1985, pp. 53–68; Galeotti, 1987a, pp. 32; Dobuzinskis, 1989, pp. 241–66; Kukathas, 1989, pp. 86–105. In relation to economic issues, see O'Driscoll, 1977, pp. 137–51.

115 Hayek, 1973–9, I, p. 59.

116 Ibid., pp. 22–24. This latter quotation (see n. 36 on p. 154) is significantly taken up again by Menger, 1883, p. 88 (Engl. trans. p. 94).

On Hayek's mention of Darwinism, see Lagueux, 1988, pp. 87–102; and Miller, 1989a, pp. 313–14. Hayek believed that Darwin had to some extent been influenced by eighteenth-century moral philosophers and by the Historical School of Law and Language; see Hayek, 1973–9, I, pp. 22–4.

117 Hayek, 1973–9, III, pp. 153–6.

118 See Hayek, 1960, pp. 62–3.

119 Ibid., p. 65.

120 Ibid., pp. 66–7.

121 Ibid., pp. 69–70. The reference here is to Humen's instruction 'to whittle down the claims of reason by the use of rational analysis'.

122 Ibid., pp. 159–61. The reference is to Polanyi, 1951.

123 See Hayek, 1973–9, II, pp. 107–8. Interestingly, the Mengerian concept of 'national economy' *Volkswirthschaft* is recalled here as being inclusive of the 'singular economies in the nation'; see pp. 184–5n. (See Menger, 1883, pp. 86–7; also Hayek, 1978, pp. 90–2.

On the implications of the Hayekian concept of catallactics, see Barry, 1979, pp. 42–53; Lachmann, 1979, pp. 69ff.; Gray, 1984a, pp. 31ff.; Shand, 1984, pp. 62–74, (also with reference to Mises).

124 See Hayek, 1973–9, II, pp. 107–9. On the substitution of the term 'economy' by 'catallactics' see also Hayek, 1978, p. 90n., where Hayek distances himself from Robbins's famous definition of 'science of economics', and one that he personally defended for a very long time:

> it seems to me appropriate only to that preliminary part of catallactics which consists in the study of what has sometimes been called 'simple economies' and to which also Aristotle's *Oeconomica* is exclusively devoted: the study of the dispositions of a single household or firm, sometimes described as the economic calculus or the pure logic of choice. (What is now called economics but had better be described as catallactics Aristotle described as *chrelatistike* or the science of wealth.)»

On the Mengerian distinction between *Volkswirthschaft*, *Wirthschaft* and *Nationalökonomie*, see Menger, 1883, pp. 44 ff. and Appendix I.

125 Hayek, 1973–9, II, pp. 109–11.

126 Ibid., II, pp. 112–13. On the Hayekian theory of catallactics, see Nemo, 1988, pp. 173–269.

127 See Hayek, 1973–79, III, p. 114.

128 Ibid., pp. 115–20.

129 Ibid., pp. 120–2.

130 Ibid., pp. 128–32.

3

FROM SOCIALISM TO TOTALITARIANISM

> We have progressively abandoned that freedom in economic affairs without which personal and political freedom has never existed in the past.
> (Hayek, *The Road to Serfdom*)

1. *Philosophical and economic sources*; 2. *The critique of socialism*; 3. *Totalitarianism.*

1. PHILOSOPHICAL AND ECONOMIC SOURCES

At the root of the interpretation of *collectivism* – a term that exponents of the Austrian School identified with *totalitarianism*[1] there lay, first and foremost, a theoretical argument concerning the limits of human knowledge, and a critique of the growing use of the method of natural science and historical knowledge in the field of social science.

When set against the backdrop of customary interpretations, the Austrian interpretation of the philosophical origins of totalitarianism presents some strikingly original aspects. This originality stands out even more if one considers the period in which the interpretation was put forward. Indeed, one might even say that in certain respects it resembles Voeglin's[2] reasoning, which was founded on analysis of the metamorphosis of gnosticism. For the theme of gnosticism may be discerned in Hayek's criticism of scientism, and it also clearly emerges in those parts of *Socialism* in which Mises pinpointed the chiliastic component of socialism. But in the eyes of the Austrians, totalitarianism was above all a phenomenon linked to the birth and spread of constructivist rationalism, as well as to the inexorable outcome of the failure of socialism. From this point of view, one could more properly speak of an affinity with the interpretation of Strauss rather than with Voegelin's thesis.

Strauss, too, held the belief that what distinguished totalitarianism from pre-modern forms of autocratic institutions was the newly arisen possibility that the development of the theoretical sciences could usher in perpetual and universal dominion over nature and human activities.[3] This view was to find expression in the modern concept of reason as lawmaker of the natural and social world, and was also expressed through confidence in the belief that proper use of reason could expedite the attainment of total knowledge, thereby solving all human problems. In his critique of modernity – although bereft of any philosophical-political outcome[4] – Strauss certainly exposed the philosophical foundations of totalitarianism. Upon reading his commentary on Xenophon's *Hiero*, one becomes only too aware that modern political science has added painfully little to the hints and ambiguous insinuations Xenophon slipped into Simonides' dialogue with Hiero.

It is perhaps in this perspective that one should read Hayek's concerns about the transformation of the concept of 'science' and its consequences. But despite any affinities between Strauss and Hayek in their analysis of totalitarianism and with their critique of historicism and scientism, their analyses truly diverged on the question of economic science. Strauss saw economic science as one of the causes of modernity, taking the latter as a form of decadence that made itself felt in the search for personal satisfaction through the pursuit of material goods. Hayek, on the other hand, was firmly of the opinion that the importance of economic science lay in the fact that, as it gained in stature, so it led to the demise of the teleocratic conception of the state of which totalitarianism itself was an expression. Their differing assessments thus derived from opposing evaluation of one aspect of modernity that both believed to be fundamental. Inasmuch as it was an attempt to overcome scarcity, Strauss viewed economic science as part of a plan aiming at control over the world, a plan that would unfailingly pave the way to totalitarianism. Any affinity thought to arise from the interpretation of totalitarianism as acceleration of the historical process by men in quest of glory, seeking to promote their subjects' welfare (and consequently reacting with contemptuous violence to the latter's dissent concerning ends and means), must therefore be incomplete.

Indeed, even the critique of historicism and of rationalistic scientism offers only apparent analogies. While it is true that the philosophy of history represented their common critical objective, Hayek nevertheless appears as the continuator of precisely the liberal economistic and evolutionistic tradition apropos of which Strauss – as can be seen in the case of Locke and Burke[5] – made no secret of his total dissent. On the other hand, Hayek by no means rejected the validity of knowledge attained through science, unlike Strauss.

In the interpretation put forward by Mises and Hayek, at the origin of totalitarianism was a union of the teleocratic conception of the state with modern science understood as dominion and design. There were also strong links with the idea of history as a cathartic process whose function is to establish on earth a 'secular' version of the kingdom of heaven, and with the diffusion of similar modes of thought in countries where the liberal tradition had been weaker. There was thus a close connection between historicism, scientism, socialism and totalitarianism. In fact, totalitarianism presents a compendium of all the aspects of modernity challenged by the Austrian School. This also explains why the difference between 'left-wing' and 'right-wing' totalitarianism ultimately boils down to technicalities concerning formal ownership of the means of production.

The above analysis, outlining the extent to which the great Western philosophical traditions are to be held responsible for opening the floodgates to the totalitarian mentality, represents a break with the tradition of political philosophy. These traditions, in particular idealism, historicism, positivism and rationalism, were considered corresponsible for the disaster. Faced with the catastrophe, Hayek and Mises – one could equally well add Popper and Strauss – realized that this could not be shrugged off as just a momentary lapse. The dissolution of the finalistic conception of history therefore led to the need for a different approach to the problem of the best political order. This development implied not only a revision of the entire tradition of political philosophy in the light of the situation that had come about, but also an awareness that tyranny is not an occasional phenomenon, but rather the endemic scourge of politics.

The reasons behind the break with mainstream traditions of the history of Western philosophy are thus shown to be twofold. On the one hand, previous traditions were held responsible for what had happened because their political philosophies had been grounded on false anthropologies, and these anthropologies had, more wittingly than unwittingly, resulted in totalitarianism. On the other hand, the discoveries of subjectivist economics concerning human action and its social consequences rendered it imperative to rethink the entire theoretical framework of the social sciences.

It follows that the Austrian interpretation of totalitarianism is by no means classifiable simply as an analysis of the latter's economic aspects or of its connections with socialism. Rather, this interpretation also provides a demonstration of the way totalitarianism is the outcome of the belief that society can be 'built'. The Austrian thesis claims that the fundamental forms of politics can be reduced to a *nomocratic model* and a *teleocratic model*. Hence the need to correlate analysis of totalitarianism with elaboration of a model of *political order* capable of combating the involution of demo-bureaucratic societies into totalitarian regimes.

Consequently, in the Austrian view neither reason nor history can be the guarantor of political philosophy. And since this means that no practical norms of action can be derived therefrom, the problem facing political philosophy is that of how to ensure that the need for an order can coexist with the need for individual freedom. In the first place, this requires that the model should be defended against the ambitions of those who would attempt to go beyond the limits of human knowledge. The critique of totalitarianism indirectly furnishes evidence that only the nomocratic model can enable *order* to coexist with *liberty*. At the same time, this very critique also shows that the prime cause of the failure of totalitarian regimes lies in the impossibility for human knowledge to control the laws of nature of society and to subject them to its own will. The hostility of totalitarian regimes towards any kind of unplanned innovation likely to disrupt their organization provides clinching historical evidence for this claim.

The starting point, once again, was represented by Menger's *Untersuchungen*. Acting as the springboard for reflections was the unusual statement that «the one-sided rationalistic liberalism» of Smith and his followers, and the «one-sidedly rationalistic mania for innovation in the field of economy» characteristic of his school, together with «partially superficial pragmatism [. . .] contrary to the intention of its representatives inexorably leads to socialism».[6]

Apart from Smith and his liberalism, the conceptual nucleus of this observation offers insight into of a number of the issues that would later be developed by Mises and Hayek. For Menger contended that if reformism founded on abstract rationalism were applied to social institutions – which were seen by abstract rationalism as nothing but the outcome of human intentions and therefore lacking in any true nature of their own – then this would unfailingly lead to socialism. That is, it would result in a form of social organization in which individuals would no longer be granted the freedom to organize their private economies as they best saw fit.[7] Such a state of affairs would stand in stark contrast to an economic system founded both on recognition that human economic activity is in general guided by «individual interests» that individuals usually recognize correctly,[8] and furthermore on awareness that human beings are not infallible or omniscient.[9]

The above themes became explicit in the first attempts by the *Katheder-sozialisten* to imagine a socialist economics such as would render the theoretical heritage of classical and neo-classical economics useless. Menger had already reacted by urging a different consideration of the relation between historical, theoretical and practical knowledge, warning that, without a valid relation to *exact science*, all *social philosophy* would prove totally bankrupt. Economic science could not, he cautioned, be founded on an ethical approach to social problems and phenomena. This would ultimately lead to subordination of economics to ethics, an eventuality that might conceivably resolve ethical problems, but those alone, and certainly not social problems.

Thus the real problem was represented by the consequences of reducing economics from a science to a tool of ethics or politics.

Echoes of these discussions can be perceived in the debate revolving around socialization that developed in Weimar Germany. In this debate the *Katheder-sozialisten*'s ideas played a fundamental role, partly on account of the way they influenced the education and training of German economists and government officials, and partly owing to the personal vicissitudes of several of those involved in the debate. Once again there surfaced an endeavour to found a new economic science that would take the German experience into account, from the *Wohlfahrtstaat* to the *Kriegswirtschaft*.

It was not only the errors into which the theoreticians of socialization fell that proved similar to those of the exponents of the Historical School of German Economists, but indeed their purposes as well: primarily their hostility towards the political consequences of the market economy. As Mises and Hayek were to point out, there is no radical break in continuity between the Reich, Weimar and National Socialism.

Thus as opposition grew among exponents of the Austrian School towards the economic theories and social philosophy that were evolving in Germany, Menger took up a critical stance towards the then unexpressed socialistic tendencies within the Historical School of German Economists. Mises, for his part, with his essay 'Die Wirtschaftsrechnung im sozialistischen Gemeinwesen', led the way towards an examination of the political-economic doctrines of collectivism, its early theories on economic planning and the impromptu ideas of the day concerning socialization. Menger and Mises (despite the latter's broad and illuminating analysis of socialism, and at least until his move to the United States) measured their ideas above all against the German experience. However, by the time Hayek came to write (when he was already teaching at the London School of Economics) the case of Germany was already beginning to appear to be the example of a more widespread mentality. Consequently, his critique of socialist economic theory did not start out from the arguments of the *Kathedersozialisten*, but from the theories of planning of Lange, Taylor and Dickinson. Similarly, during 1935–45 Hayek's writings did not focus merely on the German contribution to the rise of the totalitarian mentality, but also encompassed the repercussions of the 'Keynesian revolution' on economic, monetary and social theory[10] and study of the gnoseological presuppositions, cultural origins and political development of constructivist rationalism understood as the foundation of socialism.

2. THE CRITIQUE OF SOCIALISM

Mises

In 1921, with his essay 'Die Wirtschaftsrechnung im sozialistischen Gemeinwesen', Mises laid the basis for the so-called 'Austrian critique' of collectivist planning, taking the latter to mean centralized organization of the economy, which becomes transformed into a totalitarian regime. In this same work Mises also demonstrated the insubstantiality of theorizations concerning a socialistic economic and political order such as are furnished by the Marxistic and utopian tradition, at the same time debunking Neurath's theorizations[11] oncerning transition from a *Kriegswirtschaft* to a *Naturalwirtschaft* or a *Vollsozialisierung*.

Among the many after-effects of the Great War, Mises pinpointed one fated to gain extraordinary currency. This was the widespread popular belief that the centralized economic organization of the wartime period, blended with socialist ideals, could produce economic prosperity and social peace. In other words, political, social and economic problems could, it was felt, be overcome by 'rationalizing' the capitalist production and distribution process, and eschewing the market economy in favour of a collectivist type of economy governed by a central authority.

This essay by Mises thus set the scene for scientific discussion of the problem of socialization.[12]It resolved in negative terms the question of the possibility of a socialist economy that had already been tackled by Wieser, Barone and Pareto[13] but also concluded an era of studies on the planned economy. For in just a few years new theoretical approaches were to appear, prompted above all by Lange, Taylor and Dickinson, and, albeit in a different perspective, by the influence of Keynesian theory; and it was Hayek, rather than Mises, who would concern himself with the new approaches.[14] From both a theoretical and a historical point of view, therefore, Mises's essay forms an abiding landmark for either side, whether it be those pressing for the possibility of a planned economy, or those intending to deny any such possibility. One need only think of the debate appearing over the following few years in the *Archiv für Sozialwissenschaft und Sozialpolitik*, or Lange's claims that a statue of Mises should be erected in the central planning offices.[15]

As has been seen, Mises's essay had arisen from the desire to provide an answer to the issues put forward by Neurath. Naturally, the essay did not deal exclusively with his ideas, but Mises devoted considerable attention to them, though with a critical spirit. Matters pertaining to Neurath as a theoretician of war economics and socialization came under scrutiny, as well as the figure of Neurath as a member of the neo-positivistic movement. Significantly, the first reference to Neurath (as a theoretician of *Kriegswirtschaft*) came in the work *Nation, Staat und Wirtschaft: Beitrage zur Politik und Geschichte der Zeit*[16] the first manifestation of Mises's interest in socialism. There was thus close connection between his interest and the theoretical, practical and political dimensions of the war economy.

Just when the hopes of socialism seemed to be about to come true, Mises voiced the thoughts uppermost in the minds of so many who lacked the courage to speak out. Socialism could not work or keep its promises, he argued, because under such a system economic calculations in terms of value were rendered impossible. Furthermore, by focusing «attention solely upon painting lurid pictures of existing conditions and glowing pictures of that golden age which is the natural consequence of the New Dispensation»,[17] socialism turned out to be nothing other than a form of millenarianism. Hence its collocation within the framework of historicism.

To show his opposition towards what was considered an inevitable tendency, after Mises had analysed the impact of the experience of war economy on statal organization, as outlined in *Nation, Staat und Wirtschaft*, he seized the bull by the horns and launched into a study of the theoretical nucleus of the problem: *the possibility of a rational economic calculation in a socialist community.*

Far from sharing the belief that socialism is the «unavoidable result of human evolution», and faced with a somewhat cavalier attitude towards its social and economic aspects, Mises was much more inclined to believe that «attempts to achieve clarity on this subject need no further justification». For

> economics, as such, figures all to sparsely in the glamorous pictures painted by the Utopians. They invariably explain how, in the cloud-cuckoolands of their fancy, roast pigeons will in some way fly into the mouths of the comrades, but they omit to show how this miracle is to take place.[18]

Mises's starting point was thus the problem of ownership of the means of production and distribution of consumer goods in the socialist tradition. The lack of clarity or homogeneity in this area was to lead him, two years later, to publish the first version of *Die Gemeinwirtschaft: Untersuchungen über den Sozialismus*. Here, just as Pareto had done twenty years earlier, he reviewed the various tendencies of the movement in search of the common theoretical and historical nucleus – a nucleus which in his 1920 essay was identified as consisting of the «characteristic of socialism» whereby «the distribution of consumption goods must be independent of the question of production and of its economic conditions».[19]

In this perspective, the criteria adopted for the purpose of distributing goods among members of the socialist community were «immaterial to the fact that, in any event, the portions will be meted out by the State», by the holder of the means of production. Consequently, «it becomes utterly impossible in any socialist community to posit a connection between the significance to the community of any type of labour and the apportionment of the yield of the communal process of production». Therefore, even «remuneration of labour cannot but proceed upon an arbitrary basis».[20]

The impossibility of an economic calculation in a socialist community is thus the result of having rejected the principle of the exchange economy, i.e. the principle that makes it feasible «to base the calculation upon the valuations of all participants in trade», and «furnishes a control over the appropriate employment of goods». Equally mistaken, in Mises's view, was the belief that «in a socialist state calculation *in natura* can take the place of monetary calculation». Mises by no means denied the limits of the latter; but he believed that since it acts as a «guide through the oppressive plenitude of economic potentialities», it thereby «fulfils all the requirements of economic calculations». For in a natural economy, this calculation «can embrace consumption-goods only; it completely fails when it comes to deal with goods of a higher order». As a result, «as soon as one gives up the conception of a freely established monetary price for goods of a higher order, rational production becomes completely impossible».[21]

The conclusion was that

> without economic calculation there can be no economy. Hence, in a socialist state wherein the pursuit of economic calculation is impossible, there can be – in our sense of the term – no economy whatsoever. In trivial and secondary matters rational conduct might still be possible, but in general it would be impossible to speak of rational production any more.

If «historically speaking, human rationality is a development of economic life», socialism appears as an irrational economic system. In this case, the place of the much-maligned productive 'anarchy' of capitalism would be taken by a system of needs satisfaction guided by the state, which would lead to a system of production describable as the «senseless output of an absurd apparatus». Failure to take account of the subjective values consumers attribute to goods thus would rule out any evaluation of economic convenience. For this reason, in the socialist state «there is only groping in the dark. Socialism is the abolition of rational economy».[22]

In his examination of the various ways theoreticians and politicians had attempted to solve the problem of socialist economic structure, then, Mises was prompted by his conviction that the price mechanism is an indispensable prerequisite for an economic calculation.[23] The belief that socialism is to be preferred to the market economy on account of its greater rationality is shown to be without any foundation. But the fact of simply having demonstrated the impossibility of rational economic activity in a socialist community did not lead Mises to assume that this would in itself suffice to discredit the idea of socialism. He was well aware that his arguments would be heeded only by those who believed in socialism as a rational economic system. Those who embraced socialism on ethical or ascetic grounds would be very unlikely to allow their beliefs to be shaken merely because socialism was going to reduce the consumption of goods. Exactly the same holds true for those who hailed socialism as the long-desired overthrow of capitalism.[24]

Mises's aim, then, was to highlight the difficulties that *every* socialist economic system would find itself facing. To judge by the ensuing discussions, his essay certainly achieved its purpose of drawing attention to the theoretical foundations of the economic policies pursued by the socialist parties that had just come to power. Yet his analysis did not have the effect of exerting concrete influence over political choices. The truth of the matter was that the life-blood of the socialist ideal consisted of ethical and ideological elements, which at times were indifferent towards criticisms of an economic nature. Only part of the socialist tradition believed that socialism, true to its Marxian claims, would lead the way towards overcoming capitalism. There were substantial components that instead viewed it as a radical counterweight to all the evil capitalism had generated.

With *Socialism*, Mises therefore aimed to extend the range of his criticism, surveying the various tendencies in the socialist tradition. Divided into five parts – dealing with the relation between liberalism and socialism, the economy of a socialist community, the presumed inevitability of socialism, socialism as a moral imperative and destructivism – this monumumental work fully deserves its subtitle *An Economic and Sociological Analysis*.

The main objective Mises set himself was to underscore that *the central nucleus of socialism was a theory of the salvation and redemption of man*, which included both ethical and material aspects. Despite its various tendencies, it was therefore possible, Mises contended, to define socialism as an ideology pursuing the objective of constructing a society in which all means of production are to be socialized, and as an eschatology identifying capitalism as the sum of all evils.[25]

It did not escape Mises that socialism was a complex and highly structured *Weltanschauung* that could not be combated simply by criticizing its individual aspects. Its defeat would only be achieved if its total misguidedness could be shown. Courageously, Mises chose to pursue this path. This was, however, but the first part of his grand design. He was also aware that the elaboration of the overall image of socialism would have to be counterbalanced by elaboration of a social philosophy in opposition to socialism.

Socialism was therefore both a critique of socialist ideology, and also research into the principle of a new social philosophy which would prove victorious over the challenge of socialism and establish the relation of liberalism to the Christian churches on a completely new basis. Mises must be credited with having been the first to realize that this challenge could not be won with the social-philosophy tools of the old liberalism, based on classical political economy. Consequently, «the old liberal principles have to be submitted to a thorough re-examination», and «the general sociological and economic foundations of the liberal doctrine have to be relaid».[26]

Given the historical situation, completion of the work Menger had begun with the seminal *Untersuchungen*, on a new philosophy of social science in the light of the findings of the theory of subjective values, could be postponed no further. Questionable though Mises's interpretation of Menger may have been, he set about shaping this analysis into a system of liberal political and social philosophy capable of withstanding the advance of socialistic ideology, and of engaging in constructive debate with Christian social doctrine.

Mises's critique of socialism revolved around a fundamental argument: socialism had failed to realize that the marginalist revolution and the theory of subjective values had wrought a profound change in the interpretation of social phenomena, and of economic phenomena in particular. Oblivious of all this, socialists continued to interpret, and consequently assess, such phenomena with inadequate and misguided theoretical tools, among which the labour theory of value stood out. In this new perspective, for instance, the capitalistic mode of production was not, *pace* the socialists, an aberration. Rather – even if the origin of ownership was an act of violence – it was the best solution of economic problems, precisely because it rested upon the principle of the division of labour which lies at the root of the spontaneous rise and development of human society.[27]

Mises thus intended to point out that a social system does not necessarily prevail on account of the legitimacy of the vision of historical evolution which forms its conceptual framework, but rather on its efficiency in solving problems relating to the satisfaction of subjective human needs. He wished to demonstrate thereby that however much one may scorn the economic sphere, a society in which rational economic calculation is possible – and this is simply a tool to enable an infinite array of ends to coexist – is by far preferable to a society in which no such calculation can occur. The latter kind of society, Mises implied, could not survive for long.

As he traced the lines of the liberal society with which to counter socialist society, Mises gave expression to ideas that formed part of a theory of human action. He fashioned an anthropology grounded on a theory of choice that placed dissatisfaction and scarcity at the root of rational human action. The claim that «all human action, so far as it is rational, appears as the exchange of one condition for another» should thus be taken as meaning that every human action ensues from a subjectively rational interpretation of needs, reality, situations and ends. The error into which socialism fell was that of failing to realize that, without a calculation of value translatable into monetary terms, it would be impossible to engage in rational economic activity. Far from being the alternative to the irrationality of the market, it presented itself as «the renunciation of rational economy».[28]

Though impossible in a complex society wishing to remain so, socialism would still also have to solve the problem of the reproducibility of goods by compressing individual freedom. Far from achieving the defeat of capitalism in the promised land of milk and honey, it was therefore destined to be achievable only in limited, autarchic communities, subject to strict control by a charismatic authority; or else, as in the case of Marx's philosophy of history, it would have to transform the world into one single community. Thus the essence of socialism consisted in the contention that the means of production must be subject to the «exclusive control of the organized community». Having reached the conclusion that «this and this alone is Socialism», Mises then proceeded to examine its various types.[29]

Closely connected with the critique of socialism as an economic and social theory was that of socialism as an ideal movement. Identifying its origins in chiliasm, Mises distinguished two principal types. The first could be characterized as «an ethical, political and economic-political challenge», which found expression in the need to supplant the immoral capitalistic order with a planned economy intended to sweep away «the irrational private economic order, the anarchical production for profit». Alongside this type of socialism definable as utopian, and appearing in the shape of a goal to aim towards as being «morally and rationally desirable», there was also the type of socialism that presents itself «as the inevitable goal and end of historical evolution» that will lead «to higher planes of social and moral being». History was thus transformed into a process of «purification» of which socialism represents «perfection». Known as 'evolutionistic' or 'scientific' and held to be compatible with the utopian variant, this type of socialism was taken to be «a necessity of Nature [. . .] the inevitable outcome of the forces underlying social life». It was, at one and the same time, a historiographic method, a sociological theory and a theory of progress, «of the meaning, nature, purpose and aim of human life», from which the conclusion was drawn that historical evolution tends towards socialism.[30]

Mises regarded historical materialism not so much as a science, but rather as a form of anthropocentric metaphysics: a philosophy of history springing from a religious origin. And in this guise of a variant of the belief in a «paradisiac origin» to which man is destined to return some day, socialism transformed faith in salvation in the afterlife into «a message of earthly salvation». It was thus none other than a secular version of Christian faith in Christ as he who proclaims the kingdom of God on earth. In such ideas, and especially in their millenarian deformation into the attitude that «an earthly Kingdom of Salvation lasting one thousand years would be set up», lay the origins, Mises argued, of the idea of social and economic revolution as a cathartic experience for the whole of mankind. This suggested that from Christian chiliasm «a single step leads to the philosophical Chiliasm which in the eighteenth century was the rationalist reinterpretation of Christianity; and thence, through Saint Simon, Hegel and Weitling, to Marx and Lenin». Recognizing the vanity of a rationalistic counter-proposal to the metaphysical and chiliastic foundations of socialism, Mises thus concentrated his attention on Marxism, which in his view was «sufficiently influenced by the scientific spirit of the nineteenth century to attempt to justify its doctrine rationally».[31]

Feeling that the proponents of chiliasm were impermeable to all scientific or philosophical criticism, then, Mises concentrated his attention on the Marxist conception of society.[32] In opposition to this conception, but without referring to Menger's theories, Mises developed his own theory on the origin of society and its evolution, focusing on the division of labour as «a fundamental principle of all forms of life» and of social development. Like Hayek, he argued that «the development of human reason and the development of human society are one and the same process»; but unlike Hayek – and Menger – he claimed that «all further growth of social relations is entirely a matter of will. Society is the product of thought and will. It does not exist outside thought and will.» The Aristotelian dictum according to which man is a political animal was itself interpreted as indicating that «evolution from the human animal to the human being was made possible by and achieved by means of social co-operation and by that alone».[33]

It is on these premises that the distinction between *organism* and *organization* was created. The latter was held to be an artificial entity, the result of voluntary action, which «will not produce a living social organism» and was destined to last no longer than the will of whoever created it. While organization was grounded in authority, the organism was grounded in reciprocity. Recognition of this distinction, i.e. of the self-ordering of society and the impossibility of its organization, marked the beginnings of modern social science, forged by the trail-blazers of classical political economy. But attainment of this knowledge also meant that all attempts to organize a society are nothing but an illusion. Thus the driving force that would doom collectivist movements to failure was the fact that, however hard they might strive, they could not succeed in destroying the natural forces of social life. For

> organization is possible only as long as [collectivist movements] are not directed against the organic or do it any injury. All attempts to coerce the living will of human beings into the service of something they do not want must fail. An organization cannot flourish unless it is founded on the will of those organized and serves their purposes.

But this view of society as founded on the division of labour does not mean, in Mises's view, that society is no more than «mere reciprocity». What makes a society exist, apart from the principle of reciprocity, is that the condition of being one of its members «becomes a co-willing and action co-action». Consequently, society «is not an end but a means»: the instrument by means of which individuals attempt to achieve their own ends; and it is made possible provided that their wills become united in a «community of will». This led to disappearance of the traditional antithesis between individual and society and likewise of «the contradiction between individual principle and social principle».[34]

The idea that socialism is the inevitable future of mankind thus can be seen to derive from a conception of society based on the approach of classical political economy. In Marx this gave rise to a misunderstanding of the nature of society, and to the belief that class conflict was inevitable; moreover, it instilled the conception of private property as a hindrance to realization of the 'promised land'. Among his followers, further outgrowths of these ideas fired the conviction that with technological development satisfaction of needs would be possible only in the framework of a planned economy. Hence the belief in the greater rationalism of socialism compared to capitalism. The social theory of Marxism thus assumes the shape of an expression of the materialism of Marx's day, as a transposition of the theory of the class struggle into an interpretation of universal history, erected on the foundation of the claimed greater efficiency of socialism compared to capitalism.[35]

Marx himself, as a not very original follower of classical economists, had «the misfortune to be entirely ignorant of the revolution in theoretical economics which was proceeding during the years when he worked out his system». The result was that the volumes of *Das Kapital* subsequent to the first, «from the day they were published, were quite out of touch with modern science». Imbued with political bias, Marx interpreted society with outdated economic tools and made no attempt to come to grips with the «modern theory of value». Far from being the scientific discovery of the necessary tendency of historical evolution, Marxism went down the road towards becoming a destructive tendency threatening Western society.[36]

But Mises's critique did not restrict itself to an examination of Marxist society. Adopting an approach to religion that held it to be just another product of historically evolving social co-operation, Mises found himself grappling with the issues of Christian social doctrine. The conceptual nucleus of his critique consisted in that very historicity of religion which prevents Christianity or its «social ethics» from being placed in a privileged position with respect to the other social sciences. While its importance was not denied, religion was thus relegated to being one of the many involuntary products of human action. The factor allowing Christianity to outlive the great historical revolutions was thus not the ahistorical nature of its message but rather its neutrality towards all social systems.[37]

Mises considered that any attempt «to build up an independent Christian social ethics on the Gospels» was doomed to failure. He therefore turned to the problem of the relationship between liberalism and Christianity. His position is vividly portrayed in the question he turned over in his mind: «might not the Church reconcile itself with the social principle of free co-operation by the division of labour? Might not the very principle of Christian love be interpreted to this end?» For the impossibility of constructing a social ethics by founding it on the Gospels should indeed lead the church to contemplate the alternative of edifying ethics on the principle of free social co-operation through the division of labour. Consequently, Mises urged churches interested in the destiny of mankind to cease being among the «factors responsible for the prevalence of destructive ideals in the world today; Christian Socialism has done hardly less than atheistic socialism to bring about the present state of confusion». By the same token, Mises appealed to the Church to desist from its opposition to the liberal ideas which enable society to exist. This was in fact an offer of an alliance whose goal would be the defeat of socialism, but it was conditional on the churches' forswearing their distaste for liberalism, a distaste which had paved the way for the success of socialist ideas. By playing off socialism against liberalism, Christianity failed to notice the impossibility of achieving Christian socialism; nor did its members foresee that atheistic socialism would turn first and foremost against religion itself.[38]

But Mises did not merely call for the church to renounce its «dislike» of liberalism and economic freedom. He went as far as to invite the church to establish its foundations on these concepts and be content to exist in liberty in a liberal state, forgoing supremacy over every human activity. Strongly convinced that liberalism «transformed the world more than Christianity had ever done», he demanded that the church should cease its disapproval of modernity and its alliance with movements opposing liberalism and the market. In other words, Mises's alliance was made conditional on recognition by the church of the impossibility of Christian socialism or of an efficient society founded on Christian social doctrine. It was a question not of reaching a compromise, but rather of insistence on compliant willingness to capitulate: «a living Christianity cannot [. . .] exist side by side with Capitalism [. . .]. Christianity must either overcome Capitalism or go under.»[39]

Socialism and Christian social doctrine, however, were not the only issues Mises tackled, he also took on ethical socialism of Kantian inspiration. By pointing out that Kant had stood apart from the developments introduced into social science by Ferguson and Smith, Mises aimed to demonstrate that socialism was not heir to the Western philosophical tradition, but rather the product of the decadence of idealism and of the way society was conceived by «Kant's mysticism of duty and Hegel's deification of the State». The very fact that Kantian and neo-Kantian social philosophy approached the problem of the distribution of wealth from an ethical point of view without relating it to the problem of the production and the division of labour meant, for Mises, that it acted as an indirect support for socialism.[40]

This is clearly shown in Cohen's social philosophy. Cohen believed that in «a society based on private ownership in the means of production men serve as means, not as ends». Such a view, Mises felt, indicated that Cohen did not realize that in society every individual is both means and end to an equal extent. Similarly to Kant, Cohen failed to take note that in a social organism, where «well-being is simultaneously the condition necessary to the well-being of the others [. . .] the contrast between I and thou, means and end, automatically is overcome». Neo-Kantian arguments in favour of ethical socialism thus appear untenable, and can be reduced to the more general attitude among intellectuals of revulsion against capitalism.[41]

This line of reasoning led Mises to reject the thesis of a necessary relation between socialism and ethics. For the unfeasibility of socialism was not due to man's immorality, or to man's having been corrupted by capitalism, but rather to the fact that by not allowing economic calculation, it ended up demanding from man things «which are diametrically opposed to nature». Far from being the morally desirable system, socialism was obliged to impose its authority by force, with the additional twist of attributing its own failures to the immorality of man. Socialist critique of 'capitalist social ethics' was thus an attempt to conceal a social ethics that led to coercion and arbitrary rule.[42]

Seen from this angle, instead of representing the transition from an irrational to a rational and ethical economy, socialism was actually a form of destructivism, starting with the dissipation of capital and culminating in the moral ruin of society. It was but a vain illusion, Mises reflected, to hope that a political and social system can function and be considered moral if it is unable to make rational use of material resources.

The work *Socialism* can therefore be considered as an attempt to avert a threat looming ominously on the horizon. If *Omnipotent Government* can be seen as an analysis of what had happened, *Socialism* can be viewed as an unheeded prediction. That prediction becomes even more penetrating in the light of what is known today of the reality of the socialist countries, and of what remains of the Schumpeterian forecast of the ineluctable transition from capitalism to democracy and finally to socialism.

In other words, the collapse of socialistic systems cannot be unjustly and pathetically attributed to the erroneous ways of many 'wicked men'. Nor, for that matter, can it be ascribed to the inexperience of a human race incapable (or unworthy?) of adopting and embracing such a 'noble' ideal. The political philosophy of Mises and Hayek therefore cannot be liquidated together with socialism by claiming that now the problems are different, and that their political philosophy was, for better or for worse, inextricably bound up with the critique of socialism.[43] The truth of the matter is that the theoretical problems which prompted their reflections are still with us, and one cannot labour under the delusion that the collapse of the myth of socialism has wiped the slate clean. Cherishing this kind of attitude would be tantamount to replacing the myth of the ineluctability of socialism by the myth of the ineluctability of democracy taken as the ineluctable theoretical horizon of political philosophy.

Hayek

In presenting the English version of the most significant works on the theme of the socialist economy since the beginning of the century, Hayek's aim in the collection of essays *Collectivist Economic Planning* was to provide an overall survey of the issues involved.[44] Hayek inserted two essays of his own as the introdution and conclusion of the collection. He set himself the task of making an overall assessment of over thirty years of studies and historical experiences that had wrought a profound change in the approach to these issues, a change that resulted in the abandonment of the rudimentary gropings towards socialization that took place immediately after the Great War. But these two essays are also important in that they provide glimpse the earliest, yet already mature, outlines of arguments that would later become the nucleus of Hayek's reflection on social science philosophy.

Examination of these early statements is important, therefore, if one wishes to highlight the nature of Hayek's critique, which, to the detriment of its predominant epistemological motivations, has often mistakenly been taken as the expression of an ideological opposition. In fact, as is so often the case in Hayek, his intention was twofold. On the one hand, he analysed the problem of socialist economics from the point of view of the history of ideas, relating it to the spread of scientistic and historicistic ideology; on the other, he developed a series of theoretical considerations on the method of social science and the nature of society.

By 1935 Hayek had formed the opinion that the moment had come to consider the possibility of «a reconstruction of society on rational lines» in more dispassionate and more scientific terms than had previously been the case. He hoped thereby to call attention to the fact that «deliberate regulation of all social affairs» was preferable to the «apparent haphazard interplay of independent individuals», and to focus on the question of whether planning can achieve «the desired end». Following in the footsteps of Menger and Mises, Hayek took up the question of whether economic science «is only applicable to the problems of a capitalist society», or whether its laws are valid in all economic systems. He thus regarded planning as the economic dimension of the ambitious and extensive attempt to introduce order into the world by applying «reason to the organization of society» in order «to shape it deliberately in every detail according to human wishes and common ideas of justice».[45]

The conviction gradually unfolded for Hayek that Wieser, Pareto and Barone had already demonstrated the possibility of socialist economics.[46] He recognized that the crisis of classical political economy had produced the desire for a 'different' economic science, but this 'new' science had proved too laborious to devise. Furthermore, this crisis would not have had such adverse effects if it had not matured at the moment when the empiricist methods of the natural sciences had led to the expectation that only by the application of such methods to social science would a solution be found to human problems.[47]

This was the historical and cultural backdrop to the problem of the feasibility of socialist planning. And the certainty that one might «have much planning with little socialism or little planning and much socialism» prompted a number of thoughts in Hayek's mind. The first was that both the planning of development and the distribution of wealth «have nothing to do with the ethical aims of socialism». The second was that discussion on the necessity or otherwise of the nexus between socialism and planning was less important than being able to establish who, in a planned economy, is to decide on the principles of production and distribution. Hayek's primary critical objective was thus represented by the claim that the creation of a single central authority would be the best way «to solve the economic problem of distributing a limited account of resources between a practically infinite number of competing purposes».[48]

For Hayek, consequently, *the chief problem of planning, whether economic or social, concerned the theory of knowledge on which it was based*.[49]

Thus for Hayek, just as for Mises, the flaw inherent in the doctrine of economic planning was that it had remained anchored to the problems and issues of classical political economy. Instead of acknowledging that differing evaluations of goods originate from their scarcity compared to alternative ends, and that this produces different individual scales of value, on the contrary the theoreticians of planning founded their theories on the existence of «a single scale of values consistently followed». As a result, several theoreticians of planning wrongly thought they had solved the problem with calculations on utility that would be able «to combine the individual utility scale into a scale of ends objectively valid for society as a whole».[50]

But the end of the Great War, and the rise to power of socialist parties, heralded discussion of a «new and decisive phase». The viewpoint which came to prevail was that the planning model of war economics could also be applied successfully«to the permanent administration of a socialist economy».[51] At this juncture, the essay by Mises marked a turning point in the history of the problem. In addition to criticism of his use of the expression that «socialism was impossible», which was his way of saying that socialism «made rational calculation impossible», there came the rejoinder from the opposing camp that Mises's objections were valid only with regard to the specific form of socialism against which they were supposedly directed. This led to the rise of new theories on planning immune from Mises's criticisms. Hayek identified two main trends in this new direction. The first aimed to overcome the problem by abolishing the possibility of free choice of goods and jobs; the second endeavoured to introduce a few elements of competition into the planned economy.[52]

Hayek thus found himself facing different problems from those dealt with by Mises: early reflections on the Soviet solution, and above all mathematical formulations of the theory of economic planning. Critical assessment of the latter comprised a blend of economic and gnoseological arguments. For it was Hayek's intention to show that these arguments were unfeasible because it was impossible to concentrate both theoretical and practical knowledge in a central authority capable of adjusting prices to changing situations. Behind this reasoning lay the problem that the theoreticians of planning were desperately trying to solve, namely that of trying to avert a situation in which «every passing whim of the consumer is likely to upset completely the carefully worked out plans». Hayek therefore shifted his attention to the relation between individual freedom and planning, and to problems connected with the political framework within which collectivist economic planning can be achieved.[53]

These problems, in Hayek's opinion, would not even be resolvable within the 'pseudo-competition' system. Like socialist planning systems, this was likely to produce only a decrease in economic efficiency and consequently in productivity,[54] which in turn would have political consequences. Once again, the motif of efficiency took centre stage in the critique of socialist systems and in attendant endeavours to find a 'middle way' between the market and planning. This feverish search for a middle way was symptomatic, in Hayek's eyes, of the decadence of Western political philosophy, cheapened into the 'engineering mentality' that believed it possible to build the best social order by assembling what seemed to be the best features of the various political, economic and social systems.

The critique of the 'competitive' solution can therefore also be seen as a critique of the economic foundations of interventionism. The fallacy of compatibility between planning and freedom was thus shipwrecked on the rock of the competitive solution to the problem of planning. Not even interventionism in fact, would be able to avoid the possibility that «in the hands of an irresponsible controller even socialist planning "could be made the greatest tyranny the world has ever seen"».[55]

In those same years, Hayek did not limit his critique to the economic doctrines of socialism and interventionism, but extended his criticism to their cognitive premises as well. His conviction that diffusion of the scientistic mentality could not be combated only by challenging it from a point of view open to the risk of ideological misunderstanding led to the appearance of the essays 'Economics and Knowledge', 'The Facts of the Social Sciences', 'The Use of Knowledge in Society', 'Scientism and the Study of Society' and 'The Meaning of Competition'. These essays form one of Hayek's greatest contributions to the philosophy of social science, and the foundation of his political philosophy. In these works he dealt with the theme of the finiteness and fallibility of human knowledge,[56] its distribution and its conditions: in other words, no less than with the foundation of his liberalism and his interpretation of the history of modern and contemporary social philosophy.

In the framework Hayek worked out, all efforts of theories of planning were shown to be rendered vain by the fact that in order to achieve «plans determined upon simultaneously but independently by a number of persons», it appeared necessary that all plans should be founded «on the expectations of the same set of external events». If, on the other hand, individual expectations happened to be founded on anticipations in conflict with one another, then achievement of the plans would become impossible. And one element that contributed to just this course of development was an equivocation concerning the manner of understanding the 'data' on the basis of which the plans were elaborated. Planning theoreticians believed these 'data' to be «objective facts and the same for all people». Yet the meaning was quite the opposite: «'datum' meant given, known, to the person under consideration»[57] and this meant that their evaluation would not necessarily be univocal. Consequently, the reaction of individuals towards what the planner might well believe to be an objective 'datum' could diverge considerably from predicted reactions, thereby resulting in the débâcle of the plan. This meant that

> the assumption of a perfect market [. . .] means nothing less than that all the members of the community, even if they are not supposed to be strictly omniscient, are at least supposed to know automatically all that is relevant for their decisions. It seems that that skeleton in our cupboard, the 'economic man', whom we have exorcised with prayer and fasting, has returned through the back door in the form of a quasi-omniscient individual.[58]

The real problem of planning, then, indeed more generally the main problem of the theoretical social sciences, is thus shown to be that of the *division of knowledge*, i.e. of the way in which

> the spontaneous interaction of a number of people, each possessing only bits of knowledge, brings about a state of affairs in which prices correspond to costs, etc., and which could be brought about by deliberate direction only by somebody who possessed the combined knowledge of all those individuals.[59]

Economic planning thus appeared to be founded on the feasibility of elaborating empirical generalizations starting from mechanistically conceived individual behaviour. Essentially, this meant that generalizations were built up on a view of the 'data' of the social sciences that considered them to be real objects on a par with data of the physical world.[60] Any idea that these might be mere «pseudo-entities» never crossed the planners' minds. Transposed into the economic sphere, this gave rise to formulation of models in which

> every person's plan is based on the expectation of just those actions of other people which those other people intend to perform and that all these plans are based on the expectation of the same set of external facts, so that under certain conditions nobody will have any reason to change his plans.[61]

The search for a «general equilibrium», such as would bring about a 'perfect market', would in this framework rest on the assumption that «every event becomes known instantaneously to every member». This in its turn would mean that «all the members of the community, even if they are not supposed to be strictly omniscient, are at least supposed to know automatically all that is relevant for their decisions».[62] The eventuality that human action may be connected to individually possessed knowledge, and that this may determine subjective values and undesired consequences, was totally disregarded by theoreticians of economic and political planning.

Similar ideas on the possibility of constructing rational political and economic order were developed in 'The Use of Knowledge in Society'. In this work Hayek again stressed that the chief problem in any theory explaining the economic process was that of finding «the best way of utilizing knowledge initially dispersed among all the people», and that the solution to this problem could not consist in «erroneous transfer to social phenomena of the habits of thought we have developed in dealing with the phenomena of nature».[63] The feature that was destined to render the efforts of centralized organization vain would be precisely the circumstance that efficiency both demands «rapid adaptation to change in the particular circumstances of time and place» and also implies that «the ultimate decisions must be left to the people who are familiar with these circumstances, who know directly of the relevant changes and of the resources immediately available to meet them'.[64]

Therefore the underlying difficulty jeopardizing socialism was, Hayek pointed out, the impossibility of achieving universal control over phenomena that have repercussions on a planned system. This predicament would in its turn translate into a loss of efficiency and authoritarian bureaucratization of society.

Hayek's essays on the nature of human knowledge, the presuppositions of the theoretical social sciences and the origins of the scientistic mentality must be considered the starting point of his political philosophy. For it is here that Hayek enquired into the debate on the methods and goals of the theoretical social sciences that was evolving during the 1930s and 1940s. This was an ongoing debate characterized by the desire to organize human coexistence scientifically, and by the conviction that the decline of the liberal tradition required the elaboration of new political models.

From the point of view of economic theory, Hayek's critical objectives in those years were theories of planning and Keynesian theories.[65] From a philosophical-political point of view, the targets of his criticism comprised both totalitarian doctrines and theorizations put forward by various thinkers, notably Mannheim, who sought to lay the basis of a form of social and political planning that would be capable of overcoming the presumed limits and defects of traditional liberal policy.[66]

In his essay 'Scientism and the Study of Society', Hayek showed that this undertaking was related to the connection between radical empiricism and the conception of society as a rational organization, set up by Comte, Saint-Simon and Neurath.[67] He set out to make clear the implications that followed from the belief that society must be organized according to the demands of reason. For this belief was transformed into the

> demand for conscious control of the growth of the human mind. This audacious idea is the most extreme result to which man has yet been led by the success of reason in the conquest of external nature. It has become a characteristic feature of contemporary thought.[68]

The modern age appeared characterized by increasing predominance of the idea that what was required was «direction of everything by a super-mind». In other words, the aspiration of collectivism «which aims at conscious direction of all forces of society» was symptomatic of the state of health of modern scientific civilization.[69] Even the favourable reception enjoyed by the theory of economic planning, Hayek wrote, was «directly traceable to the prevalence of the scientistic ideas», «of the characteristic ideals of the engineers».[70]

As the manifestation of an engineering mentality, economic and political planning was to a large extent an illusion concerning the ability of reason to ensure the more effective functioning of society. The reasons why it proved illusory may be sought in the observation that if one's goal is to ensure that a system can promptly identify the most appropriate responses to constantly varying situations, then what is required is not centralized knowledge but diffused knowledge, so that reaction to a change in situation can be turned into general information. Like Menger, Hayek believed in the existence of practical knowledge as well as theoretical knowledge, maintaining that both were important for the functioning of a social system. For although conceivably «all theoretical knowledge might be combined in the heads of a few experts and thus made available to a single central authority», the same would be unlikely to happen with «knowledge of the particular, of the fleeting circumstances of the moment and of local conditions, which will never exist otherwise than dispersed among many people».[71] Once again the system would be unable to function according to the promises made and expectations generated, which in its turn would act as the cause of its authoritarian involution.

The exposure of the political implications of the failure to recognize the insuperable limits of human knowledge was, as can be seen, a constant element in Hayek's thought. From his essays in the 1930s right up to *The Fatal Conceit* he never ceased reiterating that this was the 'road to serfdom'. It was certainly no coincidence that these themes formed the specific subject-matter of 'The Pretence of Knowledge'. Here too, Hayek once more turned his attention to the question of havoc wreaked within social science by the practice of handling social and economic phenomena in the same way as the objects of natural science.[72]

Any idea that application of the results of scientific progress to social processes could make it possible «to mould society entirely to our liking» should therefore be rejected, for two orders of reasons. Firstly, it is founded on false assumptions concerning the nature of social institutions; secondly, the ensuing failure of social policies formulated on the basis of such assumptions leads to social disorder or a bureaucratic-totalitarian regime. Hence the need to attenuate the expectations associated with scientific progress. Indeed, a lessening of expectations is necessary not only to preclude science from becoming a dangerous delusion, but also because the hope that science can provide a solution for all the world's problems according to everyone's wishes would cancel any distinction between legitimate and illegitimate expectations.[73]

In opposition to those who defined the task of social science as the planning of political-economic systems, Hayek unflaggingly repeated that recognition of the insuperable limits of human knowledge

> ought indeed to teach the student of society a lesson in humility which should guard him against becoming an accomplice in men's fatal striving to control society – a striving which makes him not only a tyrant over his fellows, but which may well make him the destroyer of a civilization which no brain has designed but which has grown from the free efforts of millions of individuals.[74]

The fallacious nature of the premises of planned systems and of interventionist policies would thus, Hayek argued, bring about a whole host of adverse consequences as well as thwarting achievement of the objectives that had been singled out. This in its turn would either lead to the attempt to conceal the débâcle by resorting to terror, or else result in forms of social conflict that are controllable as long as the economic system's productivity is sufficient to allow resources to be shared out to everyone's satisfaction. In either case, failure will generate political regimes characterized by forms of struggle and decision-making different from those obtaining in a parliamentary democracy.[75] Systems propounding the need for a rational and scientific reorganization of society have a tendency to turn into totalitarian regimes, therefore, because of the impossibility of solving the problems of economic planning while at the same time also safeguarding individual freedom together with the very institutional structures in the framework of which freedom can flourish.

§3. TOTALITARIANISM

Mises

The claim that socialism would ineluctably become transformed into totalitarianism was just one aspect of the Austrian interpretation of totalitarianism and its origins. For along with his assertion that the origin of totalitarian regimes lay in socialism's inability to keep its promises, Mises had also pointed an accusing finger at the chiliastic mentality, at aversion to capitalism and liberalism and at the close connection between the spread of the 'engineering approach' and the development of totalitarian political ideas.[76]

Mises's recognition of the plurality of sources and components of totalitarianism did not always crystallize into an exhaustive philosophical-political analysis. The same reproach cannot, however, be brought against Hayek's, 'Scientism and the Study of Society', *The Counter-Revolution of Science* and *The Road to Serfdom*; or against Popper's, *The Poverty of Historicism* and *The Open Society and its Enemies* (where reference to the Hayekian approach is unmistakable).[77]

Omnipotent Government can be considered the most complete work that Mises devoted to an analysis of the sources and structure of totalitarianism. His aim in this work was twofold. On the one hand, he intended to underscore the contribution of German culture to the birth of the totalitarian state. On the other, he wished to show that German culture had begun to move in this direction under the promptings of an ideology, *étatisme*, which was alien to it. But Mises was also concerned to show that the favourable reception enjoyed by this ideology was linked both to the failure of the German liberal movement and also to the rise of Prussian political and cultural hegemony, i.e. to the growth of a force that was largely on the fringe of the German cultural tradition right up to the end of the nineteenth century. Essentially, then, Mises's intention was to show that totalitarian ideology was not only, or not so much, the outgrowth of the German cultural tradition, but rather a deviant version of the latter favoured by historical circumstances and the cultural inadequacy of German liberalism.

The aim of *Omnipotent Government* was thus to point out that «the present crisis of human civilization has its focal point in Germany», and to gain an understanding of how it could have come about that the Germany of Schiller, Goethe, Herder, Kant, Mozart and Beethoven had given way to the Germany of the «Nazi Storm Troops».[78]

The chapter devoted to the collapse of German liberalism opens with the statement that «it is a fundamental mistake to believe that Nazism is a revival or a continuation of the policies and mentalities of the *ancien régime* or a display of the 'Prussian spirit'». Nazism was not the outcome of the evolution of German cultural history–a fabrication that Nazism itself put about in order to acquire legitimacy – but rather a new phenomenon. Its development ran counter to the spread of liberal ideas in Germany. And for all Mises's insistence that «no German has contributed anything to the elaboration of the great system of liberal thought», it was precisely the spread of liberal ideas that kindled in Germans the previously non-existent national spirit.[79] But the defeat of German liberalism also showed how mistaken was the legend prophesying that capitalism would turn into militarism, imperialism and finally Nazism.[80]

Furthermore German liberalism, which was also paying the penalty for being essentially a movement of intellectuals, made its debut on the political scene contemporaneously with Bismarck, and just when the economic and political ideas of the *Kathedersozialisten* were coming into favour. The fact that German universities had been dominated by anti-liberal economic culture was to be a factor of paramount importance. This cultural climate – characterized by a sacral conception of the state and its ends – shaped the world views of the influential class of government officials and intellectuals alike.

The fact that the phenomenon of totalitarianism reached its culmination in Germany, then, was to be ascribed to a collection of cultural and historical circumstances. Germany's rather particular form of capitalistic economic development, especially, was unmatched by adequate development of institutions towards a more liberal model. However, this need not mean that 'German ideology' was the only cultural and philosophical cradle of totalitarianism. More simply, the tendency towards an increase in the powers and authority of the state, already clearly manifested throughout Europe during the nineteenth century,[81] had found a congenial environment in which it was able to thrive. Germany was accustomed to economic development directed by the government, and the influence of the Historical School of German Economists reinforced this attitude.

Although *étatisme* had already gained currency in Germany through the contributions of Fichte, Schelling and Hegel, this did not mean that it was an essentially German phenomenon. For its fundamental traits, i.e. the fact of assigning to the state «the task of guiding the citizens and holding them in tutelage», were common in those years to much of Western political culture. The victory of the statalistic mentality over liberalism was therefore the most important historical event of the last hundred years. It came about, in Mises's opinion, under the two main guises of *socialism* and *interventionism*, seen as linked by the shared aim of subordinating the individual to the state.[82] Although not disregarding the continuity between earlier German nationalism and Nazism,[83] Mises felt that the rise of the *anti-capitalist* and *anti-liberal mentality*, coupled with the fact that governments have long been in the habit of blaming the market for their failures[84] and for economic and social injustice, were the main underlying causes of the growth of totalitarian ideology.

Within the framework of *étatisme* the state was conceived as «essentially an apparatus of compulsion and coercion», and as «a necessary and indispensable institution» given the nature of man. With these premises, *étatisme* believed that its task was to work directly towards the promotion of subjects' welfare. This was linked to the conviction that rulers had greater ability than did citizens, and were better aware of their interests and their 'good'. But this foreshadowed a superhuman conception of the state, engendering its divinization and the identification of its leader with God or his delegates.[85] By sharing in such purposes, socialism, far from being the most perfect accomplishment of democracy, actually doomed the latter to extinction in a political order that refused to acknowledge any political value in individual choices. Thus every step from the market economy towards a planned economy is «necessarily a step nearer to absolutism and dictatorship».[86]

Mises found the common denominator of nationalism, socialism and Nazism to lie in their hostility towards the market system and the conviction that the only form of change is that obtained by overthrowing the system and replacing the market with a collectivist economy governed from the centre, i.e. increasing the powers and authority of the state. The arguments against totalitarianism are, in this case, identical with those against socialism. In both cases, a convincing justification for the attribution of such wide powers to the state and its representatives is utterly lacking.

The omnipotent government thus emerged, Mises contended, as the fruit of a tradition of thought – common both to nationalistic-reactionary ideologies and to social-progressivist movements – which spurns the development of individual freedom, human rights and self-determination in favour of a scenario in which human affairs are to be directed by an omnipotent government.[87] No matter if this requires instruments of coercion that would limit freedom of thought and action. Musing over what the difference might be between Laski and Alfred Rosenberg in this respect,[88] Mises thereby raised the issue of the need to investigate the totalitarian phenomenon from a less misguided perspective than that embodied in the interpretation that it was the outcome of the failure of liberal-capitalistic ideology. The object of Mises's polemic in this respect, as Murry N. Rothbard wrote, was the dominant interpretation of Nazism as, in a nutshell, the «desperate gasp of German big business, anxious to crush the rising power of the proletariat»; this was a view widespread in the United States, above all among Marxist emigrants, foremost among whom was Franz Neumann.[89] Such a view long hindered the process of shedding light on the phenomenon of totalitarianism.

Yet if the totalitarian phenomenon had multiple origins, from those dealt with above to chauvinism and the role of 'myth',[90] the predominant element on which Mises focused attention was the German experience. While not denying the role of the nationalist movement in paving the way towards the country's turmoil, Mises considered that no real danger had arisen until after 1870, when Germany realized it had become the strongest nation in Europe and set about fulfilling the historic mission to which it believed it was called.[91] German nationalism triumphed and acquired a hegemonic position at the point when figures who had been educated in the new intellectual climate burst onto the political scene. The situation was compounded by the fact that German culture was unprepared to combat a phenomenon of such dimensions.[92]

Misesian criticism did not spare the claims made by Santayana[93] of the continuity between German idealism and Nazism. For these claims, which had been taken up by Nazi intellectuals on the basis of a distinction between a genuine and a spurious German cultural tradition, were in his view quite untenable. A major reason for this was that they would require the list of genuine figures to be extended to include names such as Hitler, Goebbels, Spengler and Rosenberg, while the spurious tradition would have to include philosophers and poets such as Kant, Goethe, Schiller and Lessing. Clearly, this was an exaggeration which could not be supported even by clutching at the straws of Fichte or Hegel; for the character of «revealed philosophy» so typical of their mode of thought, inasmuch as it represented a rationalization of Protestant theology, can also be found in many English and American thinkers. And the same holds true for 'egotism', which Santayana saw as lying at the roots of German nationalism. One could equally well observe that egotism is also the starting point of the utilitarianism espoused by Smith, Ricardo, Bentham and the two Mills.

All this made it necessary to search elsewhere for the sources of nationalism. Contemplating various possible origins, Mises focused in particular on the tradition deriving from a mercantilist origin which was concerned with «the means through which the supreme good is to be attained. German nationalists are convinced that there is an insoluble conflict between the interests of the individual nations and those of a world-embracing community of nations.» According to this tradition, idealistic philosophy acted as a prop to Nazism by consisting in a critique of «utilitarian ethics and the sociology of human co-operation». This rejection of utilitarianism, a feature shared by the whole of German philosophy with the sole exception of Feuerbach, led to the idea of an implacable conflict between individual ends and social ends. Such an idea, if extended to relations between nations, has tragically notorious consequences.[94]

This supposed contrast between German economics on the one hand and Jewish and Anglo-Saxon economics on the other seemed to Mises to be bereft of a solid foundation. To some extent this was because it was also argued by Sismondi and by French and British socialists, and partly also because «arteigen German economics is almost identical with contemporary trends in other countries, e.g. with American Institutionalism». In fact it was not a case of contradiction, but rather of a misunderstanding of the nature of trade. Consequently, the continuity between the German tradition and Nazism was to be limited, in Mises's opinion, to the case of pan-Germanism and the *Kathedersozialisten*: «the plans and policies of the Nazis differ from those of their predecessors in imperial Germany only in the fact that they are adapted to a different constellation of political conditions».[95]

This negated the claim hotly defended by German social democracy that Nazism should be viewed as a development of German militarism. This was a legend devoid of truth, Mises maintained – nothing better than a crude attempt to conceal the embarrassing points of contact between the economic measures adopted by Nazism and those proposed by Marx.[96] Far better to take them as the starting point for a critical reappraisal of the role played by the socialist movement in imperial Germany. Such a reappraisal would start with the *de facto* alliance between government and trade unions against the market economy and liberal institutions, and proceed to an examination of the role played by the *Kathedersozialisten* in the teaching of social disciplines in the universities and in defining the lines of development of the German economy.[97]

Even the case of the racial myth, Mises mused, or its modern version at least, could be traced back to de Gobineau,[98] and therefore did not truly bear all the hallmarks of an authentically German product. Yet this had not prevented Nazism from exploiting some of the ideas of Stahl, Lassalle, Rathenau and Gumplowicz for its own ends. In fact this was just one of the many ambiguities of Nazism and the way it appropriated to itself ideas that it hoped would carry the masses; one such ploy, commented Mises, was the fact that it proclaimed itself Christian.[99]

During the Nazi rise to power, not only had Nazi leaders pandered to a motley array of nostalgic reminiscences of a glorified and romanticized past; also, to bolster up their cause they had exploited the situation resulting from the Weimar Republic and the lack of German liberal political culture. Through such tactics they had managed to take advantage of a series of economic and social difficulties demagogically attributed by the social-democratic governments to a market system that had never existed before in Germany in its liberal-democratic version. All these reflections led Mises to conclude that Nazi economic doctrine was anything but the historical evolution of the liberal market system. Quite the contrary: this doctrine was underlyingly a form of *étatisme*,[100] showing affinity with «Fabian and Keynesian 'unorthodoxy'».[101]

Besides his interpretation of German history as the basis for his claims, Mises also grounded his analysis on methodological considerations. He wished to perform a scientific analysis whereby facts would be explained in terms of individuals acting in pursuit of subjective ends and on the basis of limited knowledge, rather than in terms of 'collective wholes'. This led him to the observation that German aggressivness could not be considered greater than that of other peoples; nor could the character of a nation be established on the basis of statistics or of persons held to be more or less significant. In this light, Mises reflected, totalitarianism ceased to be an exclusive fruit of the German tradition and took on the complexion of a much more far-reaching problem. This wider problem encompassed the entire world, and was closely connected to the growth and increasing popularity enjoyed by that *étatist*ic mentality which posed a threat to the whole of Western civilization.[102]

Simply dismissing German culture as demonic did not represent a satisfactory response to the study of Nazi totalitarianism. Rather, analysis of the phenomenon should lead to a reassessment of the consequences of the adoption by Western civilization of political and economic interventionism. The German experience took on universal value precisely because it showed that, the greater the gap between political culture and the values of economic-political liberalism, the more serious was the risk that this culture would be doomed to evolve into totalitarianism. Any suggestion that liberalism is but the prologue to totalitarianism was therefore utterly untenable; on the contrary, liberalism appears to be the only remedy to the totalitarian tendencies innate to nationalistic and socialistic ideologies.

Mises thus asserted the pressing need for critical revision of the ideas that had guided the development of Western civilization during the previous two centuries. Unfortunately, polemically trail-blazing and thought-provoking though his analysis of totalitarianism may have been, it was not exhaustive. For as well as the matters Mises dealt with, there exists a sweeping philosophical dimension of totalitarian thought that he seems not to have treated adequately. Specifically, there is the problem of the birth and progress of modern thought. Here it is not always possible to share the interpretation urged by Mises – even though he did achieve important results in *Socialism* and in *Theory and History* – since his views are informed by a highly personal version of 'rationalism'.

Mises's fundamental philosophical problem can be stated as an enquiry into the development of the 'rational spirit' that arose with Anglo-Scottish illuminism, and it can be further spelled out as an attempt to blend it with the Kant of the *Kritik der reinen Vernunft*. For Mises, positivism, empiricism and historicism were not false and dangerous developments of the 'rationalistic spirit', but rather expressions of a different tradition that attempted to graft the new 'scientific and rationalistic' culture onto the old finalistic conception of the universe and of history.

This theme was further developed in *The Ultimate Foundation of Economic Science*. Here Mises once again took up the question of the detrimental effects exerted on the human sciences by the success of natural science, whether in terms of identification of objectives or of methodology. The cult of science pushed and promoted by positivism and logical positivism thus came to stand for the prime cause of the crisis of Western civilization, and as «the epistemological support of totalitarianism».[103]

By setting up a correlation between the spread of the cult of science and the concurrent phenomena of the rise of the 'myth of the state' and the totalitarian mentality, Mises made a stimulating attempt to reinterpret the history of Western culture and political philosophy. Yet at times his suggestions are debatable. The questions arising from his analysis are not dispelled but, if anything, reinforced by *Theory and History,* a work which reveals with startling clarity how different are the presuppositions and cultural framework of his interpretation of the history of the philosophy of social science compared to the views held by Menger and Hayek.

Hayek

The themes dealt with in 'Economics and Knowledge' and in *Freedom and Economic Systems* reappear in the essays 'The Counter-Revolution of Science' and 'Scientism and the Study of Society', showing that they had developed the full force of their potential as an explanation of political phenomena, especially of totalitarianism. It is no coincidence that these essays stem from the same period as *The Road to Serfdom*. In Hayek's view, the opposition between the market and planning was something different from and more significant than simply a debate concerning the most efficient manner of producing and distributing wealth. It was an expression of the opposition between nomocratic regimes and teleocratic regimes understood as the two fundamental forms of politics. Thus Hayek should be credited with the insightful recognition that this opposition was in fact directed against the path taken by political philosophy subsequent to the relation set up by Locke between private property and the state. Indeed, the very reconstruction of the history of the philosophy of social science can be read in this light.

The starting point of Hayek's argument always centred on the problem of the «division of knowledge», defined as «the really central problem of economics as social science».[104] In its turn, the idea of total knowledge, and its applications in the field of economics and politics with the goal of gaining control over phenomena in these fields, had already been criticized and rejected in the introductory and concluding essays to the collection *Collectivist Economic Planning*. But the optimistic vision which opens the introductory essay was destined to be cruelly betrayed, on account of the way events would unfold.[105]

In these essays *the abuse of reason* was already identified as the source of belief in the possibility of rational organization of the whole of society, with economic planning forming the hub of this organization. As a source of such a belief, Hayek pointed to the transfer onto the economic sphere of a mechanistic conception of individual and social action. This type of application emerged in connection with the positivism of Comte and Saint-Simon, reaching its apogee in contemporary «scientists agitating for a 'scientific' organization of society». What lay behind all this, as has been seen, was the 'intolerance of reason'[106] a mistaken interpretation of the 'data' of the human sciences and belief in a finalism of social institutions.[107]

The critique of the totalitarian mentality thus presupposes that if one believes the 'good society' to be the largely involuntary result of actions through which individuals seek to satisfy subjective needs, then the relation between individual interests and the interests of society must be such as to prevent either of the two from prevailing over the other. If, on the one hand, Hayek reflected, the outcome when individual interests prevail over those of the community is political unrest, and hence the end of political society, on the other hand, once the community interest is given priority over individual interests, then the result is a totalitarian regime.[108] Such a regime appears even more arbitrary since it builds its foundation on total knowledge of political reality and on absolutistic certainty of the goal; but in fact these grounds cannot be demonstrated because they do not belong to the nature of political philosophy – which is the search for the best regime, not its revelation or its imposition. Indeed, for Austrian liberalism it could not be otherwise. These observations enshrined the very essence of the view that individual and society did not represent two antagonistic terms but rather the natural starting point of philosophical reflection on politics.

After highlighting the mistakes inherent in an empiricist conception of social phenomena and the iniquities of constructivist rationalism, Hayek went on to examine the political consequences of the scientistic mentality. Among these, he listed the fact that rigorously rational social organization would involve total subordination of the individual to society, and the fact that it would leave room neither for an individual sphere regulated and protected by the law nor for economic freedom. Totalitarianism would thus be a blend of boundless trust in the ability of reason to point to the 'just political order' and of the firm conviction that all of society's ills stem from an economic organization unable to reach full efficiency. The utopian element of totalitarianism, consisting in belief in the possibility of attaining total knowledge of the world, therefore became associated with the idea that once one has found out the fundamental laws of reality, the world becomes infinitely malleable.

In this perspective, totalitarianism was seen as a consequence of conceiving civilization as a struggle between nature and man, with the ensuing failure to perceive the peculiar character of social institutions. Transposed into the world of politics, this belief was expressed as a markedly anti-liberal stance; it then grew popular by asserting that the mistaken outlook and the irrationality and immorality of the market economy were the elements preventing society from matching expectations. Hence the need for rational and scientific organization of social, economic and political affairs. It was thus no coincidence that the most relentless adversary of totalitarianism, in the latter's various historical guises, was always the connection between economic freedom and political freedom. In response to those who have criticized the connection between these two forms of freedom labouring under the delusion that the latter could exist without the former, one can adduce not only arguments of a historical order (which may be of limited weight) but also the fact that political freedom without economic freedom does not even constitute individual freedom. Freedom of conscience it may well be, but not a freedom that can be exercised, individually as well, through social institutions. More significantly, the fallacious attitude being examined here is the conviction either of those who would champion a philosophy of history and believe that freedom is destined to be realized by overcoming contingent impediments, or of those who identify economic science with political economy, neglecting all that economic science has brought to light on the subject of human action.

In this analysis, totalitarianism emerges as none other than the result – more or less intentional – of the attempt to replace history conceived as the involuntary outcome of spontaneous evolution by an alternative view. This alternative takes history as the conscious product of reason, in a scenario in which reason succeeds in identifying the 'good' and then organizes relations between individuals in such a way that the 'good' can be attained and history made to stand still. Thus in Hayek one finds a vision of the history of political philosophy described essentially as a conflict. On one side stood the *individualism* of the nomocratic conception in which the law establishes the means but not the ends of individual action. On the other stood the *collectivism* of the teleocratic conception, the outcome of which was represented by totalitarian regimes, i.e. political organizations pursuing a 'common good' that is held to be known to reason and scientifically or historically attainable.

The starting point of the analysis and critique of totalitarianism, then, focused the on progressive abandoment of «that freedom in economic affairs without which personal and political freedom has never existed in the past». Such abandonment of «the basic ideas on which European civilisation has been built»[109]occurred in favour of the socialist ideal. This led Hayek to write that

> economic control is not merely control of a sector of human life which can be separated from the rest; it is the control of the means for all our ends. And whoever has sole control of the means must also determine which ends are to be served, which values are to be rated higher and which lower, in short, what men should believe and strive for [. . .] economic planning would involve direction of almost the whole of our life.[110]

The identification of totalitarianism and collectivist planning was thus part of a broader critique of the mentality produced by the success of 'modern science', and a critical assessment of the modern conception of reason as legislator of the human world. Now as well as the heuristic value of Hayek's claims regarding the origin and nature of totalitarianism, it should be kept in mind that his problems were the classical questions of political philosophy. They concerned the quest for and definition of the best political regime, and, in the words of Strauss, can be defined as «the political question par excellence, of how to reconcile order which is not oppression with freedom which is not license».[111]

It should not be thought, however, that totalitarianism is to be identified only with socialism or collectivism. In *The Road to Serfdom*, Hayek felt no qualms about maintaining that Fascism and Nazism, far from being reactions to socialism, were manifestions of one and the same phenomenon.[112] The common aversion shown by socialism and Nazism towards liberalism, i.e. towards the doctrine that civil and political freedom is inseparable from economic freedom,[113] is a further trait that both share. For in fact definition of the essence of socialism as «a crude application of scientific ideals to the problems of society»[114] is also a rather loose – though not generic – definition of totalitarianism.

The Road to Serfdom significantly displays a quotation from Lord Acton in the introduction stating that «few discoveries are more irritating than those which expose the pedigree of ideas». Hayek proceeded further in this work with his revisitation of the most significant findings of modern political philosophy, remaining true to the inspiration that had characterized his activity as a political philosopher and historian of ideas. But this was no mere historiographic revisitation. By claiming that «we can in a measure learn from the past to avoid a repetition of the same process»,[115] and that «it seems almost as if we did not want to understand the development which has produced totalitarianism because such an understanding might destroy some of the dearest illusions to which we are determined to cling»,[116] Hayek offered a glimpse into his own interpretation of the meaning of history and its role in the process of political awareness. This interpretation went far beyond the polemical objectives of the book, reaching into the problem of an understanding of the roots of totalitarian thought.

Totalitarianism thus could not be considered merely a momentary lapse in Western civilization, nor even as its fate; rather, it was as the tragic signal of a danger latent within it which had to be averted. While the aberrations of totalitarianism are in no way the ineluctable epilogue of the liberal tradition, Hayek felt that history can be of aid to man in avoiding a series of pitfalls. The most serious stumbling-block is that of supposing the totalitarian phenomenon to be an exclusive product of German civilization rather than at least in part the result of the socialist mentality. For the affinity between Prussianism and socialism is a fact, but likewise also a confirmation of Hayekian claims.[117]

The 'road to serfdom' is heralded by the appearance and rise to prominence of the idea that planned goal-oriented development of society is to be preferred to spontaneous development, accompanied by the conviction that progress requires society to be refashioned and cast in a radically new mould.[118] In other words, the first step is the view that it is possible to maintain the civil and economic results of liberalism within a different institutional and economic framework. Seen from this vantage point, Hayek reasoned, totalitarianism resembled the tyranny of ancient times. Both sought to accelerate the process of decision-making and achieve other social targets by resorting to increased coercion. Distrust of the liberal tradition was in his view to some extent favoured

> by the uncritical transfer to the problems of society of habits of thought engendered by the preoccupation with technological problems, the habits of thought of the natural scientist and the engineer [. . .] and to impose ideals of organization on a sphere to which they are not appropriate.[119]

Scepticism was additionally fuelled by the confusion between freedom and power.[120]

Hayek felt that the cultural roots of collectivism and totalitarianism should not be sought solely in the specifics of German culture and the demoniacal forces embedded in the latter, therefore, but rather in a much more epoch-making transition. For alongside Nazism, there loomed into view Soviet Communism.[121] The affinities between these two systems prompt one to search for the origin of the phenomenon in cultural forces transcending specific national components. This need not mean, however, that «communism and fascism are essentially the same. Fascism is the stage reached after communism has proved an illusion, and it has proved as much an illusion in Stalinist Russia as in pre-Hitler Germany.» But what they did share, Hayek pointed out, was the fact of having liberalism as their common enemy,[122] as well as cherishing a substantially identical confidence in the kind of organization subsumed under the head of collectivist economic planning. This could be rephrased as placing faith in the «deliberate organization of the labours of society for a definite social goal». Differences between various types of collectivism were thus a function of «the nature of the goal» rather than of the philosophical foundation of the system, which itself consisted of the search for and definition «of a complete ethical code in which all the different human values are allotted their place». Both types of totalitarianism were triggered by the belief that it is possible and necessary to organize society on the basis of a «complete ethical code», and that such a code can be fully known. This attitude stands in sharp contrast to the individualistic-liberal system, which took the stance that

> not only do we not possess such an all-inclusive scale of values: it would be impossible for any mind to comprehend the infinite variety of different needs of different people which compete for the available resources and to attach a definite weight to each.[123]

The existence of an infinite variety of needs and of the means to satisfy them provided Hayek with the arguments he needed to refute the idea that there exists a 'social goal', a 'common aim' – definable as the 'common good' or 'general interest' – with a view to which society should be organized. But the existence of the wide variety of needs also represents the foundation of the relation between capitalism and democracy. The latter is to be seen as the political expression of the more general principle according to which individuals cannot be denied the opportunity to decide on their own interests. Democracy is thus made possible through its connection with the existence of «a competitive system based on free disposal over private property». The fate of democracy therefore appears linked to its ability to contain the expansion of government functions. Indeed, one cannot point to the subjectivity of the market economy as the factor that could put its existence in jeopardy; on the contrary, democracy is undermined by attribution to the government of functions that overstep the rules of conduct. For in such a case the democratic system would lose its character of a problem-solving procedure, to become transformed instead into a regime in which the need to take legislative measures formulated for specific categories of citizens would produce an inflation of laws and administrative measures. The upshot would be discrimination between social groups according to their political leverage, leading to social disruption and political mayhem. This would precipitate loss of «the great merit» enjoyed by the liberal tradition, namely that of reducing «the range of subjects on which agreement was necessary».[124]

These considerations left Hayek in no doubt that control over economic activity implies control over the means to attain individual ends. This in its turn involves a decision concerning which needs are to be satisfied and which not. And the argument can be extended by observing that what ends up confounding the theories of those who claim that economic planning can coexist with the democratic system is the fact that

> to be controlled in our economic pursuits means to be always controlled unless we declare our specific purpose. Or, since when we declare our specific purpose we shall also have to get it approved, we should really be controlled in everything.[125]

Accordingly, the central question of the relation between democracy and planning is represented by the possibility of the existence of individual freedom in a state that controls the means of production and steers this control towards achievement of an aim. This means that the problem always consists in establishing whether – and on what basis – individuals are to be considered tools or whether they themselves constitute ends; and whether it is up to the community or the individual to decide, to shoulder responsibility for choices. Collectivist economic planning would entail almost total control over individual and social life,[126] yet this would not automatically assure its efficiency. The myth of *abundance*, imagined as something which would flourish if only one could eliminate or introduce corrections into the economic system supposedly thwarting the myth, thus turns out to be simply a gross distortion of the facts.[127]

Consequently, Hayek went on, just as it was impossible to conceive of a totalitarian system not possessing control over economic activity, it was equally illusory to hope that a democratic system could coexist with a planned economy. For in this case economic power and political power would tend to coincide, creating a «dependence scarcely distinguishable from slavery». This in its turn would have the effect of transforming power from a diabolical tool into a goal, into an end justifying the adoption of any means whatsoever in order to attain it. Indeed, according to the customary way of thinking of the liberal tradition, which had always been averse to the concentration of powers, transformation of power from a political concept into an economic concept «means necessarily the substitution of power from which there is no escape for a power which is always limited».[128]

Given, then, that instances of it are not to be found in nature (and are infinitely less likely to occur in a complex society), realization of the «complete ethics code» and «all-comprehensive system of values» (which is indispensable for economic planning to prove successful) will not be the fruit of persuasion but of arbitrary power and unbridled use of the principle that the end justifies the means. A case in question cited by Hayek highlights the «change of meaning of words» as a feature shared by totalitarian regimes, which reduces language to a technique for swaying the masses towards pre-established goals.[129] The manipulation and anaesthetization of public opinion into stultifying uniformity are necessary to deter individualistic thinking, which would call in question the objectives of planning and with them the abilities of those in power. Thus totalitarian organization of society is not the result of a process of debate and education, but the imposition of a 'truth' through erasure of those natural differences between individuals that produce discussion, exchange and criticism.[130]

Hayek was led by these reflections to ponder on the rise of this kind of mentality, and to enquire into the role played by Germany. The answer he came up with was in many ways similar to that offered by Mises. For Hayek too, «the doctrines of National-socialism are the culmination of a long evolution of thought, a process in which thinkers who have had great influence far beyond the confines of Germany have taken part». He did not deny, or attempt to play down, the role of German intellectuals in the process that ended up with the individualistic mentality being replaced by the collectivistic approach, but he did take note that they were by «no means alone». For among their ranks, Hayek mused – as did Mises[131] – one should include Carlyle, H.S. Chamberlain, Comte and Sorel,[132] as a testimony that this particular mentality extended well beyond the bounds of German culture.

Hayek listed the ideas and works that had paved the way for the totalitarian mentality. But rather than placing great emphasis on the personal responsibility of Sombart or Plenge (to quote just two of his examples),[133] he was more concerned with demonstrating subsequent developments once these ideas had begun to take hold among intellectuals and the masses.[134] The tenet to which most credence had been given was, he felt, a belief in 'organization', in its threefold guise of economic-political organization and opposition to the individualistic concept of spontaneous order. For not only did 'organization' constitute the theoretical foundation of the so-called *Kriegswirtschaft*, but in fact similar views «were current in the offices of the German raw material dictator, Walter Rathenau». The fact that he «would have shuddered had he realized the consequences of his totalitarian economics» should not, however, obscure the enormous repercussions that his ideas had on the younger generation who were approaching adulthood in the years immediately following the Great War.[135]

Hayek considered that these thinkers, and others such as Lensch, Naumann, Spann, Freyer, Schmitt and Jünger, acted as the sources of the «immediate masters of National-Socialism, particularly Spengler and Moeller van der Bruck».[136]

One notable feature which brought together socialist thinkers, conservatives and scientists in a single political intent, though differing in content, was bitter animosity towards liberalism, springing from the desire *to establish order* in the world by starting out from what is held to be the '*just order*'. Totalitarian thought thus takes on the character of an attempt to put the shackles on change, to recoil from the historical and ephemeral dimension of human existence and anchor reality to the discovery of an ontological foundation of being.

Further confirmation of how untraumatic was the transition from Weimar socialism to National-Socialism for left-wing intellectuals comes from the circumstance that «one of the surprising features of the political emigration from Germany is the comparatively small number of refugees from the Left who are not 'Jews' in the German sense of the term».[137]

The swing among intellectuals towards a position championing the scientific organization of society cannot therefore be considered a phenomenon that reared its ugly head in Germany alone. It is no coincidence that in later works Hayek devoted to the critique of 'constructivism', references to German thinkers were rather marginal. For the belief that science can pass valid judgments in every realm of human action including the moral sphere is a recent persuasion which does not originate from German culture. The underlying conviction that the «scientist is qualified to run a totalitarian society is based mainly on the thesis that 'science' can pass ethical judgment on human behaviour».[138]

The revolt against the impersonal and at times apparently irrational laws of the market economy, and the ensuing endeavour to rationalize and control[139] such laws, in this way invariably produces «the submission to an equally uncontrollable and therefore arbitrary power of other men». Hence the implicit danger of the thesis that

> we must learn to master the forces of society in the same manner in which we have learnt to master the forces of nature. This is not only the path to

totalitarianism, but the path to the destruction of our civilization and a certain way to block future progress.

It follows that the philosophical problem implicit in analysis of the totalitarian mentality is at all times that of attempting to reconcile individual freedom «with the supremacy of one single purpose to which the whole society must be entirely and permanently subordinated».[140] For all the diversity of aims and means, totalitarian regimes and ideologies are united by their shared belief in the possibility of achieving social justice by means of transformation of the liberal political-economic system.

Above and beyond its polemical overstatements (fully understandable if one considers the historical period in which it appeared),[141] *The Road to Serfdom* can thus be considered the political elaboration of Hayek's writings on the subjects of planning, the methodology of the social sciences and the rise to prominence of the scientistic-rationalistic mentality.

But this work also demonstrated how a collectivist regime both cannot coexist with individual freedom and cannot even cope with ends and goals that differ from the concepts on which it was founded. The upshot is no mere ideological contraposition but a full-blown opposition between two philosophical systems regarding the nature of man, from which derive diametrically opposed attitudes towards the nature of political order. Totalitarianism should be rejected not only because of the outcomes to which it has given rise, but also on account of its philosophical premises. For it is founded on a false conception of human action and its ends, and holds the belief that it is possible to transcend the natural limits of human knowledge. Posing as total and definitive knowledge of man, totalitarianism is an attempt to shackle evolution of all things human. Consequently, it has absolutely nothing to do with the tradition of liberal political philosophy.

Let us now consider the overall significance of Mises's and Hayek's critique of totalitarianism in the more general context of the critique that arose in the post-war period. Their works were the first, together with those of Popper and *The Myth of the State* by Cassirer,[142] which gave an in-depth analysis of totalitarianism from a philosophical-political perspective, including an enquiry into the history of ideas. A fundamental characteristic of these works was their ability to pinpoint and highlight a necessary connection between scientism, economic planning and totalitarianism. The same theme recurs in works by Popper (who was considerably influenced by Hayek), whereas it is absent in Cassirer's work, as in other philosophical interpretations of totalitarianism, such as *On Tyranny* by Strauss, *The Origins of Totalitarianism* by Arendt[143] and *The New Science of Politics* by Voegelin. Naturally it is not the intention here to assert that these writers have anything more in common than a critique of modernity and its products, such as positivism and historicism. Overall, these are heterogeneous works addressing the issue of the origins of a phenomenon that so bitterly affected the lives of their authors, and the sources are identified in a number of different cultural circumstances: the spread of Hegelianism and Marxism, mythicization of the state, the rise of modern science, anti-Semitism and modern gnosticism.[144]

Yet two basic motifs can be identified which do tend to give these works a common denominator. The first consists in rejection of the socialist interpretation which saw totalitarianism as the tragic epilogue of the irrationality of the capitalistic-liberal system. The second, on the other hand, resides in adopting an attitude towards the phenomenon that does not start out from the vantage point of the history of institutions or politological analysis, but instead seeks to use a philosophical analysis in order to reach an assessment of, and to find underlying reasons for, totalitarianism in the evolution of Western philosophical-political culture. This entailed a critical re-examination of the foundations of the modern era, prompted by a break with the idealistic, contractualist, historicist and positivist traditions that had been predominant up to then. This turning point can therefore be considered the cradle of the revival of political philosophy understood as reflection on the 'best political order'.

Inasmuch as Mises and Hayek underscored the relation between economic and political doctrines, laying bare the political repercussions of economic choices, they made a vital contribution to an understanding of the phenomenon.

This appears particularly important because in this way they were able to counter attempts to explain away totalitarianism as the desperate last-ditch action of a doomed liberal civilization, crippled by an inexorable historical fate. As well as showing how unfounded such interpretations were, the works by Mises and Hayek also provided direct and vigorous evidence of the vitality of the liberal tradition. By shedding light on the responsibility of the socialist movement in the advent of totalitarian regimes, and likewise on the affinity between socialistic statal organization and the type of organization encountered under Nazism and Fascism, these thinkers – and let us also call to mind Röpke in this context[145] – addressed problems of the development of Western political culture and the relation between economics and politics which are still highly topical today.

This renewed attention to the interdependence of economic freedom and political freedom is the distinctive feature of the political philosophy of Mises and Hayek. Their reflections are a testimony to the fact that wherever this connection is denied or neglected, the liberal tradition itself shows signs of floundering. In a socialist system, the liberal ideal may survive as an individual ethical value, but it cannot survive as a value system. The contraposition between liberalism and socialism is not an opposition of ideals to be attained by means of economy; on the contrary, it is an opposition between two diverging conceptions of the nature and origin of social institutions.

The frequently attempted fusion of the two ideals disregards all such observations. It persists in refusing to appreciate that, from the perspective of liberalism, economic science is not a tool with which ends are to be achieved, but rather nothing less than a science that has contributed to highlighting the character and consequences of human action. All those who would fuse the two systems, preserving the best of each, go wrong in exactly the way Mises drew attention to, namely by mistaking *economic science* for *economic policy*. In so doing, they overlook the fact that since the latter is a 'practical science', i.e. a tool with which to achieve ends, it must necessarily be founded on a 'theoretical science'. In other words, this attempt at fusion appears to be conceivable – and it is no coincidence that an effort was made in this direction by Mill[146] – only in the labour-value perspective of classical economics, or in the framework of the theory of general economic equilibrium of Walras, taken as a normative model postulating complete knowledge, obtained in real time, by all agents.

Nevertheless, the features in the theses of Mises and Hayek that drew greatest criticism were not their interpretation of Communism, Nazism and Fascism as different manifestations of one and the same phenomenon, nor even the fact that they traced the philosophical and cultural origins of totalitarianism back to the application of the ideals of natural science to political society. Much more damning in the eyes of their critics was their conviction that the so-called '*middle way*' between the market system and collectivist planning was insubstantial as a theoretical model, and that it too formed a 'road to serfdom'.[147]

By pointing to this inconsistency as the major cause of the latent process of transformation of Western democracies into totalitarian regimes, Hayek and Mises came under fire from intellectuals who identified their role in society as the mission of spiritual guides, rather than seeing their function as a critique of power and opinions.

But among the fundamental aspects of the Austrian analysis of totalitarianism, one should also recall the critique of modernity. Like Strauss, and in certain respects Mises as well, Hayek felt that the horrors of totalitarianism, and indeed the time lag intervening before philosophy and political science belatedly realized what was about to happen, would not have been possible without the birth of the *constructivist mentality*. Certainly the differences between these two great interpreters of our age remain insurmountable in that they were acting within two different frameworks whose conception of the relation between revelation and philosophy differed. What they shared, however, was the position that scientism and historicism represented the principal adversaries of political philosophy, and the philosophical premises of totalitarianism. It can hardly be a coincidence that this attack should have come first and foremost from thinkers who stood aloof from the positivistic or historicist background, and were thus able to understand what was taking place. And apart from the evaluation of modernity, they also, more importantly, shared the belief that totalitarianism was not just a mishap during the course of evolution of Western civilization. In their view, totalitarianism was the fruit of the increasing credence given to the idea that the methods and cognitive aims of modern natural science could be used to resolve the problems of social science. In other words, modern science was thought to be capable of solving those problems for which traditional philosophy and political economy, deemed insufficiently 'scientific', had been unable to come up with a solution.

But if modern science had been able to reconcile unlimited subjective desires with limited resources, and then to distribute the resources in such a way as to maintain the 'subjectivity' of the choices and to ensure the coexistence of democracy and planning, it would have solved the problem of scarcity and the accompanying question of the alternative use of resources. Hence there would no longer be any need to 'choose'. And without the need to choose, the fundamental *raison-d'être* of politics would be swept away. Consequently, the unrealizability of the planned society transforms the planner into a modern tyrant who is forced to resort to violence in order to impose upon mankind what he believes to be the 'real good'.

If one stands outside the type of historicist mentality that views the past in a teleological relation to the present, however, it is possible to become aware of the mistake and avoid its repetition. This means that the 'road to serfdom' is identified with acritical acceptance of the present, with a faith in something that lies beyond the cognitive grasp of man: that dream of reason which produced the horrors of totalitarianism.

Nevertheless, Mises and Hayek were far from urging some far-fetched dream of return to a mythical golden past. They did not revile the achievements of modern science, but had every intention of focusing closely on its limits. Thus their critique of totalitarianism was both a critique of the predominant cultural trends of the last few centuries, and also a defence of an order that arises and evolves spontaneously over history.

Given this setting, totalitarianism can be seen as the product of the modern view that the 'best regime' – which for classical political philosophy constituted a desirable but unattainable goal on account of the limited nature of man – can be realized only with the tools furnished by the great strides of progress in scientific and historical knowledge achieved in the modern age. It is thereby exposed as the fond hope that the best regime will burst forth as the ultimate outcome of the struggle between *reason* and *nature*. For in the final balance, what we have in Mises and Hayek is not truly, or not merely, a critique stirred by the opposition between a free market economic model and a socialistic one. Rather, the vision that rises from the pages of their works springs from a veritable dichotomy between the *society model* and the *community model*; and this in its turn is recognizable as a classic theme of political philosophy, based on two antithetical conceptions of man and politics.

What may be termed the Austrian critique of totalitarianism thus covered a fairly extensive stretch of time, densely packed with momentous events.

Hayek, for instance, was critical of early socialist systems, and was an onlooker at the time of their collapse. This was an era of recent history that coincided with the rise and fall of socialist ideology, and with the spread of the belief that the advances of civilization obtained in the liberal world could be maintained even without the market economy.[148]

This was equally an era in which Mises and Hayek unflaggingly reiterated their interpretations and their criticisms. Yet, because for decades their ideas were essentially passed over in silence, it would be overstating the matter to claim that their ideas were of substantial import in the fall of such systems of thought. These systems fell because they were founded on false premises which produced undesired consequences, and not on account of the diffusion and success of the critique by Mises and Hayek. Their analysis rarely met with acclaim beyond the confines of the liberal tradition, and frequently exercised little influence even here. Objectively speaking, in those years the circulation of their ideas was quite limited, and they were remembered chiefly as figures from the past.[149] Nevertheless, Hayek continued to reassert his criticism of socialism, with *The Constitution of Liberty*, *Law, Legislation and Liberty* and other writings, through which he laid the basis for the revival of liberal political philosophy and made important contributions to the history of political philosophy by favourably reappraising the tradition of *order as spontaneous cultural result*. Indeed, despite not having become a 'box-office success', the penetration of their ideas was to play a key role in nurturing the rebirth of liberal political philosophy that began to make itself felt from the 1970s on.[150]

NOTES

1 See Hayek, 1944, p. 42:

> the various kinds of collectivism, communism, fascism, etc., differ between themselves in the nature of the goal toward which they want to direct the efforts of society. But they differ from liberalism and individualism in wanting to organize the whole of society and all its resources for this unitary end, and in refusing to recognize autonomous spheres in which the ends of the individuals are supreme. In short, they are totalitarian in the true sense of this word which we have adopted to describe the unexpected but nevertheless inseparable manifestations of what in theory we call collectivism.

2 See Voegelin, 1952, p. 163. Totalitarianism is here defined «as journey's end of the Gnostic search for civil theology». In the years when he was enrolled at the Faculty of Law in Vienna University, Voegelin attended the *Privatseminar* of Mises; see Mises, 1978, p. 100.

3 Strauss, 1948, pp. 26–7. On p. 22, Strauss stated that

> in contradistinction to classical tyranny, present-day tyranny has at its disposal 'technology' as well as 'ideologies'; more generally expressed, it presupposes the existence of 'science', i.e. of a particular interpretation, or kind, of science. Conversely, classical tyranny, unlike modern tyranny, was confronted, actually or potentially, by a science which was not meant to be applied to 'conquest of nature' or to be popularized and diffused.

4 See Cubeddu, 1987a, pp. 25–52.
5 See Strauss, 1953 and 1959, pp. 36ff.
6 Menger, 1883, pp. 207–8 (Engl. trans. p. 177). The importance of the passage is mentioned in Hayek, 1948, pp. 4–5n. On Smith, see also Menger, 1891, pp. 224–5:

> Ja, A. Smith geht so weit, den *Kapitalsprofit als einen Abzug vom vollen Arbeitsertrage, die Grundrente aber als ein Einkommen Solcher* zu bezeichnen, die da ernten wollen, ohne geset zu haben. Wo es sich um den Schutz der Armen und Schwachen handelt, ist der principielle Standpunkt A. Smith's zu Theile ein fortgeschrittenerer, als jener der modernen 'Social-Politiker'. Es streifen seine Ansichten an einzelnen Stellen seines Werkes geradezu an jene der modernen Sozialisten. Louis Blanc, Ferdinand Lassalle und Karl Marx berufen sich bekanntermassen unablssig auf die Theorien A. Smith's und jene seiner Schler, nicht auf jene ihrer Gegner.»

7 Menger, 1883, p. 257 (Engl. trans. p. 212).
8 Ibid., p. 47 (Engl. trans. p. 64). This however does not mean giving up the conception of the role of economic science as the activity of distinguishing between real needs and imaginary needs. That individuals are 'excellent judges' of their own interests is then explained by Menger through the fact that «economic life confronts us with regularities both in coexistence and in the succession of phenomena».
9 Ibid., p. 80 (Engl. trans. p. 88).
10 The proceedings of this contraposition are now in Hayek, 1973–9, III.
11 It is no coincidence, as Hayek wrote, that the object of his attack was represented by Neurath's theories on a collectivist economy founded on a 'natural calculus'. Hayek, 1981a, states as follows: «the crucial section on economic calculation under socialism was in fact provoked by a book by Otto Neurath published in 1919» (p. xxi). The book in question was Neurath, 1919. On the role of Neurath in the debate on planning, as well as the short but significant references in Weber, 1922b, pp. 56–7, see also Tisch, 1932, pp. 46–53; Hoff, 1949, pp. 75–80; Chaloupek, 1990, pp. 662ff.
12 On this article, and more generally on the theses of Mises and Hayek in the debate on economic calculation in the socialist economy, see Tisch, 1932, pp. 59–75, (the first scientific report of the debate); Hoff, 1949; Leoni, 1965, pp. 415–60; Buchanan, 1969, pp. 20–3; Vaughn, 1976, pp. 101–10, and 1980, pp. 536–54; Barry, 1984a, pp. 573–92; Shand, 1984, pp. 186–98; Lavoie, 1985a and 1985b; Butler, 1988, pp. 34–54; Rothbard, 1991, pp. 51–76.
13 See Wieser, 1889; Pareto, 1906; Barone, 1908.
14 Vaughn, 1976, p. 107, wrote:

> in fact it was Hayek who chose to respond to some of the more difficult problems, (Mises so-called final refutation in *Human Action* is mostly polemic and glosses over the real problem). I admit that it was Mises, neverthless, who indicated in what direction the answer to the Socialists lay.

15 See Lange, 1936, p. 53.
16 Mises, 1919, pp. 108n., 125n. (Engl. trans. pp. 134n., 154n.).
17 See Mises, 1921, p. 87 (Engl. trans. p. 88).
18 Ibid., pp. 86–7 (Engl. trans. pp. 88–9). On these aspects of the issues dealt with by Mises, even if the references are predominantly to Mises, 1981, see Albert, 1986, pp. 60–102. The technical aspects of the critique by Mises and Hayek of socialism are examined in Rothbard, 1976a, pp. 67–77, and 1992, pp. 12–22; and Hoppe, 1989.
19 See Mises, 1921, p. 88 (Engl. trans. p. 90).
20 Ibid., pp. 88–92 (Engl. trans. pp. 90–5). On this subject, see Barry, 1986a, pp. 72–4.
21 Mises, 1921, pp. 93–9 (Engl. trans. pp. 97–104). As a rejoinder to Neurath, in this

case, see p. 102 (Engl. trans. p. 108n.); Mises here objected that Neurath had failed to take into consideration «the insuperable difficulties that would have to develop with economic calculation in the socialist commonwealth». On the essay by Mises and the problems of economic calculation in a socialist economy, see Robbins, 1976, pp. 143–4.

22 Mises, 1921, pp. 100–4 (Engl. trans. pp. 105–10).

23 Ibid., pp. 105–119 (Engl. trans. pp. 111–28).

24 Ibid., pp. 119–21 (Engl. trans. pp. 128–30). On the debate surrounding his own claims on the impossibility of economic calculation in a socialist economy, see also Mises, 1924, pp. 488–500.

25 Mises, 1981, pp. 6–20. The position of H. Cohen on socialism was regarded by Mises as exemplary of how socialist ideas were accredited even by people who did not share them (see pp. 19–20).

26 Ibid., pp. 9, 418.

27 Ibid., pp. 21–32. Thus on the question of the origin of ownership too, the interpretation of Mises differed from that of Menger.

28 Ibid., pp. 96–105. The citations are on pp. 97 and 105 respectively. The observations on exchange value as the unit of economic calucation are on pp. 98–9.

29 Ibid., pp. 211–32. The citations are on p. 211. Among the various types of socialism he listed Prussian 'state socialism', military socialism, Christian socialism, the planned economy and 'guild socialism'. Christian socialism – which all Christian confessions were seen as moving towards (see pp. 223) – was taken as a variant on state socialism characterized by a theocratic organization of the state which is incompatible with the free market, hostile to capitalism and favourable to a stationary society that corresponds to the economic ideals of scholastics characterized by a search for the 'right price'. Together with the different types of socialism, Mises also included 'pseudo-socialist systems', such as 'solidarism', widespread in France on account of the influence of Gide, the various proposals for expropriation, profit-sharing, syndicalism and the various forms of partial socialism (see pp. 233–45).

30 Ibid., pp. 249–50.

31 Ibid., pp. 250–5. On the interpretation of Marxism in Mises, see Butler, 1988, pp. 55–69.

32 In this regard see also Mises, 1967, pp. 215–31.

33 Mises, 1981, pp. 256–61.

34 Ibid., pp. 261–5. In these pages Mises developed his critique of the Kantian interpretation of society as antagonism between a creative impulse and a dissolutionary impulse, attributing this interpretation to lack of knowledge on Kant's part of the theory of the harmony of interests elaborated by the classical economists.

35 Ibid., pp. 307–11.

36 Ibid., pp. 413–18. On the relation between the Austrian theory of value and Marxism, reference must naturally be made to the classic works of Böhm-Bawerk; among recent analyses, see Kauder, 1965, pp. 59–65; Meek, 1972, pp. 499–511; Shand, 1984, pp. 57–60; Chaloupek, 1986, pp. 195–221.

37 Mises, 1981, pp. 369–71.

38 Ibid., pp. 378–81.

39 Ibid., pp. 382–7.

40 Ibid., p. 388.

41 Ibid., pp. 389–98; the quotations are on p. 390.

42 Ibid., pp. 407–9.

43 A demonstration of the fact that the problems of socialism have not changed from those pointed out by Mises and Hayek is given by the statements of Elster and Moene, 1989, pp. 1–2:

Capitalism – actually existing capitalism – appears in many respects to be an ugly, irrational, wasteful way of organizing the production and distribution of goods and services [. . .] Yet today we cannot say as confidently as many socialists have in the past that it is easy to create a better system. Indeed, many would say that the question whether a better system is feasible remains unresolved. The main cause of the disenchantment of socialists is the deplorable record of central planning, which in the socialist tradition was always the panacea for the ills of capitalism [. . .] In other important respects centrally planned economies tend to do very badly. The ugliness of capitalism makes us look to central planning for a possible remedy, but the irrationality of central planning sends us back to capitalism as, probably, the lesser evil [. . .] Could, for instance, central planning be tempered by the market, or capitalism tempered by planning?.

44 The works in question are essays by Pierson, Mises, Halm and Barone.

45 Hayek, 1935, pp. 1–3. In general on Hayek's critique of socialism and economic and political planning, see Barry, 1979, pp. 179–82; Butler, 1983, pp. 66–86; Gray, 1984a, pp. 38–40; Shand, 1984, pp. 186–98. There are important annotations in Seldon, 1984, pp. xiii–xxxii, and 1990, pp. 128–33; and in Stigler, 1979, pp. 61–8.

46 This thesis had a number of authoritative backers, among them Schumpeter, 1942, p. 173 and n. (the references to Mises and Hayek are on p. 172), and 1954, p. 898 and n. Hayek's answer is in 1948, pp. 90n., 153, which contains an indication of an observation on this subject made by Pareto, 1909, pp. 233–4. The extract from Pareto is quoted again in the other writings by Hayek in which he dealt with this problem; see 1952a, pp. 43, and 212n., 1967, pp. 35, 261n., and 1978, pp. 28, 278, 303.

47 Hayek, 1935, pp. 8–14.

48 Ibid., pp. 14–17.

49 Gray, 1989, p. 174: «In its most fundamental aspects the Mises–Hayek argument against the possibility of rational economic calculation under socialism is an epistemological argument.» That the real foundation of the critique of socialism consisted of arguments of an epistemological nature was to be displayed unequivocably in *The Fatal Conceit.* This however did not mean that from the early essays to this last work Hayekian epistemology underwent no change.

50 Hayek, 1935, pp. 24–9. They thus failed, in Hayek's view, to take into account the fact that Gossen had showed as early as 1854 that the central economic authority of the communists would not be able to resolve rational calculation in the absence of private property, and that Wieser had demonstrated the impossibility of a common scale of values accepted by all. It was only in the first decade of the century that Kautsky, responding to Pierson, broke «the traditional silence about the actual working of the future socialist state». Kautsky, however, «only showed that he was not even really aware of the problem which the economists had seen». And the subsequent discussions on the economic problems of socialism added little further to solution of the problem. Only Barone, by developing «certain suggestions of Pareto's», tackled the problem of the determination of the essential magnitudes in the economic calculation of a socialist system, showing that «the tools of mathematical analysis of economic problems might be utilized to solve the tasks of the central planning authority».

51 Ibid., pp. 29–36. In the German and Austrian debate on these questions, «the most interesting and in any case the most representative» contribution was that of Neurath. But Hayek also mentioned the contribution of Bauer and the proposals of the 'Socialization Commission', in the framework of which Lederer, and «the ill-fated» Rathenau, «developed plans for socialization which became the main topic of discussion among economists». It was in this situation that the well-known

article by Mises came to attention, which boasts «the distinction of having first formulated the central problem of socialist economics» by showing that rational calculation of the resources available in an economic system is possible only if the process of price formation is expressed in money. Similar conclusions, Hayek felt, had been reached by Weber, 1922b, and Brutzkus, 1935. In those years Weber was teaching in Vienna; and Mises, 1978, pp. 69–70, relates that «we became good friends». Evidently, however, they did not face these problems, and in fact Weber, 1922b, I, p. 58, wrote that he had become acquainted with the essay by Mises only when his own was already in press, and this circumstance was upheld by Hayek. In the essay 'Soziologie und Geschichte', now in Mises, 1933, dedicated to the critique of Weberian methodology, significantly, Mises did not take up the problem again.

52 Hayek, 1935, pp. 36–8.

53 Ibid., pp. 207–17. This, observed Hayek, led some thinkers, such as M. Dobb, to the extreme and logical conclusion «by asserting that it would be worth the price of abandoning the freedom of the consumer if by the sacrifice socialism could be made possible»; see p. 215.

54 Ibid., pp. 237–41.

55 Hayek, 1940, pp. 203–7.

56 See Hayek, 1937, p. 33n. Hayek, in this respect, quoted Popper, 1935. The thesis of the influence of Popper on Hayek is based precisely on this reference; but the rest of the work does not seem to develop along Popperian lines.

57 Hayek, 1937, pp. 37–9.

58 Ibid., pp. 45–6. On the theory of *homo oeconomicus*, see also p. 11; and Hayek, 1960, p. 61.

59 Hayek, 1937, pp. 50–1. On the relation between knowledge and planning, see Kirzner, 1984, pp. 193–206; Lavoie, 1985a, pp. 52–92; Schotter, 1990, pp. 39–42.

60 Hayek, 1952a, pp. 36–8. These are the pages in which Hayek defines the individualistic and 'compositive' method of the social sciences.

61 Hayek, 1937, p. 42.

62 Ibid., pp. 45–6.

63 Hayek, 1945, pp. 78–9.

64 Ibid., pp. 83–4.

65 See Hayek, 1973–9, III. In this regard, see O'Driscoll, 1975; Lepage, 1980, pp. 417–22; Gallaway and Vedder, 1984, pp. 179–92.

66 See Mannheim, 1941. The work abounds in sentences and definitions such as:

> our opinion is that liberal mass society has reached a point in its development where continued drifting leads to disaster.
>
> (p. 113)
>
> planning means a conscious attack on the sources of maladjustment in the social order on the basis of a thorough knowledge of the whole mechanism of society and the way in which it works.
>
> It is not therefore, contrary to the nature of free democratic society if we maintain that the most satisfactory arrangement would be to fit a sphere of free creative initiative into a planned institutional framework. In the future this sphere of free creative activity must always be guided so as to guard against the possibility of distortion and breakdown.
>
> (p. 114)
>
> at the stage of planning freedom can only be guaranteed if the planning authority incorporates it in the plan itself [. . .]. Once all the instruments of influencing human behaviour have been co-ordinated, planning for freedom is the only logical form of freedom which remains.
>
> (pp. 378–9)

one of the guarantees of freedom in a planned society will be the maintenance of the individual capacity for adjustment.

(p. 379)

Far from falsifying the Hayekian approach to the relation between planning totalitarianism, these statements, the list of which could be extended) contribute to giving an idea of the kind of approach taken by theoreticians of social, economic and political planning.

67 The thinkers who prompted Hayek's reflections are Comte, Saint-Simon and Neurath. On Comte see Hayek, 1944, pp. 12, 124, and 1952a, pp. 129–55. On Saint-Simon, see Hayek, 1944, p. 18, and 1952a, pp. 105–67. On Neurath, see 1952a, p. 123.

68 Hayek, 1952a, p. 88. The champions of this «conscious control of the growth of the human mind» are indicated in Hobhouse, Needham and Mannheim, and they all share the idea of Hegelian or positivistic derivation, «that the human mind is, as it were, to pull itself up by its own boot-straps».

69 Ibid., pp. 90–1.

70 Ibid., p. 94.

71 Ibid., p. 98.

72 He did so in the lecture he gave on the occasion when he was awarded the Nobel Prize, now in Hayek, 1978. In this circumstance (see p. 28), Hayek also reiterated his critique of the reduction of economic science to mathematical economics, and once again stressed the limits, already underscored by Pareto, of the application of the mathematical method 'to arrive at a numerical calculation of prices', and he also recalled that even the «Spanish schoolmen of the sixteenth century [...] emphasized that what they called pretium mathematicum [...] depended on so many particular circumstances that it could never be known to man but was known only to God.»

73 Ibid., pp. 30–1.

74 Ibid., pp. 32–4.

75 Hayek, 1944, pp. 45ff. On the theme of the transition from democracy to socialism, the target of Hayek's criticism was represented by the thesis of H.J. Lasky, who believed that one should not admit that parliamentary democracy can constitute «an obstacle to the realization of socialism»; see p. 47n., but also p. 98, pp. 148–9.

76 In Mises, 1948, p. 113, 'social engineering', like planning, is defined as «a synonym of dictatorship and totalitarian tyranny». But see also Mises's works of 1947 and 1952. Mises, 1947, was the work referred to by Polanyi, 1951, p. 124 and n., who wrote that «Mises himself seems to move toward them [the Hayekian thesis on the relation between planned economy and totalitarianism] in his recent writing when asserting that a planned economy involves totalitarianism.»

77 See Popper, 1945, II, p. 336n. With reference to Hayek, 1939, on the problem of 'utopian engineering' and 'centralized' or 'collectivist' planning, Popper, 1945. I, p. 285n., wrote: «Hayek's criticism belongs to the realm of social technology. He points out a certain technological impossibility, namely that of drafting a plan for a society which is at once economically centralized and individualistic.» And, just a little further on:

Hayek's attitude in this book [*RS*] is so explicit that no room is left for the somewhat vague comments of my note. But my note was printed before Hayek's book was published; and although many of his leading ideas were foreshadowed in his earlier writings, they were not yet quite as explicit as in *The Road to Serfdom*. And many ideas which, as a matter of course, we now associate with Hayek's name were unknown to me when I wrote my note.

78 Mises, 1944b, p. 7. On the interpretation of totalitarianism by Mises, see Hazlitt, 1956, pp. 81–93.

79 Mises, 1944b, pp. 18–22. Among those who spread liberal ideas, Mises placed particular emphasis on Schiller. On the liberalism of Schiller and Goethe, see also p. 260.

80 Ibid., pp. 41ff.

81 Ibid., pp. 6, 44–5. This tendency had been theorized above all by thinkers such as Saint-Simon, Owen, Fourier, Pecqueur, Comte, Carlyle, Ruskin and the Fabians, and introduced into Germany by von Stein, Spielhagen and Hauptmann.

82 Ibid., p. 44.

83 Ibid., p. 1.

84 Ibid., pp. 3–5. See also Mises, 1956.

85 See Mises, 1944b, pp. 46–7. In contrast to this attitude, Mises claimed that

> With human nature as it is, the state is a necessary and indispensable institution. The state is, if properly administered, the foundation of society, of human cooperation and civilization. It is the most benefical and most useful instrument in the endeavors of man to promote human happiness and welfare. But it is a tool and a means only, not the ultimate goal. It is not God. It is simply compulsion and coercion; it is the police power.

86 Ibid., p. 53.

87 Ibid., p. 8. For Mises,

> In the history of the last two hundred years we can discern two distinctive ideological trends. There was first the trend toward freedom, the rights of man, and self-determination [. . .] In the second part of this period individualism gave way to another trend, the trend toward state omnipotence.

88 Ibid., p. 11. Starting out from the fact that «the parties of the Left and of the Right are everywhere highly suspicious of freedom of thought', Mises wondered: 'But who is "progressive" and who is "reactionary"? There is a remarkable difference with regard to this issue between Harold Laski and Alfred Rosenberg.»

89 See Rothbard, 1988, pp. 58–9.

90 Mises, 1944b, pp. 122–8.

91 Ibid., pp. 129ff. This, wrote Mises, «was the result of nationalist education. This was an achievement of authors like Lagarde, Peters, Langbehn, Treitschke, Schmoller, Houston Stewart Chamberlain, Naumann» (p. 133).

92 Ibid., pp. 129–40.

93 Ibid., p. 141. In the words of Mises:

> The popularity of the opinion that German nationalism is the outcome of the ideas of German philosophy is mainly due to the authority of George Santayana. However, Santayana admits that what he calls 'German philosophy' is 'not identical with philosophy in Germany', and that 'the majority of intelligent Germans held views which German philosophy proper must entirely despise [. . .]. According to Santayana the main source of German nationalism is egotism.

94 Ibid., pp. 140–3.

95 Ibid., pp. 145–7.

96 Ibid., pp. 149–51.

97 Ibid., pp. 155ff.

98 Ibid., p. 172.

99 Ibid., pp. 175–6 ff.

100 Ibid., pp. 224ff.

101 Ibid., p. 228.

102 Ibid., pp. 22–31ff.

103 See Mises, 1962, pp. 125–33.

104 See Hayek, 1937, pp. 50–1.

105 In the words of Hayek, 1935, pp. 1–2:

> there is reason to believe that we are at last entering an era of reasoned discussion of what has long uncritically been assumed to be a reconstruction of society on rational lines [. . .] To bring order to such a chaos, to apply reason to the organization of society, and to shape it deliberately in every detail according to human wishes and the common ideas of justice seemed the only course of action worthy of a reasonable being.

106 See Hayek, 1944, pp. 141–2 and n. Hayek intended thereby to call attention to «one feature of the intellectual development in Germany during the last hundred years» that was winning proselytes in Anglo-Saxon countries, too. On the one hand, he asserted that

> the ideal of a society organized 'through and through' from the top has in Germany been considerably furthered by the quite unique influence which her scientific and technological specialists were allowed to exercise on the formation of social and political opinions.

On the other, he pointed out that

> the way in which, in the end, with few exceptions, her scholars and scientists put themselves readily at the service of the new rulers is one of the most depressing and shameful spectacles in the whole history of the rise of National-Socialism.

The latter was in tune with a tradition begun by the famous speech of E. du Bois-Reymond in 1870.

107 See Hayek, 1952a, pp. 80ff. Particularly significant was the reference to Mengerian criticism of the 'pragmatic' interpretation of social institutions.

108 See Barry, 1984b, pp. 55–64.

109 Hayek, 1944, pp. 9–10. The fact of having forgotten the admonishments of Tocqueville and Lord Acton, according to which «socialism means slavery», thus makes it difficult to understand the origins of the totalitarian mentality, and to grasp that «the modern trend towards socialism means [. . .] a break not only with the recent past but with the whole evolution of Western civilization»: not only with the ideas of Cobden, Bright, Smith, Hume, Locke and Milton, but with the Greek and Roman Christian tradition and the individualistic tradition of Erasmus, Montaigne, Cicero, Tacitus, Pericles and Thucydides.

On the critique of the Hayekian correlation between economic freedom and political freedom, see Wootton, 1945, pp. 22–4, 140–2; but above all Finer, 1945, a work dedicated to confuting the Hayekian thesis that opens as follows: «Friedrich A. Hayek's *The Road to Serfdom* constitutes the most sinister offensive against democracy to emerge from a democratic country for many decades» (p. v); Kelsen, 1955.

110 Hayek, 1944, pp. 68–9. On the critique of planning, and on resistance to the rationalistic attitude in politics, Oakeshott, 1962, p. 21, wrote: «A plan to resist all planning may be better than its opposite, but it belongs to the same style of politics.» This type of view, as pointed out by Barry, 1979, pp. 196–7, illustrates the difference between conservatives and Hayek. On this theme, see Kukathas, 1989, pp. 179ff.; on the affinities between Hayek and Oakeshott, see Gray, 1984a, pp. 14, 53, 67, 81, 114, 130.

111 See Strauss, 1952, p. 37; on the task of political philosophy, see also, 1959.

112 Hayek, 1944, p. 3 («Few are ready to recognize that the rise of Fascism and Nazism was not a reaction against the socialist trends of the preceding period, but a

necessary outcome of those tendencies»); pp. 86–7 («Fascism and National Socialism are a sort of middle-class socialism»); pp. 124–5 («It was the union of the anti-capitalist forces of the right and the left, the fusion of radical and conservative socialism, which drove out from Germany everything that was liberal. The connection between socialism and nationalism in Germany was close from the beginning»); p. 133 («Fight against liberalism in all its forms [. . .] was the common idea which united socialists and conservatives in one common front»). On the relation between socialism and totalitarianism, see Hartwell, 1977, pp. 76–7, 92.

113 See Hayek, 1944, p. 75:

> The economic freedom which is the prerequisite of any other freedom cannot be the freedom *from* care which the socialists promise us and which can be obtained only by relieving the individual at the same time of the necessity and of the power of choice.

114 Ibid., p. 127. In this case reference is to Sombart, J. Plenge and the French origins of socialist ideas.

115 Ibid., p. 1. On these themes, see Barry, 1979, pp. 183–6.

116 See Hayek, 1944, pp. 4–5. The fact of having tried to shed light on the perverse consequences of the «dearest illusions» is perhaps what earned Hayek the accusation of being an ultra-conservative. On this charge, see Lepage, 1980, pp. 429–34.

117 Hayek, 1944, pp. 6–7.

118 Ibid., pp. 13ff. On the contrary, the fundamental principle of liberalism is that «in the ordering of our affairs we should make as much use as possible of the spontaneous forces of society, and resort as little as possible to coercion».

119 Ibid., pp. 14–17. Hayek wrote:

> the rule of freedom which had been achieved in England seemed destined to spread throughout the world. By about 1870 the reign of these ideas had probably reached its easternmost expansion [. . .] For the next sixty years Germany became the centre from which the ideas destined to govern the world in the twentieth century spread east and west. Whether it was Hegel or Marx, List or Schmoller, Sombart or Mannheim, whether it was socialism in its more radical form or merely 'organization' or 'planning' of a less radical kind, German ideas were everywhere readily imported and German institutions imitated.

120 Ibid., pp. 18ff. On p. 19n., Hayek pointed to J. Dewey as «the most explicit defender of this confusion». The theme of the confusion between freedom and power was to be developed in greater detail in Hayek, 1960, pp. 16ff.

121 See Hayek, 1944, pp. 20–3. Quoting some of the first to notice the extraordinary similarity between two regimes which for many represented instead «opposite poles», Hayek mentioned Eastman, Chamberlin, Voigt and Lippmann.

122 See Ibid., pp. 21–2. Here Hayek cited and thoroughly espoused an extract from P. Drucker, *The End of Economic Man*, 1939.

123 See Hayek, 1944, pp. 42–4.

124 Ibid., pp. 51–2. As Hayek wrote: «it is far more important to realize that only within this system is democracy possible. When it becomes dominated by a collectivist creed, democracy will inevitably destroy itself.» With regard to the mechanisms of political struggle produced by «statism» in «an age of unlimited democracy», Gray, 1984a, pp. 120–1, wrote that they tend towards

> re-creation in the context of civil society of Hobbes's state of nature. This is indeed the mechanism of Hayek's road to serfdom, a mechanism he identifies himself when in his famous book he shows why the worst are bound to come out on the top in a totalitarian state.

125 Cf. Hayek, 1944, p. 68. On the relation between planned economy and totalitarianism, with reference to this work, see Polanyi, 1951, p. 124. Despite the absence of other direct mentions, the approach to the problem of the relation between individual freedom and totalitarianism of Polanyi presents certain affinities with that of Hayek (see pp. 33, 46, 107ff., 158, 189). Agreeing with the theses of Hayek and Lippmann concerning the impossibility of bringing about coexistence between the planned economy and democracy, Jaspers, 1949, pp. 346–48n., wrote that «Lippmann and Hayek have pointed out inevitable connections which are not easy to refute with effective arguments.»

126 Hayek, 1944, p. 68–70. While recognizing that Hayekian ideas have not yet been studied seriously, Aron, 1976, expressed reservations concerning the relation he had set up between planning and totalitarianism; see pp. 118–19ff.

127 See Hayek, 1944, pp. 73–4.

128 Ibid., pp. 107–9. In general on the Hayekian analysis of totalitarianism and its polemical objectives, see Douglas, 1984, pp. 103–18.

129 See Hayek, 1944, pp. 115–18. On these aspects, see Butler, 1983, pp. 83–5.

130 See Hayek, 1944, pp. 122–3.

131 See Mises, 1944b, pp. 44, 45, 126, 133, and 1981, pp. 528ff.

132 See Hayek, 1944, p. 124.

133 Ibid., pp. 125ff.

134 The case in point – see Hayek, 1952a, pp. 25–7 – was an example of how the spread of ideas can induce an individual to act. On this matter, see Buckley, 1977, pp. 95–106.

135 Hayek, 1944, pp. 129.

136 Ibid., pp. 129–34. On Schmitt, see also pp. 59n., 139; 1960, pp. 485n., 487n.; 1973–9, I, pp. 71, 139, 161–62n., 179n., II, pp. 144, 167n., 191n, and III, pp. 125, 192–3n., 194–5n. In Hayek, 1944, Spengler and Moeller van der Bruck («the patron-saint of National-Socialism») were seen as the typical examples of how the mixture of socialism, Prussianism and aversion to liberalism was destined to evolve into National Socialism. Concerning Spengler, Hayek wrote that in *Prussianism and Socialism* «he merely gave expression to ideas widely held by German socialists which will now be evident»; of Moeller van der Bruck, that his Third Reich «was intended to give the Germans a socialism adapted to their nature and undefiled by Western liberal ideas».

137 Hayek, 1944, p. 137n.

138 Ibid., pp. 141–3. Carr and Waddington were considered emblematic figures of the diffusion of these ideas in English culture. This critique is mentioned in Popper, 1957, p. 159n.

139 As well as scientism, Hayek pinpointed another source of the diffusion of totalitarian ideas as consisting in the attempt to make future events depend on union of the forces of organized capital with workers' organizations. Hayek's polemic thus tackled not only the movement of ideas that led to totalitarianism, but also the monopolistic organizations of capitalists. He explicitly wanted to avoid being «suspected of any tenderness toward the capitalists». The monopolistic organization of firms and trade unions constituted a danger for the liberal-democratic state, because they shifted decision-making power outside the bounds of representative organs. See Hayek, 1944, pp. 144–9.

140 Ibid., pp. 152–3.

141 The most complete analysis of *The Road to Serfdom* is Barry, *et al.*, 1984 which contains essays by Seldon, 1984, pp. xv–xxxii and by Giussurarson, 1984, pp. 1–23, dedicated to the historical, cultural and academic period in which it is set. The intellectual climate in which the book appeared is sketched by Gray, 1984b, pp. 25–42. Barry, 1984a, pp. 43–64, draws attention to the responsibility of Mill

in the conversion of intellectuals to statism. Shearmur, 1984, pp. 65–85, compares and contrasts the explanations given by Hayek, Marx and Weber of the tendencies at work in modern societies. The highly topical nature of Hayek's exposure of the dangers involved in the 'Middle Way', is treated by Burton, 1984, pp. 87–115. Vaughn, 1984, pp. 117–42, deals with the problem of the ability of Hayek's evolutionistic conception to restore the liberal tradition in a world that is increasingly moulded by a capillary system of diffusion of ideas through the mass media.

142 Cassirer, 1946. On the differences between the interpretations of totalitarianism by Cassirer and Hayek, see Douglas, 1984, p. 105.

143 See Arendt, 1951.

144 That these were non-homogeneous interpretations did not, of course, escape the attention of their authors. Further confirmation of this divergence is given by the lack of reciprocal citations in their works. On the other hand, there is no lack of reciprocal book reviews. Only between Popper and Hayek was there a more closely intermeshed dialogue. Since some of them knew each other personally, this fact is rather curious, but it is explained by taking into account that an affinity of political ideas can be established only between Mises, Hayek and Popper.

145 See Röpke, 1942, 1944, 1947 and 1959.

146 Generally, Hayek (like Menger and Mises) missed no opportunity to underline the profound differences between the 'liberalism' of Mill and the authentic liberal tradition, going so far as to cast doubt on whether he could actually be considered a liberal thinker. As well as Hayek, 1951b, see for example: 1948, p. 11; 1952a, pp. 140, 178, 186, 200, 261 (on his relations with Comte), 158 (on his relations with Saint-Simon), 202 (on moral relativism); 1960, p. 61 «The *homo oeonomicus* was explicitly introduced, with much else that belongs to the rationalist rather than to the evolutionary tradition, only by the younger Mill»); 1967, p. 245; 1978, p. 127 (in the important essay 'Liberalism', where Mill is mentioned only on this page), 302; 1973–9, II, pp. 64 (from social justice to socialism), 98 (social justice); 1988, pp. 52 (collocation in constructivism), 65 ('saint of rationalism'), 148–9 (on the monocausal explanation, and on the fact that «he probably led more intellectuals into socialism than any other single person»). On the relation of Hayek with Mill, see Gray, 1984a, pp. 95–103.

147 On this aspect, see Machlup, 1977, pp. 39–40.

148 Among the many expressions of this belief, see the discussion of Hayekian theses in Kelsen, 1955.

149 In this regard, one may cite the example of the way their critique of totalitarianism failed to spread among historians of the phenomenon, or of the definition of Hayek in Quinton, 1967, p. 2, as a «magnificent dinosaur».

150 See Bosanquet, 1983, pp. 26–41; Barry, 1986a, p. 2; Gray, 1986, p. 42.

4

THE FATE OF DEMOCRACY

> Organizations are possible only as long as they are not directed against the organic or do it any injury [. . .] All attempts to coerce the living will of human beings into the service of something they do not want must fail. An organization cannot flourish unless it is founded on the will of those organized and serves their purposes.
> (Mises, *Socialism*)

1. *Law and politics*; 2. *Interventionism and the fate of democracy*; 3. *The mirage of social justice*

§ 1. LAW AND POLITICS

Between the publication of *The Constitution of Liberty* and *Law, Legislation and Liberty*, Hayek realized that the traditional doctrine of liberal constitutionalism[1] was no longer capable of safeguarding the principle of the *rule of law* against the threat of being overwhelmed by the concept of popular sovereignty, a concept akin to the secularization of divine omnipotence. Furthermore, interventionism had produced new forms of political aggregation and dynamics, which had afforded a glimpse of an alarming rift opening up between real political practice and constitutional forms. Faced with the phenomenon of legislative hypertrophy and the bankruptcy of interventionism, Hayek set himself the task of combating the influence of the constructivist mentality in the juridical sciences,[2] in order to restore the distinction between *law* and *rules of organization*.

Hayek thereby took a stand against several widespread tendencies in contemporary social philosophy, namely: democratic theory, which holds that the law depends on a decision by the legislator; the interventionism produced by Keynesian and socialistic economic theories, and the theory of the 'democratic rule of law' as it had developed above all through the influence of Kelsen's juridical and political philosophy.

In Hayek's assessment, this situation could not be resolved by simply updating constitutional doctrine so as to ensure that it would conform to political practice. Rather, a complete rethinking of the philosophy of public law was called for.

Within the broad sweep of the history of ideas, this conceptual framework constituted the object of his argument. If one turns to a philosophical appraisal, with the intent of fathoming the connection of catallactics with constitutional doctrine, Hayek's problem can be analysed as that of avoiding transformation of subjectivism into a relativism that would inhibit formation of an *order*. But he was also anxious to avoid the pitfall of allowing the quest for the best regime to turn into the *construction* of an organization by a majority. For as he saw it, the tendency towards legislative regulation of every form of associative life was none other than the result of democratic interventionism: a version of *constructivism*.

Directing his thoughts towards new constitutional forms, Hayek determined to quash the tendency to consider social reality as infinitely mouldable by abstract reason and by majority decisions that recognize no limits to their sphere of authority and their powers.

In *Law, Legislation and Liberty*, his aim was thus to demonstrate that the classical tripartition of power had failed because governments everywhere have overstepped the powers assigned to them by the constitution they invoke, and have done so with perfectly legal means. Such excesses, Hayek argued, had set the stage for growing disbelief in the existence of an independent system of justice. They also provided a foothold for legislation that did not disavow coercion, even condoning its use as a means to achieve particular ends. Furthermore, the task of establishing the rules of conduct and of expressing the government had been attributed to the legislative assembly itself. Hence the rueful conclusion that «the first attempt to secure individual liberty by constitutions has evidently failed», and the need to make a critical review of the interpretation of democracy as a doctrine holding that the majority can legislate on every particular subject.[3]

This theme effectively constituted a leitmotiv in Hayek's thought that can be picked out as early as *The Road to Serfdom*.[4] Even in this work Hayek had shown that the crucial element blurring the distinction between totalitarian state and democratic state was the fact that the law had become a tool for the accomplishment of political ends. Having started out as «utilitarian machinery» with the avowed goal of furthering the development of individuality, it had now become transformed into a «'moral' institution». Significantly, the relationship between the lack of limits in the field of legislation, on the one hand, and totalitarianism, on the other, had begun with legislation aiming to produce particular effects by selecting the ends and imposing them upon individuals. In this way the state had been transmuted into a tool for the imposition of moral and practical behaviour. The paradoxical conclusion of such a doctrine is that «the Nazi or any other collectivist state is 'moral', while the liberal state is not».[5]

At the root of the dissolution of the boundary between democracy and tyranny lay the huge popularity of the belief that economic planning would allow a more efficient use and fairer distribution of resources. This in its turn gave rise to the ethical need for state intervention through legislation directed towards the fulfilment of social goals that would be binding on the members of society. Schmitt, «the legal theorist of National Socialism», was therefore quite right in elaborating a theory that «opposes to the liberal Rechtsstaat (i.e. the Rule of Law) the national-socialist ideal of the *gerechte Staat* (the just state)». In fact, however, substantive justice of this kind involves discrimination among people, so that «any policy aiming at a substantive idea of distributive justice» leads to destruction of the rule of law and hence to totalitarian political organization.[6]

The fatal threat to democracy was thereby identified as the lack of any limits placed on legislation. «By giving the government unlimited powers the most arbitrary rule can be made legal: and in this way a democracy may set up the most complete despotism imaginable.» Therefore, in affirming that in a totalitarian regime the rule of law does not exist, Hayek was concerned less to deny the lawfulness of such a government's actions, than to emphasize a foregone conclusion. Given a situation in which «the use of the government's coercive powers will no longer be limited and determined by pre-established rules», the result cannot be other than a form of tyranny. It follows that the rule of law is identified with the limiting of legislation «to the kind of general rules known as formal law».[7]

As early as *The Road to Serfdom*, then, Hayek was well aware that the dangers posing a threat to democratic regimes consisted in failing to set unbreachable limits on legislative activity, and in preferring to rely on modifiable rules.

It was no aversion for democracy that enflamed Hayek's writings, then. On the contrary, he was driven by concern for its destiny. Hayek firmly believed that the struggle to affirm the «true and original meaning» of democracy should be carried on despite the fact that democracy, counter to expectations, had not «proved to be a certain protection against tyranny and oppression». It is therefore the facts that he presented – facts that no political theory can afford to ignore – that lead one to become disenchanted with democracy, and to reassess it as a «convention which enables any majority to rid itself of a government it does not like». Yet even in this understanding of the term, it conserves an «inestimable value».[8]

With *The Constitution of Liberty*, Hayek aimed to address this whole range of issues through a systematic exploration of political philosophy, elaborating a treatise on the best regime which can be considered among the most significant works of twentieth century liberalism. Numerous features of this work show it to be a landmark in the revival of liberalism – a milestone in the turn-around of an attitude that for decades had focused almost exclusively on defending itself, nearly always unsuccessfully, against the onslaughts of Marxism and interventionism.

One of the undisputed merits of Hayek to emerge from this discussion – and the same is true of Mises – is that he fully understood that the reconstruction of liberalism would have to start principally from a re-examination of the entire Western political tradition. A reconsideration of the relationship between *economic freedom* and *political freedom* was urgently necessary to ensure that analysis would no longer be founded on the philosophical background constituting the milieu in which the liberalism of classical political economy thrived and spawned its 'labour theory of value'. Instead, it should be grounded on the findings of subjectivist economics. A further merit of Hayek's work, seen slightly differently, is that it testifies to his shift towards an evolutionistic conception of phenomena and social institutions.

The period of interest in this discussion is the century which saw the decline of the liberal conception of the state. The earlier view of the state as a body whose goal was to remove obstacles that prevent society from drawing advantage from individual talents had given way to the conviction that all members of society should have equal initial opportunity and the same chance of success. The 'social state', Hayek argued, had brought about the subordination of individuals to society. As a result, the idea of individual freedom had been overshadowed by the belief that «government knows best how individual capacities can be used».[9]

A profound change had thus come about in the way the law was conceived, and reflection on this change became part and parcel of Hayek's enquiry into the process of corruption of political philosophy. This discipline had arisen in an age when practical and theoretical activity was set in a cosmological perspective, but now had to re-elaborate its own premises in order to avoid being reduced to sociology, history or theology. Such was the philosophical-political problem Hayek found himself grappling with, and as such his critique of modern trends in the philosophy of law should be evaluated. For his objective was not to elaborate a 'critical history of contemporary philosophy of law'; rather his aim was to find out the extent to which certain ideas in the field of law had contributed to the crisis of political philosophy.[10]

The issue of the use and social distribution of knowledge and abilities also had a bearing on reflections concerning the law, in that both knowledge and abilities were invoked to map out the distinction between *coercion* and *power*.[11] Arguing that power was required for the maintenance of the social order and consequently for elaboration of the distinction between law, coercion and order, Hayek resolved to sever his links with the liberalism of Milton, Burke, Acton and Burckhardt, who «have represented power as the archdevil».[12] His starting point was the fundamental principle of the liberal theory of law proclaimed by Savigny – «one of the great legal scholars of the last century». Hayek embarked on this series of reflections by asserting that 'the rule whereby the indivisible border is fixed within which the being and activity of each individual obtains a secure and free sphere is the law'. Far from resigning himself to the idea of forsaking the conception of the law as the foundation of freedom, Hayek explicitly set about its restoration.[13]

The object of Hayek's criticism was the way the concept of law as the spontaneous evolution of conduct rules had been replaced by a very different concept of law as human plans directed towards the achievement of specific ends. In other words, confusion had risen between «abstract rules» or «laws» and «specific or particular commands». One striking characteristic of the modern age, he felt, was precisely its replacement of *the law* («a 'once-and-for-all' command that is directed to unknown people and that is abstracted from all particular circumstances of time and place and refers only to such conditions as may occur anywhere and at any time») by *commands* directed towards particular subjects and for the achievement of specific ends.[14]

Faced with this situation, Hayek felt that it was desirable to have a state in which it was the laws that governed and not men: one where power would be limited to the implementation of general and abstract rules, while authority would be understood as the power «of enforcing the law».[15] The legislator's task would not be «to set up a particular order but merely to create conditions in which an orderly arrangement can establish and ever renew itself». One such condition would be that of assuring a certain regularity of behaviour by means of laws.[16]

Hayek's efforts to reconstruct the origins of the concept of rule of law, then, aimed to show that current tendencies essentially amounted to deviations from the tradition that could be considered the characteristic of Western civilization.[17]

In this effort towards reconstruction Hayek dwelt in particular on the doctrine of the *Rechtsstaat*. The theoretical and historical significance of this model (in which one might detect influence of the ideas of Kant and Humboldt) consists in its having drawn attention to the political and juridical necessity of making the administrative apparatus of the state into a *subject* of the law. In this battle, as is well known, German liberalism leapt into the fray with only meagre success. But the lawmakers of the time had clearly understood that the real threat to the survival of the *Rechtsstaat* did not come from the existence of a monarch or a legislator, but rather from the existence of «an elaborate administrative apparatus» that either was not subject to the law, or enjoyed a special discipline. In this manner they had anticipated the problem of our own times in which «the power of the professional administrator [. . .] is now the main threat to individual liberty».[18]

Reconsideration of these experiences thus led Hayek to conclude that the rule of law

> constitutes a limitation on the power of all government, including the powers of the legislature. It is a doctrine concerning what the law ought to be, concerning the general attributes that particular laws should possess. This is important because today the conception of the Rule of

> Law is sometimes confused with the requirement of mere legality in all government action. The Rule of Law, of course, presupposes complete legality, but this is not enough.

The concept of the rule of law was thus «a meta-legal doctrine or a political ideal» which was «part of the moral tradition of the community, a common ideal shared and unquestioningly accepted by the majority».[19]

The historical era in which Hayek was writing, however, was characterized by the hegemony of anti-liberal ideologies that not only called into question the achievements of the rule of law but actually jeopardized its very survival. Hence the 'restoration' of the distinction between *politics* and *law* became the cornerstone of a plan for constitutional reform aiming to establish effective «legal limits of administrative discretion».[20] It was a plan that presupposed the distinction between law and enactment of the legislative authority, as well as the end of the deplorable habit of using the term 'law' to define what «has been resolved in the appropriate manner by a legislative authority». This line of reasoning entailed the need to entrust «the task of laying down general rules and the task of issuing orders to the administration to distinct representative bodies and [to subject] their decisions to independent judicial review so that neither will overstep its bounds».[21]

If the law is entrusted with the task of averting violations of the private sphere, this need not mean that the state should take no interest in economic questions. It does mean, though, that there exist certain typologies of means that are best avoided in that they cannot be justified through motivations of public utility. The rule of law, Hayek contended, should be conceived as a «criterion which enables us to distinguish between those measures which are and those which are not compatible with a free system». Seen thus, the problem for Hayek no longer consisted in the extent of state intervention in the economic sphere, but rather in the «nature» of that intervention. For while certain activities undertaken by the state are likely to enhance the smooth functioning of the market, some will be no more than barely compatible with it, and yet others will hamper and throttle it. On this basis Hayek then went on to argue in favour of the validity even in the economic sphere of the principle that «a free society demands not only that the government have the monopoly of coercion but that it have the monopoly only of coercion and that in all other respects it operate on the same terms as everybody else».[22]

The decline of the law did not, however, begin as a consequence of the crisis of *laissez-faire* (whose ideology Hayek did not care to defend, in any case) but rather sprang from the unfolding of a much broader set of circumstances in which once again German affairs and culture were prominent. It was here that a reaction was sparked off that challenged the tradition of the rule of law and of the *law of nature* («the framework within which our central problems have been mainly discussed»). The dispute centred partly on the issue of 'jurisprudence of interests' and the doctrines of historicism, but was kindled above all by legal positivism. The upshot was that the common matrix of the schools of natural law, seen as consisting in the 'existence of rules which are not of the deliberate making of any lawgiver' was replaced by a purely formal conception of the *Rechtsstaat* «which required merely that all action of the state be authorized by the legislature». Kelsen's 'pure theory of law' marked the culminating point of this process: «the definite eclipse of all traditions of limited government».[23]

In *The Constitution of Liberty*, the critique of Kelsenian doctrines for their role in leading towards that uncertainty in legal matters that is so characteristic of the modern age was not yet as radical as in *Law, Legislation and Liberty*. However, Hayek noted the influence of Kelsen's teachings on those who viewed the principle of the rule of law as an unacceptable restriction on the power of the majority; and he focused attention on the passages where Kelsen had called for an end to individual freedom in favour of collective freedom, and for the 'emancipation of democratism from liberalism'. Indeed, Hayek's critique did not restrict itself to the sphere of political influence but amounted to a full-blown attack on the pivotal idea of the Kelsenian system, namely:

> the identification of the state and the legal order. Thus the *Rechtsstaat* becomes an extremely formal concept and an attribute of all states, even a despotic one. There are no possible limits to the power of the legislator, and there are no 'so-called fundamental liberties'; and any attempt to deny to an arbitrary despotism the character of a legal order represents 'nothing but the naiveté and presumption of natural-law thinking [. . .] Even the distinction between jurisdiction and administrative acts is practically obliterated. In short, every single tenet of the traditional conception of the Rule of Law is represented as a metaphysical superstition.

In this manner Kelsen's theories had thrown open «the doors to the victory of the fascist and bolshevist will of the State». The positivist doctrine according to which «the state must not be bound by the law» was once again shown to lie at the heart of anti-liberal and totalitarian ideologies.[24]

Naturally the decline of the idea of the rule of law was also influenced by other matters and other juridical doctrines which Hayek neither overlooked nor underestimated.[25] Yet the chief object of his criticism remained the theories of his one-time teacher at the University of Vienna.

The Constitution of Liberty thus aimed to show the superiority of the principles of the rule of law compared to all attempts to replace it by the 'rule of men'. Subsequently, faced with the havoc wreaked by the spread of the rational constructivist mentality in the field of law, Hayek reached the conviction that mere updating was quite inadequate. For after classical liberal constitutionalism had lost the first round, there was clearly little reason to hope it would win the second simply by re-entering the contest with the same instruments as before against an adversary which in the meantime had mustered hefty reinforcements.

Hence the attempt by *Law, Legislation and Liberty* to re-establish liberalism on a more rigorous search for and definition of its essence. Tackling the issues of the nature of the law, of order and of constitutionalism in an evolutionalist perspective, Hayek reinterpreted the classical problems of political philosophy. At the centre of his reflections lay the destiny of liberal institutions in the era of all the new patterns of organized social interests that had sprung up following the rise of theories of the *welfare state*. His outlook was deeply pessimistic as he contemplated the seriousness of the situation, as is shown by his assertion that

> the predominant model of liberal democratic institutions, in which the same representative body lays down the rules of just conduct and directs government, necessarily leads to a gradual transformation of the spontaneous order of a free society into a totalitarian system conducted in the service of some coalition of organized interests.[26]

Consequently, it was necessary, Hayek argued, to re-examine the concept that legislation is a means to obtain desired changes in society which conform to a «coherent design». For this concept brings with it the fear that «if the principles which at present guide that process are allowed to work themselves out to their logical consequences, law as we know it as the chief protection of the freedom of the individual is bound to disappear». Among the causes of this transformation Hayek ranked the substitution of public law for private law in the role of guide of jurisprudence: a substitution which had had the effect of subordinating private law to «the rules of organization of government».[27]

Once again a situation had arisen that provided evidence of the way the field of law experienced repercussions of the constructivist mentality that was favourable to greater state intervention in the social sphere. As a result of this mentality, a dense jungle of legislative measures had sprung up, extending throughout society, producing a new function of the law. The idea that the task performed by the lawmaker was 'revolutionary' thus became associated with the idea that the 'wisdom' of the law was an attribute of the democratic legislator rather than of the juridical tradition.

The increasing prestige of the anti-liberal mentality in the field of juridical science eventually resulted in victory for Schmitt's views, the goal of which was «concrete order formation». The law was no longer understood as being a set of «abstract rules which make possible the formation of a spontaneous order by the free action of individuals through limiting the range of their actions», but instead as «the instrument of arrangement or organization by which the individual is made to serve concrete purposes».[28]

Surveying the impasse, which he felt to be the prelude of a 'juridical totalitarianism' and of politically faceless tyranny, Hayek did not restrict himself to a critique of the «interventionist fallacy» of legal positivism in its guise as an aspect of constructivist rationalism. He maintained that the law did not derive «from the will of a legislator» but was instead something that «existed for ages before it occurred to man that he could make or alter it». In this perspective, the «law, in the sense of enforced rules of conduct, is undoubtedly coeval with the society». For «only the observance of common rules makes the peaceful existence of individuals in society possible».[29]

Thus even in the evolution of law two opposing traditions were identified. The positions they embodied were, respectively, deliberate production of the law by human will, and independence of the law. The former, clearly enough, represents the object of his criticism (among other reasons, because in the modern age it has come to be identified with the formation of the modern state which has laid claim to absolute power of lawmaking), while the latter is the tradition of *natural law*.[30]

As a complex of *abstract rules of conduct* independent of any particular goal, the law must therefore be applicable «to an unknown number of further instances» which «enable an order of actions to form itself wherein the individuals can make feasible plans».Yet this process, for all its *spontaneity*, was not *natural* but *cultural*. As such it could flounder and was therefore in need of continual and rapid correction. But the corrections introduced could not always be drawn from 'case law', especially when «wholly new circumstances» had come into play, since case law was at times «too slow to bring about the desirable adaptation». Hence the need for legislation to be understood as constant and step-by-step perfecting of the abstract rules of conduct by lawmakers and legislators; hence also the need to refrain from rejecting legislation and thereby also from entrusting the formation of law to spontaneous evolutionism, for this would lead to a loss of the distinction between 'good law' and 'bad law'.[31]

Hayek, then, did not conceive of evolution as a biological process which, contradicting Hume's laws, would transform *de facto* reality into a positive 'datum', but neither did he view it as the product of reflection and rational construction. Rather, his depiction of evolution was of a process «in the course of which spontaneous growth of customs and deliberate improvements of the particulars of an existing system have constantly interacted».[32]

The function of the law thus cannot be identified with the protection of individual expectations, but rather with the provision of guarantees in the use of certain means. In this connection, Hayek ascribed great importance to unforeseeable changes in knowledge, given that they were likely to have a twofold effect. Not only would they induce the emergence of new ends which would in their turn make it impossible to guarantee all individual expectations, but they would also make it possible to forestall the lack of elasticity that so frequently occurs whenever new situations arise, even resulting in the fossilization of behaviour and threatening to precipitate «breakdown of the whole order». For not all rules are capable of assuring an order, and «the obedience to unsuitable rules may well become the cause of disorder».[33]

Consequently, the less the rules of conduct set themselves concrete objectives to attain, the more effective they will be. They should confine themselves to favouring an abstract order allowing individuals to formulate expectations which, on the basis of their knowledge, have «a good chance of being correct». The task of the law is to decide «which expectations must be assured in order to maximize the possibility of expectations in general being fulfilled». In so doing, it will have to make «a distinction between such 'legitimate' expectations which it [. . .] must protect and others which it must allow to be disappointed». The foundation of every universal rule of conduct, and likewise the guarantee of order, will reside in a delimitation of the areas of individual action: «law, liberty and property are an inseparable trinity».[34]

From such considerations Hayek concluded that «the law indeed does not serve any purpose but countless different purposes of different individuals»; it is not a means to achieve ends «but merely a condition for the successful pursuit of most purposes». A relation between ends and rules cannot and must not subsist: «the order of actions is a factual state of affairs distinct from the rules which contribute to its formation». For this reason «*an abstract order can be the aim of the rules of conduct*».[35]

It follows that the target of Hayek's polemics was not so much the concept of legislation itself as the manner in which it was conceived in modern times. It had become associated, Hayek argued, with the rise of the absolutistic bureaucratic state, the latter thereby coming to represent the exclusive source of the law. A conception of this type fosters the belief that it is necessary for there to be «a supreme legislator whose power cannot be limited», together with the idea that «anything laid down by that supreme legislator is law and only that which expresses his will is law».[36]

The outcome of the lack of distinction between «universal rules of just conduct and the rules of organization of government» was a pernicious confusion between *private* and *public* law, i.e. a blurring of the demarcation between the principal duties of the government. For one of the characteristics of the modern age, Hayek felt, was that it tends to obscure the borders between «the enforcement of the universal rules of just conduct» and «the direction of the organization built up to provide various services for the citizens at large».[37]

It was therefore becoming imperative, in Hayek's view, to introduce distinctions into what is denominated 'law'. The term *nomos* should be used to designate «a universal rule of just conduct applying to an unknown number of future instances and equally to all persons in the objective circumstances described by the rule», while the term *thesis* should denominate «any rule which is applicable only to particular people or in the service of the ends of rulers». This effectively required restoration of the distinction between private and public law.[38] It also entailed the need for modification in the conception of constitutional law, in the sense that instead of being considered «the source of all other law», constitutional law should be viewed as a «superstructure erected to secure the maintenance of *the law*». For if one were to attribute to the constitution the character of law in the material sense, this could even lead to a conception of the law as a political measure aiming at the achievement of economic and social results, hence to the «*transformation of private law into public law by 'social legislation'*».[39]

All this has indeed come to pass. The conception of *social legislation* as having a guiding function, leading «private activity towards particular ends and to the benefit of particular groups», has transformed the state into a dispenser of benefits. The state has been charged with the task of removing the sources of malcontent, no heed being paid to the legitimacy of malcontent. The upshot has been a radical change in political life and the goals of legislation. This change has not stopped short of making the legitimation of government dependent on the latter's ability to satisfy every subjective aspiration of social groups.[40]

Mulling over the ideas put forward in *What is Justice?*, Hayek reopened his never completely abated polemics against Kelsen. If «nature can be neither just nor unjust», since «nothing that is not subject to human control can be just (or moral)», then «the desire to make something capable of being just is not necessarily a valid argument for our making it subject to human control». Hayek intended to show thereby that if «only situations which have been created by human will can be called just or unjust, the particulars of a spontaneous order cannot be just or unjust». On the contrary, and despite its good intentions, an organization aiming to attain the good, conceiving its members as tools to reach this end, will unquestionably be unjust. Consequently, one can speak of 'social' or 'distributive' justice only within the perspective of an *organization*, but definitely not in the perspective of an *order*;[41] furthermore, inasmuch as it is bound to consider its members as tools, no organization can claim to be 'just'.

If this was the outcome of the confusion between law and direct government, then the need to distinguish between them became a pressing political problem calling for urgent solution. Such a distinction was precisely what Hayek set out to establish on the basis of the criterion of universalizability of rules, itself resting on consideration of the «rules of justice as prohibitions and as subject to a negative test». The background of ideas informing the stance adopted by Hayek was, of course, Kant's philosophy of law and Popper's conception of the «laws of nature as prohibitions». The affinity here resided, according to Hayek, in the common conviction that «we can always only endeavour to approach truth, or justice, by persistently eliminating the false or unjust, but can never be sure that we have achieved final truth or justice».[42]

In this manner, an order would be identified not with mere *biological growth*, but with a cultural process that, in its endeavour to preserve the fundamental value of abstractness of the rules and their universal applicability, would require constant improvement. This was the process that Hayek identified as the foundation of liberalism.

Opposition to legal positivism and its legacy therefore focused on the nature of the «objective criteria of justice», on the issue of their being either 'negative' or 'positive', and in addition on the way justice and its attendant problems tended to be conceived as «a matter of will, or interests or emotions». It follows that Hayek's animosity towards legal positivism was not stirred simply by motives of a theoretical character. But to the extent to which such motives did subsist, they show Hayek's concern to speak out against the attempted assimilation of liberalism to legal positivism; for if such an assimilation were to be carried through, this would portend the end of liberalism. In other words, according to Hayek the relation between the two movements cannot be analysed as compenetration or continuity, but rather as one of genuine opposition. The spread of legal positivism had led to the decline of classical liberalism, he contended, replacing it by a sort of «constructivist pragmatism» – inspired by James, Dewey and Pareto – which, «profoundly anti-liberal» though it might be, represents «the foundations of that pseudo-liberalism which in the course of the last generation has arrogated the name».[43]

Law, Legislation and Liberty thus shows Hayek resuming his attack on the ideology of legal positivism for which he had set the stage in *The Constitution of Liberty*. In *Law, Legislation and Liberty*, not only did he plan to demonstrate that legal positivism is «a naive expression of the constructivist fallacy» and that its thesis regarding the origin of the law from a «will of the legislator is simply false», but he also intended to make clear what political consequences were likely to ensue from the conception of the state as an *organization*.[44]

Legal positivism was guilty, in Hayek's eyes, of the same erroneous stance as Weber, who considered that «'order' is throughout something which is 'valid' or 'binding', which is to be enforced or contained in a maxim of law». Following in the steps of the socialists and positivists, Weber viewed order «anthropomorphically» as organization, Hayek argued. And since in Weber's position little or no importance is ascribed to the existence of a spontaneous order, with the law seen only as *taxis* rather than as *cosmos*, he «blocks for himself the access to the genuine theoretical problems of a science of society».[45]

The same held true, Hayek reasoned, for the Kelsenian conception of the law founded on the belief that «the legislator creates the *content* of that law and in doing so has a completely free hand». For Kelsen used the term 'order' not only to indicate «the 'norms' prescribing a particular arrangement» but also to describe «a factual state of affairs». In so doing, Kelsen made a series of mistakes such as that of taking «existence» as a synonym of «validity», deriving the latter logically «from some act of will of the ultimate authority», and used «the terms 'creating', 'setting' or 'positing' (*erzeugen* or *setzen*) to include everything that is 'constituted by human acts'». All these arguments then led him to consider both «the products of human design» and also «spontaneous growths as the rules of language or moral or etiquette», as 'set, that is, positive norms'.[46]

In this perspective, Hayek did not attribute any particular interest to the question of the scientific nature of the 'pure theory of law', or to the various problems surrounding its relation to 'normative science', its meaning and its empirical or logical-mathematical nature. He confined himself to observing that an examination of these questions from an epistemological point of view «would show that Kelsen's conception of a 'science' which 'seeks to discover the nature of law itself' rests on what Karl Popper has called 'methodological essentialism'». The conclusion was that «the 'pure theory of law' is thus one of those pseudosciences like Marxism and Freudianism which are represented as irrefutable because all their statements are true by definition but tell us nothing about what is the fact». Yet these were not the primary issues for Hayek. He was far more anxious to expose the political consequences of the identification of *existence* with *validity*, and of the transformation of the concept of legal coercion from a means to ensure observance of the universal rules of just conduct into a means for the achievement of particular ends. For in this manner Kelsen's legal positivism had assumed the guise of a *socialist ideology*. More specifically, it had turned into a form of constructivism characterized by the thesis of the «omnipotence of the legislative power». It was now no less than «an ideology born out of the desire to achieve complete control over social order, and the belief that it is in our power to determine deliberately, in any manner we like, every aspect of this social order».[47]

Far from being the philosopher of democracy, Kelsen is thus revealed as the one who supplied the legal tools to modern *totalitarian democracy*. Hayek diagnosed these tools as consisting in the theorizing of the power of the legislator as unlimited power, in failing to consider individual freedom as an irrevocable value and in transforming political freedom into the «collective freedom of the community». Inasmuch as Kelsenian legal positivism held the will of the majority to be unlimited, it presented itself as «the chief ideological support of the unlimited powers of democracy». It followed, Hayek argued, that the factors determining the 'law' would be first and foremost the political ends of the aforesaid majority. But this would leave legislative regulation totally unconstrained by any theoretical limit, thereby precluding the possibility of a rational evaluation of the human interests that have come into conflict. Kelsen, then, effectively handed over the power of resolving social problems and political debate to a majority: in other words, to what could be considered the modern form of a physical clash. The result could hardly be other than a form of relativism out of which ominous political developments were to loom up.[48]

Consequently, Hayek contended, Kelsen's claim to be able to «unmask all other theories of law as ideologies and to have provided the only theory which is not an ideology» appeared quite unfounded. For in fact he accomplished nothing more than replacing one ideology by another. Moreover, by postulating that «all orders maintained by force are orders of the same kind, deserving the description (and dignity) of an order of law», legal positivism played a part in undermining the defences of the «guardians of the law» against the «advance of arbitrarian government». In this, Hayek shared the misgivings voiced by Gustav Radbruch and Emil Brunner. In particular, his position was scarcely different from that of Brunner, who claimed that 'the totalitarian state is simply and solely legal positivism in political practice'. A certain bitterness may therefore be detectable in Kelsen's finding that 'from the point of view of the science of law, the law (*Recht*) under the Nazi government was law (*Recht*)'. But if the science of law and political philosophy had fallen into the dramatic plight of possessing no theoretical tools to distinguish among regimes, part of the blame must lie squarely on his shoulders.[49]

To avert disquieting prospects of this kind, Hayek believed it was necessary to recognize that they are bound up with an erroneous conception of the law. What was at issue was not an ineluctable destiny of democracy, but rather a false conception of democracy and of the relation between politics and law. A remedy could be found by resuming the debate concerning relations between law on the one hand and morals and politics on the other, taking up the discussion again from the point at which the deviation induced by legal positivism had been introduced.

For with order conceived as spontaneous evolution, such problems would assume a somewhat different shape. It would then become feasible to deal with the question of the lawfulness of the imposition of moral rules on individual dissenters. No longer would the attitude go unchallenged whereby a justification for coercion is sought through appeal to the latter's function as an instrument to defend the private domain. Nor could coercion be justified by exempting from the control of law all «actions which affect nobody but the individuals who peform them».[50]

Yet the aspects which appear to be of paramount importance are the interpretation and favourable reassessment of the 'law of nature'. In a move to parry legal positivism, which had had the affrontery to use this term to denominate theories of law counter to his own, Hayek put forward once again the law of nature, with the meaning that the law is 'the product not of any rational design but a process of evolution and natural selection, an unintended product whose function we can learn to understand, but whose present significance may be wholly different from the intentions of its creators'. The ideas whose presence can be felt here belong less to the tradition of modern natural right – which in the Hayekian framework tends to coincide with rationalism – than to the Humeian concept of *natural law* (which in fact is explicitly mentioned). For in conformity with the lines of reasoning set forth above, Hayek did not believe that the rules of conduct are 'natural' (in the sense of belonging to an «external and eternal order of things»), nor that they are «permanently implanted in an unalterable nature of man, or even in the sense that man's mind is so fashioned». Yet he stopped far short of maintaining that they are «the product of a deliberate choice» by man. As fundamental components of the social order, he argued, the rules of conduct, «are not dependent on any one person's decision and will often not be alterable by any concrete act of will». Accordingly, in rejecting both the interpretation of «law as construct of a supernatural force» and equally its interpretation as «the deliberate construct of any human mind», Hayek planned to open up an evolutionistic perspective that had very little in common with rationalistic theories of the law or nature or with legal positivism.[51]

The critique of legal positivism was thus first and foremost a demonstration of the consequences resulting from its hypotheses concerning the nature of law. Indeed, it was not Hayek's intention to compose a history of contemporary philosophy of law, or to write an essay on the incongruities and mistakes of Kelsen. His real design was to shed light on the way legal positivism and Kelsen himself had contributed to the decadence of political philosophy, sapping its capacity to combat relativism and totalitarianism

The crucial point around which the dispute centred was the question of whether the Kelsenian doctrine of legal positivism could be considered as also constituting a solution to the repercussions it had generated. Hayek wished to highlight the truth of the belief that there exist no alternatives to the relativistic foundation of democracy. If the law is conceived as an organization imposed by a majority, and the prerogatives of sovereignty are thereby conferred upon it, the end result, as in the case of Weber, ultimately stifles «the access to the genuine theoretical problems of a science of society». All that is accomplished is the transfer of political and social antagonism, deemed to be ineradicable, into juridical forms.

Essentially, then, Hayek intended his critique of the theories of Kelsen to act as a spotlight trained on the unbridgeable gap between liberalism and the theory of democracy as value, together with the dangers stemming from the latter.

§ 2. INTERVENTIONISM AND THE FATE OF DEMOCRACY

Even before the symptoms of decadence of the Western political tradition began to be manifested in the field of law, they had started to make themselves felt in the field of social philosophy with the success of what Mises and Hayek defined as *interventionism, étatisme* and the '*middle way*'.[52] If the judgment they passed on the economic-political form of socialism was bereft of any uncertainties when they asserted that it paved the way straight to totalitarianism, no less peremptory was their judgment on the consequences of the spread of this mentality. The doctrine of interventionism claimed that there exists a system of economic co-operation, which is feasible as a form of economic organization, that is neither capitalistic nor socialist. This supposed 'middle way' was conceived as an organization based on private ownership of the means of production, though government intervention was envisioned, by means of commands and prohibitions, in the exercise of ownership rights.

Mises did not restrict himself to contesting the efficiency of an economic organization of this type. He went as far as to challenge its very feasibility, emphasizing that the subject-value theory is valid not merely in the framework of a market system, but in every economic system.[53]

This argument was to figure as a constant element in the work of Mises, constituting the premise of his critique of interventionism. Viewing interventionism as a product of the *anti-capitalistic mentality*[54], he assessed it as an attempt to overcome the contraposition between capitalism and socialism in a social model characterized by a *mixed economy* that would compound the advantages but not the disadvantages of the two.

The critique of interventionism is thus one aspect of the awareness that the foundations of social science and of political philosophy were being undermined, and that this quandary would be impossible to resolve without calling on the findings of subjectivist economics. Interventionism itself, on the other hand, gave the impression of being hidebound, held in the leash of the old theories, believing socialism and capitalism to be reconcilable. It failed to realize that although their conciliation was a problem that could be meaningful within the framework of classical political economy, it was meaningless in an economic system founded on the sovereignty of the consumer.

As a model aiming to reconcile highly sensitive economic, political and ethical issues, interventionism undeniably achieved enormous popularity in its various formulations. But the truth is that it was still primarily an economic policy: an attempt at problem-solving without a solid theoretical basis. Mises and Hayek thus devoted their efforts to showing up the fragility of its theoretical premises and the incompatibility of its outcome with the maintenance of a democratic system.

In the short term, this was a contest in which the theses of Mises and Hayek fought a losing battle.[55] What was supposed to be a 'cultural operation', one of the most radically innovative[56] ever attempted within the sphere of social science, was mistaken for the lament of the old guard bemoaning the passing of the 'old' liberalism and expressing hostility towards the 'new' liberalism that was opening to the requirements and social problems of its day. In the era of the hegemony of Marxist and 'progressive' culture – the obtuseness and harshness of which fell not far short of equalling the prevailing tenor of totalitarian regimes – Mises and Hayek found themselves confronted by a wall of indifference and ostracism. The man who at the outset of the 1930s had been the most celebrated economist after Keynes was now downgraded to not much better than a pamphleteer.

As well as distinguishing between interventionism and socialism, Mises identified two fundamental types of interventionism; and he decided that both were condemned to fail or degenerate into chaos because of their claim to be able to achieve their objectives, while flouting the universal, necessary and a priori laws of economics. Interventionism thus took on the appearance of the modern version of identification of the state with God, and of confusion between will and power.[57] In reducing economic science to economic policy, interventionism believed it would be able to achieve its political and social ends by making price determination dependent on politicians instead of the market. It did not realize that «democracy is inextricably linked with capitalism. It cannot exist where there is planning.» Interventionism therefore appeared as a glorified version of the illusory belief that a planned system can be democratically governed.[58]

Planning and interventionism, Mises argued, are forms of political control incompatible with the market economy and democracy. They are attempts to press economic science and the laws of the market into service to fulfil the ethical aim of redistribution of wealth. Thus interventionism is not a compromise between socialism and capitalism, but rather a system in its own right whose theories on price control lead to socialism.[59]

Liberalism can therefore be analysed as a response to the question of whether the interests of individuals or those of rulers should become predominant in society. Clearly both can go wrong, but this was not the crux of the matter. The central question, in Mises's opinion, was the need to choose between «spontaneous action of each individual versus the exclusive action of the government»: between «freedom versus government omnipotence». For behind intellectuals' propensity to plan there lay the design to deprive individuals of the power to make their own 'subjective' decisions in order to propel them towards choices held to be 'objective'.[60] The main objective of liberalism would thus be to criticize the dogma of the inevitability of omnipotent government.

The essays gathered together in *Planning for Freedom* show Mises setting himself the task of endowing the expression 'planning for freedom' with a meaning different from that of social-economic planning that aspires to substantial freedom and equality. On the contrary, planning as Mises envisaged it meant striving towards the removal of the impediments to individual freedom, inasmuch as the latter would further economic prosperity.[61] His reflections in this collection are therefore chiefly a development of his critical observations on the problem of bureaucratization. Mises again took up the Weberian theme of the 'steel cage' as the fate of the process of rationalization, but in the Misesian assessment it was less a case of its fate than simply a situation that could and had to be overcome.

The phenomenon of bureaucratization now moved centre stage in the political arena of the time, becoming a classic example of the conflict between individual freedom and the bureaucratic state.[62]

Given the universal scope of this phenomenon, the explanation of bureaucratism could not be divorced, in Mises's opinion, from the phenomenon of interventionism. Through the latter «the tyrannical rule of an irresponsible and arbitrary bureaucracy» was taking the place of the democratic system by subjecting civilian life to regulations in the form of government decrees and regulations – not laws, it should be noted. The propensity towards government control over economic activity and education was passed off as a panacea for all ills, and as an inevitable and positive historical tendency. Accordingly, without any constitutional modifications, a class of government officials drew their legitimation from the belief that greater state intervention was required for the sake of relieving social and economic injustice, and thereby they appropriated the tasks of legislative power.[63] Hence the aversion of bureaucracy for the market and free enterprise. One may conclude, Mises contended, that contrary to the theorizations of those who would have us believe that bureaucratism is simply the way capitalism tries to arrest its own decline, it is not in fact the necessary evolution of the market, but is instead a tool to usher in the totalitarian state.[64]

From a different perspective, the study of bureaucratism reveals how socialist utopias degenerate into totalitarianism. For when politicians are entrusted with the power to establish artificial prices, the eventual outcome is the same as the results of a planned economy, in which abolition of economic calculation degenerates into chaos[65] Mises contended that the stimulus to select the solution felt to be most suitable from the economic point of view is in abeyance in bureaucratized systems as well, a feature which causes wastage of resources instead of profit. A decrease in investment possibilities results, the repercussions of which will be paid by future generations.[66] The bureaucratization of society is therefore not the price of democracy, but rather its negation, since it implies tearing down its two pillars: «the primacy of the law and the budget». With the people and their representatives deprived of the power to decide how much and when to spend, and this power attributed to the bureaucrats, a slide towards a regime that can scarcely be considered democratic is insidiously set in motion. And indispensable though bureaucracy may be for the purposes of governing, the key element to which a democratic government needs to pay the utmost care in order to ensure its own survival is containment of the expansion of bureaucracy.[67]

The apprehensions voiced by Mises are therefore similar to those of Hayek in *The Road to Serfdom.* Both spoke out against the danger that if state affairs are conducted according to principles other than those of the market, the outcome may well result in a non-democratic state. The most urgent requirement at this point, in Mises's view, was to go back to the problem of who should be in command in a democratic society, to enquire whether the system of bureaucratic control or that of economic freedom was likely to be more efficient.[68] It was imperative to prevent the solution of economic problems being entrusted exclusively to professionals. Democracy would become impossible if citizens were not in a position to form their own opinion on the main problems.[69]

Faced with the success of the new conceptions of the law and of interventionist policies inspired by the concept of 'social justice', Hayek too began to explore the question of the fate of democracy.[70] The fact that, contrary to expectations, democracy «has not proved to be a certain protection against tyranny and oppression», together with the existence of a «growing loss of faith in democracy among thinking people», led him to a series of despondent reflections. Considering democracy as a «convention which enables any majority to rid itself of a government it does not like», Hayek expressed disbelief in the possibility of a *democratic political philosophy*. Yet democracy still had an «inestimable value»; while far from being *the* ideal political regime, it was nevertheless«a wholesome method of arriving at widely acceptable political decisions», a «convention». Its defects would come to light when all this was overlooked, with democracy being transformed into a «pretext for enforcing substantially egalitarian aims». Equally fallacious, in Hayek's eyes, was the assumption that attributing the task of controlling government activity to the majority would prove to be the most satisfactory means of dispensing with the constitutional safeguards set up specifically to limit government powers. For under this assumption democracy would be converted from its nature as a method into a theory of a political regime with the characteristic of placing no limits on the power of the majority.[71]

Modern democratic doctrine was thus a sign of the decadence of the age and should be subjected to a series of criticisms endeavouring to take it back to its original meaning.[72] It is undeniable that the lack of norms having the function of limiting the majority's power of coercion led Hayek to prefer «non-democratic government under the law to unlimited (and therefore essentially lawless) democratic government». The central point, however, was the conviction that a democracy lacking any limits was unable to reflect the will of the majority, and could be exploited for «gratification of the *will* of the separate interest groups which add up to a majority». This was a congenital defect, and Hayek, unlike so many 'reformers' of democratic theory – even those who were critical of its degeneration into a bureaucratic regime – believed it could be corrected only by leading it back to a 'method' underpinned by the tradition of liberal and market constitutionalism. The «great tragedy» of democracy thus consisted in the fact of its having entrusted one single assembly with the power both of controlling the government and of establishing what should be considered as 'law'. For the outcome, crudely disguised as the «pious belief that such a democratic government will carry out the will of the people», effectively empowered government to bypass the law.[73]

Democracy is in this way one of the many terms that has taken on a different meaning from its original content. Initially it «meant no more than that whatever ultimate power there is should be in the hands of the majority of the people or their representatives. *But it said nothing about the extent of that power.*» Consequently, from the fact that «the *opinion* of the majority should prevail it by no means follows that their *will* on particular matters should be unlimited».[74]

From this point of view, the attribution of unlimited power to the people or their representatives appears to be the consequence of the blurring of borders between *opinion*, *will* and *truth*, as well as being the result of a lack of awareness of the limits of human knowledge. This was a danger that the great theorists of representative government had tried to sidestep with the theory of the separation of powers; Hayek proposed to thwart it by distinguishing between *nomos* and *taxis*,[75] and by differentiating the powers of the two representative assemblies. In Hayek's framework, this should take place with the exclusion of the parties (who should concern themselves only with «matters of concrete *will*, the satisfaction of the particular interest of the people who combine to form them») from formation of the *nomos*. In fact, this process should not be placed «in the hands of representatives of particular interests but in the hands of a representative sample of the prevailing opinion, persons who should be secured against the pressure of particular interests». Consequently, noting that «democracy and limited government have become irreconcilable conceptions», it was necessary to search for a new expression to embody the concept of «limited democracy». The objective should be to leave supreme authority to the «opinion of the *demos*» but to prevent «the naked power of the majority, its *kratos*» from doing «rule-less violence to individuals». Invoking Locke, Hayek thus declared that «the majority should rule (*archein*) by 'established *standing laws*, promulgated and known to the people, and not by extemporary decrees'»; associating *demos* and *archein*, this complex of rules could be defined as *demarchy*.[76] Democracy, Hayek believed, would be saved only by curbing its tendency, held by many to be ineluctable, to become distorted and end up as «totalitarian democracy».[77]

Hayek placed a quotation from Hume as an epigraph above the paragraph of *Law, Legislation and Liberty* in which he most systematically expounded his model of a constitution. This question is, naturally, highly significant of his intentions:

> in all cases it must be advantageous to know what is the most perfect in the kind, that we may be able to bring any real constitution or form of government as near it as possible, by such gentle alterations and innovations as may not give too great a disturbance to society.

If this is not sufficient to absolve Hayek from the charge of having forsaken his principles and having himself carried out an operation of 'constitutional engineering',[78] it should additionally be stressed that his chief concern was to stimulate debate on two centuries of constitutional experiences. These had been centuries in which the general hope was that separation of legislative from executive and judicial could prove sufficient «to subject government and the individuals to rules of just conduct».[79]

But this hope had been vain, Hayek reflected, and its result had come to be identified with the limits of the liberal-democratic constitutional experience. These limits could be overcome, however, by elaborating a constitutional model which «in normal times» would oblige individuals «to do particular things only in accordance with the recognized rules of just conduct designed to define and protect the individual domain of each». One of its salient characteristics would be a fundamental clause «not intended to define the functions of government but merely to define the limits of its coercive powers». The other would be the proposal to entrust «the task of stating the general rules of just conduct to a representative body, distinct from the body which is entrusted with the task of government»,[80] one which, moreover, is differently composed.

Following in the footsteps of eighteenth-century theorists of representative government, Hayek believed that the legislative assembly should not be representative of 'factions', but rather should reflect the «general opinion about what is right». This objective could be reached by recourse to a special electoral system that would render its components «independent from the support of any particular group». The task of such an assembly should be constitutionally limited «to passing general laws», so that «any specific or discriminating order it issued would be invalid». The peculiarity of a legislative assembly of this kind – a sort of chamber of the wise not alien to reflection on political philosophy – should thus consist in its independence in the face of the constant flux of passions, fashions and the multitudes clamouring for gratification. The elaboration of criteria and procedures for eligibility was directed towards averting the risk of this public office being transformed into yet another form of concentration of power, and ensuring that the natural bargaining processes of democratic practice did not take on an endemic character.

Hayek, therefore, wanted to prevent the fusion of «legislative and the governmental power in the same assembly» from creating a power that «in a free society no authority should possess». The way to obtain this result was to entrust central government with responsibility for foreign policy, and transform regional or local government «into business-like corporations» in competition with each other to win citizens over to their cause, offering them «the highest benefits compared with the price charged». The power of the government should in its turn be limited by norms to be established by the legislative assembly, which the government would have no power to change. Essentially, its function should be reduced to administration of the resources assigned to it for the purpose of providing citizens with various services, but it should not be able to establish the level of tax revenue to finance such services.[81]

The legislative assembly would thus be accompanied by a governing assembly; «employees of government and all who received pensions or other support from government» would be debarred from taking part in electing the assembly. Finally, a constitutional court would complete the picture.[82]

Here, too, what induced Hayek to formulate these proposals was the need to combat the influence of the «totalitarian-positivist conception» of Bacon and Hobbes, and to foil the impact of the «constructivism of Cartesian rationalism». For an opposition had developed between democratic theory and liberalism which could be overcome only by means of a constitutional form capable of distinguishing «the truly legislative from the governmental task», and by distinguishing «between distinct legislative and governmental assemblies». The solution to the problem could no longer be the creation of two «assemblies of essentially the present character, and merely charged with different tasks».[83]

Faced with a type of democratic practice that had transformed government into an expression of the «varied interests of a conglomerate of pressure groups whose support the government must buy by the grant of special benefits, simply because it cannot retain its supporters when it refuses to give them something it has the power to give»,[84] Hayek turned to the problem of the containment of power and the *dislodging of politics.* In so doing, he came to grips with the two mainstays of the development of modern political ideas. The first was the tendency to identify 'state' and 'society', granting priority to the state while conceding that «societies form but states are made».[85] The second was represented by the effects of submitting each and every choice to governmental power, resulting in the transformation of politics into «a tug-of-war for shares in the income pie». This rendered «decent government» impossible, with the upshot of turning politics into a dirty word and widening the rift between rulers and citizens.[86]

The need for constitutional reform, Hayek contended, is a consequence of the limits and possible outcomes of democratic theory. The focus of discussion thus became the philosophical foundations of contemporary democratic theory, but what needed to be clarified was whether it was a *method* or a *value*. Hayek regarded it as a method, and contended that it was precisely its being taken as a value that had brought about its transformation into the 'tyranny of majority'.

These considerations aside, the concept of democracy as a value arose in a different context from that in which it was subsequently applied. Its equivocality and the cause of the unexpected consequences of its realization perhaps lay in its origin as a 'communitarian' concept and in its implementation in a 'societarian' context. In this perspective, it appears meaningless to attempt to rationalize democracy by avoiding any association of its negative consequences with its philosophical equivocality, or with the consequences of attributing absolute power to the presumed holder of sovereignty.

Hayek therefore has the merit of having highlighted the way the evolution of the concept of democracy is closely connected to theories of human knowledge which are no longer tenable.

The fate of democracy appears to be linked to its capacity to keep legislative power distinct from government power.[87] This is the framework in which one should interpret Hayek's the proposals regarding the *constitution of a liberal state*. These proposals reflected the concerns that had already surfaced in *The Road to Serfdom*, regarding the destiny of personal freedom in democratic systems which at that time appeared strongly conditioned by collectivist ideologies. The Schumpeterian thesis of the necessary outcome of democracy as socialism therefore holds true only if democracy is taken as a form of government characterized by the progressive expansion of government control over economic and social activity and by the absence of any limit to the power of the majority.[88]

The insurmountable difference between liberalism and democracy thus does not specifically reside in the problem of equality and the fight against privilege. Rather, it concerns the powers of the state and the decision as to who is to govern. From a philosophical point of view, therefore, coexistence of the two traditions is by no means a foregone conclusion. But while it is difficult to imagine a liberal method abandoning the democratic regime to become authoritarian, one can readily envisage a democratic regime giving up its liberal principles and turning into an authoritarian regime. Thus the possibility of democracy consists chiefly in endorsing the liberal thesis on the limitation and partition of powers, and then in stemming the tide of interventionism which renders the bureaucratic apparatus increasingly independent of any democratic control.

Hayek essentially feared – and this is one of the possible readings of his proposals for constitutional change – that the defects of a certain manner of understanding democracy could end up throwing discredit on the democratic model as well. This would open the floodgates to a despotic regime which the ruling political class could impudently aid and abet to cover up responsibility for its own mistakes. He therefore wished to forestall any eventuality that the outcome of a theory of government, an outcome long foreseen and feared by the liberal tradition, could be considered the degenerative processes of a civilization.

The work of Hayek is thus coherently characterized, from as early as the critique of Lasky in *The Road to Serfdom*,[89] as an exposé of the consequences of a one approach to the understanding of democracy.[90] It was particularly timely in a period when democratic theory was boastfully puffing up its credentials as the ineluctable horizon of debate on the *best regime*. And all this was happening without any measures being taken to correct any of its multiplicity of defects.

The need had arisen to restore the term 'democracy' to its original meaning of a *method* for making political decisions and for the peaceful change-over of rulers, as well as for the establishment by majority of general norms only, valid for everyone, but not of what is right in particular cases. All the shortcomings outlined here, together with the increasing interventionism of the state in its guise of dispenser of benefits to this or that social group, had transformed politics into a constant process of bargaining, the object of which was the distribution of benefits to groups that changed according to the majorities. Having come to depend on the strength of groups clamouring for intervention favourable to their demands in return for votes, the decision-making process of the government had reached the utmost degree of exposure to corruption.[91]

In Hayek's opinion, the origin of these developments lay above all in the success of socialist ideology. But the collapse of this ideal leaves wide open the problem of how to find an antidote to so many years of a hegemony which seems to have become more deeply ingrained in Western thinking and culture than it did in the mentality and culture of those who actually experienced socialism. Before declaring that the collapse of socialism has obliterated the relevance of Hayek's teachings,[92] and more generally those of the Austrian School, one would do well to reflect on this circumstance. The truth is that what has nothing more to say is the 'liberal' critique of socialism, not liberal critique.

Similarly, one would be well advised to reconsider the problems of democratic theory in the perspective of the relation set up by Mises between democracy and market economy. Viewing democracy as the only method capable of satisfying subjective expectations and ensuring that they coexist peacfully, Mises felt that since the market economy subordinates the production of goods to the requirements of consumers, it is the only possible form of democracy.

As evidence of the insubstantiality of the thesis of continuity between liberal capitalism and totalitarianism, Mises stressed that in the capitalistic system «the entrepreneurs and capitalists are the servants of the consumers».[93] In this perspective, *the real democracy is the market.*[94] Thus from a conception of capitalism as «economic democracy» – as a system in which, instead of the producers, the consumers «would decide what was to be produced and how» – there derived a conception of social status as the result of a judgment passed by consumers and expressed through the mechanism of the market. Mises reasoned that, if the characteristic of the capitalistic system is that it recognizes no privileges other than those defined by the favour of the consumers,[95] then the market takes on the nature of an instrument of *social criticism*. The preference for the system of private property must therefore find its justification in greater efficiency compared to rival systems.[96].

The presumed contrast between liberalism and democracy was thus to be seen as the result of a misunderstanding of the meaning of the democratic constitutional form. For the value of democracy, according to Mises, derives not so much from its being founded on respect for the «natural and inborn rights of man», or from the assumption of its being the best realization of the ideals of equality and liberty, as from its capacity «to make peace, to avoid violent revolutions». Viewed from this angle, democracy is necessary for «attainment of the economic aims of man», an achievement which «presupposes peace» and is therefore compatible with liberalism. Indeed, «the essence of democracy is not that everyone makes and administers laws, but that lawgivers and rulers should be dependent on the people's will in such a way that they may be peaceably changed if conflict occurs». Therefore democracy does not consist in the «limitless rule of the *volonté générale*» but in a method directed to the achievement of individual ends independently of the state. Consequently, Mises argued, «only within the framework of Liberalism does democracy fulfil a social function. Democracy without Liberalism is a hollow form.» Rejecting the conception that would found the state «purely on political might», Mises also rejected the idea that the legislator admits of no limits, and can make the law depend on his will.[97] Mises then went on to conclude that the foundation of democracy did not lie – *pace* Kelsen – in its being «the result of a policy of compromise or of a pandering to relativism in questions of world-philosophy», but in its nature as an ineluctable requirement for the «peaceful development of the state».[98]

Since it possessed no philosophical foundation, democracy drew its legitimation, Mises reflected, from the fact of being the only system capable of keeping the social peace that is indispensable if man is to attain his economic ends. For this reason democracy must be set in a framework of liberalism and capitalism, since it is the only system able to subordinate the interests of producers to those of consumers, with reciprocal advantages for both.[99]

This kind of approach, as outlined by Mises, smoothed out the contrasts between those who owned the means of production and the consumers, a gap which had previously constituted a limit to the acceptance of democracy by classical liberalism. Even the aspiration of socialism to be accredited as a way of overcoming the contradictions of capitalism and democracy appeared as a matter arising from and to be explored within the confines of classical political economy.

The model of economic democracy worked out by Mises did, however, suffer from the flaw of deriving *order* from the satisfaction of individual needs. It did not allow a distinction between the sphere of satisfaction of subjective needs, on the one hand, and the political sphere on the other, the latter taken as the guarantee of the formation of an order based on abstract rules. Its limits were exposed by Hayek when, quoting a passage from Mises's *Theory and History* –

> The ultimate yardstick of justice is conduciveness to the preservation of social co-operation. Conduct suited to preserve social co-operation is just, conduct detrimental to the preservation of society is unjust. There cannot be any question of organizing society according to the postulate of an arbitrary preconceived idea of justice. The problem is to organize society for the best possible realization of those ends which men want to attain by social co-operation. Social utility is the only standard of justice. It is the sole guide of legislation.[100]

– he declared he could not follow Mises down this road. Hayek considered that one should view the problem of modification of the rules and of «their consistency or compatibility with the rest of the system from the angle of their effectiveness in contributing to the formation of the same kind of overall order of actions which all the other rules serve». That is, the issue required a point of view different from the 'rationalist utilitarianism' espoused by Mises.[101]

The approach charted here tended to see democracy as a co-operative system allowing the achievement of all subjective ends within the framework of the state. It thus led to a downgrading of the political sphere in the latter's function as the proper place for decisions regarding the compatibility of particular values with the abstract values by means of which order is rendered possible. The limits of such an approach are that, in a system characterized by limited resources, the upshot may well be a tug of war between particular ends and hence degeneration of the system.

Awareness of these risks led Hayek to reject the view that democracy could be founded on an assumption of relativism of values, or that it could be made to rest on a conception of society and the state that drew its legitimation from the possibility of satisfying these values. Mises, on the other hand, who conceived the state as the direct result of individual wills, could do no more than evaluate individual aims from the perspective of their usefulness for the purposes of achieving other advantages. The fact is that not all individual advantages are also useful to society; hence the need for a distinction between the individual sphere and the political sphere. But in Mises such a distinction fails to emerge, because he believed that society should be organized so as to fulfil the aims that individuals propose to achieve through social co-operation.

Beyond these differences, however, Mises and Hayek shared a wary outlook towards the attempt by democratic theory to create a model of the state wherein both political and economic institutions would differ from either the liberal or the social-collectivist model. Mises and Hayek regarded this attempt as the ultimate outcome of the statalistic and scientistic mentality that had gained currency as liberalism fell into disfavour among intellectuals. They rejected this option, although it was considered by many political scientists to be the only alternative to the success of socialism, for they judged it capable of aggravating social and economic problems, and also feared it could reveal itself to be a form of totalitarianism more sophisticated and more insidious than Communism or Nazism.

Once again, the spectre of the desire to elaborate a different political, economic and social form from that obtaining under liberal capitalism was rearing its ugly head. This was the same desire that the Austrians had already identified and criticized in the ideological programme of the Historical Schoool of German Economists. It was an attempt that benefited from the aversion of intellectuals towards a society in which their social status was made to depend upon the market, thereby depriving them of ancient privileges.[102] Hence their hostility to the market and the assiduousness of their reflection on the need to elaborate a different model from that of the market, deemed to be irrational and vulgar.

This attitude of Mises and Hayek towards interventionism is thus but one aspect of their critique of constructivism. The same critical outlook led them into their strenuous polemic against the ideas of Keynes. For in their opinion the latter's theories represented the best attempt to elaborate a political economy for interventionism. They immediately realized that these ideas could – voluntarily or involuntarily – engender consequences very different from those on account of which the ideas had been elaborated. Even Keynes, then, despite the influence of his ideas between 1930 and 1980, is no more than an example, albeit perhaps the most significant, of a mentality. It is no coincidence that his ideas were successful during the historical period in which liberalism enjoyed least favour and the political, social and economic hegemony of interventionism reached an all-time high.[103]

Since it consisted of a fusion of the ideal elements of socialism and liberalism, interventionism aimed to repel the advance of Marxist socialism in order to create a new political-economic-social model that was to constitute the foundation of democracy. Yet, for all its success, the attempt to make interventionism the foundation of democracy, and to interpret it not as an empirical compromise between liberalism and socialism but rather as the third of the fundamental political forms, rested on weak and fragile theoretical premises. In vain did Mises and Hayek call attention to its possible consequences for political insitutions and individual freedom, and to the fact that the economy could not be treated as a *tool* for the attainment of ethical and political ends.

Democratic regimes are therefore the outcome of a crisis that has affected political philosophy ever since the early years of the century. The crisis is still keenly felt today, in spite of the disappearance of the socialist model – against which interventionism was supposed to constitute a bulwark, not disdaining weighty concessions to demagogy if the need arose – from the historical and theoretical scene. No firm solution seems yet to have become established, and it appears more urgent than ever to reconsider the belief that the state must intervene in the economic and social sphere in order to guarantee the realization of subjective expectations. By the same token, it is vital to take a critical look at the idea that the state is free to intervene without any mandatory regard for repercussions that such expectations might have on the overall order of rules and on maintenance of the rules, the only concern being the technical possibility of the fulfilment of expectations. The need to revise this approach is confirmed by the fact that such fulfilment can generate order only if expectations are evaluated on the basis of universalizable rules of conduct; and the state and the world of politics may not have the ability to perform this evaluation. In other words, at the present historical moment, the reduction of government to a mere representation of interests can only produce an organization; it cannot give birth to an order.

Building on the Hayekian critique of the concept of politics that has now found favour, and therefore above all on his critique of democracy, re-examination of the predominant role assumed by politics can be delayed no further. In any case, politics can no longer lay claim to being the most important sphere of the theoretical social sciences, and no longer can it be considered the most comprehensive body of knowledge.

From this point of view, the model of economic democracy proposed by Mises presents itself as a radicalized blueprint that holds democracy to be a tool for guaranteeing the compatibility and pursuit of individual ends without the need for state intervention. It is possible to interpret this model as theorizing a form of democracy that is not susceptible of turning into a «democratic bureaucracy». But Hayek's criticisms also point to the fact that democratic theory needs a much more profound revision than was offered by Mises when he merged it with subjectivist economics.

The crisis of democratic theory also appears to be confirmation of the Austrian thesis according to which the basic opposition between political models is between '*spontaneous order*' and '*organization*', between *nomos* and *taxis*. And it provides evidence for the Austrian claim that democracy is a *method*, not an alternative model to liberalism and socialism.

Nevertheless, delegitimation of the statal interventionistic-democratic model by virtue of theoretical argumentation by no means resolves the problem of its influence. But given that the period has passed in which compelling motives of caution and appropriateness could be invoked in order to close ranks around the lesser evil, the problem now arises of the need to reconsider a model which those very motives contributed to validating as the only one possible. Naturally, as has been seen, neither Hayek nor, much less, Mises planned or even meditated a return to a universe of political concepts lacking that of democracy.[104] Such a misreading of their thought would mean totally overlooking the fact that the *theory of subjective values* is the foundation of their political philosophy and of their conception of the best political order. Indeed, their greatest contribution to political philosophy can be recognized as the emphasis they placed on the need for the concepts of state, government, law and democracy to be revised within the scope of the findings of the theory of subjective values.

Their intention was essentially to demonstrate that, since the expression 'social justice' is meaningless from the point of view of *subjectivist economics*, interventionism has no *raison d'être*. Inasmuch as it strives to prevent prices and incomes from acting as indicators of information and of social utility, they argued, it is forced either to assign to these indicators a political value that provides false and misleading suggestions for market operators, or else to resuscitate theories on the 'just price' or 'just value'. It follows that interventionism cannot be defined as a perfecting of the market system. On the contrary, it has to be assessed as a distinct system which will definitely not lead to the realization of *economic democracy*; it is bound to usher in an attempt by intellectuals, or by socio-political groups capitalizing on their majority position, to exploit the market as an instrument for the maintenance of political or social hegemony.

Mises and Hayek perceived from the start that this could easily be the prelude to a new form of serfdom. This serfdom would be the consequence of a crisis of legitimacy affecting political power and originating from the inability to meet all demands. One can choose not to discriminate among values, thereby affirming their compatibility only within the framework of a constantly expanding economic system. But this expansion is not compatible with abolition of the information-providing price mechanism, and demands sufficient accumulation of capital. The latter in its turn is incompatible with a policy of income redistribution inspired by criteria of 'social justice'. Two possible solutions can be contrived at this stage. The first consists in the introduction by the political-bureaucratic class of a system of discrimination among needs. The second resides in the formation of a majority aggregation of social groups sharing the goal of safeguarding acquired privileges. With neither solution does any genuine body of democratic ideals survive.

Yet these considerations were unable to prevent the misunderstanding whereby the political philosophy of Mises and Hayek was mistaken for nostalgic yearning for an idealized past. For a protracted period contemporary political reflection thus deprived itself of the conceptual tools indispensable for a proper understanding of the phenomenon of totalitarianism. By the same token, it failed to grasp the nature of the corporativistic involution of the democratic regime, even while this involution was reducing democracy to an electoral system stripped of any influence over the determination or control of government policy.[105] Seen in this perspective – as a forewarning of what was likely to ensue from the application of interventionist policies inspired by the idea of social justice understood as 'distributive justice' – their work is one of the fundamental documents for a true interpretation of our age.

§3. THE MIRAGE OF SOCIAL JUSTICE

Criticism of the premises and outcome of democratic theory induced Hayek to examine the relationship that had come to obtain between *democracy* and *justice*. This relationship did not simply arise from considering democracy as 'value', but indeed stood as its one and only justification. Yet the result was that the identification of political philosophy with democracy ultimately reduced the former to the status of ideology (i.e. to an attempt to justify a model of political regime). Furthermore, the fact of imagining the democratic system to be the only political system capable of resolving the problem of social justice also means that it has to be examined from the point of view of its empirical results. Such an enquiry is bound to lead to the question of whether democracy is truly the 'best political order', and one will wish to inspect its actual achievements in order to assess its claim to be a third solution to the dichotomy of *order* vs *organization*.

Hayek's exploration of the theme of social justice thus eventually led him to tackle the relationship between *political philosophy* and *justice*. He went on to speculate whether the task of political philosophy should be that of elaborating a model of a 'just' social order, what the term 'just' signified in the sphere of politics and what was the real meaning of the expression 'social justice'.

From the philosophical point of view, the problem he faced was the question whether the term 'social justice' still possessed any meaning within the perspective of *catallactics*. In other words, might it not be better considered as an «atavism»[106] that found its true expression in a conception of society as a finalistic *organization* and was therefore essentially meaningless in a society understood as *spontaneous order*? This query in its turn raised the need to ascertain whether it was preferable to have a *teleocratic* or a *nomocratic* society.

In carrying out a critical review of the *theory of social justice* – i.e. of the confused and contradictory meanings assumed by the expression – Hayek proposed to show that its fusion with democratic theory would lead to a form of totalitarianism. In such a political regime, rewards would be proportional to individuals' contribution to the achievement of the ends around which society was organized. By agreeing to act as a tool for the realization of social justice, democracy would forsake its nature as a political system in which all individual aims can coexist and be achieved, and allow itself to be turned into a teleocratic organization.

What has been overlooked in this ongoing debate is that, the more particular the ends, the more difficult it will become – in a democracy – to reach an agreement regarding their achievement and division of the costs incurred. Therefore individuals aiming to draw advantage from the attainment of these ends must be excluded from the ranks of those entrusted with the task of choosing among rival ends. For the 'common good' of a social order must be endowed with *abstract* nature. There must be no confusion between 'common good' and concrete purposes, rather, the former must be identified as residing in an agreement concerning what means are utilizable for the pursuit of individual ends. Hence the superiority of the classical liberal solution over the democratic solution. The classical liberal solution takes the *common good* to be the set of rules of conduct which leave both the content of actions and also the subjects who will draw benefit therefrom quite unaffected, thereby allowing a wide variety of purposes. General welfare is to be identified with the «abstract order of the whole which does not aim to the achievement of known particular results but is preserved as a means for assisting in the pursuit of a great variety of individual purposes».[107]

Nevertheless, *The Mirage of Justice* did not take as the target of its criticism the work by Rawls, *A Theory of Justice*, whose positions, Hayek felt, showed «differences [. . .] more verbal than substantial».[108] It focused instead on the more recent and more sophisticated form of that collectivistic mentality that had long been at the centre of his critical attention. Given Hayek's philosophy of the social sciences it is clear that his critical arguments simply kept abreast of the times. Above all, he took account of the fact that collectivistic ideology no longer expresses itself with the language of Marxism, but with a more sophisticated language: that of *liberal* ideology.

His first critical objective was to tackle the meaning that the spread and popularization of the mixture of Marxism, collectivism, radicalism and constructivism had attributed to the fundamental concepts of political philosophy. The appeal to a tradition divested of its specific content and reduced to being a mere prelude of the contemporary era thus appeared as the distinctive feature of a new form of *historicism* incapable of justifying itself in any other way than by asserting its own continuity with the ostensible glory days of yore.

Many, indeed some of the most important, pages of *Law, Legislation and Liberty* and *The Fatal Conceit* were dedicated to this reconstruction of the true liberal tradition. Throughout, Hayek is constantly aware that the battle against socialism would stand no chance of success unless a battle were also engaged, and won, on the front of the history of ideas. Only thus would the interpretation of the past and of the meaning of political concepts not remain the exclusive purview of socialist and constructivist intellectuals.

Accordingly, many of the essays subsequent to *The Constitution of Liberty* set themselves the task of 'restoring' the principles of liberal political philosophy and bringing it up to date with the times. This was necessary to defend it against the insincere inroads of liberals, socialists and constructivist rationalists who masqueraded as the heirs and revivers of its historical heritage.

The first difficulty Hayek encountered was the problem of restoring to the various terms their original meaning, rescuing them from confusion and ambiguity. In this endeavour, *The Mirage of Justice* tackled the most difficult issue. For the theme of social justice had become ensnared in an interpretative monopoly held by liberal intellectuals whose strong point lay in the belief that social justice, in their understanding of the term, was the foundation and the goal of democracy.

Hayek's starting point was thus represented partly by the meaning that terms such as 'common good' and 'general welfare' had taken on, and also by the mistaken belief that «all collective interests are general interests of the society». His criticism was directed at the idea that the state – while possessing no conceptual tools to evaluate the compatibility of collective interests with the general interest of society – should foster general welfare. General welfare in this case would wave the banner of the interests of whatever political, social or electoral force chose to uphold it. In opposition to the current tendency which (in the best of hypotheses) views political parties as organizations whose goal is to win advantages and privileges from the state on behalf of the groups they 'represent', Hayek emphasized that

> the whole history of the development of popular institutions is a history of continuous struggle to prevent particular groups from abusing the governmental apparatus for the benefit of the collective interest of these groups. This struggle has certainly not ended with the present tendency to define as the general interest anything that a majority formed by a coalition of organized interests decides upon.

Justice cannot therefore reside in giving greater amounts to those who enjoy greater political power, but instead «requires that what each group receives out of the common pool should be roughly proportional to what it is made to contribute». Hayek believed it was fitting to entrust this decision to a democratic government; his belief, however, was motivated only by the hope that such a government would pay greater attention to the public interest than would any other form of government. But a decision of this kind must be backed up by some empirical evidence, and does not in any case entail the requirement that the 'general interest' has to be defined by a majority.[109]

Having identified that the connective fabric of a society resides not so much in an impossible community of aims, but rather in the abstract rules regulating individual actions, Hayek elaborated a model of society capable of preventing social conflict from reaching a level of virulence that would render the formation of order impossible. The starting point of his political philosophy was the impossibility of a political organization directed towards the achievement of a particular end through the use of legislative means. Indeed, any society imposing a hierarchy of binding ends on its members and failing to recognize a multiplicity of individual ends and of independent decision-making centres could not even be defined as a free society.[110]

Consequently, the central problem of political philosophy is not bound up with the discovery of concrete universal rules around which to organize society as an organic whole. On the contrary, the basic issue is that of encouraging the development of those norms which are endowed with abstract beneficial effects for the entire society. These rules will receive all the more endorsement the more they succeed in being abstract, i.e. the less foreseeable their particular outcomes: 'only if applied universally, without regard to particular effects, will they serve the permanent preservation of the abstract order, a timeless purpose which will continue to assist the individuals in the pursuit of their temporary and still unknown aims'.[111]

The birth and development of the rules of conduct are therefore not linked to the desire to provide human actions with an organization and a *taxis* on the basis of their known consequences, but to the impossibility of foreseeing all the consequences of an action. In contrast with utilitarianism, which aimed at the creation of a society wherein norms would be closely coordinated with intended results, Hayek stressed that these norms originated from social evolution. For this reason, he argued, they are measures «to prevent frequent causes of minor disturbances of the social order but not rare causes of its total disruption». They are not «part of a plan of action but rather equipment for certain unknown contingencies».[112]

Political philosophy has the aim of assuring the coexistence of free individual ends with the requirements of order inherent in a system. It will need to to evaluate norms from the point of view of their «consistency or compatibility» with other recognized norms which tend towards the «formation of a certain kind of order of actions». Essentially, then, the aspects contributing crucially to the soundness of a system lie in close compenetration of these norms. This circumstance in its turn limits the possibility of introducing norms from other systems which could regulate a particular circumstance in a more satisfactory manner. So there derives «no absolute system of morals independent of the kind of social order in which a person lives, and the obligation incumbent upon us to follow certain rules derives from the benefits we owe to the order in which we live». This does not however necessarily entail that a system of norms cannot or should not be improved in the direction of an «open or 'humanistic' society».[113]

The criterion for the introduction of change into society is therefore the 'universalizability' of norms understood as «compatibility with the whole system of accepted rules». Hence the need to evaluate the rules in such a way as to look beyond whatever results they may or may not yield in the short term, thereby judging them according to the results forecast over the long run. From a juridical-political point of view, the distinctive feature of the *nomocratic society* would then be the limitation of «coercion wholly to the enforcement of rules serving a long run order». From the gnoseological point of view, the foundation of the 'open society' would be the diffusion «of an evolutionary or critical rationalism that is aware not only of the powers but also of the limits of reason» – of a rationalism, that is, which also acknowledges reason as «a product of social evolution». It follows that freedom «means that in some measure we entrust our fate to forces which we do not control».[114]

What is commonly indicated today by the expression 'social justice' is none other than a sophisticated version of what used to be called 'distributive justice'. This was a concept that had found a theorizer in Mill, who did not notice that it led «straight to full-fledged socialism». But as well as problems of an economic and political nature linked to the concept of social justice, Hayek also identified a moral issue consisting in the rightness of submission to a power committed to coordinating «the efforts of the members of society with the aim of achieving a particular pattern of distribution regarded as just». As he mused on these matters, Hayek reached the conclusion that the way the market distributes advantages and disadvantages could be considered 'just' or 'unjust' only «if it were the result of a deliberate allocation to particular people. But this is not the case.» Consequently, «to demand justice from such a process is clearly absurd, and to single out some people in such a society as entitled to a particular share evidently unjust».[115]

Evaluation of the respective advantages of the liberal tradition and of social justice thus cannot be performed merely on the basis of the abstract righteousness or otherwise of their intents. Instead it must take account of their consequences. From this point of view, while the liberal tradition restricts itself to demanding «just action by individuals», the tradition of social justice «more and more places the duty of justice on authorities with power to command people what to do». The former develops a concept of social order which is viable even without presupposing that righteousness and justice govern human aims and social relations. The latter – overestimating mankind, less in terms of man's moral attributes as of his cognitive abilities – ultimately constructs a finalistic concept of order that is viable only by means of increasing coercion. The outcome is that «the prevailing belief in 'social justice' is at present probably the gravest threat to most other values of a free civilization». Indeed, Hayek pronounced the doctrine of social justice to be an imposition of types of behaviour: a sort of political obligation to be virtuous. Recalling the teachings of Gibbon, who warned that moral or religious beliefs could destroy a civilization, Hayek now proposed to submit this doctrine «to ruthless rational dissection». He resolved to analyse it so as to expose the dangers inherent in the adoption and application to a society of its principles.[116]

The tradition of social justice represents the legacy of the centuries-old tradition of Western civilization that has always opposed liberalism, the same tradition that found a mouthpiece in the social doctrine of Catholicism, also in the *polizei Staat*. Herein lies the essence of Hayek's contention that the reintroduction of a principle of 'distributive' or 'substantive justice' neither was nor could be an antidote to the defects of the liberal society. Quite the contrary: it was the cause of the ills liberalism wished to avert.

These political-philosophical criticisms were integrated by considerations regarding the compatibility of the concept of social justice with a spontaneous process. Here, Hayek explored the meaning of the concept of social justice «in a market order» and the compatibility between market order and a «pattern of remuneration based on the assessment of the performance or the need of different individuals or groups by an authority possessing the power to enforce it». The negative conclusion he reached was grounded in the circumstance that in a market order, «the concept of 'social justice' is necessarily empty and meaningless, because in it nobody's will can determine the relative incomes of the different people, or prevent that they be partly dependent on accident». As a result, the expression could be meaningful only in a context not presupposing freedom, i.e. in «a directed or 'command' economy in which individuals are ordered what to do».[117]

The function of salaries, Hayek argued, could not truly consist in remunerating individuals for what they have done, for their lavish efforts, or their merits or individual needs. Rather, salaries act as an indication of «what in their own as well as in general interest they *ought* to do». This line of reasoning is an application to the complex of the social sciences of the approach through which the Austrian School succeeded in shifting attention, within the field of political economy, from the producer to the consumer as the source of 'value'. As a consequence, the value of a service for whoever receives it «will often have no relation to [. . .] individual merits or needs» of the producer; and «it is not good intentions or needs but doing what in fact most benefits others, irrespective of motive, which will secure the best reward».[118]

Hayek developed his critique on the basis of these arguments, highlighting the fact that the realization of social justice was the cause of far more ills than it managed to remedy. Foremost among such ills was the denaturing of the tenets of the rule of law, together with the trend towards concentrating in the hands of rulers a plethora of powers that would be extremely difficult to control. The myth of equality thus concealed within it the danger of the total submission of vast masses to an élite that directed the public economy and controlled private economies. Aspiration to an «equality of material position», in Hayek's eyes, could be fulfilled only «by a government with totalitarian powers».[119]

But if «in a society of free men whose members are allowed to use their knowledge for their own purposes the term 'social justice' is wholly devoid of meaning or content», this does not necessarily mean that it is «an innocent expression of good will toward the less fortunate». Indeed, Hayek viewed this as «a dishonest insinuation that one ought to agree to a demand of some special interest which can give no real reason for it». The expression is «intellectually dishonest», then, and its continual use «is not only dishonest and the source of constant political confusion, but destructive of moral feeling». Therefore the concept of social justice, in Hayek's judgment, was the product of morals indifferent to the social consequences. The application of the ideals of social justice to a political and moral system would be unable to produce «a functioning order, capable of maintaining the apparatus of a civilization which it presupposes». It is thus no coincidence that political systems based on malfunctioning moral systems are unknown; for «societies which try them rapidly disappear». The connection between *moral order* and *political order* is thereby spelled out as an application of the «atrocious idea that political power ought to determine the material position of the different individuals and groups». From here it is but a short step to the conclusion that the theory of social justice is none other than a sophisticated form of the socialist ideal, an ideal which, for all its presumed good intentions, metamorphoses into a political organization that will be unable to refrain from increasing rulers' discretionary power. Far from being its fulfilment, social justice is hereby revealed as a vision of politics thoroughly opposed to liberalism; whereas the latter, on the contrary, «brought about the greatest reduction of arbitrary power ever achieved». Hayek's verdict was that when Rawls used the term 'social justice', he simply compounded the confusion.[120]

Such was the emphasis placed on the concept of social justice, Hayek claimed, that it had contributed to changing the general attitude towards society and the state. It had led to the dissemination of «a feeling that [individuals] have a claim in justice on 'society'», and of the demand that society should provide certain particular goods. This was what lay behind the growth of a new conception of society and government, but the trend also gave rise to a proliferation of subjective expectations that became known as «new positive 'social and economic' human rights». Although «it is equally meaningless to speak of right in the sense of a claim on a spontaneous order» – unless one wishes to assert that «somebody has the duty of transforming that cosmos into an organization and thereby to assume the power of controlling its results» – the outcome is that «an equal or even higher dignity» is attributed to such rights, yet without any indication of who must shoulder the responsibility for seeing to their satisfaction, or how this can be carried out.[121]

The mirage of social justice, as sketched out in Hayek's writings, has become «a powerful incantation». Emotional states of bygone times hover in the background, «threatening to destroy the Great Society». They have brought with them the risk of pushing society back into the dark ages of tribalism from which liberalism sought to ransom Western civilization. Defence of the interests of those who aim to maintain, or aspire to, privileged social and economic positions thus transforms the myth of social justice into a form of social disintegation. And what started out as an ideal inspired by noble-spiritedness and altruism threatens to be transformed into a hindrance to social progress: «a mere pretext for claims for privileges by special interests» and a «slogan used by all groups whose status tends to decline».[122]

Once again, Hayek's main concern was to avert the risk that the democratic state would be transformed into a totalitarian state by acting in favour of the attainment of moral aims through the use of coercive tools. His critique offered a pressing invitation to reflect on the impossibility of a middle way miraculously managing to combine the best aspects of both liberalism and socialism. To attempt to steer a middle course in this manner would be to behave as if they were not founded on two completely different conceptions of political coexistence.

Among the causes of the diffusion of the mirage of social justice therefore is the inability of political philosophy to make a definitive statement on values and on the feasibility of realizing individual expectations. The withdrawal from this sphere on the part of political philosophy, its abandonment of human action to the realm of uncertainty, has left government at the mercy of the occasional convergence of majorities. Political practice has thus effectively disavowed a guiding philosphical idea in favour of the quest for legitimation through the attempt to content all people: from the 'new subjects' to those who have to be protected against a type of progress that has had to become ceaseless and perpetual precisely so as to maintain the possibility of satisfying each and every subjective aspiration. Once again, all this is the result of the incapacity of political philosophy to make statements concerning values, the result of its having abandoned them to the sphere of individual conscience or religion.

NOTES

1 On Hayek 1960, as well as the essays contained in *Ordo*, 1979, see Albert, 1978, pp. 132ff., 138–64, and 1990, pp. 269–70; Vaughn, 1984, pp. 117–42; Barry, 1989, pp. 267–82. As a critique of the Hayekian approach to the relation between evolutionism and constitutionalism, see Buchanan, 1975, pp. 183n., 191n., 194.

2 On the relation set up by Hayek between *liberty*, *law*, *order* and *constitution*, see: Hamowy, 1971, pp. 352ff.; Dietze, 1977, pp. 107–46; Barry, 1979, pp. 76–101; Cunningham, 1979; Butler, 1983, pp. 106–31; Gray, 1984a, pp. 56–78; Hoy, 1984, pp. 68–118; Radnitzky, 1987a, pp. 17–46; Shenfield, 1987, pp. 77–93; Brittan, 1988, pp. 80–92; Kukathas, 1989, pp. 131–64; Shand, 1990, pp. 101–6.

3 See Hayek, 1973–79, II, pp. 1–2. An anticipation of these themes can already be

found in 'The Constitution of a Liberal State', now in Hayek, 1978, pp. 98–104.

4 See Hayek, 1944, p. 54. Here the distinction between a free country and a country dominated by arbitrary power is seen to consist in observance of the «great principles known as the Rule of Law», understood as a complex of «rules fixed and announced beforehand» that are binding on government.

5 Ibid., pp. 55–7.

6 Ibid., pp. 57–9. On these aspects of the constitutional doctrine of Schmitt, see also Hayek, 1960 p. 485n., and 1973–9, I, p. 71 and n. on pp. 161–2.

7 See Hayek, 1944, pp. 61–2. On the treatment of the problem in this work, see Dietze, 1977, pp. 108–10, 113–18, 120, 125–6, 132–4; and Shand, 1984, pp. 189–91.

8 See Hayek, 1978, p. 152.

9 Hayek, 1960, pp. 92–3.

10 On this issue, see Bobbio, 1977, pp. 23, 123ff.; Raz, 1979, pp. 185–211; Viola, 1987, pp. 129–61, 163–8, 173–8. However, they are perhaps not so much interested in the true Hayekian objective as in his philosophy of law and the implications of the latter in particular sectors of jurisprudence. On the political implications of the juridical philosophy of Hayek, see Robilant, 1989, pp. 103–21; and Shearmur, 1990a, pp. 106–32.

11 Hayek, 1960, pp. 133–5. The first consists in preventing a person «from making the greatest contribution that he is capable of to the community»; the second, taken as the coordination of efforts of individuals who have voluntarily united to pursue an end, is not an evil in and of itself, but it becomes a scourge when it is transformed into «the power to coerce, to force other men to serve one's will by the threat of inflicting harm».

12 Ibid., p. 134.

13 Ibid., p. 148. As well as Savigny and, obviously, Hayek, in this case the reference is to Menger, 1883, see n. 3 on p. 452. In this perspective he thus has a connection to the 'debate on codification'.

14 See. Hayek, 1960, pp. 149–50.

15 Ibid., pp. 153–5. On the relation between coercion and freedom in connection with these pages, see Miller, 1989b, pp. 26ff.

16 Hayek, 1960, pp. 160–1.

17 Ibid., p. 181.

18 Ibid., pp. 196–202.

19 Ibid., pp. 205–6.

20 Ibid., p. 212.

21 Ibid., p. 207.

22 Ibid., pp. 220–2.

23 Ibid., pp. 234–8.

24 Ibid., pp. 238–9.

25 Ibid., pp. 239–49.

26 Hayek, 1973–9, I, p. 2.

27 Ibid., pp. 65–7.

28 Ibid., pp. 69–71.

29 Ibid., pp. 72–4.

30 Ibid., pp. 74–84.

31 Ibid., pp. 85–9.

32 Ibid., pp. 100–1.

33 Ibid., pp. 102–5.

34 Ibid., pp. 106–7.

35 Ibid., pp. 112–14.

36 Ibid., p. 91.

37 Ibid., pp. 131–4.

38 Hayek, 1978, pp. 76–7.
39 Hayek, 1973–9, I, pp. 134–41.
40 Ibid. pp. 141–4.
41 Ibid., II, pp. 31–3 and n. on p. 158.
42 Ibid., pp. 42–3 (Ital. trans. pp. 235–6). In particular, as regards Kant and the affinity with his conception of law, see the note on pp. 166–7. Here Hayek observes that

> Kant probably did not, as is generally assumed, discover the principle of the categorical imperative in morals and afterwards apply it to law, but [. . .] he rather found the basic conception in Hume's treatment of the Rule of Law and then applied it to morals. But while his brillant treatment of development of the ideal of the Rule of Law with its stress on the negative and end-independent character of the legal rules seems to me to be one of his permanent achievements, his attempt to turn what in law is a test of justice to be applied to an existing body of rules into a premise from which the system of moral rules can be deductively derived was bound to fail.

There is here a clear declaration of affinity with Kantian philosophy of law, attenuated by the circumstance of unmeditated knowledge, but also the awareness that the Kantian attempt «was bound to fail». On this reference to Kant by Hayek, see MacCormick, 1982, p. 6 and n. The thesis of the influence of Kant's political philosophy on Hayek – see Gray, 1984a, pp. 62ff.; and Kukathas, 1989, pp. 31–41 – cannot avoid taking this observation into account. More generally – even though one can interpret Hayek's critique of democracy as a resumption of the distinction (which however is not only Kantian) between republic and despotism – it must take account of the fact that his political philosophy pays little attention to the Kantian concept of *summum bonum*; nor does it appear assimilable to Kantian *finalism*. Faced with this situation, especially considering the role that finalism has in his political philosophy, even the demand for universalization of the rules, even if it was taken up again by Kant, appears to be of limited relevance. One is tempted to think that it is a methodological affinity divested of the implications that the philosophy of religion has for the philosophy of law and of morals and for the political philosophy of Kant. Yet, even taking into account all the differences that Hayek identified between his philosophy of law and that of Kant, these pages lead one to a different view of Kant from the one that in other works, e.g. Hayek, 1967, p. 94, had led Hayek to place him within the framework of constructivist rationalism.

43 Hayek, 1973–9, II, p. 44.
44 Ibid., pp. 44–8.
45 Ibid., pp. 48–9 and n. on p. 170. For a comparison between the theses of Weber and Hayek regarding the process of rationalization and bureaucratization, its consequences for individual freedom and its outcome as socialism and totalitarianism, see Bottmore, 1985, pp. 46–53, 69–71. Hayek's critique of the Weberian concept of 'organization' seems, however, to limit the value of this affinity.
46 Hayek, 1973–9, II, pp. 48–9 and n. on p. 170.
47 Ibid., pp. 49–53 and n. on pp. 171–2.
48 Ibid., pp. 53–4.
49 Ibid., pp. 54–6.
50 Ibid., p. 57.
51 Ibid., pp. 59–60. In the note on p. 174, Hayek quotes a fragment of the *Treatise* by Hume which is significant for an understanding of what Hayek himself meant by the term 'natural'. As Hume wrote:

> 'where an invention is obvious and absolutely necessary, it may as properly be said to be natural as anything that proceeds immediately from original principles,

without the intervention of thought or reflection. Though the rules of justice be *artificial*, they are not *arbitrary*. Nor is the expression improper to call them *Laws of Nature*; if by natural we understand what is common to any species, or even if we confine it to mean what is inseparable from the species'.

There follows the quotation from a fragment by Popper, 1945, which states that «nearly all misunderstandings can be traced back to one fundamental misapprehension, namely, to the belief that 'convention' implies 'arbitrariness'».

52 In this connection see Littlechild, 1978.
53 Mises, 1933, pp. 191–2 (Engl. trans. p. 207).
54 A compendium of the reflection on the origin, development, extension and implications of the anti-capitalistic mentality is in Mises, 1956.
55 See Lepage, 1980.
56 And rightly so, even if «the word revolution is not quite appropriate to Hayek's intellectual world» Nishiyama, 1984, pp. xxxvii–lxviii, talks of 'the Hayekian Revolution'.
57 See Mises, 1947, pp. 481–9. On the theme of interventionism in Mises, see Rothbard, 1962 and 1970; Lavoie, 1982, pp. 169–83.
58 Mises, 1981, pp. 490–4. On the impossibility of a 'middle way' see also Mises, 1952, in particular pp. 18ff., and 40ff. The belief in the possibility of a middle way between socialism and capitalism appears to be due to an «unfortunate influence which originated from J.S. Mill», Cairnes and Laski. But Mises believed that no compromise at all was possible between the two systems, and that there exists no third system as a stable condition of a social order. On the idea of the middle way, see Burton, 1984, pp. 87–115.
59 Mises, 1952, pp. 21–7.
60 Ibid., pp. 43–7.
61 Ibid., pp. 1–2, and 1956.
62 Mises, 1944a, p. iii.
63 Ibid., pp. 3ff.
64 Ibid., pp. 2, 9–12, 17.
65 Ibid., pp. 18–23.
66 Ibid., p. 30.
67 Ibid., p. 30.
68 Ibid., pp. 74, 106.
69 Ibid., pp. 119ff.
70 On Hayek's interpretation of interventionism and welfare-state-like dangers to freedom and democracy, see Hirschman, 1991, pp. 110ff.
71 Hayek, 1978, pp. 152–4. On the relation between democracy and 'spontaneous order', see diZerega, 1989, pp. 206–40.
72 On the Hayekian relation between rule of law and liberal democracy, see Becker, 1982, pp. 161–70.
73 Hayek, 1978, pp. 154–5.
74 Ibid., p. 92.
75 Hayek was referring here to Oakeshott, who,

> in his oral teaching, has long used the terms *teleocratic*, and (*teleocracy*) and *nomocratic*, and (*nomocracy*) to bring out the same distinction. A teleocratic order, in which the same hierarchy of ends is binding on all members, is necessarily a made order or organization, while a nomocratic society will form a spontaneous order.

See Hayek, 1973–9, II, p. 15. Probably, in this circumstance, Hayek was taking up again the thesis expounded in the essay 'The Confusion of Language in Political

Thought', of 1967, now in Hayek, 1978, and did not notice that *On Human Conduct* appeared in 1975.

76 See Hayek, 1978, pp. 93–7. On these aspects of Hayek's critique of democracy, see Nemo, 1988, pp. 329–58.

77 See Hayek, 1978, p. 162.

78 See Hayek, 1973–9, III, p. 105. On this problem, see Zintl, 1983, and Buchanan, 1987a, pp. 75ff.

79 Hayek, 1973–9, III, p. 105.

80 Ibid., pp. 109–11.

81 Hayek, 1978, pp. 158–62.

82 Hayek, 1973–9, III, pp. 109–27; the quotation is on p. 119. See also Hayek, 1978, pp. 159–60.

83 Hayek, 1978, pp. 158–9. On the proposal of a new constitutional model as an instrument to control the extension of government powers, and thus to save liberal democracy, see Barry, 1979, pp. 190ff., and 1990; Butler, 1983, pp. 121–31; Gray, 1984a, pp. 127–8. On the relevance of Hayek's theses in the debate on the form and limits of state action, see Held, 1986, pp. 2–3, and 1987, pp. 247–54.

84 See Hayek, 1973–9, III, pp. 128–9.

85 Ibid., pp. 139–41.

86 Ibid., pp. 149–52.

87 On the problem of limited government in Hayek, see Jasay, 1989, pp. 296ff.

88 For a comparison between the position of Schumpeter and those of Mises, Hayek and Popper with regard to the presumed inevitability of socialism, see Albert, 1986, pp. 60ff.

89 Hayek, 1944, pp. 62–3 and n.

90 See Barry, 1979, pp. 186–90; and Hoy, 1984, pp. 93–115.

91 See Hayek, 1973–9, III, pp. 5–17, and 98–104,

92 See Dahrendorf, 1990, pp. 31ff.

93 Mises, 1944b, p. 49 wrote:

> In an economic order based on private ownership of the means of production the market is the focal point of the system. The working of the market mechanism forces capitalists and entrepreneurs to produce so as to satisfy the consumers' needs as well and cheaply as the quantity and quality of material resources and of manpower available and the state of technological knowledge allow [. . .] Within the market society the working of the price mechanism makes the consumers supreme [. . .] Within the market society each serves all his fellow citizens and each is served by them. It is a system of mutual exchange of services and commodities, and mutual giving and receiving. In that endless rotating mechanism the entrepreneurs and capitalists are the servants of the consumers.

94 Ibid., p. 137.

95 See Mises, 1981, p. 11, and 1944a, pp. 20ff.

96 See Mises, 1981, pp. 27ff.

97 Ibid., pp. 58–65.

98 Ibid., p. 71.

99 Ibid., pp. 399ff. On the differences between Mises and Hayek regarding the rationalistic foundation, (for Mises) of liberalism, see Hayek, 1981a, p. 28.

100 Mises, 1957, p. 54. The passage is cited in Hayek, 1973–9, III, pp. 204–5n.

101 Hayek, 1973–9, III, pp. 167 and n. on pp. 204–5.

102 In this connection, see Jouvenel, 1954, pp. 91–121, in Hayek, 1954. On this work, see Hartwell, 1977, pp. 73–93, and 1987, pp. 1–17.

103 On the contraposition between Keynes and the Austrians, and on the dissolution

of consensus accorded to the Keynesian system, see Shand, 1984, pp. 147–55.

104 On the position of Mises and of Hayek towards democracy, see Barry, 1986a, pp. 79–80.

105 This has resulted in Mises and Hayek being included in the framework of the so-called New Right; see Bosanquet, 1983; O'Gorman, 1986, pp. 52–3; Held, 1987, p. 254. Although he placed Hayek, like Nozick, in the movement of the New Right, Held recognized that they «have contributed significantly to a discussion about the appropriate form and limits of state action». In other authors, a sort of ideological prejudice has led to a misunderstanding of the positions of Mises and Hayek, which even culminated in an erroneous delineation of the issues they were tackling. This is the case, for instance, with Dunleavy and O'Leary, 1987, pp. 86–95, 130–5, 273–4.

106 This theme is treated in the essay 'The Atavism of Social Justice', of 1976, now in Hayek, 1978.

107 See Hayek, 1973–9, II, pp. 3–5. An interesting and fertile comparison between the Catholic tradition of the 'common good' and the Austrian conception is to be found in Novak, 1989, pp. 78–80, 86–7, 162–3.

108 Hayek, 1982, p. xvii.

109 Ibid., II, pp. 6–8.

110 Referring to the terminology of Oakeshott, Hayek always distinguished between *teleocratic* societies and *nomocratic* societies, setting up a correspondence between the former and a *taxis* and between the latter and a *cosmos*; see ibid., p. 15, and also, 1978, p. 89 and n.

111 Hayek, 1973–9, II, pp. 15–17.

112 Ibid., pp. 17–23, citations on pp. 22, 23.

113 Ibid., pp. 24–7.

114 Ibid., pp. 27–30.

115 Ibid., pp. 62–5. The critique of social justice has been one of Hayek's themes that has aroused greatest interest, but also the greatest number of doubts and negative reactions. In the works of Barry, 1979, pp. 124–50; of Butler, 1983, pp. 86–105; of Gray, 1984a, pp. 61–75; of Shand, 1984, pp. 212–17, and 1990, pp. 125–31; of Crowley, 1987, pp. 194–6; of Flew, 1987, pp. 93–112; of Nemo, 1988, pp. 181–8; and of Kukathas, 1989, pp. 46–83, while different particular issues are highlighted in these various authors, and in a more or less critical perspective, there is a scientific treatment of the problem and its implications. The exact presuppositions of this critique within Austrian economic theory are not always made clear, however, and indeed Hayek himself did not always explicitly specify them.

116 See Hayek, 1973–9, II, pp. 65–7.

117 Ibid., pp. 67–70.

118 Ibid., pp. 71–2.

119 Ibid., pp. 82–3.

120 Ibid., pp. 96–100. On the comparison between Hayek and Rawls see Barry, 1979, pp. 143–47. His conclusion, although written before the various modifications of Rawls's thought, seems to be the most balanced assessment. Yet the same can probably not be said of the words of Crowley, 1987, pp. 200–2, who places Hayek «in the liberal tradition of Kant and Rawl», with a crucial distinction regarding the scepticism of Hayek concerning individual rationality. Kukathas, 1989, pp. 65–79, 169–72, focuses his analysis on a demonstration of the differences between the two, and rightly observes that «both see themselves as liberals, the ultimate difference between them is that they represent two different theories of *individualism*» (p. 79).

121 See Hayek, 1973–9, II, pp. 101–3.

122 Ibid., pp. 133–42; the quotations are on pp. 133, 140–1. Radnitzky, 1985, after

a penetrating critique, carried out in a perspective drawing inspiration from Hayek, of the «systematic distortion» of the concept of justice outlined by Rawls (pp. 26ff.), wrote that «*the best means to destroy the market economy, and therefore in the long run not only welfare, but also one of the premises of the Open Society, is the concept of "social justice"*» (p. 47). More clearly than the previously cited scholars, Radnitzky thus correctly highlighted the fact that the difference between Hayek and Rawls was far more radical than even Hayek himself had thought at first.

5

THE LIBERALISM OF THE AUSTRIAN SCHOOL

Freedom means that in some measure we entrust our fate to forces which we do not control.
(Hayek, *Law, Legislation and Liberty*, II)

1. *Philosophical foundations of Austrian liberalism*; 2. *Mises*; 3. *Hayek*; 4. *Epilogue*

§ 1. PHILOSOPHICAL FOUNDATIONS OF AUSTRIAN LIBERALISM

An examination of the philosophical foundations of the Austrian School's liberalism must consider both its approach to the problem of the nature and role of political philosophy in society, and the position of political philosophy within the framework of the social sciences. Naturally this involves an appraisal of the Austrian approach vis-à-vis the various tendencies of constructivist rationalism, but also in comparison with the philosophical-political trends that proposed to 'rehabilitate' the practical function of political philospphy. Critique of the tradition of constructivist rationalism is – as has been seen – a constant and essential feature of the work of the Austrian School. No less important to the present discussion, especially in view of the problem of modernity, is some reference to elements that distinguish the Austrian School from other contemporary attempts to rehabilitate political philosophy as *scientia practica*.

One may concentrate too intensely on the considerable attention that was devoted to exploring the *possibility of political philosophy* in an era whose hallmark was the widespread popularity of the mentality bred by historicism and scientism. But by doing so, one may be misled into classing the Austrian School as belonging to multi-faceted movement that sought the re-accreditation of political philosophy as *scientia practica*. In fact, these are two distinct perspectives grounded on very different premises, with strongly diverging outcomes. The exponents of the Austrian School certainly believed that critical reflection on the theoretical foundations and practical function of political philosophy could be delayed no further. But they differed in their understanding of economics as a *science* which had opened up new horizons for the understanding and explanation of human action and its products. In their view this had contributed to undermining the traditional conception of political philosophy and the state.

According to the theorists of *scientia practica*, economics – whenever they happen to take it into consideration, which means hardly ever – is essentially a tool for the achievement of particular ends. By contrast, Mises and Hayek insisted that catallactics could not be made to serve particular ends. Thus the liberalism of these Austrian thinkers drew its origin from the process that led economics to make a bid for independence from ethics and politics, in favour of the elaboration of a systematic theory of human actions and an interpretation of those social institutions which were changing the theoretical framework of the social sciences. Their liberalism can therefore be assessed as the end result of the Lockean turning point. For, with ownership established as the foundation of the state – i.e. a non-political phenomenon, or a manner of satisfying individual needs – the stage was set for the evolution of liberal theory firstly towards a critique, and then subsequently into delegitimation, of the primacy of politics over the other social sciences.

It follows that, according to the Austrian School, the possibility of political philosophy is by no means linked to a rejection of modernity, because political philosophy is essentially a reflection on the best political order. Such reflection may well be rendered more complicated by modernity and its products, but it will not thereby be nullified. The demonization of modernity is only a signal of the inability to elaborate a political philosophy, with responsibility for this impasse being attributed either to historicism, or to the crisis of modernity, or else to the so-called 'process of secularization'. Without denying these responsibilities, however, this inability may be seen primarily as the result of the failure of a tradition: the tradition that placed politics at the summit of a presumed hierarchy of the social sciences in the belief that it is the duty of politics to evaluate, direct and organize every sphere of human action. Consequently, the problem of political philosophy has to be tackled within the framework of modernity itself, by examining it from a perspective free from any finalistic conception of history, one which is capable of interpreting it as human reflection on matters and ends pertaining to human coexistence. In this perspective, both historicism and scientism can be characterized as typical products of modernity, but they do not represent its only and ineluctable outcome.

The Austrian School's approach thus provided the first delineation of a solution to the problem of the foundation and possibility of political philosophy. Theirs was a solution that differed sharply from other suggestions of their day. It can be analysed into a *theoretical* part (the problem of the nature of political order), a *historical* part (interpretation of the history of modern political philosophy) and a *practical* part (the social philosophy of liberalism as the best solution of political problems).

The shape of this tradition can thus be outlined as a conception of political philosophy running counter to several different trends. Its opposition to the various outcomes of constructivist rationalism was indeed paralleled by its divergence from the view that would refound political philosophy by returning to classicity. (For those who espoused the latter view failed to take into account that their concept of *oeconomica* not only was no longer tenable but could not even be replaced by another without shattering the system.) A further objection to this view was that it would interpret modernity as a process of secularization leading to nihilism, or to what Strauss defined as a return to God in the desire to escape from a world now deprived of meaning.[1] More generally, the Austrian School's political philosophy marks out quite a different approach from the attempts of those who declined to view it as human understanding of human products but then went on to explore it in search of something which it should not be the duty of philosophy to seek. This was the result of having gradually whittled away the boundary between philosophy and revelation by rationalizing or 'secularizing' the latter.[2]

Modernity therefore cannot be said to represent the cessation of philosophy and of political philosophy seen as a rational human enterprise. Nor can it be said to leave in its place nothing but a form of nihilism, or relativism, opening the floodgates to voluntaristic irrationalism or political theology.

Furthermore, insistence on the theme of secularization to the degree of making it one of the central points of modern political philosophy eventually leads to a false portrayal of modernity. The assessment of political philosophy becomes far too bound up with theological issues, so that philosophy becomes deformed, and the impression is given that it is condemned to failure should it stray too far from the fold of theology. One might even be led to think that the issues and indeed the fundamental concepts of politics originated from Christianity. Quite the opposite is the case. At the roots of modern political philosophy there lay an attempt to rethink philosophy following the fragmentation and political failure of the pre-Renaissance Christian world: an attempt to work out a concept of political order that would take account of the fact that classical cosmology was now untenable and that nothing similar could replace it.[3]

One may well acknowledge that philosophy, inasmuch as its nature is enquiry and exploration, consists in nothing more than the effort to provide solutions for new problems, or for new features of perennial problems, without claiming to establish a definitive solution. Yet abandoning this approach would be tantamount to forsaking philosophy itself. This is a prospect that would open up far more problems than it is capable of solving, and in any case in our field it would reduce political philosophy either to political theology, or to a form of historical fatalism; or else would doom it to watch as values admitting of no statements – about which it would in fact be meaningless to make statements – were locked in deadly struggle.

Rather than explaining the question of modern political philosophy in terms of secularization, one would do well to ask why the predominance of religion over politics is waning. Why and how was a point of reciprocal autonomy reached at the root of which lie both the birth of economic science and also the birth and rise of modern natural science? Such a query is equivalent to enquiring into the 'problematic situation' of political philosophy between the fifteenth and the seventeenth centuries. And it is by no means a foregone conclusion that all can be explained in terms of *secularization*. Consequently, the reduction of the 'problematic situation' of political philosophy to its relation to revelation succeeds in explaining very little.

The critique of modernity put forward by Menger, Mises and Hayek thus did not focus on the aspiration towards scientific knowledge, but rather aimed to fight against extension of the inductivist method to the theoretical social sciences. For like all historical trends, modernity too is an unintentional product of human action. It is not eschatological in character, nor is it the fulfilment of a *telos*. It is simply a trend which, for those who elect to stand outside the framework of historicism, can be halted and changed.

Consequently, the Austrian School's philosophy of the social sciences can be interpreted as an alternative to modernity in the latter's guise as an outcome of positivism, historicism and irrationalism, and it can be considered as *critical rationalism*, as *rational praxis*.[4]

As has been seen, an analysis of the Austrian School that holds it to be an example of the application to politics of a type of knowledge and methodology that arose in a specific economic framework does not seem compelling. Even less does it seem warranted to interpret its political philosophy as an attempt to legitimate the market economy speculatively. A more fitting description of its genuine contribution to political philosophy is as the transition from the theory of subjective values to a theory of the best political order. It did not content itself (except perhaps in the case of Mises) with verification and justification of the fact that, if the subjectivity of values represents the supreme value, a statal organization must be elaborated that will allow all subjective values to be fulfilled. The Austrian School went further, returning to the classical theme of the possibility of conciliating an '*order which is not oppression with freedom which is not licence*'. This is the crux of the school's philosophical problem (and of Hayek's in particular). In agreement with Strauss, there can be no doubt that it is the problem *par excellence* of political philosophy as a human undertaking.

This broad spectrum of issues can also be interpreted as an attempt to overcome the limits of the influential Weberian vision, given that the latter admitted of no other possibility than the 'deadly struggle' between values and spheres of value, thus remaining aloof from political philosophy. By *values*, Hayek meant «what may guide a person's action throughout most of his life as distinct from the concrete ends which determine his action at a particular moment». In this manner, *values* are distinguished from *ends* (objects on which attention is consciously focused and which «will normally be the result of the particular circumstances in which he finds himself at any moment»). Values thereby become intersubjective models, of which the proponents may at times be unaware; furthermore, these models can be culturally transmitted, and like all cultural products, they can be critically discussed. This shows that values, as an expression of a culture or a tradition, can guide individual actions better that the subjective computability of the consequences of an action. Thus in the abstract understanding of the term, values are the elements that render possible «a peaceful existence of the order of an Open Society». It follows that the condition for existence of the latter resides in its members possessing «common opinions, rules and values», rather than in the existence of «a common will issuing commands directing its members to particular ends». The larger the society, the more its common values «must be confined to abstract and general rules of conduct. The members of an Open Society have and can have in common only *opinions* on values but *not* a *will* on concrete ends».[5]

A further contribution by the exponents of the Austrian School to political philosophy can be identified in their quest for a solution to the problem of the cognitive objectivity of the theoretical social sciences. They did not conceive of politics as a struggle between alternative visions, but rather aimed to pass judgment on values by assessing their universalizability, their desired and undesired consequences, and realization costs as well. Political philosophy would come into play when no spontaneous solution to social problems came to the fore. Its premise is thus the conviction that the best solution to problems can derive only from comparison and critique of the proposed solutions. For this is the method that best enables one to make use of the theoretical and practical knowledge randomly diffused throughout society. It follows that the scope of political philosophy is restricted to the social dimension of individual problems. Its task is to ensure that individual solutions are worked out in a more general dimension such as will allow the formation and maintenance of an order that relies on individual contributions as the building blocks for the solution of common problems.

Since such a model prescribes no specific goals, it is compatible with the fallibility of knowledge. It is therefore more easily modifiable upon the appearance of unexpected situations.

Thus the political philosophy and liberalism of the Austrian School are linked, on the one hand, to the latter's claims regarding the consequences for human knowledge of the revolution of subjectivist economics, and, on the other, to the impossibility that any form of centralization of theoretical and practical knowledge can become the nerve centre by means of which society can be guided towards some end. The implications of this approach support the assertion that there can exist no political philosophy that makes boast of superior wisdom and thereby proclaims its fitness for tackling the formulation of a hierarchy of goals and values.

The Austrian School's liberalism, then, did not aim to establish the best allocation of resources for the purposes of common benefits. Instead it left the decision as to individual rewards to the process of catallactics. The maximization of individual utility was not a dogma but an instrument securing benefits for the whole of society. Individual success then became a reward granted by society to whoever manages to furnish the best solution to a problem experienced by the set of individuals of whom society is composed.

The pivotal element in this political model is the *political* conviction that reliance on individual contributions, and the appeal for such contributions to come forward, is the best means to solve political problems. In other words, this model aimed to prevent the political sphere from overlapping onto the individual sphere, and to avert the risk that this, together with confusion between politics, morals, law and economics, might precipitate the situation into totalitarianism or chaos.

The starting point of the Austrian School's political philosophy is thus the fact of the fallibility of human knowledge, together with recognition that knowledge is scattered throughout society. The object of political philosophy is seen as reflection on the abstract rules of conduct within the framework of which all individuals can pursue their own individual ends. Political philosophy therefore has as its object only those individual actions which entail social repercussions, and its aim is the maintenance of order but not of the latter's contents. Consequently, the values and ends to which it turned its attention are the values and ends which could shatter order or set out to modify it.

In this way, politics loses its character as an instrument for the allocation of goods and services according to the importance of the social groups producing them. It is transformed into a critical function, whose essential role is to forestall the eventuality that any momentary condition of power may modify the universal rules of conduct in the struggle to hold on to a dominant position. The problem of politics is not to establish «*Who should rule*?» but rather to furnish a satisfactory answer to the question: «*How can we so organize political institutions that bad or incompetent rulers can be prevented from doing too much damage?*».[6] Hence the need to recall that «the rulers are always certain personalities. And, whatever class they may once have belonged to, once they are rulers they belong to the ruling class».[7]

§ 2. MISES

The leitmotiv running throughout Mises's reflection on liberalism consists of the attempt to tailor theoretical foundations and political practice to the findings of *subjectivist economics.* Apart from the various criticisms that can be levelled at this type of foundation, one can hardly deny its coherence with epistemological doctrine – praxeology[8] – and its perspicacious and innovative finding that it was not only socialistic theories but subjectivist economics as well that had led to the crisis of classical liberalism.

The basic characteristic of this approach was thus the conviction that liberalism is not an ideology or political practice, but a rationalist political philosophy founded on a theory of human action and society. And as a political philosophy it cannot stoop to theoretical and practical compromise with political ideologies, not even when they represent the hegemonic cultural and political forces. Mises saw clearly that the popular dissemination of ideas was no guarantee of their veracity, and that consequently history could not be taken as a measure of the validity of theories. For the untenability of historicism led him to disbelieve in the existence of inevitable processes, maintaining instead that there exists nothing other than historical trends linked to the fact that individuals often have limited knowledge of the consequences of their actions. Furthermore, individuals often prefer to appease immediate needs with unthinking disregard for the effects this could have on the satisfaction of the selfsame needs in the future.

The fact that the historical, social and ideological contingencies that had come to pass in his own age could signal the definitive downfall of liberal ideals thus had no theoretical relevance, as Mises saw it. In this perspective, the crisis of liberalism was not a symptom of its being supplanted by later historical and philosophical developments; instead it was a testimony of the fact that it was unable to adapt its foundations so that they would match the discoveries of subjective economics. It was therefore urgent, Mises argued, to dispel the misunderstanding which held that the crisis of classical economy entailed the failure of the liberal ideal. Subjective economics was not an abandoment of liberalism, but rather a more exhaustive response to theoretical problems – primarily the problem of *value* – which classical economics had not succeeded in resolving.[9]

Even Menger, writing in the early period, had shown the insubstantiality of economic science if the cultural and theoretical heritage of the individualistic tradition were discarded. Mises made the same kind of critical observations vis-à-vis socialistic economy, accusing the latter of ignoring the accomplishments of the theory of subjective values. The opposition thus came to lie in the contrast between a social philosophy that had endorsed the findings of economic science concerning human action and, on the other hand, one that disregarded these findings, considering marginalism as the last-ditch attempt by the bourgeoisie to legitimate and maintain its hegemonic position. If the problem was one of greater production and a more just distribution of wealth, it followed that the best solution could not derive from the part that was dragging its heels. Accordingly, socialism could not be considered the way to overcome the limits of classical economics, but was instead a mistaken outcome of the predicament in which the latter was ensnared: an aspect of the crisis, not its resolution. The definitive statement on the Marxist (and classical) theory of labour-value had already been made by Böhm-Bawerk, and Mises[10] extended the scope of his critique to the theories of socialization.

Therefore the solution could not be sought, contrary to the belief of many at the time, in a blend of liberalism and socialism, or in a generic 'opening up' of liberalism to socialistic ideals. For the latter was a perspective fraught with confusion, and was to be resisted. The spread of the historicist mentality thus led to the mistaking of a *de facto* sitation – deriving from an erroneous representation and understanding of the problem – for an ineluctable historical trend, against which it seemed vain to strive. In the face of this tendency, all that seemed possible was to endeavour to salvage some remnants of the conquests of liberal civilization. Mises's critique of historicism aimed to show the havoc the latter wreaks in the understanding of social phenomena and trends. For these are undeniably products of historical evolution (i.e. consequences of the way individuals have tried to solve the problems and likewise of the spread of ideas, whether true or false), but this does not mean that such trends are also evidence of finalism in history.

Mises took up arms in *Socialism* against this approach to the problem, and he continued to wage his battle right up to his death. The historical ending of socialism thus has limited value, it is none other than the generalized recognition of a failure that from a theoretical point of view was long predicted. And socialism collapsed precisely because it was founded on an anthropological falsehood, and also because, unable as it was to solve the problem of reproduction of capital, it generated not welfare but, on the contrary, poverty. As a solution to the problem of political order, socialism had already shown all its weaknesses long before being discarded by historical evolution, when it had come under the scrutiny of those areas of economic and philosophical-political reflection that had opted to stand aloof from the perspective of historicism.

The problem of liberal political philosophy, then, was one of stimulating awareness that evolution is not endowed with any particular aim, and that in the absence of an aim history cannot be thought to be a judge of human affairs and values. What remains are trends and beliefs that have to be subjected to evaluation by reason in the light of their consequences. When this critique focuses on the individual sphere, it must assess realizability and cost of ends; when, on the other hand, it turns its attention to society, it must appraise universalizability of ends.

The role of tradition (as a complex of prudential norms) is therefore to perform the first critical assessment of innovations springing from the evolutionary process. Consequently, given that every type of human action is a transition from a situation held to be unsatisfactory to one held to be an improvement, it is not the task of political philosophy to guide the process towards the achievement of an end. Rather, it should highlight the unintentional results of human actions. In so doing, political philosophy will make use of the a priori theorems of praxeology.

Set against this backdrop of problems and issues, political philosophy ultimately becomes identified with the liberal tradition, once the errors of classical liberalism have been amended. Other solutions to the problem of political order are unable to reconcile the subjectivity of values with the requirement of universalizable norms of conduct, and are therefore false or inadequate. Despite the credence they may gain, they are doomed to be stranded on the fringe of reflection in political philosophy taken as a rational enterprise. Yet their popularity may still constitute a political problem.

In *Socialism*, in the light of these considerations, Mises interpreted the failure of socialism as due to a mistaken economic and anthropological theory. As a result of this, he argued, the value of «social interdependence» underscored by liberal social philosophy had passed unnoticed. This was not, however, to be taken as suggesting that the state of health of the latter, in those years, was any better. Undeniably, liberalism had to be credited with establishing the basis of modern social science, showing that society was not a «mysterious and incomprehensible» formation explainable only by attributing its development to «divine will guiding human destinies from outside», i.e. by invoking a conception long since abandoned even in natural science. But these credentials were not sufficient to defeat socialist ideology. Identifying «the last great expressions» of the finalistic conception of society as residing in «Kant's *Nature*, which leads humanity towards a special aim», in «Hegel's *World Spirit*» and in «Darwinian *Natural Selection*», Mises took the first steps towards charting an outline of the new liberalism which was to reaffirm the conception of human society as «a product of will and action»:[11] as «an issue of the mind».[12]

Using different expressions from those of Menger, and likewise from those that would later be penned by Hayek, Mises built the foundation of liberalism on a conception of society. The superiority of this society consists not so much in its capacity to function even though individuals may not be virtuous, as in the fact that it would not be founded on ethical values different from eudemonism seen as social co-operation. He underscored that the deleterious influence of socialistic ideals could be combated by elaborating a social philosophy capable of allowing liberalism to regain the prestige it had lost, above all among intellectuals.

But the chief criticism levelled by Mises against contemporary philosophers, namely the accusation that they purported to be dealing with social philosophy without having any knowledge of economic science, also highlighted the fact that when deprived of an economic foundation, liberalism ceases to be a political force, and becomes reduced to a 'religion' of a handful of intellectuals. Cultivating the illusion that it can survive as an ideal force in any regime means nothing more than undermining its worth as a political philosophy.

These erroneous views were not the only conceptions of the foundations of liberalism that Mises intended to discredit. He also aimed to explode the belief that the crisis of *laissez-faire* was to be interpreted as the downfall of liberalism. It did not escape him that it was no longer possible, nor even advantageous, to tie liberalism down to the classical economic theory already coming under fire from marginalism. The cornerstones of this break with tradition are represented by the emphasis placed by Mises on rejecting the charge that liberalism conceives society as a collection of 'atoms', and by his endeavour to expose the misunderstanding concerning the role of the system of ownership in a liberal society. The objection put forward to parry the first accusation consisted in reaffirming that liberal society is founded on the system of the division of labour, and that far from 'atomizing' society, it encourages the formation of strong cohesive bonds, since it makes the satisfaction of individual needs dependent on satisfaction of the needs of the other members of society.[13] To tackle the misconception centring around the system of ownership, on the other hand, Mises pointed out that in the liberal society the system of property has a social function, since it is placed in the hands of those who best know how to obtain the maximum benefit from it on behalf of common prosperity, thereby abolishing privileges and static situations.[14]

As well as contesting the above misconceptions that distorted the picture of liberalism, Mises also dissented from sociological Darwinism and from the claims regarding the origin of society advanced by «social theories which are based on natural law» and which «start from the dogma that human beings are equal». Such theories hold that «since all men are equal», they must «be treated as members of society with full rights». Mises, on the contrary, countered these statements by asserting that «to liberalism the concepts man and social man are the same», and that these rights are therefore deducible from the criterion of social utility, i.e. from the advantages that accrue to each individual from the fact of treating others justly.[15] In this perspective,

> the policy of Liberalism is the policy of the common good, the policy of subjecting particular interests to the public welfare – a process that demands from the individual not so much a renunciation of his own interests as a perception of the harmony of individual interests.[16]

These themes recur in *Liberalism*, where Mises expounded the principles of the liberal conception of economic and social order, analysing the meaning assumed by the term 'liberalism' in the twentieth century. His plan was to show that *Sozialpolitik* and the New Deal were not part of that tradition, but rather belonged to the socialistic tradition.[17] Taking cognizance of the illusory nature of the optimistic beliefs of classical liberalism, according to which the path that has marked out the evolution of society points towards constant progress,[18] Mises set himself the task of bringing liberalism into harmony with subjectivist economics.

In this framework, Mises put forward the view that the foundations of liberalism were to be identified in the conception of human society as an association of individuals working together for the purpose of co-operative actions, and also in the theory according to which at the origin of civilization lies the division of labour.[19] It follows that, by virtue of the solution to the relation between *property*, *freedom* and *peace*, liberalism was the social system providing all individuals with a chance to achieve 'fulfilment'.[20]

Through this solution, understood as the twofold concept of social peace and peace among states,[21] was born a social process – in which the primary concern of producers is to satisfy consumers' demands – out of what was reckoned by other social philosophies to be an irreconcilable conflict between the owners of the means of production and proletarians.[22] Far from being the ideology of exploitation, by making economic and social status depend on the ability to satisy demand for goods and services, liberalism presented itself as a social philosophy characterized by continual social mobility.[23] This interpretation of the market became the pivotal element of Mises's liberalism: a yardstick against which to evaluate human actions, distinguishing between those actions that increase and those that weaken or call into question co-operation and social peace.[24] In this manner, the market system was seen as the most effective instrument to override the natural inequalities between individuals and indeed to obtain public benefits therefrom. It was transformed into an instrument serving the purpose of averting – with coercion if necessary – any risk that this peaceful means of conflict resolution could be undermined.[25]

Granted these premises, Mises accepted the democratic principle, viewing it as «the form of political constitution which makes possible the adaptation of the government to the wishes of the governed without violent struggles». Thus the state obtained its justification on the basis of its role as guarantor of social peace and individual freedom.[26] But in order to ensure that the state does not overstep its bounds, society must be characterized by the diffusion of private property. This in its turn reduces the individual's need of the state, thereby standing as the one and only tool that can successfully counteract the natural aversion of rulers towards the limitation of their power constituted by private property.[27]

In Mises's opinion, however, the term 'liberalism' had undergone a series of distortions produced by the attempt to fuse its social doctrine with other ideologies of our age. Indeed, there appeared to be a bid by such ideologies to take over an ideal tradition which had come to be identified with the modern way of life. Faced with these repeated onslaughts, Mises stressed the need to maintain the distinction between liberalism, on the one hand, and socialism or interventionism, on the other; he showed that their respective foundations are grounded in theories of human action that appear to be absolutely unreconcilable. Hence the unfoundedness of the claim by interventionism to be the final culmination of liberalism and its fusion with socialism and democracy.

These themes recur throughout Mises's discussion of liberalism, and in *Human Action* the approach is largely unchanged from that in *Socialism* and *Liberalism.* Here too liberalism is said to have been founded on a conception of society understood as «division of labor and combination of labor». But unlike the interpretation found in Hayek, society is understood as «the outcome of conscious and purposeful behavior», and while excluding any contract, it has the aim of reaching «definite singular ends». It is «an outcome of human action, i.e. of a conscious aiming at the attainment of ends»: «the outcome of a purposeful utilization of a universal law determining cosmic becoming, viz., the higher productivity of the division of labor». For Mises,

> the question[s] whether society or the individual is to be considered as the ultimate end, and whether the interests of society should be subordinated to those of the individuals or the interests of the individuals to those of society, are fruitless.[28]

The foundation of liberalism is thus seen to reside in the doctrine of the division of labour. Mises believed that this doctrine inspired a whole series of crucial tenets: «the spiritual, moral and intellectual emancipation of mankind inaugurated by the philosophy of Epicureanism»; the replacement of a «heteronomous and institutionalist ethics» by «an autonomous rational morality»; the assumption that laws and legality originated from social co-operation and not from «unfathomable decrees of Heaven»; and finally, the vision of social dynamics as co-operation rather than as unreconcilable antagonism. Liberal social doctrine, inasmuch as it is «based on the teachings of utilitarian ethics and economics», «aims at democratic government».[29]

Liberalism is therefore «a political doctrine [. . .] not a theory», which aims to apply «the theories developed by praxeology and especially by economics to definite problems of human action within society». It «is not neutral with regard to values» but informs individuals «about the means suitable to the realization of their plans». Naturally, Liberalism is not indifferent to spiritual and intellectual aspirations. But it believes that the most fitting strategy is to create a milieu in which the flowering of individual creativity will not be cramped and repressed, but on the contrary will be inspired to greater heights, so that within the limits of feasibility, man will be freed from material toil. The history of Western civilization thus coincides with the rise to splendour of the liberal civilization, whose greatest accomplishment lies not so much in its series of great scientific and artistic triumphs, but rather in having made «the great works and great thoughts accessible to the common man».[30]

Among the properties of liberalism, Mises also listed the fact that it was «based upon a purely rational and scientific theory of social co-operation». This was not to be taken as meaning that it was atheistic, however, nor hostile to religion: simply that it was «radically opposed to all systems of theocracy». The relation between liberalism and religion, Mises reflected, was thus one of tolerance founded on the neutrality of liberalism vis-à-vis religious beliefs that do not interfere «with the conduct of social, political, and economic affairs». But if religion takes on the characteristics of a form of theocracy («an insight not open to examination by reason and to demonstration by logical methods», which claims «to organize the earthly affairs of mankind according to the contents of a complex of ideas whose validity cannot be demonstrated by reasoning»), this relation can become one of opposition. Although religion may on occasion have assumed theocratic forms, Mises believed that there subsisted no incompatibility between the rationalism of liberalism and the rules of behaviour obtaining in private affairs and inspired by the gospel teachings. Ranking liberalism above religion, Mises also assigned to the former the task of preventing church intervention in secular affairs from reaching the point of conflict between these two powers. The separation between church and state was therefore due to the need for an institution that would safeguard rational discussion concerning social problems.[31]

The position espoused by Mises was no less than a passionate defence of the conquests of the liberal civilization. In an era in which its fortunes seemed to be ebbing, Mises proudly proclaimed its merits and defended it against unjust and false accusations. But in this noble reaffirmation of ideals and historical merits, expressed when liberalism faced the charge of having favoured the advent of totalitarian regimes, one can also read a criticisim of the inadequacies of the social philosophy of classical liberalism. For the latter had been incapable of reacting against the reproach that it had acted in defence of the privileged castes, and had implicitly accepted the Marxistic vision of society, thereby coming to represent, in the eyes of the masses, the ideology of the ruling class.

Mises's reponse to this crisis was to revitalize liberal social philosophy. The historical conditions, even his own academic and cultural isolation, were not conducive to the reception of his proposals, at times even in liberal circles. This was partly because in those years liberal culture appeared to be afflicted by a sense of inevitable defeat. Such an attitude could be sensed in the works of many who, while proclaiming themselves liberals, confined themselves either to backing no longer acceptable and outdated perspectives, or else to snubbing the heritage of tradition in a vain and myopic endeavour to seem 'open' to the new age. Often in peremptory terms, exposing himself to the risk of being accused of following in the steps of Marxism in equating the economy with the driving force of historical, political and social evolution, Mises insisted that no political philosophy can effectively seek after the best regime if it is divorced from the establishment and development of the system of division of labour and social co-operation.

§ 3. HAYEK

With the publication of *The Constitution of Liberty* in 1960, Hayek systematically explored the issues of political philosophy in a treatise on the best regime that is one of the most significant twentieth-century documents of liberalism.[32] This work is notable also as the turning point in the almost exclusively defensive war that liberalism had waged – and not always successfully – against Marxism and interventionism. Hayek's intention was thus to reconsider its philosophical foundations and its history, and above all to endow it with an economic theory that would take account of what had happened in the meantime.[33]

The Constitution of Liberty also heralds Hayek's transition to a mature evolutionistic conception of social phenomena and institutions. It was no coincidence that here he once more stated his conviction that «freedom is not a state of nature but an artifact of civilization» which «did not arise from design» or by precise intent. Hayek thus distinguished liberalism into two traditions:

> one empirical and unsystematic, the other speculative and rationalistic – the first based on an interpretation of traditions and institutions which had spontaneously grown up and were but imperfectly understood, the second aiming at the construction of a utopia, which has often been tried but never successfully.

Faced with the overwhelming predominance of the second tradition together with its outcome, Hayek planned to champion a positive assessment of the first tradition, in the conviction that it could provide an antidote to the ills of our age.[34]

A return to the teachings of Mandeville, Hume, Smith, Ferguson and Menger, on the subject of the role of reason and the origin of human institutions, appeared to Hayek to be the first and indispensable step towards the revival of liberalism. The discovery that institutions are «the result of human action but not the execution of human design» had enabled these thinkers «to comprehend how institutions and morals, language and law, have evolved by a process of cumulative growth», and how, in the same context, «human reason has grown and can successfully operate». Hayek therefore wished to underscore that this tradition – the authentic liberal tradition – differs from the individualism of Cartesian ancestry and from the latter's assumption «of an independently and antecedently existing human reason that invented these institutions». Yet it could not be identified with the belief that «civil society was formed by some wise original legislator or an original 'social contract'», in which Hayek discerned the origin of «totalitarian democracy».[35]

It was not Hayek's intention, however, to dispute the stimulus given to the growth of civilization in Europe as a result of the critical use of reason. He merely wished to call attention to the cautionary message implicit in the words of Montesquieu, who stated that «'la raison même a besoin de limites'». 'Constructivist rationalism' was thus, in Hayek's eyes, «an illegitimate and erroneous exaggeration of a characteristic element of the European tradition» – even though its leading figures included no less than Plato, Descartes, Hobbes, Rousseau, Hegel, Marx and the exponents of positivism. There could be no doubt that it was the most important philosophical tradition of the West, but it could not be regarded as the only school of thought. For alongside this mainstream tradition another, less ambitious trend could be observed, namely the philosophical tradition from which liberalism had arisen. To this tradition, Hayek claimed, as well as the thinkers already cited, belonged Aristotle, Cicero, Saint Thomas and, among his own contemporaries, the founder of 'critical rationalism', Popper. A special position was occupied by certain others, on account of the influence exerted on them by Rousseau and French rationalism; Hayek referred here to Humboldt, Kant, Bentham and the English utilitarians.[36]

This intentional simplification has the virtue of highlighting the pattern of opposition between the two traditions and the ensuing political consequences. If any fault can be found in Hayek's account, it does not reside in having oversimplified, but in having underestimated the German philosophical tradition, whose major exponents figured only in minor roles in both schools of thought. Indirect confirmation is thereby furnished of the claim that the Austrian School stood apart from German culture and from the outcome of the latter's political and social philosophy. But this was not the focal point of Hayek's attention; for his real concern was to assert once again that the crisis of the constructivist-rationalist tradition could not and should not be mistaken for a crisis of Western political philosophy.

This interpretation of the history and destiny of Western political philosophy came to the fore in the essay 'Liberalism'. Here Hayek underscored that the pressing necessity to keep the two main traditions separate could admit of no further delay. Deliberate or involuntary intermingling of these components, he argued, had led first to the gradual loss of the spirit manifested at the outset, and subsequently to the eclipse of the liberal ideal. Drained by debate regarding its own character and foundations, liberalism had failed to provide an adequate response to the criticism levelled against it. Bound up as it was with a certain interpretation of classical political economy, for better or for worse, it had run the risk of suffering the latter's own fate.

Hayek's interpretation of the history of liberalism thus evinced the desire to show that it was founded on a conceptual core which, if left unfulfilled, would transmute it into something other than itself, or even doom it to extinction. Set beside this, the fact that this history can also be seen as an attempt by Hayek to furnish historical legitimation for his own liberalism pales into insignificance. For one cannot fault Hayek when he asserts that the revival of liberalism would not have been possible without the theory of subjective values and without fusion of the Scottish theory of social institutions with Mengerian theory. And it cannot be denied that it was Hayek himself who successfully carried out this fusion. By the same token, he was responsible for the most seminal attempt to establish the theoretical nucleus of liberalism, distinguishing it from other movements that had usurped the term. Contemporary liberalisms that ignored the contribution of Austrian marginalism have not succeeded in doing anything of the kind.

As part of the theoretical foundations of liberalism, then – along with the older conceptions of freedom, the concept of natural rights, the theory of sovereignty and the separation of powers, and the problems of justice and equality – Hayek also introduced the theory of *spontaneous order*, together with a renewed approach to the relation with democratic tradition. What stands out above all is the definition of the central core of liberal doctrine, i.e. the assumption from which «all liberal postulates» derive. This was the conviction that

> more successful solutions of the problems of society are to be expected if we do not rely on the application of anyone's given knowledge, but encourage the interpersonal process of the exchange of opinion from which better knowledge can be expected to emerge.

In the general process of discussion and critical assessment, economic freedom performs a function as important as intellectual freedom. For if it is true that it is «the mind which chooses the ends of human action, their realization depends on the availability of the required means, and any economic control which gives power over the means also gives power over the ends».[37]

The problem liberalism faced was thus of understanding what it is that links common welfare to individual egoism. It was not a question of founding liberalism on a concept of 'natural freedom' that would consider every social constraint as a restriction on individual freedom; what was required, instead, was to encourage the birth and advancement of institutions committed to guaranteeing life, freedom and ownership, and to guiding individual efforts towards socially beneficial aims. It was no part of this liberalism's mission to defend *laissez-faire*;[38] rather, its objective was the defence of a critical appraisal of the functions and limits of statal action, endeavouring to ward off social evil rather than to foster the social good.

The value of freedom therefore consists «mainly in the opportunity it provides for the growth of the undesigned». But far from considering tradition as unalterable, or «assuming that those who created the institutions were wiser than we are», Hayek's liberalism was founded on the conviction that «the result of the experimentation of many generations may embody more experience than any one man possesses».[39]

Hayek exploited the unforeseeability of the outcome that individual contributions can give to this process, and the principle of equality before the law, to underscore the points in common between «traditional liberalism and the democratic movement», and to trace the distinction between *liberalism* and *democracy*. He did not believe that their respective goals tended to coincide, or that liberalism was superseded, in historical or philosophical-political terms, by democracy. If liberalism held that the powers of the state must be as restricted as possible, democratic theory on the other hand, according to Hayek, held that the only limit should be that of the majority: «liberalism is a doctrine about what the law ought to be, democracy a doctrine about the manner of determining what will be the law». Thus liberalism's espousal of democratic principles confined itself to an acceptance of «majority rule as a method of deciding». The overwhelming flaw of democratic theory derived in his view from its having been «developed with some ideal homogeneous community in view and then applied to the very imperfect and often arbitrary units which the existing states constitute». Consquently, it «is not an ultimate or absolute value and must be judged by what it will achieve. It is probably the best method of achieving certain ends, but not an end in itself.»[40]

Hayek accordingly took a critical stance towards that particular brand of democratic rhetoric that had caused mayhem in political philosophy by ruling that the problem of the best political order was to be resolved within democratic theory. The result had been both the blurring of boundaries between a form of regime and political philosophy and also the lack of distinction between the two concepts, as a result of which the concept of democracy had been rendered generic and vacuous. Besides, Hayek could not accept the idea that the political philosopher should feel bound by the opinion of the majority, being reduced to no more than an official carrying out the majority will. He therefore put in a plea for the autonomy and independence of political philosophy, claiming that its task consists in showing «possibilities and consequences of common action», and in elaborating «comprehensive aims of policy as a whole which the majority have not yet thought of». In other words, liberal political philosophy is «the art of making politically possible the seemingly impossible».[41]

Hayek did not simply reiterate the difficulties inherent in the relation between political philosophy and democracy. In a period when hegemonic reflection on politics belonged to that empiricist and positivistic political science that had reduced the field of investigation of politics to verification of «questions of fact», he once again emphasized that the task of political philosophy is one «of deciding between conflicting values». For the political philosopher «cannot allow himself to be limited by the positivism of the scientist, which confines his functions to showing what is the case and forbids any discussion of what ought to be». Such a situation would have transformed political philosophy into an ideology with the aim of legitimating the democratic model that had become established in those years. A historical model of political regime would have been mistaken for philosophical reflection on the best regime.[42]

All this means that the political philosopher must stand equally aloof both from power and from the *demos*, and must take up a critical attitude towards both. The political philosopher can «often serve democracy best by opposing the will of the majority» rather than trying to provide democracy with a philosophical justification. In fact, it is precisely the unpopularity of his opinions which are the hallmark, in a democratic regime, of the validity of his position and his role. «It is by insisting on considerations which the majority do not wish to take into account, by holding up principles which they regard as inconvenient and irksome, that he has to prove his worth.» The most serious hazard that political philosophy, democracy and freedom have to contend with is therefore an underestimation of the dangers that stem from conferring upon rulers the task of pursuing particular ends.[43]

Revival of the liberal tradition also implied a redefinition of the duties of the state. Here Hayek's position differs from those who have subscribed to the thesis of the 'minimal state', frequently understood as privatization of the state. Hayek, by contrast, argued that the state primarily fulfils the function of guarantor of order, and additionally that of performing tasks indispensable for the functioning of a '*great society*' whenever these are insufficiently remunerated and cannot be carried out via the market. These arguments did not amount to reintroducing by the back door of practical considerations the interventionism that had been thrown out in theory; rather, they were simply recognition that the market, like all human productions, cannot solve everything.[44]

Hayek's liberalism was therefore as far removed from interventionistic democracy as it was from *conservatism*. Indeed, it was Hayek himself, in 'Why I Am Not a Conservative', (the Postscript to *The Constitution of Liberty*), who clearly traced a distinction that would become more accentuated in *Law, Legislation and Liberty*,[45] with the defence of *catallactics* as a social order that was not finalistic but open to innovation.[46] Once again, the basis for this distinction lay in the turning point represented by subjectivist economics, whereby the position of individuals and social groups was made to depend on the dynamics of the market. But this position has not been given due consideration by those who accuse Hayek of being a conservative, with the result of offering an imprecise and misleading portrayal of his social philosophy.[47]

In 'Why I Am Not a Conservative', conservatism is defined as «a legitimate, probably necessary, and certainly widespread attitude of opposition to drastic change». It is thus a political attitude running counter to liberalism, which latter «is not averse to evolution and change; and where spontaneous change has been smothered by government control, it wants a great deal of change of policy». Consequently, liberalism is not a social philosophy wishing «to preserve things as they are», but the belief «that what is most urgently needed in most parts of the world is a thorough sweeping-away of the obstacles to free growth».[48]

Hayek's liberalism (and more generally that of the Austrian School»),[49] thus interpreted, steps forth as an alternative to conservatism. The latter, Hayek felt, interpreted historical evolution and modernity as a process of decadence which had to be checked in order to set the course of history back on the right track. Yet this did not imply that its caution in the face of innovation and the effects of change on the overall social structure was totally unfounded. Hayek stopped far short of claiming that there could be nothing to learn from conservative thinkers such as Coleridge, Bonald, de Maistre, Möser and Donoso Cortes. Politically reactionary though they might have been, they had highlighted «the value of the grown institutions we know». But despite this acknowledgment, Hayek also felt that their contribution to the study of social phenomena went no further than that. Their «fear of change» could not be shared, and neither could their «timid distrust of the new as such», since both attitudes led them «to use the powers of government to prevent change or to limit its rate to whatever appeals to the more timid mind». The main theoretical limit of conservatism, then, resided in its inability to formulate «a general conception of how a social order is maintained». It is no coincidence that in the attempt to overcome this limitation conservatism invokes the teachings of thinkers such as Burke, Macaulay, Tocqueville, Lord Acton and Lecky, all of whom, one may note, «certainly considered themselves liberals».[50]

What distinguishes the two political philosophies is therefore the problem of coercion and arbitrary power. These are deemed by the conservative to be instruments that honest and wise rulers may use to pursue just ends, without being «too much restricted by rigid rules». For similarly to socialism, conservatism believes that even moral and religious ideals can be subjected to coercion for the attainment of ends regarded as desirable, and that «in any society there are recognizably superior persons whose inherited standards and values and position ought to be protected and who should have a greater influence on public affairs than others». It thereby tends «to defend a particular established hierarchy». Liberalism, on the other hand, takes the view that «moral beliefs concerning matters of conduct which do not directly interfere with the protected sphere of other persons do not justify coercion». Therefore, since it is not egalitarian, it proclaims that «no respect for established values can justify the resort to privilege or monopoly or any other coercive power of the state in order to shelter such people against the forces of economic change». As a consequence, the élites «have to prove themselves by their capacity to maintain their position under the same rules that apply to all others»[51] who are members of society.

Here too, the line of demarcation between the two schools of thought is shown by the different value ascribed to the market. In the eyes of liberalism the market essentially stands for a system of transfer of information and knowledge, whereas conservatism regards it above all as fomenting disintegration of social values, and feels it ought to be controlled and directed. The inability of conservative thought to understand the reasons of social change has driven its proponents to defend the values they believe in by appealing to «the authority of supernatural sources of knowledge», of which they confidently believe themselves to be the repository.[52] These diverging attitudes have generated a radically different outlook towards the conception of *political philosophy*. Liberalism holds it to be founded on ignorance and on the quest for an explanation of phenomena that elude understanding, yet it stops short of espousing political immobilism. Therefore, though «*quieta non movere* may at times be a wise maxim for the statesman, it cannot satisfy the political philosopher». Striving «to free the process of spontaneous growth from the obstacles and encumbrances that human folly has erected», the political philosopher must not shrink back before the opinion of the majority; but with his capacity for persuasion he must endeavour to win the support of whoever is ready «to examine critically the existing and to change it wherever necessary». It follows that his task «can only be to influence public opinion, not to organize people for action».[53]

Nevertheless, Hayek's liberalism should not be identified with the anarchic or libertarian connotation that is a characteristic trait of certain versions of the revival of American liberalism in particular. For Hayek's thought developed out of the European tradition according to which the state is not so much 'our enemy'[54] as a product of human action whose aim is to guarantee peaceful coexistence and the attainment of individual ends in the framework of law.

Thus Hayek's liberalism should be distinguished not only from conservativism, but also from *libertarianism*[55] and from *anarcho-capitalism*.[56] Although the foundations and development of libertarianism and anarcho-capitalism have a debt to the Austrian School, and even more so to the Chicago School – and perhaps more to Mises than to Hayek – two undeniably different conceptions of the state stand out. For Hayek's conception (but not that of Mises) lacks that utilitarian interpretation of the state which, by contrast, does put in an appearance at times in libertarianism and anarcho-capitalism. Hayekian liberalism ranks as part of the tradition whereby the state is seen as an instrument that will ensure the evolution of a spontaneous order. The task assigned to the state, in Hayek, thus extends far beyond the mere guarantee of private law, rising to the function of guarantor of a pre-political order. Any move to recast this order in a different mould by political means is a gamble in the wake of which comes the peril of transforming the state into a tool of oppression.

This is no idle speculation, but follows from recognition that political knowledge constitutes only a part of a more complex body of knowledge that is unequally distributed throughout the various spheres of human action. Consequently, politics is not entitled to assume the guiding function of humanity. Far from it, for one can in fact summarize the teachings of the Austrian School as a demonstration that every time the attempt to overstep these bounds has been ventured, politics has been turned into a tool of oppression, incapable, in any case, of achieving the objectives it set itself. In this sense, the Austrian School has unequivocally shown the outcome of the tradition that upholds the primacy of politics. The moot point that still remains is how to transform these insights into a new articulation of the various spheres of human action, with the aim of pursuing the formation and maintenance of an *order*.

Critique of the 'mirage of social justice' is accordingly one aspect of this broader and intricate web of issues. The point is that to fix wealth-distribution parameters according to a design that fails to take into account the unforeseeability of change, in a world dominated by uncertainty regarding the possible outcome of human actions – or indeed assuming that it is possible to guide such changes – would be tantamount to stifling any kind of social development, or confining the latter within a prearranged pattern even more tightly bound to political power. In practical terms, this would mean spurning the idea that the optimal use of knowledge scattered throughout society is closely connected with individual freedom to choose ends. The concept of a government that establishes what opportunities are available to all people, and in particular places utmost emphasis on equality, appears therefore to be the very opposite of the idea of a free society. Furthermore, if the role that an individual or his or her offspring are to play in the future is fixed in advance, this is likely to arouse far greater discontent than would be generated in a society where the future is linked to individual capacities and to the ability to foresee which activities will yield greatest material and moral satisfaction.

In conclusion, if

> the overall order depends on the use of knowledge possessed by the individuals and used for their purposes, it becomes clear that the role of government in that process cannot be to determine particular results for particular individuals or groups, but only to provide certain generic conditions whose effects on the several individuals will be unpredictable.[57]

§ 4. EPILOGUE

The liberalism of the Austrian School closes one phase in the history of liberalism, and opens another. Its generalization of the findings of the *theory of marginal utility*[58] as the foundation of liberal political philosophy opened up new perspectives and marked the end of old-style liberalism. The older liberalism had not been able to withstand the frequently unfair criticisms levelled against it on account of the way it had provided ideological backing for the despised *laissez-faire* capitalism. Nor had it withstood the new social science unfolding as an outgrowth of positivistic ideas, nor even the blending of historicism and socialism into a salvation-bestowing vision of becoming. These extremely unfavourable historical circumstances were, if anything, further aggravated by awareness that the theoretical principles of classical liberalism were by now thoroughly outworn. Faced with this legacy, the embattled leaders of the Austrian School perceived that the future depended above all on their ability to elaborate a new philosophy of the social sciences.

Together with this theoretical refoundation, there arose a new interpretation of the history of liberal thought, centred on a positive reappraisal of the tradition of *spontaneous order*. The latter came to be seen, especially in Hayek, as the essence of liberalism. As a result of this new trend, certain figures, felt to be too closely linked to rationalism and utilitarianism, were relegated to the backwaters of the history of liberalism, while others, such as Burke and Savigny, were elevated to the ranks of fully fledged liberal thinkers. Naturally, this 'new history' of liberalism has both merits and shortcomings; but it cannot be denied that it represents a conceptual structure graced by coherence and originality, which stands as a historical and theoretical milestone.

If Hayek can be faulted, it is for having at times singled out individual German liberal thinkers rather than making reference to the entire tradition of German liberalism. The point at issue is that of ascertaining whether there effectively existed a 'liberal tradition' as such within German culture, or whether it was not perhaps a case of individual liberal thinkers. From this point of view, the Austrian School as a whole appears to have been characterized from its outset by opposition to 'German culture', regarding the latter as anti-liberal. This opposition did not, however, rule out the possibility of welcoming into the fold of the liberal tradition individual thinkers such as Kant, Humboldt and Savigny.

Within the perspective of historical references, a comparison between Hayek and Mises reveals important differences linked to Hayek's criticism of Mises for establishing the foundations of his liberalism in too rationalistic and utilitarian a fashion. For when Mises embarked on the undertaking of mapping out a history of liberalism, the background on which he drew differed both from the kinds of reference introduced by Hayek and also from those mentioned by Menger. It should therefore be no cause for surprise that Mises felt closer to exponents of the rationalistic and utilitarian tradition, whom Menger and Hayek, on the other hand, deemed to be alien to their own spirit. Furthermore, even when all three did pass a positive verdict on the same authors, their motivations differed. Nevertheless, if for no other reason than that of chronological sequence, it was Mises who initiated the renewal of liberalism that was later to be continued and developed by Hayek.

The theory of the origin and development of social institutions worked out by Menger in the *Untersuchungen* appears as a focal point which, despite the different assessments made by Mises and Hayek, laid the foundation for a new liberalism, and heralded the critique of historicism and scientism from which the Austrian School's political philosophy arose. The latter can thus be accounted an attempt to chart a new role for political philosophy following the tragic – and predicted – failure of historicism and constructivist rationalism. Moreover, it was also a response to the realization that the Mengerian theory of the birth of social institutions (language, money, law, the state, religion, etc.), if accepted, would spark off a revolution in the articulation of the social sciences, a redefinition of the relations holding between them and the end of the primacy of politics.

It follows that the polemical stance taken up by the exponents of the Austrian School, against those who strove to deduce practical norms of individual and political action from the presumed discovery of the meaning and laws of historical becoming, cannot be thought of as lying on the fringe of the problems of political philosophy and the latter's relation with history. Glancing back to the dawn of political philosophy, one notes that just as the idea of history as becoming and as finality was completely unknown at that time, so also the idea of a reason bestowing order on the world was inconceivable; equally outlandish was the idea that every desire had a right to be fulfilled. In the face of these odds, political philosophy found itself defenceless when pitted against the onslaughts of the philosophy of history, naturalistic rationalism and the relativism of values. In the subsequent enterprise of 'restoration' the Austrian School played a role that cannot be overlooked.

In other words, Mises and Hayek not only saw that the restoration of liberal philosophy would have to contend with historicism, scientism and constructivist rationalism. But indeed, they realized that it could not even be attempted unless an effort were made to overcome the cumbersome legacy of the past, embodied by the theory of labour-value, *laissez-faire* and *homo oeconomicus*, all of which, in varying degrees, had up to then formed part of the cultural trappings of liberalism. The old liberalism had been incapable of renewing itself because, in the endeavour to rid itself of the image of defender and heir of that type of capitalism, it also forswore the idea that it was rooted in a theory of the relation between the individual and society. By contrast Mises and Hayek opposed attempts to throw out ignominiously a wealth of social, political, economic and civil conquests comparable only to the accomplishments of Christianity. Confident they had succeeded in overcoming the limitations of classical liberalism, they once again championed the validity of liberal political philosophy.

The century that is drawing to a close has kindled a ferment of ideas that seem to have a bearing on some of the controversies that have animated philosophical reflection over the last 200 years. Anyone still cultivating the idea of «world history» as the «world's court of judgment»[59] might be tempted to think that history has issued its verdict on the age-old controversy between those whom, borrowing a phrase from Hayek or Oakeshott, one might define as the theorists of the *nomocratic regime* and the theorists of the *teleocratic regime*: a judgment on the central theme of political philosophy in its meaning as quest for the *best political order.*

It would be naive, indeed fallacious, to imagine that an era is being heralded in which the debunking of outworn myths will unveil the truth before our eyes. However, it is arguable that unless one believes that political reflection should remain totally indifferent in the face of the development and historical manifestation of its concepts, there are lessons to be learned from the present state of affairs. The first is that political philosophy is not a form of ideology; nor can it be reduced to historical knowledge, or naturalistic knowledge. If by political philosophy one has in mind the philosophical quest for the best political regime – a human undertaking, in other words, guided by reason and experience – then one is in a far better position today to make a lucid appraisal of several strands of thought thrown up by a century of deliberation. These strands are: the belief that political philosophy was the ideological expression of class conflict; attempts to present it as accredited through research and the ensuing discovery of the goal of history; and finally, the belief that problems of civil coexistence derive from the failure to apply the methods and knowledge of natural science in this sphere.

For it has become self-evident that practical norms guaranteeing the success of individual and collective action cannot be deduced from the study and presumed discovery of the laws of historical becoming. It is equally plain that the application of scientific discoveries to society can do no more than solve a few political-social problems, and even then only at the cost of creating new ones, some of which are even more disturbing.

Marxist historicism was one of the chief 'paradigms' that constituted part of the distinctive features of modernity. Its dissolution and increasing doubts about the 'wonder-working' effects of the social application of scientific discoveries focus attention once again on the specificity of political reflection and its theoretical premises. Consequently, political philosophy is now free to return to its task as the human quest for the best political regime, but naturally this also raises anew the issue of what should be taken as the 'best political order'. It is in this perspective that the contribution of the Austrian School to the revival of political philosophy must be evaluated.

Indeed, the entire history of modern political philosophy can be seen as a debate centring on two different approaches to the problem of the best political order. The first views politics as the point at which philosophy establishes order in the complex of social relations. The second believes that social relations themselves are capable of producing an order understood as a set of inter-individual relations (for instance, the division and organization of labour) such that abstract advantages can be guaranteed to members of a society and, more generally, the outcome of an action can be rendered foreseeable. A salient characteristic of this latter approach is the belief that political interaction is only one of the possible types of inter-individual relations, and that no valid reasons can therefore be adduced to justify its predominance over the others.

Historical experience is not a criterion of truth, but only one of the possible ways of attempting, in the manner of Popper, to confute theories (or at least to display some of their limits). Thus, if one of the characteristics of an 'order' is its persistence over time, historical experience reveals that attempts to impose an order on human relations, or rather, to 'order' them in advance of achievement of an end, are destined to be transformed into a series of acts of coercion which in the course of time will degenerate into a form of chaos. What is manifested, in this case, is the necessary outcome of the attempt to order society on the basis of knowledge conceived as having reached completion and no longer susceptible of correction or modification. The problem can also be seen as concerning the capacity of philosophy to foresee and direct change. If one takes the position that this is impossible, then it follows that all attempts to conceive the relation between thought and reality as two distinct elements obeying different and distinct logics and evolutionary processes – which nevertheless imply the subordination of reality to abstract reason – will have negative effects on the problem of political order.

More particularly, it is perhaps fitting, conceivably even necessary, to ask wherein lies the claim of politics to *confer order* on society. This entails two further questions. The first, of a theoretical character, is linked to the foundation of 'political knowledge', and concerns the presuppositions on the basis of which it is believed that this knowledge is superior to other types of knowledge concerning human facts, for instance morals, religion and economics. The second, of a historiographic nature, concerns historical evolution and the outcome of that majority trend in political philosophy which has privileged the *state* at the expense of *society*, making the former its chief object of reflection. In this, the fact that, while society is a natural entity, the state is an artificial and at times random entity, has been overlooked.

The main lesson to be learned from the work of Hayek is that the time has now arrived to draw appropriate conclusions from the failure of the age-old attempt to 'legitimate the bastard'.[60] These conclusions cannot be limited to a repudiation of those tendencies of political philosophy whose failure is painfully obvious. The conclusions must extend to a reflection on all the other tendencies that have made the state the main object of debate, attributing to it the capacity to order society, understood as the focal point of individual subjectivity and of the conflict that can be reconciled only in the perspective of higher values.

Reflection, in other words, must tackle the belief that politics is capable of creating or realizing an *order*, and that it must coincide with the statal sphere.

Upon closer inspection, this rethinking does not imply a reformulation of the nature and tasks of political philosophy. The latter is still understood as enquiry into the best political regime, and as philosophical and critical reflection on the great cultural, economic, ethical and technological-scientific issues of an era, to the extent to which they impinge on the political dimension. But regardless of which of these two perspectives is adopted as the standpoint from which to make an assessment of political philosophy – for the two perspectives are complementary – the main theme of political philosophy still remains that of *order*. The element of controversy, if any, concerns the point at which the requirement of order comes to the fore. In other words, the essential question is: whether order is a spontaneous product of social dynamics which, as such, is already manifested in society; or whether, by contrast, should one happen to regard society as constitutionally incapable of producing order and predominantly an expression of conflict, order would then be the main task and philosophical justification of the state – a product of the state.

Modern political-philosophical reflection is concerned with these two different conceptions of order. On the one hand, the liberal tradition of the Austrian School tends to consider order a spontaneous, non-natural but cultural production of society. The task of the state, in this framework, is to act as guarantor of the rules of civil coexistence. On the other hand, other political traditions, for all the differences they evince, hold the conviction that order has to be imposed on society, since the latter is seen as unable to perceive anything beyond the interests of the social groups making up society, and incapable of overcoming what is interpreted as the unreconcilable clash between such interests.

The great dichotomy between the *nomocratic* and the *teleocratic* model thus appears not only as a criterion of analytic simplification, but also as a seminal interpretative canon of the history of modern political philosophy. It ultimately embodies the unceasing debate concerning the primacy of society or the state, and the nature and goal of civil coexistence. Acceptance of the one or the other of the two models strongly influences the nature and function of politics. Adopting the standpoint of the nomocratic model leads to a drastic scaling down of the function of politics, given that the latter would thereby lose its role as supreme 'architectural science'. If, however, one adopts the framework of the teleocratic model, the role of politics will clearly be reinforced.

The outcome of these considerations has been that all attempts to restrict or deny individual freedom on account of the high number of negative consequences ascribed to it have been fated to prompt the elaboration, indeed at times the establishment, of political organizations with aspects even less desirable than those which were supposedly to be avoided. If in the case of liberal political philosophy the risk was that the political philosopher could be reduced to one who endeavours to endow the complex of individual volitions with philosophical legitimation, in the other case he was transformed into a counsellor of the prince or a figure who imposed on men what they themselves were unable to know. In the latter case, however, the question of the truth of what was to be imposed still remained open. There was an abiding risk that the imposed wisdom might not only fail to be welcomed by the *demos* but actually be false. In either case, political philosophy was ultimately divested of its role as the crucial link between truth and opinion, the instrument of which is education; moreover, in no way could this approach promote civil coexistence, given the philosopher's refusal to use force.

The fact that the option of force is barred to political philosophy clearly does not mean that philosophical legitimation of individual wills is the only alternative possible. Yet it would be mistaken to assume that this was the perspective in which the Austrian School evolved. Rather, the latter's concern was to ensure that individual wills took part in a process of discussion and critical research, the results of which eventually limit the absoluteness of these wills, transforming them into elements for the creation of an order. The very scarcity of goods compared to the infinity of needs and ends is seen as limiting the absoluteness of wills, transforming them into elements of a dynamic order. In this case, however, politics is stripped of its role as arbitrator between individual expectations that have entered into conflict, thereby itself becoming one of the individual expectations from which, through a process of comparison and contrast, an order is produced.

The Austrian School's major contribution to the theory of order resides precisely in its having demonstrated that the conflict between individual expectations does not concern questions of life or death – which would lead to radicalizing and absolutizing expectations – but rather things, or quantities, taken singly. Furthermore, in the perspective of the theory of subjective values these things can be exchanged for others according to the principle of marginal utility. Thus according to the theory of subjective values the abundance of goods becomes the presupposition for a peaceful solution to conflicts. Such goods do not consist exclusively of material goods, however. Rather, material goods can be exchanged for other types of goods, and the more goods there are available, the less value attaches to them. Naturally, this exchange activity needs to be regulated by rules aiming to prevent a position of advantage from being transformed into privilege or into a position of strength from whence the rules can be changed to the advantage[61] of some particular group.

The essence of these observations is to highlight the Austrian School's important contribution on the problem of civil coexistence. Insistence on the issue of the relation between individualism and economic efficiency may suggest that the 'great society' that Mises and Hayek had in mind was none other than a society in which the prosperity produced by the market would allow all its members greater subjective freedom: a society where the sovereignty of the consumer and individual prosperity would appear to be the premise for a freedom knowing no bounds or limits. But the truth is that the economic science which lay at the root of the Austrian School's social philosophy was far from identifying economic action with the consumption of goods. In fact Menger believed that «we perform an economic action inasmuch as we provide the means necessary for satisfaction of our needs, and we thereby assure the possibility of consumption at a future date, but not through the very fact that we consume».[62] This places tight restrictions on consumption, with undeniable consequences of a political nature, and it eventually led Hayek to identify the task of political philosophy as that of distinguishing between individual expectations which are likely to be satisfiable and those that are not. This in turn means evaluating individual expectations in the perspective of the formation of an order that can also be understood as the 'common good' of civil society, i.e. as something different from consumption regarded as an end in itself.

Certainly, the concept of increasing individual prosperity as a means to provide rules through which to deal with social conflict is one possible solution to the problem of civil coexistence. For no civil coexistence can be sustained unless the material conditions of individual and collective existence are met and stabilized. Yet it is a solution that produces more problems than it solves. In its modern version, the relation between the sphere of needs satisfaction and that of civil coexistence is identified with the problem of liberalism: how to avoid the formation of a *lawless rabble*. One may therefore view the social philosophy of the Austrian School as a fertile attempt to utilize material prosperity and leisure time for a process of liberal education.

Still unresolved, however, is the role of political philosophy. As the quest for the 'political good', it has only limited knowledge concerning those goods whose exchange promotes order and those which are detrimental to order. It cannot elaborate a hierarchy of ends to act as a yardstick against which individual behaviour can be measured. All it can say is that certain types of behaviour favour the formation of order, while others act as an impediment or thwart it.[63] It follows that political philosophy can only supply suggestions concerning the likelihood of certain individual expectations being realized.

But these expectations are precisely the ones that can be abstractly universalized, and the way they pattern into a hierarchical order cannot be different from the Mengerian arrangement of three orders of needs satisfaction. Admittedly, as Mises later showed, the Mengerian scheme is at times abstract, an 'ideal type' which does not rule out the possibility that in certain concrete cases life itself may be sacrificed to the affirmation of ideal, cultural, religious or other kinds of values. Any hierarchy of ends setting itself the goal of creating an order would ultimately, in the best hypothesis, render society rigid, looking with disfavour on all ferments of innovation that could cast doubt on the legitimacy or rationality of the hierarchy. For this hierarchy could not be other than the result of what is known, on the assumption that it is possible to draw normative implications of a universal and eternal nature from particular experiences; but it could not rule out the rise of innovations that could jeopardize the hierarchy by impugning the relation between its various parts.

Political philosophy thus evinces its main limitation: the fact of its being a theory of choice poised between a past and a future which are both only partially known. Besides from the practical point of view, the search for a general agreement regarding a hierarchy of concrete ends would soon prove impossible and would in any case bind individuals to their initial preferences, while nevertheless not excluding the possibility of a change in knowledge.

Seen differently, the cessation of the primacy of politics involves a rethinking of the concept of political obligation. A reformulation of the concept of *order* is required. In this perspective, political philosophy would lose the function of *architectural science*, although preserving the no-less-important *critical function* as a critique of both power and opinions.

It would be superficial and over-optimistic to interpret recent historical events as the definitive demise of the utopian mentality and the victory of democratic-liberal ideals. On closer examination, Marxism can be considered a tragic attempt to blend the utopian and millenarian mentality with the tradition of Western rationalism. Possibly the most important lesson to be drawn from its failure (the conciliation of classical economic theory with Hegelian historicism) is that even when politics has no antagonists, it is unable to produce a lasting order. It can only produce an organization, more or less efficient, more or less brutal, which will endure as long as there is an obligation to believe in its pretentious ideological foundations, i.e. as long as it is in a position to impose this model of organization by force. But when confidence in this ideology begins to falter, the model of organization itself will inexorably become crippled. Founded on a false interpretation of human action and economic dynamics, Marxism – counter to its own theoretical presuppositions – has actually been a desperate attempt to consider every aspect of human life from the political point of view: an attempt to subordinate every aspect of human life to the realization of an ethical-political ideal (substantial equality). That this ideal has crumbled so tragically raises the query of whether politics is truly able to produce an order and educate to virtue: whether there might not be spheres of human life obeying distinct rules and necessities which can be ignored only at one's own peril if the intention is to construct lasting social order.

This implies a return to a problem which has long seemed intractable despite innumerable attempts to exorcise it by affirming the 'primacy' of politics: the twofold question as to the conditions required for order, and the relation of such conditions to the statal model. Such a stimulus to reappraise the function of politics constitutes perhaps the most seminal and most topical aspect of the Austrian School's legacy.

Far too often political philosophy has confined itself to theorizing models of the state which are deemed more or less 'just' or 'rational', thus evading the problem of the truthfulness of precisely the assumptions concerning human action which could have rendered such a state possible. In other words, the problem of the desirability of a model has too frequently been divorced from the problem of its feasibility. By regarding economics as political economy, the end result has been to ascribe little or no importance to the findings of economic science concerning the relation between the subjectivity of the various modes of needs satisfaction and their cultural, social, political and ethical repercussions.

On the contrary, there has been a constant battle to relegate this to a sort of material sphere of existence independent of the political sphere, ostensibly because it was in any case imperative to look beyond this sphere in order to study the problems of civil coexistence from a supposedly 'loftier' and 'more philosophical' ideal perspective. The impression is almost conveyed of a conviction that a political order could persist without the satisfaction of its fundamental material requirements, or without there being any relation between such an order and needs satisfaction.

The whole line of reasoning was taken so far that it was ultimately overlooked that the state was nothing more than an instrument for the guaranteeing of precisely the very human freedom without which virtue can have no existence, i.e. for guaranteeing pre-political requirements.

Debate on these issues also lost sight of the fact that any state choosing to ignore these conditions would soon degenerate into an intolerable tool of arbitrary power, coercion and oppression. As such it would either produce a rabble or else be interpreted as a burden that had to be thrown off. This became all the more likely the more the state displayed an inefficiency that was in effect the direct result of the inaccuracy of its theoretical premises, i.e. of the attempt to engage in political reflection independently of a theory of human action, or to found politics on a false interpretation of the latter.

To become aware that politics is incapable of producing an order, one need only look at the failure of political regimes founded on planned economies. But even if this kind of regime could show itself capable of producing an efficient model of organization directed towards the achievement of a goal, the model would still deny human freedom and all that derives therefrom. This would not be a 'good order'.

From a different persepective, the question arises whether a political theory can in effect be founded on a false theory of human action: the question, that is, of the relation between economics and politics. At the root of the failure of Marxism there lies the circumstance of having tried to construct a political ordering on false economic assumptions concerning human action, as well as the fact of having considered economics an expedient for the realization of political ends deriving from presumed knowledge of the meaning of historical becoming.

It follows that the failure of Marxism stands not only as the failure of an ideology, but also as the failure of a mode of thought characterizing both Marxism and also the various other ideologies that have considered order to be an exclusive production of politics (or the state). The mistake is to confound order with *organization*, i.e. with a type of arrangement of society oriented towards the achievement of specific ends. This misunderstanding is tantamount to viewing politics as the repository of a form of knowledge to which all other knowledge must be subordinated. The need to break out from this intolerable and unjustified conception of politics thus also calls for a profound rethinking of the other political models that have embraced this basic assumption; this in effect means all the political models from Machiavelli onwards that have conceived of the state as an instrument for the moral and material elevation of man.

Naturally, it is not the intention here to maintain that the error into which Marxism fell was that of founding a presumed correct intuition, such as that of the relation of culture and philosophy to the means of production, on a mistaken economic theory and on a philosophy of history. Nor is there any wish to claim that a return to the manner in which Smith approached the relation between the economy and culture would suffice to solve the problem. What is truly of interest is to see whether the prospects opened up by the generalization of the principle of marginal utility, in the 'Austrian' version of the theory of subjective values, to the whole set of the theoretical social sciences can shed any new light on the problem of *political order*. The claim put forward here is that this principle – which, as has been seen, entails a distinction between 'real needs' and 'imaginary needs'– has awakened new and fertile avenues of research into the theory of human action. These in their turn have a direct – if often neglected – bearing on the philosophy of the social sciences in general, and on political philosophy in particular. In fact, although the theory of subjective values may well be the foundation of an economic theory, it is primarily a theory of human action that helps shed light on the way individual wills work together for the production of social institutions and, consequently, for the development of an order.

The final observation to be made is that this model of order will not be the result of the exact answer to the question concerning who should govern; for this would mean deriving the best political order from the laws enacted by those who on various counts are reputed to be possibly the 'best rulers'. Rather, order will spring from the 'rule of law', understood as the regime aiming to prevent oppression. It follows that both the question of political obligation and also that of representation now appear as secondary problems. They may be seen as manifestations of the hope that the best solution to the political problem can derive from the best choice of rulers: in other words, as manifestations of the belief that political order can be the product of an electoral system.

It is in its response to attempts to found democratic theory on a new epistemology, or to rethink it totally in order to transform it into a political model finally capable of providing credible answers to the challenges of the various eras, that the teachings of the Austrian School reveal their true topicality.

NOTES

1 See Strauss, 1965, Preface.
2 The best analysis of this manner of thinking is still that of Albert, 1968.
3 I am referring to the interpretation of the birth of modern political philosophy in Strauss, 1953 and 1959, pp. 36ff., substantially agreeing with the analysis but not with the conclusions.
4 Obviously the two expressions are used in the meaning ascribed to them by Albert, 1968 and 1978.
5 See Hayek, 1978, pp. 87–8.
6 See Popper, 1945, I, p. 121.
7 See Popper, 1963, p. 345.
8 On Mises's liberalism, as well as Butler, 1988, pp. 103–18, see Baumgarth, 1976, pp. 79–99. Baumgarth claims that although the merit of Mises is that of having pointed out that liberal thought was inadequate to his age, having shown the mistakes of classical liberalism (p. 82), and also having shown the inextricable nexus between liberalism and the market, p. 88, he actually developed a pragmatic rather than an ethical justification of liberalism (p. 89), which weakens its ideal force.
9 On the character of Mises's liberalism, see Vaughn, 1976, pp. 101–10; Vaughn too believed that his main limitation was that of having founded the liberal state on economic efficiency and not on an ethical justification (p. 110).

10 In Mises, 1981 the references to Böhm-Bawerk are on pp. 27n., 115, 123n., 299n., 316n., 362n.
11 Ibid., pp. 465–9.
12 Ibid., p. 461.
13 Ibid., pp. 273–6.
14 Ibid., pp. 277ff.
15 Ibid., pp. 281–4.
16 Ibid., p. 456.
17 See Mises, 1976, pp. xiiiff.
18 Ibid., p. 157.
19 Ibid., p. 18. On these pages, see Novack, 1989, p. 80, but also pp. 156, 161–3, 169.
20 See Mises, 1976, p. 5.
21 Ibid., p. 19. On peace as the goal of liberalism's domestic and foreign policy, see pp. 105ff.
22 Ibid., pp. 20ff. The liberal solution to the problem of social conflict thus showed, in Mises's opinion, the untenability of the claims of Marx and Ricardo concerning the irreconcilability of interests between social groups (pp. 162–4).
23 Ibid., pp. 183–8.
24 Ibid., pp. 24ff.
25 Ibid., pp. 28–37.
26 Ibid., pp. 40–58; the quotation is on p. 42.
27 Ibid., pp. 60–70.
28 See Mises, 1948, pp. 143–5.
29 Ibid., pp. 146–50. This type of government is believed to be the only tool «for the peaceful adjustment of government to the will of the majority», and for this reason Mises rejected the solution to the political problem given by universalism and collectivism, because they were, in his view, «systems of theocratic government». On these themes, see also Mises, 1962, pp. 92ff.
30 See Mises, 1948, pp. 153–5.
31 Ibid., pp. 155–7.
32 On this work, see Hamowy, 1961, pp. 28–31; and Robbins, 1963, pp. 90ff. Hayek responded to their criticisms in 1973–9, I, p. 170n. Above and beyond total or partial dissension on specific points, the most detailed analyses of Hayekian liberalism are those of Miller, 1979, pp. 242–67; Crowley, 1987; Gissurarson, 1987; Kukathas, 1989. Bobbio, 1986, p. 63, writes that

> Hayek's thought, expounded in numerous works that can arguably be considered the *summa* of contemporary liberal doctrine, represents an authoritative confirmation of what was the original nucleus of classical liberalism: a theory of the limits of the power of the state, derived from presupposition of rights or interests of the individual, prior to formation of political power.

33 On the Hayekian critique of the «objectivist labour theory of value» of classical-liberalism, see Gray, 1984b, pp. 34ff. Gray maintained that «these defects in the intellectual foundations of classical liberalism were largely remedied by the Austrian School». After having accused Mill of contributing to the decline of the liberal tradition, he went on to say that «It was only with the work of the Austrian School that the conception of economics as science of catallaxy or exchange, together with the subjective theory of economic value, allowed the shaky intellectual foundations of liberalism to be strengthened», (pp. 34–5).
34 See Hayek, 1960, pp. 54–6.
35 Ibid., pp. 56–8. The reference is naturally to the classic reconstruction by J.L. Talmon, *The Origins of Totalitarian Democracy*.
36 See Hayek, 1967, pp. 93–4. The interpretation of and position assigned to Kant in

this work appears different from the interpretation that Hayek, as has been seen, was to offer in 1973–9.

37 Hayek, 1978, pp. 147–9.

38 On the affinity with Milton Friedman, Koerner, 1985, p. 311, wrote that «Hayek and Friedman, then, argue in favour of classical liberal principles of lassez-faire.» On Hayek and Friedman, see Gray, 1984a, pp. 88–91; and Barry, 1986a, pp. 2–3.

39 Hayek, 1960, pp. 61–2. These themes form the focal point of the essay by Gray 'Hayek on Liberty, Rights and Justice', in 1989, pp. 89ff., which concludes with the statement (p. 100):

> The result of my discussion of the various strands of argument in Hayek's case for liberty is that, quite apart from the inadequacies of his conception of liberty, none of his arguments to its value secures the universability and certainty that he seeks for liberal principles. The programmatic conclusion of any critical appraisal of Hayek's social philosophy is that its failure illustrates the confusion of categories involved in any attempt to develop a liberal ideology with claims on the allegiance of all rational men. Liberalism is to be regarded as a form of moral and political practice, a species of partisanship, rather than as a deduction from conceptual analysis or from rationally certified principles.

40 See Hayek, 1960, pp. 103–6.

41 Ibid., p. 114.

42 Ibid., pp. 114–15.

43 Ibid., pp. 115–17.

44 Hayek, 1973–9, III, pp. 41–64.

45 In this connection, see Pirie, 1987, pp. 147–67. Pirie stated (p. 164):

> Hayek recognizes that societies change; that is what evolution is all about. But it is evolution, not revolution which makes change take place successfully. This, too, is part of the conservative political tradition [. . .] In his later work we see how his ideas mesh with the political ideas which conservatives have stood for and worked for.

46 A clear indication of what distinguishes Hayek's thought from conservativism is implicit in the judgment on *The Road to Serfdom* by Oakeshott, 1962, p. 21, that «A plan to resist all planning may be better than its opposite.»

47 For an interpretation of Hayek as a conservative political philosopher – ranking Hayek within the New Right does not, in general, imply his being considered a conservative – see Dahrendorf, 1979; on p. 29, referring to the claims put forward in Hayek, 1960, Dahrendorf describes Hayek as «an author who is commonly defined as a liberal and who symbolizes, in my view, the conservative character of a limited and truncated liberal theory»; Ward, 1979; Minogue, 1987, pp. 127–45. Harbour, 1982, pp. 109, 155, ranks Hayek, together with Mises and Milton Friedman, as a 'libertarian' conservative. On the conservative movement, see Kirk, 1986.

48 See Hayek, 1960, pp. 397–9.

49 Sennholz, 1978, pp. 170ff., writes that Mises was always aware of what distinguished his liberalism from traditionalist and conservative thought which declared liberalism, collectivism, utilitarianism, positivism, socialism, capitalism and individualism to be at the root of the decadence of Western civilization.

50 Hayek, 1960, pp. 399–410.

51 Ibid., pp. 401–3.

52 Ibid., pp. 406–7.

53 Ibid., pp. 410–11.

54 This is suggested by the wording of the title of Nock's book, 1935, in which American history is interpreted as a progressive increase in statal power and a

progressive erosion of individual freedom. It is no coincidence that in a review of *The Road to Serfdom* Nock accused Hayek of not being a «whole-hogger» anti-statist; see Nock, 1945, p. 4.

55 The most significant document of this movement, which boasts a large number of figures, is Rothbard, 1973. On the relation between liberalism and libertarianism, see Lepage, 1978, and above all Barry, 1986a.

56 The manifesto of this movement, which in the opinion of some thinkers also includes Nozick, can be considered to be the work by Friedman, 1989.

57 Hayek, 1973–9, II, pp. 8–13.

58 In this connection, Popper could be ranked within the framework of the scientific programme of the *Untersuchungen* when, in 1976, pp. 117–18, he showed that he embraced its programme in his comments apropos of the 'zero method', indicating that in *The Open Society* his aim was «*to generalize the method of economic theory (marginal utility theory) so as to become applicable to the other theoretical social sciences*».

59 Hegel, 1821, § 340. (Engl. trans. § 340, p. 216).

60 The expression is from Meinecke, 1924, p. 411.

61 Herein lies, on closer inspection, the affinity and close compenetration between the rule of law and the market. There can be no liberal philosophy if one of the two is denied, and when such an eventuality does happen, for example by placing the state, or ethics, above the law and above economics, the confines of liberalism are overstepped.

62 See Menger, 1923, p. 62.

63 One of the most penetrating investigations of this problem to date – and more generally of the problem of the rule of law and the dichotomy between private law and public law – is still that carried out by Leoni, 1961; see in particular the essay 'The Law as Individual Claim', pp. 189–203. In general, besides the very occasional references – see Hayek, 1973–9 – Hayek's debt to Leoni is arguably greater than at first appears. See however Hayek, 1969, pp. 23–7; and Stoppino, 1962, pp. 162–80.

BIBLIOGRAPHY

Albert, H. (1957) 'Theorie und Prognose in den Sozialwissenschaften', reprinted in Topitsch, E. (ed.) (1984) *Logik der Sozialwissenschaften*, Königstein Ts.: Athenäum.

—— (1963) 'Modell-Platonismus: Der neoklassische Stil des ökonomischen Denkens in kritischer Beleuchtung', reprinted in Topitsch, E. (ed.) (1984) *Logik der Sozialwissenschaften*, Königstein Ts.: Athenäum.

—— (1968) *Traktat über kritische Vernunft*, Tübingen: J.C.B. Mohr (Paul Siebeck).

—— (1973) 'Macht und öekonomisches Gesetz', reprinted in Albert, H. (1976) *Aufklärung und Steuerung*, Hamburg: Hoffmann & Campe.

—— (1977) 'Die Einheit der Sozialwissenschaften', reprinted in Topitsch, E. (ed.) (1984) *Logik der Sozialwissenschaften*, Königstein Ts.: Athenäum.

—— (1978) *Traktat über rationale Praxis*, Tübingen: J.C.B. Mohr (Paul Siebeck).

—— (1986) 'Ist der Sozialismus unvermeidbar', in Albert, H., *Freiheit und Ordnung*, Tübingen: J.C.B. Mohr (Paul Siebeck).

—— (1987) *Kritik der reinen Erkenntnislehre: Das Erkenntnisproblem in realistischer Perspektive*, Tübingen: J.C.B. Mohr (Paul Siebeck).

—— (1988) 'Hermeneutics and Economics: A Criticism of Hermeneutical Thinking in the Social Sciences', *Kyklos* 41, 4.

—— (1990) 'Die Verfassung der Freiheit: Bedingungen der Möglichkeit sozialer Ordnung', in Marquard, O. (ed.) *Einheit und Vielheit*, Hamburg: Felix Meiner Verlag.

Alchian, A. (1977) 'Uncertainty, Evolution and Economic Theory', in Alchian, A., *Economic Forces at Work*, Indianapolis: Liberty Press.

Alter, M. (1982) 'Carl Menger and Homo Oeconomicus: Some Thoughts on Austrian Theory and Methodology', *Journal of Economic Issues* 16, 1.

—— (1990a) *Carl Menger and the Origins of Austrian Economics*, Boulder, San Francisco and Oxford: Westview Press.

—— (1990b) 'What Do We Know about Menger?', in Caldwell, B.J. (ed.) *Carl Menger and His Legacy in Economics*, annual supplement to vol. 22, *History of Political Economy*, Durham and London: Duke University Press.

Anderson, B.M. (1911) *Social Value: A Study in Economic Theory Critical and Constructive*, quotation from 1966 edn, New York: Kelley.

Andrews, J.K. Jr (ed.) (1981) *Homage to Mises*, Hillsdale, Mich.: Hillsdale College Press.

Antiseri, D. (1984) 'Fatti, teorie e spiegazioni in Carl Menger e Karl Popper', *Nuova civiltà delle macchine* 2, 1.

—— (1987) 'Individualismo metodologico e autonomia della sociologia', in Antiseri, D., Infantino, L. and Boniolo G. (eds) *Autonomia e metodo del giudizio sociologico*, Rome: Armando.

Antiseri, D. and Pellicani, L. (1992) *L'individualismo metodologico*, Milan: Angeli.

Antonelli, E. (1953) 'Léon Walras et Carl Menger à travers leur correspondance', *Economie appliquée*, 6, 2.

Arendt, H. (1951) *The Origins of Totalitarianism*, New York: Harcourt Brace.

Aristotle, (1966) *Topica*, Engl. trans. E. S. Forster, London: Heinemann.

—— (1968a) *The Metaphysics*, Engl. trans. H. Tredennick, London: Heinemann.

—— (1968b) *The Nicomachaean Ethics,* Engl. trans. H. Rackham, London: Heinemann.

—— (1968c) *Parts of Animals*, Engl. trans. A. L. Peck, London: Heinemann.

—— (1982) *Eudemian Ethics*, Engl. trans. M. Wood, Oxford: Clarendon Press.

—— (1988) *The Politics*, Engl. trans. S. Everson, Cambridge: Cambridge University Press, reprint 1990.

Aron, R. (1976) *Essai sur les libertés*, Paris: Calmann-Lévy.

Ashcraft, R. (1987) 'German Historicism and the History of Political Theory', *History of Political Thought* 7, 2.

Barone, E. (1908) 'Il Ministro della produzione nello stato collettivista', *Giornale degli economisti* 37, trans. in Hayek, F.A. von (ed.) (1935) *Collectivist Economic Planning: Critical Studies on the Possibilities of Socialism*, London: George Routledge & Sons.

Barry, N.P. (1979) *Hayek's Social and Economic Philosophy*, London: Macmillan.

—— (1982) 'The Tradition of Spontaneous Order', *Literature of Liberty* 5.

—— (1984a) 'The Economics and Philosophy of Socialism', *Il Politico* 49, 4.

—— (1984b) 'Ideas *versus* Interests: The Classical Liberal Dilemma', in Barry, N. *et al.*, *Hayek's 'Serfdom' Revisited*, London: Institute of Economic Affairs.

—— (1986a) *On Classical Liberalism and Libertarianism*, London: Macmillan.

—— (1986b) 'The Concept of "Nature" in Liberal Political Thought', *Journal of Libertarian Studies* 7, 1.

—— (1989) 'The Liberal Constitution: Rational Design or Evolution?', *Critical Review* 3, 2.

—— (1990) 'The Road to Freedom: Hayek's Social and Economic Philosophy', PPE Lectures, 2, Department of Economics, University of Vienna.

Barry, N., Burton, J., Giussurarson, H., Gray, J., Shearmur, J. and Vaughn, K. with Seldon, A. (1984), *Hayek's 'Serfdom' Revisited*, London: Institute of Economic Affairs.

Baumgarth, W. (1976) 'Justification of the Liberal Order', in Moss, L. S. (ed.) *The Economics of Ludwig von Mises: Toward a Critical Reappraisal*, Kansas City: Sheed & Ward.

Becker, W. (1982) *Die Freiheit, die wir meinen: Entscheidung für die liberale Demokratie*, Munich and Zurich: Piper.

Berger, P.L. (1986) *The Capitalist Revolution: Fifty Propositions about Prosperity, Equality, and Liberty*, New York: Basic Books.

Birner, J. (1990) 'A Roundabout Solution to a Fundamental Problem in Menger's Methodology and Beyond', in Caldwell, B.J. (ed.) *Carl Menger and His Legacy in Economics*, annual supplement to vol. 22, *History of Political Economy*, Durham and London: Duke University Press.

Blaug, M. (1980) *The Methodology of Economics*, Cambridge: Cambridge University Press.

Bloch, H.S. (1940) 'Carl Menger: The Founder of the Austrian School', *Journal of Political Economy* 48, 3.

Bobbio, N. (1977) *Dalla struttura alla funzione: Nuovi studi di teoria del diritto*, Milan: Edizioni di Comunità.

—— (1986) *Liberalismo e democrazia*, Milan: Angeli.

Boehm, S. (1982) 'The Ambiguous Notion of Subjectivism. Comment on Lachmann', in Kirzner, I.M. (ed.) *Method, Process, and Austrian Economics*, Lexington: Lexington Books.

—— (1990) 'The Austrian Tradition: Schumpeter and Mises', in Hennings, K. and Samuels, W.J. (eds) *Neoclassical Economic Theory, 1870 to 1930*, Boston and Dordrecht: Kluwer.

Böhm-Bawerk, E. von (1890) 'The Historical vs the Deductive Method in Political Economy', *Annals of the American Academy of Political and Social Science* 1.

—— (1896) 'Zum Abschluss des Marxschen Systems', in Boenigk, O. von (ed.) *Staatswirtschaftliche Arbeiten, Festgaben für Karl Knies*, Berlin: Haering.

—— (1921) *Kapital und Kapitalzins*, ed. F. von Wieser, Jena: Fischer.

Boland, L.A. (1982) *The Foundations of Economic Method*, London: Allen & Unwin.

Boos, M. (1986) *Die Wissenschaftstheorie Carl Mengers, Biographische und ideengeschichtliche Zusammenhänge*, Vienna: Hermann Böhlaus Nachf.

Bosanquet, N. (1983) *After the New Right*, London: Heinemann.

Bostoph, S. (1978) 'The Methodological Debate between C. Menger and the German Historicists', *Atlantic Economic Journal* 6, 3.

Bottmore, T. (1985) *Theories of Modern Capitalism*, London: Allen & Unwin.

Brittan, S. (1988) *A Restatement of Economic Liberalism*, London: Macmillan.

Brough, W.T. and Naka, S. (1984) 'Man, the Market and the Transfer State', in Leube, K.R. and Zlabinger, A.H. (eds) *The Political Economy of Freedom: Essays in Honor of F.A. Hayek*, Munich and Vienna: Philosophia Verlag.

Brown, R. (1984) *The Nature of Social Laws*, Cambridge: Cambridge University Press.

Brutzkus, B. (1935) *Economic Planning in Soviet Russia*, London: George Routledge & Sons.

Bryant, C.G.A. (1985) *Positivism in Social Theory and Research*, London: Macmillan.

Buchanan, J.M. (1969) *Cost and Choice: An Inquiry in Economic Theory*, quotation from 1978 edn, Chicago: University of Chicago Press.

—— (1975) *The Limits of Liberty: Between Anarchy and Leviathan*, Chicago: University of Chicago Press.

—— (1982a) 'The Domain of Subjective Economics: Between Predictive Science and Moral Philosophy', in Kirzner, I.M. (ed.) *Method, Process, and Austrian Economics*, Lexington: Lexington Books.

—— (1982b) 'Order Defined in the Process of its Emergence', *Literature of Liberty* 5.

—— (1987a) 'Cultural Evolution and Institutional Reform', in Buchanan, J.M., *Liberty, Market and State*, Brighton: Wheatsheaf.

—— (1987b) *Liberty, Market and State*, Brighton: Wheatsheaf.

Buchanan, J.M, and Tullock, G. (1962) *The Calculus of Consent: Logical Foundations of Constitutional Democracy*, Ann Arbor: University of Michigan Press.

Buckley, W.F. Jr (1977) '*The Road to Serfdom*: The Intellectuals and Socialism', in Machlup, F. (ed.) *Essays on Hayek*, London: Routledge & Kegan Paul.

Burgalassi, M. (1992) 'Appunti sulla metodologia weberiana e la Scuola Austriaca', *Quaderni di storia dell'economia politica* 10, 2.

Burton, J. (1984) 'The Instability of the "Middle Way"', in Barry, N. *et al.*, *Hayek's 'Serfdom' Revisited*, London: Institute of Economic Affairs.

Butler, E. (1983) *Hayek: His Contribution to the Political and Economic Thought of Our Time*, quotation from 1985 edn, New York: Universe Books.

—— (1988) *Ludwig von Mises: Fountainhead of the Modern Microeconomics Revolution*, Aldershot: Gower

Butler, E. and Pirie, M. (eds) (1987) *Hayek on the Fabric of Human Society*, London: Adam Smith Institute.

Caldwell, B.J. (1988a) 'Hayek's Transformation', *History of Political Economy* 20, 4.

—— (1988b) 'La méthodologie de Hayek: description, évalutation et interrogations', in Dostaler, G. and Ethier, D. (eds) *Friedrich Hayek: Philosophie, économie et politique*, Montreal: ACFAS.

—— (ed.) (1990) *Carl Menger and His Legacy in Economics*, annual supplement to vol. 22, *History of Political Economy*, Durham and London: Duke University Press.

Cassirer, E. (1946) *The Myth of the State*, New Haven: Yale University Press.

Cesa, C. (1986) 'Sulle idee politiche della scuola storica', *Annali della Scuola Normale Superiore di Pisa* S. III, 16, 1.

Chaloupek, G.K. (1986) 'Marxistische Kritik an der Österreichischen Schule', in Leser, N. (ed.) *Die Wiener Schule der Nationalökonomie*, Vienna: Böhlaw.

—— (1990) 'The Austrian Debate on Economic Calculation in a Socialist Economy', *History of Political Economy* 24, 4.

Clontz, J.M. (1988) 'Popper's Philosophy of Science and Classical Austro-Marginalism', Working Paper no.5, Faculty of Economics, Kyoto University.

Collini, S., Winch, D. and Burrow, J. (1983) *That Noble Science of Politics: A Study in Nineteenth-Century Intellectual History*, Cambridge: Cambridge University Press.

Craver, E. (1986) 'The Emigration of the Austrian Economists', *History of Political Economy* 18, 1.

Crowley, B.L. (1987) *The Self, the Individual, and the Community: Liberalism in the Political Thought of F.A. Hayek and Sidney and Beatrice Webb*, Oxford: Clarendon Press.

Cubeddu, R. (1984) 'Otto Neurath e la filosofia politica del Circolo di Vienna', *Il pensiero politico* 17, 2.

—— (1985) 'Fonti filosofiche delle *Untersuchungen über die Methode der Socialwissenschaften* di Carl Menger', *Quaderni di storia dell'economia politica* 3, 3.

—— (1987a) 'La critica della modernità in Leo Strauss', *Filosofia* S. III, 38, 1.

—— (1987b) 'Popper et l'Ecole Autrichienne', *Economies et Sociétés,* Série PE, 8, *La pensée de Karl Popper et la science économique.*

Cunningham, R.L. (ed.) (1979) *Liberty and the Rule of Law*, College Station and London: Texas A&M University Press.

Dahrendorf, R. (1979) *Intervista sul liberalismo in Europa,* ed. V. Ferrari, Bari: Laterza.

—— (1990) *Betrachtungen über Revolution in Europa*, Stuttgart: Cotta.

De Vecchi, N. (1990) 'La Scuola viennese di economia', in Becattini, G. (ed.) *Il pensiero economico: temi, problemi e scuole*, Turin: Unione Tipografica Editrice Torinese.

Diamond, A.M. Jr (1988) 'The Austrian Economics and the Late Hapsburg Viennese Milieu', *Review of Austrian Economics* 2.

Diemer, A. (ed.) (1968) *Beiträge zur Entwicklung der Wissenschaftstheorie im 19. Jahrhundert*, Meisenheim am Glan: Verlag Anton Hain.

Dietze, G. (1977) *Hayek on the Rule of Law*, in Machlup, F. (ed.) *Essays on Hayek*, London: Routledge & Kegan Paul.

—— (1985) *Liberalism Proper and Proper Liberalism*, Baltimore and London: Johns Hopkins University Press.

diZerega, G. (1989) 'Democracy as Spontaneous Order', *Critical Review* 3, 2.

Dobretsberger, J. (1949) 'Zur Methodenlehre C. Mengers und der österreichischen Schule', *Zeitschrift für Nationalökonomie* 12.

Dobuzinskis, L. (1989) 'The Complexities of Spontaneous Order', *Critical Review* 3, 2.

Dolan, E.G. (ed.) (1976) *The Foundations of Modern Austrian Economics*, Kansas City: Sheed & Ward.

Dostaler, G. and Ethier, D. (eds) (1988) *Friedrich Hayek: Philosophie, économie et politique*, Montreal: Association Canadienne-Française pour l'Avancement des Sciences.

Douglas, J.D. (1984) 'The Road to Modernist Slavery', in Leube, K.R. and Zlabinger A.H. (eds) *The Political Economy of Freedom: Essays in Honor of F.A. Hayek*, Munich and Vienna: Philosophia Verlag.

Dunleavy, P. and O'Leary, B. (1987) *Theories of the State: The Politics of Liberal Democracy*, London: Macmillan.

Egger, J.B. (1978) 'The Austrian Method', in Spadaro L.M. (ed.) *New Directions in Austrian Economics*, Kansas City: Sheed Andrews & McMeel.

Ekelund, R.B. (1970) 'Power and Utility: The Normative Economics of Friedrich von Wieser', *Review of Social Economy* 27.

Ekelund, R.B. Jr. and Hébert, R.F. (1983) *A History of Economic Theory and Method*, Auckland: McGraw-Hill.

Ekelund, R.B. Jr. and Thornton, M. (1987) 'Wieser and the Austrian Connection to Social Economics', *Forum for Social Economics* 16, 2.

Elster, J. and Moene, K.O. (eds) (1989) *Alternatives to Capitalism*, Cambridge and Paris: Cambridge University Press.

Eucken, W. (1938) 'Ueberwindung des Historismus', *Schmoller Jahrbuch* 62, 2.

—— (1940) *Grundlagen der Nationalökonomie*, Jena: Fischer.

Faucci, R. (1988) 'Gustav Schmoller e la Scuola storica in Italia', *Quaderni di storia dell'economia politica* 6, 3.

Ferry, L. and Renaut, A. (1985) *Philosophie politique*, vol. III, Paris: Presses Universitaires de France.

Finer, H. (1945) *The Road to Reaction*, quotation from 1963 edn, Chicago: Quadrangle Books.

Flew, A. (1987) 'The Mirage of Social Justice', in Butler, E. and Pirie M. (eds) *Hayek on the Fabric of Human Society*, London: Adam Smith Institute.

Friedman, D. (1989) *The Machinery of Freedom: Guide to a Radical Capitalism*, La Salle: Open Court.

Fuerle, R.D. (1986) *The Pure Logic of Choice*, New York: Vintage.

Galeotti, A.E. (1987a) 'L'insorgenza delle regole e dell'ordine nella teoria sociale di F.A. Hayek', *Politeia – Contributi per la discussione* 14.

—— (1987b) 'Teoria politica e modi di spiegazione: Il caso dell'individualismo metodologico', in Veca, S. (ed.) *Filosofia politica e società: Utilitarismo e teoria della giustizia*, Naples: Bibliopolis.

—— (1988) *Individuale e collettivo: L'individualismo metodologico nella teoria politica*, Milan: Angeli.

Gallaway, L.E. and Vedder, R. (1984) 'The Market Place and Macroeconomic Planning', in Leube, K.R. and Zlabinger A.H. (eds) *The Political Economy of Freedom: Essays in Honor of F.A. Hayek*, Munich and Vienna: Philosophia Verlag.

Gentile, F. (1989) (ed) *Interpretazione e decisione: Diritto ed economia*, Milan: Giuffrè.

Gide, C. and Rist, C. (1909) *Histoire des doctrines économiques*, quotation from the 1920 edn, Paris: Recuil Sirey.

Gioia, V. (1990) *Gustav Schmoller: la scienza economica e la storia*, Galatina: Congedo.

Giussurarson, H.H. (1984) 'The Only Truly Progressive Policy . . . ', in Barry, N. *et al.*, *Hayek's 'Serfdom' Revisited*, London: Institute of Economic Affairs.

—— (1986) *Hayek's Conservative Liberalism*, Los Angeles: Garland.

Gordon, D. (1986) *Hermeneutics versus Austrian Economics*, Auburn: Ludwig von Mises Institute.

Gram, H.N. and Walsh, V.C. (1978) 'Menger and Jevons in the Setting of post-von Neumann-Sraffa Economics', *Atlantic Economic Journal* 6, 3.

Grassl, W. and Smith, B. (eds) (1986) *Austrian Economics: Historical and Philosophical Background*, London: Croom Helm.

Gray, J. (1984a) *Hayek on Liberty*, quotation from the 1986 edn, Oxford: Blackwell.

—— (1984b) 'The Road to Serfdom: Forty Years On', in Barry, N. *et al.*, *Hayek's 'Serfdom' Revisited*, London: Institute of Economic Affairs.

—— (1986) *Liberalism*, Minneapolis: University of Minnesota Press.

—— (1989) *Liberalisms*, London and New York: Routledge.

Greaves, P.L. Jr (1974) *Mises Made Easier: A Glossary for Ludwig von Mises' Human Action*, Dobbs Ferry, NY: Free Market Books.

Grinder, W.E. (ed.) (1977) *Capital, Expectations, and the Market Process*, Kansas City: Sheed Andrews & McMeel.

Haberler, G. (1981) 'A Vienna Seminarian Remembers', in Andrews, J.K. Jr (ed.) *Homage to Mises*, Hillsdale, Mich: Hillsdale College Press.

Hahn, H., Neurath, O. and Carnap, R. (1929) *Wissenschaftliche Weltauffassung – Der Wiener Kreis*, Vienna: Artur Wolf Verlag.

Haller, R. (1986) 'Emanuel Herrmann: On an Almost Forgotten Chapter of Austrian Intellectual History', in Grassl, W. and Smith, B. (eds) *Austrian Economics: Historical and Philosophical Background*, London: Croom Helm.

Hamowy, R. (1961) 'Hayek's Concept of Freedom', *Individualist Review* 1, 1.

—— (1971) 'Freedom and the Rules of Law in F.A. Hayek', Il Politico 21, 2.

Hansen, R. (1968) 'Der Methodenstreit in den Sozialwissenschaften zwischen Gustav Schmoller und Karl Menger', in Diemer, A. (ed.) *Beiträge zur Entwicklung der Wissenschaftstheorie im 19. Jahrhundert*, Meisenheim am Glan: Verlag Anton Hain.

Harbour, W.R. (1982) *The Foundations of Conservative Thought: An Anglo-American Tradition in Perspective*, Notre Dame and London: University of Notre Dame Press.

Hartwell, R.M. (1977) 'Capitalism and the Historians', in Machlup, F. (ed.) *Essays on Hayek*, London: Routledge & Kegan Paul.

—— (1987), 'Hayek and the Historians', in Butler, E. and Pirie, M. (eds) *Hayek on the Fabric of Human Society*, London: Adam Smith Institute.

Häuser, K. (1988) 'Historical School and "Methodenstreit"', *Zeitschrift für die gesamte Staatswissenschaft* 144.

Hayek, F.A. von (1926) 'Friedrich Freiherr von Wieser', now in Spiegel, H.W. (ed.) (1952) *The Development of Economic Thought: Great Economists in Perspective*, New York: Wiley, and London: Chapman & Hall.

—— (1933) 'Carl Menger', in Menger, C. (1933–6) *The Collected Works of Carl Menger*, ed. F.A. von Hayek, 4 vols, Reprints of Scare Tracts in Economics and Political Science nos 17–20, London: London School of Economics and Political Science, vol. I.

—— (ed.) (1935) *Collectivist Economic Planning: Critical Studies on the Possibilities of Socialism*, London: George Routledge & Sons.

—— (1937) 'Economics and Knowledge', now in Hayek, F.A. von (1948) *Individualism and Economic Order*, London: George Routledge & Sons.

—— (1939) *Freedom and the Economic System*, Chicago: University of Chicago Press.

—— (1940) 'Socialist Calculation III: The Competitive "Solution", now in Hayek, F.A. von (1948), *Individualism and Economic Order*, London: George Routledge & Sons.

—— (1942–4) 'Scientism and the Study of Society', now in Hayek, F.A. von (1952) *The Counter-Revolution of Science: Studies on the Abuse of Reason*, Glencoe: Free Press.

—— (1944) *The Road to Serfdom*, London: George Routledge & Sons, quotations from reprint 1979.

—— (1945) 'The Use of Knowledge in Society', now in Hayek, F.A. von (1948) *Individualism and Economic Order*, London: George Routledge & Sons.

—— (1948) *Individualism and Economic Order*, London: George Routledge & Sons.

—— (1951a) 'Comte and Hegel', now in Hayek, F.A. von (1952a) *The Counter-Revolution of Science: Studies on the Abuse of Reason*, Glencoe: Free Press.

—— (1951b) *John Stuart Mill and Harriet Taylor: Their Friendship and Subsequent Marriage*, London: Routledge & Kegan Paul.

—— (1952a) *The Counter-Revolution of Science: Studies on the Abuse of Reason*, Glencoe: Free Press.

—— (1952b) *The Sensory Order: An Inquiry into the Foundations of Theoretical Psychology*, London: Routledge & Kegan Paul.

—— (1954) *Capitalism and the Historians*, London: Routledge & Kegan Paul, and Chicago: University of Chicago Press.

—— (1960) *The Constitution of Liberty*, London: Routledge & Kegan Paul, quotations from the 1978 edn, Chicago: Henry Regnery.

—— (1967) *Studies in Philosophy, Politics and Economics*, London: Routledge & Kegan Paul.

—— (1968a) 'The Austrian School', in Sills, D.L. (ed.) *International Encyclopedia of the Social Sciences*, vol. IV, New York: Macmillan and Free Press, 458–62.

—— (1968b) 'Menger, Carl', in Sills, D.L. (ed.) *International Encyclopedia of the Social Sciences*, vol. X, New York: Macmillan and Free Press, 124–7.

—— (1969) 'Bruno Leoni the Scholar', in Scaramozzino, P. (ed.) *Omaggio a Bruno Leoni*, Quaderni della revista *Il Politico* no. 7, Milan: Giuffrè.

—— (1972) *A Tiger by the Tail: The Keynesian Legacy of Inflation*, compiled and introduced by S.A. Shenoy, London: Institute of Economic Affairs.

—— (1973) 'Liberalism', in Hayek, F.A. von (1978) *New Studies in Philosophy, Politics, Economics and the History of Ideas*, London: Routledge & Kegan Paul.

—— (1973–9) *Law, Legislation and Liberty*, 3 vols, London: Routledge & Kegan Paul; vol. I, *Rules and Order*, 1973; vol. II, *The Mirage of Social Justice*, 1976; vol. III, *The Political Order of a Free People*, 1979.

—— (1974) 'The Pretence of Knowledge', Nobel Memorial Lecture, now in Hayek, F.A. von (1978) *New Studies in Philosophy, Politics, Economics and the History of Ideas*, London: Routledge & Kegan Paul.

—— (1976) 'Tribute to Ludwig von Mises', in Mises, M. von (1984) *My Years with Ludwig von Mises*, 2nd enlarged edn, Cedar Falls, Iowa: Center for Future Education.

—— (1978) *New Studies in Philosophy, Politics, Economics and the History of Ideas*, London: Routledge & Kegan Paul.

—— (1981a) 'Foreword' to Mises, L. von, *Socialism: An Economic and Sociological Analysis*, Indianapolis: Liberty Press.

—— (1981b) 'Vorwort zur deutschen Ausgabe', in Mises, M. von, *Ludwig von Mises, Der Mensch und Sein Werk*, Munich: Philosoplia Verlay.

—— (1982) 'Consolidated Preface' to one-volume edn of *Law, Legislation and Liberty*, London: Routledge & Kegan Paul.

—— (1983) *Knowledge, Evolution, and Society*, London: Adam Smith Institute.

—— (1988) *The Fatal Conceit: The Errors of Socialism*, London: Routledge; *The Collected Works of F.A. Hayek*, ed. W.W. Bartley III, vol. I.

—— (1989) *Order – with or without design?*, excerpts from the writings of Friedrich A. Hayek compiled and introduced by. N. Moldofsky, comment by S.A. Shenoy, London: Centre for Research into Communist Economies.

Hazlitt, H. (1956) 'The Road to Totalitarianism', in Sennholz, M. (ed.) *On Freedom and Free Enterprise: Essays in Honor of Ludwig von Mises*, Princeton: Van Nostrand.

Hébert, R.F. (1990) 'Commentary' to Streissler, E., 'Menger, Böhm-Bawerk, and Wieser: The Origins of the Austrian School', in Hennings, K. and Samuels, W.J. (eds) *Neoclassical Economic Theory, 1870 to 1930*, Boston and Dordrecht: Kluwer.

Hegel, G.W.F. (1821), *Grundlinien der Philosophie des Rechts*, Berlin: Nicolaischen; Engl. edn, *Hegel's Philosophy of Right*, trans. T.M. Knox, London: Oxford University Press, 1967.

Heine W. (1983) *Methodologischer Individualismus: Zur geschichtsphilosophischen Begründung eines sozialwissenschaftlichen Konzeptes. C. Menger, J.A. Schumpeter, M. Weber, F.A. von Hayek, K.R. Popper*, Würzburg: Könighausen-Neumann.

Held, D. (1986) 'Introduction' to Held, D. and Pollitt, C. (eds) *New Forms of Democracy?*, London: Sage.

—— (1987) *Models of Democracy*, Cambridge: Polity Press.

Held, D. and Pollitt, C. (eds) (1986) *New Forms of Democracy*, London: Sage.

Hennings, K. and Samuels, W.J. (eds) (1990) *Neoclassical Economic Theory 1870 to 1930*, Boston and Dordrecht: Kluwer.

Hennis, W. (1987) 'A Science of Man: Max Weber and the Political Economy of the German Historical School', in Mommsen, W.J. and Osterhammel, J. (eds) *Max Weber and His Contemporaries*, London: Allen & Unwin.

—— (1991) 'The Pitiless "Sobriety of Judgment": Max Weber between Carl Menger and Gustav von Schmoller – the Academic Politics of Value Freedom', *History of the Human Sciences* 4, 1.

Hicks, J.R. and Weber W. (eds) (1973) *Carl Menger and the Austrian Economics*, Oxford: Clarendon Press.

Hirschman, A.O. (ed.) (1991) *The Rhetoric of Reaction: Perversity, Futility, Jeopardy*, Cambridge, Mass.: Harvard University Press.

Hodgson, G.M. (1991) 'Hayek's Theory of Cultural Evolution: An Evaluation in the Light of Vanberg's Critique', *Economics and Philosophy*, 7, 1.

Hoff, T.J.B. (1949) *Economic Calculation in the Socialist Society*, London: William Hodge; quotations from the 1981 edn, Indianapolis: Liberty Press.

Hoppe, H.H. (1989) *A Theory of Socialism and Capitalism: Economics, Politics, and Ethics*, Boston, Dordrecht and London: Kluwer.

Howey, R.S. (1960) *The Rise of the Marginal Utility School: 1870–1889*, Lawrence: University of Kansas Press.

Hoy, C.M. (1984) *A Philosophy of Individual Freedom: The Political Thought of F.A. Hayek*, Westport: Greenwood Press.

Hutchison, T.W. (1953) *A Review of Economic Doctrines: 1870-1929*, Oxford: Clarendon Press.

—— (1973) 'Some Themes from "Investigations into Method"', in Hicks, J.R., Weber W. (eds) *Carl Menger and the Austrian Economics*, Oxford: Clarendon Press.

—— (1981) *The Politics and Philosophy of Economics: Marxists, Keynesians and Austrians*, Oxford: Blackwell.

Ingram, J.K. (1888) *A History of Political Economy*, New York: Kelley.

Jaffé, W. (ed.) (1965) *Correspondence of Léon Walras and Related Papers*, Amsterdam: Royal Netherlands Academy of Sciences and Letters.

—— (1976) 'Menger, Jevons, and Walras De-homogenized', *Economic Inquiry* 14, 4.

Jasay, A. de (1989) 'Is Limited Government Possible?', *Critical Review* 3, 2.

Jaspers, K. (1949) *Vom Ursprung und Ziel der Geschichte*, quotation from 1983 edn, Munich: Piper.

Johnson, G.R. (1990) 'Hermeneutics: A Protreptic', *Critical Review* 4, 1–2.

Johnston, W.M. (1972) *The Austrian Mind: An Intellectual and Social History, 1848–1938*, Berkeley: University of California Press.

Jouvenel, B. de (1954) 'The Treatment of Capitalism by Continental Intellectuals', in Hayek, F.A. von (ed.) *Capitalism and the Historians*, London: Routledge & Kegan Paul, and Chicago: University of Chicago Press.

Kauder, E. (1953a) 'Genesis of the Marginal Utility Theory: From Aristotle to the End of the Eighteenth Century', *Economic Journal* 63.

—— (1953b) 'The Retarded Acceptance of the Marginal Utility Theory', *Quarterly Journal of Economics* 67, 4.

—— (1957) 'Intellectual and Political Roots of the Older Austrian School', *Zeitschrift für Nationalökonomie* 57, 4.

—— (1959) 'Menger and His Library', *Economic Review* 10, 1.

—— (1961) 'Freedom and Economic Theory: Second Research Report on Menger's Unpublished Paper', *Hitotsubashi Journal of Economics* 2, 1.

—— (1962) 'Aus Mengers nachgelassenen Papieren', *Weltwirtschaftliches Archiv* 89, 1.

—— (1965) *A History of Marginal Utility Theory*, Princeton: Princeton University Press.

Kelsen, H. (1955) 'Foundations of Democracy', *Ethics* 66, 1.

Keynes, J.M. (1891) *The Scope and Method of Political Economy*, quotations from the 1930 edn, London: Macmillan.

Kirk, R. (1986) *The Conservative Mind: From Burke to Eliot*, Chicago: Gateway Editions.

Kirzner, I.M. (1976a) 'On the Method of Austrian Economics', in Dolan, E.G. (ed.) *The Foundations of Modern Austrian Economics*, Kansas City: Sheed & Ward.

—— (1976b) 'Philosophical and Ethical Implications of Austrian Economics', in Dolan, E.G. (ed.) *The Foundations of Modern Austrian Economics*, Kansas City: Sheed & Ward.

—— (1981) 'Mises and the Renaissance of Austrian Economics', in Andrews, J.K. Jr (ed.) *Homage to Mises*, Hillsdale, Mich.: Hillsdale College Press.

—— (ed.) (1982) *Method, Process, and Austrian Economics*, Lexington: Lexington Books.

—— (1984) 'Prices, the Communication of Knowledge, and the Discovery Process', in Leube, K.R. and Zlabinger A.H. (eds) *The Political Economy of Freedom: Essays in Honor of F.A. Hayek*, Munich and Vienna: Philosophia Verlag.

—— (1986a) 'Ludwig von Mises and Friedrich von Hayek: The Modern Extension of Austrian Subjectivism', in Leser, N. (ed.) *Die Wiener Schule der Nationalökonomie*, Vienna: Böhlau.

—— (ed.) (1986b) *Subjectivism, Intelligibility and Economic Understanding. Essays in Honor of Ludwig Lachmann on His Eightieth Birthday*, London: Macmillan.

—— (1990a) 'Commentary' to Boehm, S., 'The Austrian Tradition: Schumpeter and Mises', in Hennings, K. and Samuels, W.J. (eds) *Neoclassical Economic Theory 1870–1930*, Boston and Dordrecht: Kluwer.

—— (1990b) 'Menger, Classical Liberalism, and the Austrian School of Economics', in Caldwell, B.J. (ed.) *Carl Menger and His Legacy in Economics*, annual supplement to vol. 22, *History of Political Economy*, Durham and London: Duke University Press.

Kley, R. (1992) 'F.A. Hayeks Idee einer spontanen sozialen Ordnung: eine kritische Analyse', *Kölner Zeitschrift für Soziologie und Sozialpsychologie* 44, 1.

Koerner, K.K. (1985) *Liberalism and its Critics*, London and Sydney: Croom Helm.

Kraus, O. (1905) 'Die Aristotelische Werttheorie in ihren Beziehungen zu den Lehren der modernen Psychologenschule', *Zeitschrift für die Gesamte Staatswissenschaft* 61, 4.

—— (1937) *Die Werttheorien. Geschichte und Kritik*, Brunn and Vienna: Roher.

Kukathas, C. (1989) *Hayek and Modern Liberalism*, Oxford: Clarendon Press.

Lachmann, L.M. (1966) 'Die geistesgeschichtliche Bedeutung der österreichischen Schule', *Zeitschrift für Nationalökonomie* 27.

—— (1969) 'Methodological Individualism and the Market Economy', in Streissler, E. (ed.) *Roads to Freedom: Essays in Honor of Friedrich A. von Hayek*, London: Routledge & Kegan Paul.

—— (1970) *The Legacy of Max Weber*, London: Heinemann.

—— (1977) 'The Significance of the Austrian School of Economics in the History of Ideas', in Grinder, W.E. (ed.) *Capital, Expectations, and the Market Process*, Kansas City: Sheed Andrews & McMeel.

—— (1978) 'Carl Menger and the Incomplete Revolution of Subjectivism', *Atlantic Economic Journal* 6, 3.

—— (1979) 'The Flow of Legislation and the Permanence of Legal Order', *Ordo* 30.

—— (1982) 'Ludwig von Mises and the Extension of Subjectivism', in Kirzner, I.M. (ed.) *Method, Process, and Austrian Economics*, Lexington: Lexington Books.

—— (1986) *The Market as an Economic Process*, Oxford: Blackwell.

Lagueux, M. (1988) '"Ordre spontané" et darwinisme méthodologique chez Hayek', in Dostaler, G. and Ethier, D. (eds) *Friedrich Hayek: Philosophie, économie et politique*, Montreal: Association Canadienne-Française pour l'Avancement des Sciences.

Laird, J. (1929) *The Idea of Value*, quotation from the 1969 edn, New York: Kelley.

Lange, O. (1936) 'On the Economic Theory of Socialism', *Review of Economic Studies* 4, 1.

Lavoie, D. (1982) 'The Development of the Misesian Theory of Interventionism', in Kirzner I.M. (ed.) *Method, Process, and Austrian Economics*, Lexington: Lexington Books.

—— (1985a) *National Economic Planning: What Is Left?*, Cambridge, Mass.: Ballinger.

—— (1985b) *Rivalry and Central Planning: The Socialist Calculation Debate Reconsidered*, Cambridge: Cambridge University Press.

—— (1986) 'Euclideanism versus Hermeneutics: A Reinterpretation of Misesian Apriorism', in Kirzner, I.M. (ed.) *Subjectivism, Intelligibility and Economic Understanding: Essays in Honor of Ludwig Lachmann on His Eighteenth Birthday*, London: Macmillian.

—— (ed.) (1990a) *Economics and Hermeneutics*, London and New York: Routledge.

—— (1990b) 'Understanding Differently: Hermeneutics and the Spontaneous Order of Communicative Processes', in Caldwell, B.J. (ed.) *Carl Menger and His Legacy in Economics*, annual supplement to vol. 22, *History of Political Economy*, Durham and London: Duke University Press.

Leoni, B. (1961) *Freedom and the Law*, Princeton: Van Nostrand; 3rd expanded edn, Indianapolis: Liberty Fund, 1991.

—— (1965) 'Il problema del calcolo economico nell'economia di piano', *Il Politico* 16, 3.

Lepage, H. (1978) *Demain le capitalisme*, Paris: Hachette.

—— (1980) *Demain le libéralisme*, Paris: Hachette.

Leser, N. (ed.) (1986a) *Die Wiener Schule der Nationalökonomie*, Vienna: Böhlau.

—— (1986b) 'Der zeitgeschichtliche Hintergrund des Wien und Österreich im fin-de-Siecle', in Leser, N. (ed.) *Die Wiener Schule der Nationalökonomie*, Vienna: Böhlau.

Leube, K.R. and Zlabinger, A.H. (eds) (1984) *The Political Economy of Freedom: Essays in Honor of F.A. Hayek*, Munich and Vienna: Philosophia Verlag.

Littlechild, S. (1978) *The Fallacy of the Mixed Economy*, London: Institute of Economic Affairs.

—— (ed.) (1990) *Austrian Economics*, vol. I, Aldershot: Edward Elgar.

Lukes, S. (1968) 'Methodological Individualism Reconsidered', *British Journal of Sociology* 19, 1.

MacCormick, N. (1982) *Legal Right and Social Democracy. Essays in Legal and Political Philosophy*, Oxford: Clarendon Press.

—— (1985) 'Alcuni problemi circa l'ordine spontaneo', in Ricossa, S. and de Robilant, E. (eds) *Libertà giustizia e persona nella società tecnologica*, Milan: Giuffrè.

Machlup, F. (ed.) (1977a) *Essays on Hayek*, London: Routledge & Kegan Paul.

—— (1977b) 'Hayek's Contribution to Economics', in Machlup, F. (ed.) *Essays on Hayek*, London: Routledge & Kegan Paul.

Madison, G.B. (1990) 'How Individualistic Is Methodological Individualism?', *Critical Review* 4, 1–2.

Mäki, U. (1990a) 'Carl Menger's Conception of Economics as an Exact Science', paper for the Symposium on the Methodology of Carl Menger, London, King's College, January.

—— (1990b) 'Mengerian Economics in Realist Perspective', in Caldwell, B.J. (ed.) *Carl Menger and His Legacy in Economics*, annual supplement to vol. 22, *History of Political Economy*, Durham and London: Duke University Press.

Mannheim, K. (1941) *Man and Society in an Age of Reconstruction*, quotations from the 1980 edn. London: Routledge & Kegan Paul.

Marini, G. (1977) 'La polemica con la scuola storica nella "Filosofia del diritto" hegeliana', reprinted in Marini, G. (1987) *Storicità del diritto e dignità dell'uomo*, Naples: Morano.

—— (1982a) 'La codificazione in Germania', reprinted in Marini, G. (1987) *Storicità del diritto e dignità dell'uomo*, Naples: Morano.

—— (1982b) 'Il metodo di Savigny in alcuni giudizi dell'anno 1883', reprinted in Marini, G. (1987), *Storicità del diritto e dignità dell'uomo*, Naples: Morano.

—— (1987) *Storicità del diritto e dignità dell'uomo*, Naples: Morano.

Marquard, O. (ed.) (1990) *Einheit und Vielheit*, Hamburg: Felix Meiner Verlag.

Meek, R.L. (1972) 'Marginalism and Marxism', *History of Political Economy* 4, 2.

Meinecke, F. (1924) *Die Idee der Staatsräson in der neueren Gesghichte*, Munich and Berlin: R. Oldenbourg, quotation from the 1957 edn.

—— (1936) *Die Entstehung des Historismus*, Munich and Berlin: R. Oldenbourg.

Menger, C. (1871) *Grundsätze der Volkswirtschaftslehre*, Vienna: Wilhelm Braumüller; reprinted in Menger, C. (1968–70) *Gesammelte Werke*, ed. F.A. von Hayek, Tübingen: J.C.B. Mohr (Paul Siebeck), vol. I; bibliography of Menger, C., in vol. IV; Engl. trans. *Principles of Economics,* Glencoe: Free Press, 1950; reprinted New York: New York University Press, 1981.

—— (1883) *Untersuchungen über die Methode der Socialwissenschaften, und der politischen Oekonomie insbesondere*, Leipzig: Duncker & Humblot; reprinted in Menger, C. (1968–70), *Gesammelte Werke*, ed. F.A. von Hayek, Tübingen: J.C.B. Mohr (Paul Siebeck), vol II; Engl. trans. *Problems of Economics and Sociology*, Urbana: University of Illinois Press, 1963; reprinted as *Investigations into the Method of the Social Sciences with Special Reference to Economics*, New York: New York University Press, 1985.

—— (1884) *Die Irrthümer des Historismus in der deutschen Nationalökonomie*, Vienna: Alfred Hölder; reprinted in Menger, C. (1968–70), *Gesammelte Werke*, ed. F.A. von Hayek, Tübingen: J.C.B. Mohr (Paul Siebeck), vol. III.

—— (1887) Review of E. von Philippovich, *Ueber Aufgabe und Methode der politischen Oekonomie*, Freiburg i.B.: J.C.B. Mohr, 1886, *Zeitschrift für privates und öffentliches Recht der Gegenwart* 14.

—— (1889a) 'Friedrich List', reprinted in Menger, C. (1968–70), *Gesammelte Werke*, ed. F.A. von Hayek, Tübingen: J.C.B. Mohr (Paul Siebeck), vol. III.

—— (1889b) 'Grundzüge einer Klassifikation der Wirtschaftswissenschaften'; reprinted in Menger, C. (1968–70) *Gesammelte Werke*, ed. F.A. von Hayek, Tübingen: J.C.B. Mohr (Paul Siebeck), vol. III; Engl. trans. 'Toward a Systematic Classification of the Economic Sciences', in Sommer, L. (ed.) *Essays in European Economic Thought*, Princeton: Van Nostrand, 1960.

—— (1891) 'Die Social-Theorien der classischen National-Oekonomie und die moderne Wirthschafstpolitik', reprinted in Menger, C. (1968–70), *Gesammelte Werke*, ed. F.A. von Hayek, Tübingen: J.C.B. Mohr (Paul Siebeck), vol. III.

—— (1892) 'Geld', reprinted in Menger, C. (1968–70), *Gesammelte Werke*, ed. F.A. von Hayek, Tübingen: J.C.B. Mohr (Paul Siebeck), vol. IV.

—— (1923) *Grundsätze der Volkswirtschaftslehre*, ed. K. Menger, Vienna: Hölder-Pichler-Tempsky AG.

—— (1926–55) *Katalog der Carl Menger-Bibliothek in der Handels-Universität Tokio*, 2 vols, Tokyo: Bibliothek der Handels-Universität Tokio.

—— (1981) *Principles of Economics,* New York: New York University Press.

—— (1985) *Investigations into the Method of the Social Sciences with Special Reference to Economics*, New York: New York University Press.

Menger, K. (1979) *Selected Papers in Logic and Foundations, Didactics, Economics*, Dordrecht: Reidel.

Menzel, A. (1927) *Friedrich Wieser als Soziologe*, Vienna: Julius Springer.

Milford, K. (1988a) 'Menger's Solution of the Problem of Induction: On the History of Methodological Thought in Economics', Working Paper no. 8806, Department of Economics, University of Vienna.

—— (1988b) *Zu den Lösungsversuchen des Induktionsproblems und des Abgrenzungsproblems bei Carl Menger*, Vienna: Verlag der Österreichischen Akademie der Wissenschaften.

—— (1990) 'Menger's Methodology', in Caldwell, B.J. (ed.) *Carl Menger and His Legacy in Economics*, annual supplement to vol. 22, *History of Political Economy*, Durham and London: Duke University Press.

—— (1991) 'Nationalism, Volkgeist, and the Methods of Economics: A Note on Ranke, Roscher and Menger', PPE Lectures, 7, Department of Economics, University of Vienna.

Miller, D. (1989a) 'The Fatalistic Conceit', *Critical Review* 3, 2.

—— (1989b) *Market, State and Community*, Oxford: Clarendon Press.

Miller, E. (1979) 'The Cognitive Basis of Hayek's Political Thought', in Cunningham, R.L. (ed.) *Liberty and the Rule of Law*, College Station and London: Texas A & M University.

Minogue, K.R. (1987) 'Hayek and Conservatism: Beatrice and Benedick?', in Butler, E. and Pirie, M. (eds) *Hayek on the Fabric of Human Society*, London: Adam Smith Institute.

Mises, L. von (1919) *Nation, Staat und Wirtschaft: Beiträge zur Politik und Geschichte der Zeit*, Vienna: Manzsche Verlags – und Universitäts-Buchhandlung; Engl. trans. *Nation, State, and Economics*, New York and London: New York University Press, 1983.

—— (1921) 'Die Wirtschaftsrechnung im sozialistischen Gemeinwesen', *Archiv für Sozialwissenschaft und Sozialpolitik* 47; Engl. trans. in Hayek, F.A. von (ed.) (1935), *Collectivist Economic Planning: Critical Studies on the Possibilities of Socialism*, London: George Routledge & Sons.

—— (1924) 'Neue Beiträge zum Problem der sozialistischen Wirtschaftsrechnung', *Archiv für Sozialwissenschaft und Sozialpolitik* 51; Engl. trans. in Mises, L. von (1981) *Socialism: An Economic and Sociological Analysis*, Indianapolis: Liberty Press.

—— (1926) 'Sozialliberalismus', in Mises, L. von (1929) *Kritik des Interventionismus*, Jena: Gustav Fischer.

—— (1929) *Kritik des Interventionismus: Untersuchungen zur Wirtschaftspolitik und Wirtschaftsideologie der Gegenwart*, Jena: Gustav Fischer; Engl. trans. *A Critique of Interventionism*, New Rochelle, NY: Arlington House, 1977.

—— (1931a) 'Die psychologischen Wurzeln des Widerstandes gegen die nationalökonomische Theorie', in Mises, L. von (1933) *Grundprobleme der Nationalökonomie*, Jena: Gustav Fischer.

—— (1931b) 'Vom Weg der subjektivistischen Wertlehre', in Mises, L. von (1933) *Grundprobleme der Nationalökonomie*, Jena: Gustav Fischer.

—— (1933) *Die Grundprobleme der Nationalökonomie: Untersuchungen über Verfahren, Aufgaben und Inhalt der Wirtschafts – und Gesellschaftslehre*, Jena: Gustav Fischer; Engl. trans. *Epistemological Problems of Economics*, Princeton: Van Nostrand, 1960, and New York: New York University Press, 1976.

—— (1940) *Nationalökonomie: Theorie des Handelns und Wirtschaftens*, Genf: Editions Union; 1980 edn, Munich: Philosophia Verlag.

—— (1944a) *Bureaucracy*, New Haven: Yale University Press.

—— (1944b) *Omnipotent Government: The Rise of the Total State and Total War*, New Haven: Yale University Press; quotations from 1969 edn, Westport: Arlington House.

—— (1947) *Planned Chaos*, Irvington-on-Hudson, NY: Foundation for Economic Education; reprinted as 'Epilogue' in Mises, L. von (1981) *Socialism: An Economic and Sociological Analysis*, Indianapolis: Liberty Press.

—— (1949) *Human Action: A Treatise on Economics*, New Haven: Yale University Press; quotations from rev. 1966 edn, Chigago: Contemporary Books. This is not the translation, but a different version of Mises, L. von (1940) *Nationalökonomi Theorie des Handelns und Wirtschaftens*, Genf: Editions Union; 1980 edn, Munich: Philosophia Verlag.

—— (1952) *Planning for Freedom, and Other Essays and Addresses*, South Holland, Ill.: Libertarian Press, quotations from enlarged 1980 edn.

—— (1953) *The Theory of Money and Credit*, New Haven: Yale University Press; Engl. trans. and enlarged edn of Mises, L. von (1912) *Theorie des Geldes und der Umlaufsmittel*, Munich and Leipzig: Duncker & Humblot.

—— (1956) *The Anti-Capitalistic Mentality*, Princeton: Van Nostrand.

—— (1957) *Theory and History: An Interpretation of Social and Economic Evolution*, New Haven: Yale University Press.

—— (1961) 'Epistemological Relativism in the Sciences of Human Action', in Schoeck, H. and Wiggins, J.N. (eds) *Relativism and the Study of Man*, Princeton: Van Nostrand.

—— (1962) *The Ultimate Foundation of Economic Science: An Essay on Method*, Princeton: Van Nostrand.

—— (1967) 'A Hundred Years of Marxian Socialism', in Mises, L. von (1990) *Money, Method, and the Market Process*, ed. R.M. Ebeling, Norwell and Dordrecht: Kluwer.

—— (1969) *The Historical Setting of the Austrian School of Economics*, New Rochelle, NY: Arlington House.

—— (1976) *Liberalism: A Socio-Economic Exposition*, Kansas City: Sheed Andrews & McMeel; formerly published as *The Free and Prosperous Commonwealth: An Exposition of the Ideas of Classical Liberalism*, Princeton: Van Nostrand, 1962, Engl. trans. of *Liberalismus*, Jena: Gustav Fischer, 1927.

—— (1978) *Notes and Recollections*, ed. H.F. Sennholz, South Holland, Ill.: Libertarian Press.

—— (1980) *Planning for Freedom, and Other Essays and Addresses*, South Holland, Ill.: Libertarian Press.

—— (1981) *Socialism: An Economic and Sociological Analysis*, critical and enlarged edn, Indianapolis: Liberty Press; first Engl. edn, London: Jonathan Cape, 1936; first German edn, *Die Gemeinwirtschaft: Untersuchungen über den Sozialismus*, Jena: Gustav Fischer, 1922.

—— (1990) *Money, Method, and the Market Process*, ed. R.M. Ebeling, Norwell and Dordrecht: Kluwer.

Mises, L. von and Spiethoff, A. (eds) (1931) *Probleme der Wertlehre*, part 1, *Schriften der Vereins für Sozialpolitik* 183, 1, Munich and Leipzig: Duncker & Humblot.

Mises, M. von (1981) *Ludwig von Mises. Der Mensch und sein Werk*, Munich: Philosophia Verlag; with a bibliography of L. von Mises.

—— (1984) *My Years with Ludwig von Mises*, 2nd enlarged edn, Cedar Falls, Iowa: Center for Futures Education..

Mitchell, W.C. (1969) *Types of Economic Theory from Mercantilism to Institutionalism*, New York: Kelley.

Mommsen, W.J. and Osterhammel, J. (eds) (1987) *Max Weber and His Contemporaries*, London: Allen & Unwin.

Mongin, P. (1988) 'Aspects d la méthodologie économique et de la théorie des choix entre 1930 et 1960', Document no. 159, Laboratoire d'Economie Politique, Ecole Normale Supérieure, Paris.

Morgenstern, O. (1927) 'Friedrich von Wieser', *American Economic Review* 17, 4.

—— (1931) 'Die drei Grundtypen der Theorie des subjektiven Wertes', in Mises, L. von and Spiethoff, A. (eds) *Probleme der Wertlehre*, part 1, *Schriften des Vereins für Sozialpolitik* 183, 1, Munich and Leipzig: Duncker & Humblot.

—— (1976) 'The Collaboration between Oskar Morgenstern and John von Neuman on the Theory of Games', *Journal of Economic Literature* 14, 3.

Moss, L.S. (ed.) (1976), *The Economics of Ludwig von Mises: Toward a Critical Reappraisal*, Kansas City: Sheed and Ward.

Nadeau, R. (1986) 'Popper, Hayek et la question du scientisme', *Manuscrito* 9.

—— (1987) 'La thèse subjectiviste de Hayek: Sur la notion d'ordre sensoriel et son rapport à la méthodologie économique', Cahiers d'épistémologie: no.8706, Université du Québec à Montréal.

—— (1988) 'L'économique et la question de ses limites', in Dostaler, G. and Ethier, D. (eds) *Friedrich Hayek: Philosophie, économie et politique*, Montreal: Association Canadienne-Française pour l'Avancement des Sciences.

Nagel, E. (1961) *The Structure of Science*, London: Routledge & Kegan Paul, reprint 1982.

Negishi, T. (1989) *History of Economic Theory*, Amsterdam and New York: North–Holland.

Nemo, P. (1988) *La société de droit selon F.A. Hayek*, Paris: Presse Universitaires de France.

Neurath, O. (1919) *Durch die Kriegswirtschaft zur Naturalwirtschaft*, Munich: Georg D.W. Callwey.

Nishiyama, C. (1979) 'Anti-Rationalism or Critical Rationalism', *Ordo* 30.

—— (1984) 'Introduction' to Nishiyama, C. and Leube, K.R. (eds) *The Essence of Hayek*, Stanford: Hoover Institution Press.

Nock, A. (1935) *Our Enemy, the State*, New York: Morrow.

—— (1945) Review of F.A. von Hayek, *The Road to Serfdom*, London: George Routledge & Sons, 1944, *Economic Council Review of Books*, February.

Novak, M. (1989) *Free Person and the Common Good*, Lanham, New York and London: Madison Books.

Nozick, R. (1977) 'On Austrian Methodology', *Synthese* 36, 2.

Nyiri, J.C. (1986) 'Intellectual Foundations of Austrian Liberalism', in Grassl, W. and Smith, (eds) *Austrian Economics: Historical and Philosophical Background*, London: Croom Helm.

Oakeshott, M. (1962) *Rationalism in Politics*, London and New York: Methuen.

—— (1975) *On Human Conduct*, Oxford: Clarendon Press.

O'Driscoll, G.P. Jr (1975) 'Hayek and Keynes: A Retrospective Assessment', Staff Paper no. 20, Department of Economics, Iowa State University; prepared for the Symposium on Austrian Economics, University of Hartford, 22–28 June.

—— (1977) 'Spontaneous Order and the Coordination of Economic Activities', *Journal of Libertarian Studies* 1, 2.

—— (1986) 'Money: Menger's Evolutionary Theory', *History of Political Economy* 18, 4.

O'Gorman, F. (1986) *British Conservatism: Conservative Thought from Burke to Thatcher*, London and New York: Longman.

Ordo (1979) XXX, *Zur Verfassung der Freiheit*, Festgabe für Friedrich A. von Hayek zur Vollendung seines achtzigsten Lebensjahres.

Osterhammel, J. (1987) 'Varieties of Social Economics: Joseph A. Schumpeter and Max Weber', in Mommsen, W.J. and Osterhammel, J. (eds) *Max Weber and His Contemporaries*, London: Allen & Unwin.

Paqué, K.H. (1990) 'Pattern Prediction in Economics: Hayek's Methodology of the Social Sciences Revisited', *History of Political Economy* 22, 2.

Pareto, V. (1897) *Cours d'économie politique*, Lausanne: F. Rouge.

—— (1906) *Manuele di economia politica*, Milan: Società Editrice Libraria; French edn, *Manuel d'économie politique*, *Oeuvres complètes*, vol. VII, Geneva: Droz.

Parsons, S. (1990) 'The Philosophical Roots of Modern Austrian Economics: Past Problems and Future Prospects', *History of Political Economy* 20, 2.

Pellicani, L. (1988) *Saggio sulla genesi del Capitalismo: Alle origini della modernità*, Milan: Sugarco.

Pfister, B. (1928) *Die Entwicklung zum Idealtypus: Eine methodologische Untersuchung über das Verhältnis von Theorie und Geschichte bei Menger, Schmoller und Max Weber*, Tübingen: J.C.B. Mohr (Paul Siebeck).

Pheby, J. (1988) *Methodology and Economics*, London: Macmillan.

Philippovich, E. von (1886) *Ueber Aufgabe und Methode der politischen Oekonomie*, Freiburg i.B.: Akademische Verlagsbuchhandlung von J.C.B. Mohr (Paul Siebeck).

Pirie, M. (1987) 'Why F.A. Hayek Is a Conservative', in Butler, E. and Pirie, M. (eds) *Hayek on the Fabric of Human Society*, London: Adam Smith Institute.

Polanyi, M. (1951) *The Logic of Liberty*, reprint 1980, Chicago: University of Chicago Press.

Popper, K.R. (1935) *Logik der Forschung*, Vienna: Julius Springer.

—— (1945) *The Open Society and its Enemies*, 2 vols, London: Routledge & Kegan Paul, reprint 1973.

—— (1957) *The Poverty of Historicism*, London: Routledge & Kegan Paul, reprint 1972.

—— (1963) *Conjectures and Refutations*, London: Routledge & Kegan Paul, reprint 1976.

—— (1965) *Das Elend des Historizismus*, Tübingen: J.C.B. Mohr (Paul Siebeck).

—— (1976) *Unended Quest: An Intellectual Autobiography*, London: Fontana/ Collins.

Quinton, A. (1967) 'Introduction' to Quinton, A. (ed.) (1967) *Political Philosophy*, Oxford: Oxford University Press.

Radnitzky, G. (1984) 'Friedrich von Hayeks Theorie der Evolution spontaner Ordnungen und selbstorganisierender Systeme', *Sonderdruck aus Hamburger Jahrbuch für Wissenschafts – und Gesellschaftspolitik*, 'Die ungeplante Gesellschaft', 29.

—— (1985) 'Sul fondamento epistemologico della filosofia della Società aperta', in Ricossa, S. and de Robilant, E, (eds) *Libertà giustizia e persona nella società tecnologica*, Milan: Giuffrè.

—— (1986), 'Ordine ed evoluzione nella teoria sociale di Hayek', *Il Mulino* 35, 6.

—— (1987a) 'The Constitutional Protection of Liberty', in Butler, E. and Pirie, M. (eds) *Hayek on the Fabric of Human Society*, London: Adam Smith Institute.

—— (1987b) 'An Economic Theory of the Rise of Civilization and its Policy Implications: Hayek's Account Generalized', *Ordo* 38.

Radnitzky, G. and Bartley, W.W. III (eds) (1987) *Evolutionary Epistemology, Rationality, and the Sociology of Knowledge*, La Salle, Ill.: Open Court.

Raz, J. (1979) 'The Rule of Law and its Virtues', in Cunningham, R.L. (ed.) *Liberty and the Rule of Law*, College Station and London: Texas A & M University Press.

Ricci, D.M. (1984) *The Tragedy of Political Science*, New Haven: Yale University Press.

Rickert, H. (1899) *Kulturwissenschaft und Naturwissenschaft*, Tübingen: J.C.B Mohr (Paul Siebeck); quotation from 1926 edn.

Ricossa, S. and de Robilant, E. (eds) (1985) *Libertà giustizia e persona nella società tecnologica*, Milan: Giuffrè.

Ritzel, G. (1950) *Schmoller versus Menger: Eine Analyse des Methodenstreits im Hinblick auf den Historismus in der Nationalökonomie*, Frankfurt a.M.: Buchdruckerei Enz & Rudolph KG.

Robbins, L. (1963) *Politics and Economics*, London: Macmillan.

—— (1976) *Political Economy: Past and Present. A Review of Leading Theories of Economic Policy*, London: Macmillan.

Robilant, E. di (1989) 'Economia, Diritto e persona nella società complessa', in Gentile, F. (ed.) *Interpretazione e decisione: Diritto ed economica*, Milan: Giuffrè.

Röpke, W. (1942) *Die Gesellschaftskrisis der Gegenwart*, Erlenbach and Zurich: Eugen Rentsch.

—— (1944) *Civitas Humana*, Erlenbach and Zurich: Eugen Rentsch.

—— (1947) *Die Krise des Kollektivismus*, Erlenbach and Zurich: Eugen Rentsch.

—— (1959) *Gegen die Brandung*, Erlenbach and Zurich: Eugen Rentsch.

Rosenberg, A. (1988) *Philosophy of Social Science*, Oxford: Clarendon Press.

Rosner, P. (1990) 'To What Extent Was the Austrian School Subjectivist? A Note on Carl Menger', PPE Lectures, 3, Department of Economics, University of Vienna.

Rothacker, E. (1920) *Einleitung in die Geisteswissenschaften*, Tübingen: J.C.B. Mohr (Paul Siebeck).

Rothbard, M.P. (1962) *Man, Economy, and State: A Treatise on Economic Principles*, Princeton: Van Nostrand.

—— (1970) *Power and Market: Government and the Economy*, Menlo Park, Calif.: Institute for Humane Studies.

—— (1973) *For a New Liberty: The Libertarian Manifesto*, reprint New York: Libertarian Review Foundation.

—— (1976a) 'Ludwig von Mises and Economic Calculation under Socialism', in Moss, L.S. (ed.) *The Economics of Ludwig von Mises: Toward a Critical Reappraisal*, Kansas City: Sheed & Ward.

—— (1976b) 'New Light on the Prehistory of the Austrian School', in Dolan, E.G. (ed.) *The Foundations of Modern Austrian Economics*, Kansas City: Sheed & Ward.

—— (1980) 'The Essential von Mises', in Mises, L. von, *Planning for Freedom, and Other Essays and Addresses*, South Holland, Ill.: Libertarian Press.

—— (1988) *Ludwig von Mises: Scholar, Creator, Hero*, Auburn: Ludwig von Mises Institute.

—— (1991) 'The End of Socialism and the Calculation Debate Revisited', Review of Austrian Economics 5.

—— (1989) 'The Hermeneutical Invasion of Philosophy and Economics', *Review of Austrian Economics* 3.

—— (1992) 'The Present State of Austrian Economics', working paper from the Ludwig von Mises Institute, Auburn.

Rothschild, K.R. (1986) 'Die Viennaer Schule im Verhältnis zur klassischen Nationalökonomie, unter besonderer Berücksichtigung von Carl Menger', in Leser, N. (ed.) *Die Wiener Schule der Nationalökonomie*, Vienna: Böhlau.

—— (1989) 'The Hermeneutical Invasion of Philosophy and Economics', *Review of Austrian Economics* 3.

Savigny, F.C. von (1814) *Vom Beruf unsrer Zeit für Gesetzgebung und Rechtswissenschaft*, Heidelberg: Mohr & Zimmer.

Scaramozzino, P. (ed.) (1969) *Omaggio a Bruno Leoni*. Quaderni della rivista Il Politico, no. 7, Milan: Giuffrè.

Schiera, P.A. (1987) *Il laboratorio borghese*, Bologna: Il Mulino.

Schmoller, G. (1883) 'Zur Methodologie der Staats- und Sozialwissenschaften', *Schmollers Jahrbuch* NF, 8, 3; reprinted in *Zur Literaturgeschichte der Staats- und Sozialwissenschaften*, Leipzig: Duncker & Humblot, 1888.

Schneider L. (1963) 'Introduction' to Menger, C. (1985) *Investigations into the Method of the Social Sciences with Special References to Economics*, New York: New York University Press.

Schoeck, H. and Wiggins, J.N. (eds) (1961) *Relativism and the Study of Man*, Princeton: Van Nostrand.

Schön, M. (1987) 'Gustav Schmoller and Max Weber', in Mommsen, W.J. and Osterhammel, J. (eds) *Max Weber and His Contemporaries*, London: Allen & Unwin.

Schotter, A. (1990) *Free Market Economics*, Oxford: Blackwell.

Schumpeter, J.A. (1908) *Das Wesen und der Hauptinhalt der theoretischen Nationalökonomie*, Leipzig: Duncker & Humblot.

—— (1914) 'Epochen der Dogmen – und Methodengeschichte', in *Grundriss der*

Sozialökonomie, section 1, part 1, Tübingen: J.C.B. Mohr (Paul Siebeck).
—— (1942) *Capitalism, Socialism and Democracy*, New York: Harper & Brothers.
—— (1951) *Ten Great Economists from Marx to Keynes*, New York: Oxford University Press.
—— (1954) *History of Economic Analysis*, London: Allen & Unwin.
Schütz, A. (1932) *Der sinnhafte Aufbau der sozialen Welt*, reprint Vienna: Springer, 1960.
Seldon, A. (1984) 'Before and after *The Road to Serfdom*: Reflections on Hayek in 1935, 1944, 1960, 1982', in Barry, N. *et al.*, *Hayek's 'Serfdom' Revisited*, London: Institute of Economic Affairs.
—— (1990) *Capitalism*, Oxford: Blackwell.
Selgin, G.A. (1988) 'Praxeology and Understanding: An Analysis of the Controversy in Austrian Economics', *Review of Austrian Economics* 2.
Sennholz, H.F. (1978) 'Postscript' to Mises, L. von, *Notes and Recollections*, ed. H.F. Sennholz, South Holland, Ill.: Libertarian Press.
Sennholz, M. (ed.) (1956) *On Freedom and Free Enterprise: Essays in Honor of Ludwig von Mises*, Princeton: Van Nostrand.
Shand, A.H. (1984) *The Capitalist Alternative. An Introduction to Neo-Austrian Economics*, New York and London: New York University Press.
—— (1990) *Free Market Morality: The Political Economy of the Austrian School*, London and New York: Routledge.
Shearmur, J. (1984) 'Hayek and the Wisdom of the Age', in Barry, N. *et al.*, *Hayek's 'Serfdom' Revisited*, London: Institute of Economic Affairs.
—— (1986) 'The Austrian Connection: Hayek's Liberalism and the Thought of Carl Menger', in Grassl, W. and Smith, (eds) *Austrian Economics: Historical and Philosophical Background*, London: Croom Helm.
—— (1990a) 'From Dialogue Rights to Property Rights: Foundations for Hayek's Legal Theory', *Critical Review* 4, 1–2.
—— (1990b) 'From Hayek to Menger: Biology, Subjectivism, and Welfare', in Caldwell, B.J. (ed.) *Carl Menger and His Legacy in Economics*, annual supplement to vol. 22, *History of Political Economy*, Durham and London: Duke University Press.
Shenfield, A. (1977) 'Scientism and the Study of Society', in Machlup, F. (ed.) *Essays on Hayek*, London: Routledge & Kegan Paul.
—— (1987) 'Hayek on Law', in Butler, E. and Pirie, M. (eds) *Hayek on the Fabric of Human Society*, London: Adam Smith Institute.
Silverman, P. (1990) 'The Cameralist Roots of Menger's Achievement', in Caldwell, B.J. (ed.) *Carl Menger and His Legacy in Economics*, annual supplement to vol. 22, *History of Political Economy*, Durham and London: Duke University Press.
Smart, W. (1891) *An Introduction to the Theory of Value on the Lines of Menger, Wieser, and Böhm-Bawerk*, reprint New York: Kelley, 1966.
Smith, B. (1986) 'Austrian Economics and Austrian Philosophy', in Grassl, W. and Smith, (eds) *Austrian Economics: Historical and Philosophical Background*, London: Croom Helm.
—— (1990a) 'Aristotle, Menger, Mises: An Essay in the Metaphysics of Economics', in Caldwell, B.J. (ed.) *Carl Menger and His Legacy in Economics*, annual supplement to vol. 22, *History of Political Economy*, Durham and London: Duke University Press.
—— (1990b), 'On the Austrianness of Austrian Economics', *Critical Review* 4, 1–2.
—— (1990c) 'The Question of Apriorism', Austrian Economics Newsletter, Fall.
Spadaro, L.M. (ed.) (1978) *New Directions in Austrian Economics*, Kansas City: Sheed Andrews & McMeel.
Spiegel, H.W. (1971) *The Growth of Economic Thought*, revised and expanded edn, Durham: Duke University Press, 1983.

Stark, W. (1944) *The History of Economics in its Relation to Social Development*, London: Kegan Paul, Trench, Trubner.

Stigler, G.J. (1937) 'The Economics of Carl Menger', *Journal of Political Economy* 45, 2.

—— (1979) 'Why Have the Socialists Been Winning?', *Ordo* 30.

Stoppino, M. (1962) 'Liberty and the Rule of Law', *Il Politico* 12, 1.

Strauss, L. (1948) *On Tyranny: An Interpretation of Xenophon's Hiero*, reprint Glencoe, Ill.: Free Press.

—— (1949) 'Political Philosophy and History', in Strauss, L. (1959) *What Is Political Philosophy and Other Studies*, reprint Westport: Greenwood, 1976.

—— (1952) *Persecution and the Art of Writing*, reprint Chicago and London: University of Chicago Press, 1988.

—— (1953) *Natural Right and History*, Chicago and London: University of Chicago Press.

—— (1959) *What Is Political Philosophy and Other Studies*, reprint Westport: Greenwood, 1976.

—— (1965) *Spinoza's Critique of Religion*, New York: Schocken Books.

Streissler, E. (ed.) (1969a) *Roads to Freedom: Essays in Honour of Friedrich A. von Hayek*, London: Routledge & Kegan Paul.

—— (1969b) 'Structural Economic Thought: On the Significance of the Austrian School Today', *Zeitschrift für Nationalökonomie* 29, 2.

—— (1972) 'To What Extent Was the Austrian School Marginalist?', *History of Political Economy* 4, 2.

—— (1986) 'Arma virumque cano. Friedrich von Wieser, der Sänger als Ökonom', in Leser, N. (ed.) *Die Wiener Schule der Nationalökonomie*, Vienna: Böhlau.

—— (1988) 'The Intellectual and Political Impact of the Austrian School of Economics', *History of European Ideas* 9, 2.

—— (1990a) 'The Influence of German Economics on the Work of Menger and Marshall', in Caldwell, B.J. (ed.) *Carl Menger and His Legacy in Economics*, annual supplement vol. 22, *History of Political Economy*, Durham and London: Duke University Press.

—— (1990b) 'Menger, Böhm-Bawerk, and Wieser: The Origins of the Austrian School', in Hennings, K. and Samuels, W.J. (eds) *Neoclassical Economic Theory, 1870 to 1930*, Boston and Dordrecht: Kluwer.

Streissler, E. and Weber, W. (1973) 'The Menger Tradition', in Hicks, J.R. and Weber W. (eds) *Carl Menger and the Austrian Economics*, Oxford: Clarendon Press.

Sugimura, K. (1926) 'Inquiry into Menger's Methodology of Social Science', *Shogakukenkyu*.

Tabarrok, A. (1990) 'Subjective Value Theory: A Reformulation', *Austrian Economics Newsletter*, Fall.

Taylor, T.C. (1980) *An Introduction to Austrian Economics*, Auburn: Ludwig von Mises Institute.

Tenbruck, F.H. (1959) 'Zur Genese der Methodologie Max Webers', *Kölner Zeitschrift für Soziologie und Sozialpsychologie* 11.

Tessitore, F. (1981) *Profilo dello storicismo politico*, Turin: Unione Tipografica Editrice Torinese.

—— (1987) *Il senso della storia universale*, Milan: Garzanti.

Tisch, K. (1932) *Wirtschaftsrechnung und Verteilung im zentralistisch organisierten sozialistischen Gemeinwesen*, Wuppertal and Elberfeld: H. Scheschinski.

Topitsch, E. (ed.) (1984) *Logik der Sozialwissenschaften*, Königstein Ts.: Athenäum.

Vanberg, V. (1981) *Liberaler Evolutionismus oder Vertragstheoretischer Konstitutionalismus*, Tübingen: J.C.B. Mohr (Paul Siebeck).

—— (1986) 'Spontaneous Market Order and Social Rules: A Critical Examination of F.A. Hayek's Theory of Cultural Evolution', *Economics and Philosophy* 2.

Vannucci, A. (1990) 'La "rivoluzione marginalistica" nelle scienze sociali: alcune osservazioni', *Quaderni di storia dell'economia politica* 8, 1.
Vaughn, K.I. (1976) 'Critical Discussion of the Four Papers', in Moss, L.S. (ed.) *The Economics of Ludwig von Mises: Toward a Critical Reappraisal*, Kansas City: Sheed & Ward.
—— (1978) 'The Reinterpretation of Carl Menger: Some Notes on Recent Scholarship', *Atlantic Economic Journal* 6, 3.
—— (1980) 'Economic Calculation under Socialism. The Austrian Contribution', *Economic Inquiry* 18.
—— (1982) 'Subjectivism, Predictability, and Creativity: Comment on Buchanan', in Kirzner, I.M. (ed.) *Method, Process, and Austrian Economics*, Lexington: Lexington Books.
—— (1984) 'The Constitution of Liberty from an Evolutionary Perspective', in Barry, N. *et al.*, *Hayek's 'Serfdom' Revisited*, London: Institute of Economic Affairs.
—— (1990) 'The Mengerian Roots of the Austrian Revival', in Caldwell, B.J. (ed.) *Carl Menger and His Legacy in Economics*, annual supplement vol. 22, *History of Political Economy*, Durham and London: Duke University Press.
Viola, F. (1987) *Autorità e ordine del diritto*, Turin: Giappichelli.
Voegelin, E. (1952) *The New Science of Politics*, Chicago: University of Chicago Press.
Ward, B. (1979) *The Ideal Worlds of Economics*, New York: Basic Books.
Watkins, W.N. (1952) 'Ideal Types and Historical Explanation', *British Journal for the Philosophy of Science* 3.
—— (1957) 'Historical Explanation in the Social Sciences', *British Journal for the Philosophy of Science* 8.
—— (1976) 'The Human Condition: Two Criticisms of Hobbes', in Cohen, R.S., Feyerabend, P.K. and Wartofky, M.W. (eds) *Essays in Memory of Imre Lakatos*, Dordrect: Riedel.
Weber, M. (1903–6) 'Roscher und Knies und die logischen Probleme der historischen Nationalökonomie', in Weber, M. (1922a) *Gesammelte Aufsätze zur Wissenschaftslehre*, Tübingen: J.C.B. Mohr (Paul Siebeck), reprint 1985.
—— (1904) 'Die "Objektivität" sozialwissenschaftlicher und sozialpolitischer Erkenntnis', in Weber, M. (1922a) *Gesammelte Aufsätze zur Wissenschaftslehre*, Tübingen: J.C.B. Mohr (Paul Siebeck), reprint 1985.
—— (1906) 'Kritische Studien auf dem Gebiet der kulturwissenschaftlichen Logik', in Weber, M. (1922a) *Gesammelte Aufsätze zur Wissenschaftslehre*, Tübingen: J.C.B. Mohr (Paul Siebeck), reprint 1985.
—— (1908) 'Die Grenznutzlehre und das "psychophysische Grundgesetz", in Weber, M. (1922a) *Gesammelte Aufsätze zur Wissenschaftslehre*, Tübingen: J.C.B. Mohr (Paul Siebeck), reprint 1985.
—— (1918) 'Der Sinn der "Wertfreiheit" der soziologischen und ökonomischen Wissenschaften', in Weber, M. (1922a) *Gesammelte Aufsätze zur Wissenschaftslehre*, Tübingen: J.C.B. Mohr (Paul Siebeck), reprint 1985.
—— (1922a) *Gesammelte Aufsätze zur Wissenschaftslehre*, Tübingen: J.C.B. Mohr (Paul Siebeck), reprint 1985.
—— (1922b) *Wirtschaft und Gesellschaft*, Tübingen: J.C.B. Mohr (Paul Siebeck), reprint 1982.
Weiss, F.X. (1924) 'Zur zweiten Auflage von Carl Mengers *Grundsätzen*', *Zeitschrift für Volkswirtschaft und Sozialpolitik* NF, 4.
White, L.H. (1977) *The Methodology of the Austrian School of Economists*, New York: Center for Libertarian Studies; quotation from the 1984 edn, Auburn: Ludwig von Mises Institute.
—— (1985) 'Introduction' to Menger, C., *Investigations into the Method of the Social Sciences with Special Reference to Economics*, New York: New York University Press.

—— (1990) 'Restoring an "Altered" Menger', in Caldwell, B.J. (ed.) *Carl Menger and His Legacy in Economics*, annual supplement to vol. 22, *History of Political Economy*, Durham and London: Duke University Press.

Wicksell, K. (1921) 'Carl Menger', in Wicksell, K., *Selected Papers on Economic Theory*, ed. E. Lindahl, Cambridge, Mass.: Harvard University Press.

Wieser, F. von (1889) *Der natürliche Wert*, Vienna: Hölder.

—— (1891) 'The Austrian School and the Theory of Value', *Economic Journal* 1, March.

—— (1914) 'Theorie der gesellschaftlichen Wirtschaft', in *Grundriss der Sozialökonomik*, vols 1 and 2, Tübingen: J.C.B. Mohr (Paul Siebeck).

—— (1926) *Das Gesetz der Macht*, Vienna: Springer.

Wootton, B. (1945) *Freedom under Planning*, London: Allen & Unwin.

Yagi, M., (1981) 'Menger on Ricardo: C. Menger's Notes on Ricardo's *Principles of Political Economy*', *Okayama Economic Review* 13, 1.

—— (1992) 'Carl Menger as Editor: Significance of Journalistic Experience for His Economics and for His Later Life', *Revue européenne des sciences sociales*, 30, 92.

Yeager, L.B. (1984) 'Utility, Rights, and Contract: Some Reflections on Hayek's Work', in Leube, K.R. and Zlabinger, A.H. (eds) *The Political Economy of Freedom: Essays in Honor of F.A. Hayek*, Munich and Vienna: Philosophia Verlag.

—— (1989) 'Reason and Cultural Evolution', *Critical Review* 3, 2.

Zamagni, S. (1982) 'Sui fondamenti metodologici della scuola austriaca', *Note economiche* 3.

Zintl, R. (1983) *Individualistische Theorien und die Ordnung der Gesellschaft. Untersuchungen zur politischen Theorie von J.M. Buchanan und F.A. von Hayek*, Berlin: Duncker & Humblot.

Zöller, M. (1979) 'Handeln in Ungewissheit: F.A. v. Hayeks Grundlegung einer freiheitlichen Sozialphilosophie', *Ordo* 30.

NAME INDEX

Note: page references in italics indicate entries to be found in notes sections of the text.

SUBJECT INDEX

Note: page references in italics indicate entries to be found in notes sections of the text.